International Library of and the New Medicine

C000134469

Volume 82

Founding Editors

Thomasine Kimbrough Kushner, Berkely, USA

David C. Thomasma, Dordrecht, The Netherlands

David N. Weisstub, Montreal, Canada

The book series *International Library of Ethics, Law and the New Medicine* comprises volumes with an international and interdisciplinary focus. The aim of the Series is to publish books on foundational issues in (bio) ethics, law, international health care and medicine. The volumes that have already appeared in this series address aspects of aging, mental health, AIDS, preventive medicine, bioethics and many other current topics. This Series was conceived against the background of increasing globalization and interdependency of the world's cultures and governments, with mutual influencing occurring throughout the world in all fields, most surely in health care and its delivery. By means of this Series we aim to contribute and cooperate to meet the challenge of our time: how to aim human technology to good human ends, how to deal with changed values in the areas of religion, society, culture and the self-definition of human persons, and how to formulate a new way of thinking, a new ethic. We welcome book proposals representing the broad interest of the interdisciplinary and international focus of the series. We especially welcome proposals that address aspects of 'new medicine', meaning advances in research and clinical health care, with an emphasis on those interventions and alterations that force us to re-examine foundational issues.

More information about this series at http://www.springer.com/series/6224

Mark Eccleston-Turner · Iain Brassington
Editors

Infectious Diseases in the New Millennium

Legal and Ethical Challenges

 Springer

Editors
Mark Eccleston-Turner
School of Law
University of Keele
Keele, UK

Iain Brassington
School of Law
University of Manchester
Manchester, UK

ISSN 1567-8008   ISSN 2351-955X   (electronic)
International Library of Ethics, Law, and the New Medicine
ISBN 978-3-030-39821-7   ISBN 978-3-030-39819-4   (eBook)
https://doi.org/10.1007/978-3-030-39819-4

This Springer imprint is published by the registered company Springer Nature Switzerland AG
The registered company address is: Gewerbestrasse 11, 6330 Cham, Switzerland

In loving memory of Paul William Turner

Contents

Introduction

Mark Eccleston-Turner and Iain Brassington

1   Introduction

At a number of points in the twentieth century, bold proclamations were made to the effect that the era of infectious diseases was coming to a close, and that humanity would soon no longer be afflicted by the microbes and viruses which had plagued humanity hitherto. The most notable of these comments came in 1962, when the noted virologist Sir McFarland Burnett stated that "[b]y the end of the Second World War it was possible to say that almost all of the major practical problems of dealing with infectious disease had been solved".[1] A few years later, in 1970, the Surgeon-General of the United States of America, William H. Stewart, claimed that it was "time to close the book on infectious diseases, declare the war against pestilence won, and shift national resources to such chronic problems as cancer and heart disease".[2]

Looking back, these comments may seem naïve; however, they were not as wild as they may appear—and it is tempting to bask in some of their optimism even now. Smallpox—the last natural case of which was reported in 1977, and which was declared eradicated in 1980[3]—provides the paradigmatic example of humanity being able to eliminate at least one of the thousand natural shocks that flesh is heir to. The eradication of polio has been promised for some time now, and though that

---

[1] Brachman (2003).

[2] Spellberg and Taylor-Blake (2013).

[3] World Health Organisation, 'Smallpox' https://www.who.int/csr/disease/smallpox/en/ last accessed: 22nd December 2018.

M. Eccleston-Turner (✉)
School of Law, Chancellor's Building University of Keele, Staffordshire, UK
e-mail: m.r.eccleston-turner@keele.ac.uk

I. Brassington
School of Law, Univesity of Manchester, Manchester, UK
e-mail: iain.brassington@manchester.ac.uk

© Springer Nature Switzerland AG 2020
M. Eccleston-Turner and I. Brassington (eds.), *Infectious Diseases in the New Millennium*, International Library of Ethics, Law, and the New Medicine 82, https://doi.org/10.1007/978-3-030-39819-4_1

aim does keep slipping through our fingers, it is still tantalisingly close. Not all infectious diseases will be eliminated in the foreseeable future, but programmes of vaccination intended to reduce their prevalence have made an important difference for the better, and continue to do so; innovations such as antibiotic drugs historically gave reason to think that the mortality and morbidity rates associated with other diseases could be slashed. Finally, improved surveillance and reportage provided the means to make better public health interventions. A host of infectious diseases that had caused widespread misery throughout human history had, in the hundred years preceding Burnett's and Stewart's comments, either been eradicated, or largely brought under control.[4] Why not take that as a sign for the future?

However, events in the closing couple of decades of the twentieth century and the first decade or so of the 21st have eroded such hope. The years since Burnett's and Stewart's comments saw the emergence and spread of new diseases such as HIV/Aids, hepatitis C, Sudden Acute Respiratory Sydrome (SARS), Middle East Respiratory Syndrome (MERS) and a number of haemorrhagic fevers; they saw too the resurgence of diseases once considered confined to the history books or controllable, such as cholera and malaria. Indeed, as we write this Introduction, the second largest ever outbreak of Ebola virus disease continues to impact the Democratic Republic of the Congo and a pandemic of COVID-19 coronavirus shows very little sign of ending.,[5] Moreover, we are also faced with very real prospect of many antibiotics ceasing to be effective, rending even routine surgery a potentially life-threatening prospect.[6]

It therefore seems an appropriate time to reflect on the state of our responsiveness to the threat of infectious diseases in the early twenty-first century, and determine what, if any, lessons we can learn from the recent past. What are the problems that remain that need to be addressed by policymakers? To this end, this collection draws together scholars from across the globe, and across disciplines to create a multi-disciplinary perspective on what, if any, lessons we can learn from such infectious diseases in the new millennium.

2   Themes

It is a commonplace to point out that humanity is the only species that has the slightest regard for national borders. Microbes do not stop to get their passports stamped. However, the scope of moral concern is not defined by jurisdictional boundaries either: if the suffering of a compatriot wholly unknown to us has any moral claim to our attention at all, then surely so does the suffering of a foreigner. Even if we think that compatriots should for some reason count for more than foreigners, it does not follow that foreigners count for nothing; they still have a moral gravity that can,

---

[4]Brachman, (n 1).
[5]World Health Organisation (2018).
[6]World Health Organisation (2014).

does, and should influence our behaviour. Is this kind of cosmopolitanism anything more than a fashion, though—and a dying one at that? One might think that there are signs that this is the case. Donald Trump's inaugural address as President of the United States told listeners that

> a nation exists to serve its citizens. [...] From this day forward, a new vision will govern our land. From this moment on, it's going to be America First.[7]

Admittedly, to say that a nation exists to serve its citizens does not mean that it may not serve others: Trump might have meant that a nation exists *primarily* to serve its citizens, or—which is not the same thing—to serve its citizens *primarily*. Likewise, "America first" is compatible with "and others close behind". But these imputations are departures from what he said; and it is fair to infer from his words—and his behaviour since—a certain looking inwards, perhaps bordering on isolationism. Neither is this attitude unique to the 45th President: we write this at a time when populist movements throughout the developed world are making hay from parochialism of one sort or another.

But even the most hyperbolically or childishly isolationist policy platform has a reason to care about disease in other lands. As noted, pathogens do not recognise borders, and are not halted when the people or the winds, animals, and rivers carrying them cross from one state to another. An outbreak of disease in a country may incentivise the movement of people, which will spread its reach further. It may cause economic damage—which will itself incentivise migration, and which has knock-on effects for other countries anyway. Closing borders in this sort of situation may be counterproductive: the incentive to move will remain, but if all migrants are rendered illegal by the stroke of a pen, the incentive to seek treatment that might help prevent an outbreak in the host country will be nullified. A policy of national self-interest means, then, that states have an indirect interest in what happens in their neighbours, like it or not. To treat illness as anything other than a transnational problem is therefore not only morally questionable, but—if they stop to think about it for a moment—too short-sighted even for today's populists. Parochialism can be *too* parochial.

But if diseases are not neatly confined to states, what does this mean in reality?

One of the prevailing themes of this collection is the fact that the detection, response, and control of infectious diseases has moved clearly beyond the state-based paradigm, and now encompasses a range of non-state actors. While in some respects this is nothing new—the Pan American Health Organisation and the International Health Office of the League of Nations were both created in the early 1900s, and the World Health Organisation was created in 1948,—responses to infectious disease outbreaks in the twenty-first century have been characterised by the presence of an ever more diverse range of actors, carrying out an ever more diverse range of tasks in place of the state. Included in this is the increasing role of the United Nations and through the securitisation of global health agenda, which has resulted in two Security Council Resolutions concerned with infectious diseases. The first, Resolution 1308 in 2000, recognised the potential of the Aids epidemic, if unchecked, to pose a risk to

---

[7]Trump (2017).

stability and security, and largely focused on the potential of HIV/Aids to affect the health of UN peacekeeping personnel.[8] Resolution 2177, passed in 2014 in regards to the West African Ebola outbreak,[9] was the first Resolution to acknowledge a health issue as an ongoing threat to peace and security, and was also the impetus for the creation of the United Nations' first ever health-related mission: the United Nations' Mission for Ebola Emergency Response (UNMEER).

The increased role of the United Nations in matters of public health has not been entirely without its problems. UN forces became an unwitting vector for infectious disease in Haiti in 2010, introducing the cholera bacterium to the country and thereby causing a serious outbreak of the disease. This was something that the UN attempted to cover up for nearly six years.[10] This episode is considered in detail in this anthology by Adam Rainis Houston, who argues that the containment of cholera is at the heart of a longstanding legal principle, which the UN violated. While there may be things that we can learn from cholera as we respond to threats such as Ebola, what remedy might be available to the people of Haiti in the meantime is not obvious: Houston's conclusion is that Haiti's first encounter with cholera "has resulted in much legal debate but little justice". This episode is not the only one considered in the anthology to consider Haiti in the context of public health: Mason Maier, Evans and Phelan's paper notes the harm done to that country by policies intended to curb the spread of HIV.

Of course, the UN is not the only non-state actor to respond to public health emergencies, as is shown by the role of organisations such as Médecins Sans Frontières[11] and the Red Cross[12] in responding to—inter alia—the West African Ebola outbreak in 2014. But the involvement of a multitude of actors, with heterogeneous structure, liabilities, and legal standing on the international stage is not without its added complexities. Notably, not all agencies are civilian: as Kamradt-Scott notes, military involvement in public-health related interventions brings a raft of problems of its own. Civilian agencies have reason to be wary of military involvement, not the least of the reasons for which is that such involvement may erode trust and, at best, make aid agencies look partial. Military organisations, too, have reasons to be wary of getting too involved in aid work: their primary responsibility is to their national governments. And yet there are times when civil and military bodies must work together. Moreover, military bodies come with their own medical teams, which are—Kamradt-Scott notes—presumably beholden to some standard of medical ethics; and the Hippocratic ideal of doing no harm is a relevant consideration. The doctrine of doing no harm can be taken to mean simply that healthcare professionals

---

[8]UNSC (2000, 2011).

[9]UNSC Res 2177 (18th September 2014) UN Doc/S/Res/2177.

[10]Katz (2016).

[11]Hofman and Au (2017).

[12]See: The International Red Cross and Red Crescent Movement Response to the West African Ebola Outbreak 2014 by Christy Shucksmith-Wesley p. 70.

ought not to harm when they can avoid it.[13] But it is—at least sometimes—interpreted as a contributory consideration in the idea that it is the job of the medical professional to *allow* no harm, or to be *beneficent*, not just non-maleficent.[14] This being so, it is plausibly part of the job of the military medic actively to pursue health, too. But how might one reconcile military loyalties with a perceived moral obligation to intervene? And what about things that militaries can do that other agencies cannot?

> For example, were militaries to reconnoitre mobile phone text-messaging to identify potential infectious disease outbreaks in a health crisis, would this be ethically sound given that it is a breach of individuals' privacy?

There being a public health emergency might make a difference to how we should answer this question; it might make a difference to how we answer other questions. It might not. As things stand, there is little guidance, let alone explicit rules, to govern how military agencies should act during a health crisis.

This does not mean, of course, that things are always much more straightforward when the military is not involved. Christy Shucksmith-Wesley's chapter considerers some of the complications surrounding the Red Cross' work, with particular reference to its interactions with bodies such as the WHO. Using the 2014 Ebola outbreak as her reference, she compares the ability of the Red Cross and other organisations to respond to emerging crises. Once again, we are led to the conclusion that there is more that needs to be done when it comes to regulating and organising NGO roles. "New ground," she argues, "needs to be broken in the future coordination of humanitarian responses to infectious disease." Spotting a problem, and diagnosing it correctly, will not yield a solution—one possibility is that there should be one overarching coordinating body, though Shucksmith-Wesley would herself not necessarily be in favour—but it is a vital first step in working out what to do next.

The 2014 Ebola outbreak, with a particular emphasis on the WHO's role and response, also motivates Eccleston-Turner and McArdle's chapter. Their exploration of the criteria for declaring—and the obligation to declare—a Public Health Emergency of International Concern echoes, in important ways, the themes raised in the opening paper of this anthology, concerning the obligation to act to limit cholera's spread. Though the paper is ostensibly a piece of legal analysis, it is nevertheless true that it points us towards important themes from political philosophy and international relations: what is the nature—indeed, the ontology—of a transnational body? In what sense can an organisation have duties and responsibilities? How can those duties and responsibilities be enforced? And, in the final analysis, what would justice look like if and when those duties and responsibilities are not properly discharged? After all, those who are most vulnerable to illnesses such as Ebola are overwhelmingly people who live in the greatest economic and political precarity already, in countries whose

---

[13] We take it as a given that never harming is an implausible demand, since surgery inevitably does harm in the pursuit of a longer-term good: the injunction must be interpreted as "do no harm without good reason".

[14] See Beauchamp and Childress (2013) passim.

governments are least able (and sometimes least willing) to press the case on behalf of their citizenry.

"There are numerous practical limitations to finding and giving effect to any determination of responsibility in relation to an international organisation like the WHO," Eccleston-Turner and McArdle write, continuing:

> Not only is there a question about a lack of judicial fora before which cases on breach of international law by international organisations could be brought, but there is also the question of practical consequences arising from actions before such courts, if one with appropriate jurisdiction could be identified. A determination of responsibility gives rise to an obligation to make reparation. The extent to which this is possible in the present case, both in terms of enforcement, and of where any money would be drawn from in order to make such reparation, is highly questionable.

Clearly, it would be fallacious to suggest that since responsibility implies obligation, and obligation may be unenforceable, there is *modus tollens* no responsibility. Not the least of the reasons for this is that unenforceability of an obligation doesn't stop there being an obligation at all. All the same: if responsibilities cannot be enforced, then one might think that there is *to all intents and purposes* nothing much to be said about them: that they are purely notional. This also seems as though it must be incorrect, though, both as a matter of jurisprudence and as a matter of ethics. Working out how one might resolve this problem looks to be a major task, though no less important for that.

In short, all these papers indicate that there is a lack of formal structures in place to hold international actors to account for the power they exercise on the global stage.

A second major theme of this volume is innovation in global health, and the manner in which that innovation occurs. As has been noted elsewhere, "[i]nnovation is essential to address the complex problems in global health today – widening inequity, changing patterns of disease burden, the impacts of conflict, migration, natural disasters, and climate change."[15] This collection considers two interlinked elements of the innovation process.

The first element, addressed in the chapters by Minssen and Nordberg,[16] and by Gopinathan, Peacocke, Gouglas, Ottersen and Røttingen,[17] concerns how innovation might be properly incentivised and rewarded in such a way as to generate the greatest possible good in the most just way possible. At present, we currently lack an effective vaccine or treatment for a number of infectious diseases, not least of all, COVID-19. Neglected tropical diseases affect more than 1.4 billion people in low-income countries, and a growing number of microbial organisms are becoming resistant to available drugs. This problem is compounded by another: poor access in developing countries to those products that do exist. These problems of access are a factor in low immunisation rates, and a correspondingly high prevalence of vaccine-preventable diseases, resulting avoidable morbidity and mortality. Getting intellectual property rights right is central to addressing these challenges, as intellectual property rights

---

[15]Mannell et al. (2018).

[16]p. 130.

[17]p. 164.

have the potential to incentivise innovation in a market, but also to inhibit access to the resulting products. Two chapters here address these interlocking issues in detail, highlighting why traditional market-based forces do not offer an adequate solution to either of these problems.

Minssen and Nordberg confront the relationship between the IP system and the need for pharmaceutical innovation in the context of antimicrobial resistance to currently available drugs, claiming that the former hinders (or, at best, does not foster) our ability to respond to that need. This is a pressing issue, given that there are almost three quarters of a million deaths worldwide every year that are attributable to antimicrobial resistance, and warnings that this will only get worse in future unless there is a significant breakthrough. But new antibiotics do not promise significant rewards for their developers

> due to limits on sales imposed by national conservation plans, the existence of a strong generic market functioning as substitute products, the fact that health regulations and reimbursement procedures encourage the use of the less expensive drug, and the short duration of treatment.

It is tempting to add to this list an observation that the people most vulnerable to infectious disease are often the world's poorest; but if surgical disinfection procedures are rendered ineffective by antimicrobial resistance, it will be the world's wealthy who suffer as well. This is not, then, just a problem that will impact on people somewhere vaguely "out there". For Minssen and Nordberg, what is really needed is a combination of push and pull factors that will stimulate development in a way that the legal framework we have currently does not.

Meanwhile, Gopinathan et al. focus more directly on a strategy for providing vaccines for emerging diseases: the Coalition for Epidemic Preparedness Innovations (CEPI). This initiative, which includes governmental and non-governmental bodies, was announced in 2017, with the aim of stimulating vaccine development. One particularly striking aspect of their paper is that they examine CEPI—and, by extension, other strategies to encourage the development of medical interventions—in terms of claims about justice, and intergenerational justice in particular. There is a parallel, they suggest, between the way that a phenomenon such as anthropogenic climate change can be seen, and the way that our success or lack of success in facilitating medical innovations can be seen. If ACC can plausibly be presented as an intergenerational injustice, then so (pari passu) can collective failures in respect of disease prevention and treatment. More,

> [i]nvoking the concept [of intergenerational equity] for epidemic preparedness and protection against infectious diseases would make the case that present generation has benefited from vaccines developed by the previous generation, and accordingly, the present generation should do the same for future generations. Moreover, since vaccine development takes a long time, and the present generation has experienced the consequences of outbreaks and acquired knowledge about the value of vaccines in preventing such outbreaks, the present generation should be compelled to invest today for the sake of preventing human suffering in the future.

It is not a given that being the beneficiary of some good from Alice means that one is under an obligation to provide a comparable good to Bob (and the idea that one could be compelled to do so). Nevertheless, we might think all the same that there is a sense in which decency means that we owe it to Bob to provide him with some good, and that Bob may have a legitimate criticism of our character if we take the benefits from Alice without passing anything on. And if that is true for Bob, it may also be true for future generations. After all, if we think that there is a good moral reason to—say—try to minimise (or even reverse) our carbon emissions for the sake of merely possible future people, the same kind of consideration is not obviously inapplicable when we're talking about new vaccines or antibiotics. The point is this: if we think that future generations are of any moral importance at all—and most of us, to some degree, do think that—then we would seem to have to acknowledge that it is not implausible to recognise at the very least *a moral reason* to support measures that incentivise steps to maximise their wellbeing. (How we compare the moral pull of people in distant lands and people in distant places, given the claim above that people in distant places do exert *some* pull, would be a matter for further consideration.)

The second element relates to the commercialisation of scientific research. In this context, the chapters by Nicholas Evans and Michelle Rourke consider how 'pure' scientific research builds towards innovations in infectious diseases.

Rourke's aim is directed squarely at the concept of viral sovereignty, "the concept that virus samples isolated from within the territorial boundaries of a Nation State are the sovereign property of that State", which she treats as generating problems that are yet to be resolved. She traces the evolution of the concept through the legal and policy responses to H5N1 influenza, MERS, Ebola, Zika and H7N9 influenza. Countries, she argues, "own their viruses in the very same sense that they own the birds in their skies". It does not follow from that they own the data about those viruses, although there are good moral and practical reasons to think that data-sharing should be encouraged. Importantly, though, she warns against romanticism concerning data-sharing, noting that the benefits of such protocols generally accrue to the wealthy rather than the poor. Once again, though, this may not be desirable given certain intuitions about global justice, and given that the world's poorest are often the most vulnerable to illness, and might be most vulnerable to the power of a few politically and economically powerful actors to take control of the benefits that are there to be had from data. Likewise, while insisting on sample-sharing has a certain intuitive appeal, she asserts that that "completely ignores the demands of LMICs for equitable benefit-sharing". There is a sense in which unfettered research may be contrary to justice.

Another potential problem with unfettered research is that of "dual use dilemma"—the possibility that entirely legitimate research may be coopted for entirely nefarious ends. Allow that there is a good reason to manipulate the genes in a virus to make it more transmissible, as a way of understanding how likely that might be in the wild. Allow, too, that there is good reason to publish research. In so doing, though, one puts into the public domain insight that may be used in a deliberately harmful way. How ought regulators and ethicists to deal with this sort of situation? How should we balance goods—including the good of scientific freedom—with potential harms?

Evans notes in his paper that even framing the question in these terms smuggles in all manner of assumptions. Not the least of these is that risks and benefits can be balanced on the same fulcrum:

> We typically and perhaps justifiably tend to think of risks and benefits as straightforwardly comparable or commensurate. But this need not be the case. [I]t isn't clear that the kinds of benefits we typically describe for dual-use infectious disease research – saving lives – are morally equivalent to the typical risks we assign to dual-use research in terms of lives lost.

And it's not only that harms and benefits may be different in kind: there may be different kinds of harm, and different kinds of benefit. Trying to balance the pros and cons may be not so much simple as simplistic. Evans suggests that we should adopt what he calls a "position of pluralism" when it comes to the ethics of dual-use research, but using policy, through funding decisions, to bias research towards that which provides the clearest benefit for the lowest foreseen dual-use potential, commensurate with scientific freedom.

In the final chapter of this collection, we return to a focus on the state, but through a particular lens—that of human rights. The chapter by Mason Meier, Evans and Phelan "examines the evolving link between infectious disease control and human rights, analysing rights-based approaches to preventing, detecting, and responding to infectious disease outbreaks". They take as their starting point the observation that "public health efforts to prevent, detect, and respond to infectious disease outbreaks continue to employ mechanisms that infringe individual rights", such rights covering bodily integrity, freedom of movement, and privacy. At the same time, measures such as vaccination, quarantine, and monitoring are quite plausibly important measures if we are to take seriously another ostensible right: the so-called "right to health" (or, perhaps more accurately in this context, the right not to be deprived of one's health). These sets of rights-claims appear to be in tension; the question, then, is whether and how they can be reconciled. Likewise, individual rights may be in tension with states' rights (and obligations) to protect their citizens.

One of the problems here, of course, is defining what we mean by rights in the first place. Are rights generated by legal *fiat*, or are they things that one has irrespective of the legal dispensation, and that any decent legal system ought to recognise and strive to realise? If some rights belong to one category and others to the other, how can we compare them? For the purposes of their paper, rights are taken to be expressed in law, but there is a hint that they are not exclusively the products of law. "Assuring the realisation of human rights in public health," the authors write, will require that we assess

> whether infection control policies, programmes, and practices pose the least threat of infringing on human rights while posing the greatest opportunity to realise health-related human rights.

If human rights are posits of lawmakers and nothing else besides, a statement like this would not make sense. There would be no need to worry about a policy infringing on a human right, because endorsing that policy would mean that one no longer had that right, and that there was therefore nothing to infringe. So there must be (we may infer) something more fundamental—something bankable by the individual against the state. This represents an approach to infectious diseases born out of a growing interesting in human rights in healthcare, and the putative right to health. It returns our focus to the person, the individual, who is caught up in the devastating impact infectious diseases can have on lives.

3 Lucky All the Time: Addressing the Challenges of Infectious Disease

Notwithstanding the more optimistic ideas mentioned at the beginning of this introduction, and whatever optimism we may try to salvage from them, it is abundantly clear that the era of infectious diseases has not come to a close. The most that we can hope to say with any degree of good faith is that the list of diseases that may kill us in the twenty-first century is not *quite* the same as the list of diseases that killed us in the twentieth. Smallpox is no longer be a worry, and polio—with luck and a following wind—is at least on its way to extinction, and is even now not a worry for most. Even HIV might be conquered: if providing antiretroviral drugs can reduce viral load to undetectable levels, making transmission near impossible, the reservoir of the virus in the human population will gradually fade away as those who are infected die of other causes. UNAids published its 90-90-90 target in 2014, which aimed to ensure that by 2020, 90% of HIV cases would be diagnosed, of which 90% would be on treatment, of which 90% would be virally suppressed. "Modelling suggests that achieving these targets by 2020 will enable the world to end the AIDS epidemic by 2030."[18] As we write this in early 2019, this target may seem a touch optimistic—in 2017, treatment was being accessed by just short of 60% of people living with HIV.[19] Still, the general point stands that the virus is not as invulnerable to human action as we may have feared a generation ago.

But SARS, MERS, and COVID-19 have shown us that new pathogens are waiting in the wings, and flu has shown us that old enemies will keep on returning. In the grand scheme of things, the damage that these illnesses have done has been relatively small so far; but in the age of mass global travel, it is surely not implausible to think that a truly devastating global pandemic with truly mass mortality may be just a few sneezes away. A widely-reported statement issued by the IRA in 1984 reminded the British government that bomb-setters only have to be lucky once; the security services have to be lucky all the time. Something similar might be said in this context. Indeed, infectious diseases remain one of the top five causes of years of life lost around the globe.[20]

---

[18]UNAids, 90-90-90: An Ambitious Treatment Target to Help End the AIDS Epidemic (available via http://www.unaids.org/en/resources/documents/2017/90-90-90).

[19]Figures via http://www.unaids.org/en/resources/fact-sheet, as of 10.1.19.

[20]GBD 2016 Causes of Death Collaborators (2017).

That said, while infectious diseases have changed in the twenty-first century, so has infectious disease control and response. In many ways, the world is much better prepared for the next major infectious disease outbreak: medical interventions continue to improve; surveillance and response is more accurate and quicker than it has ever been. Even so, and partly because we don't know exactly where it'll come from, we remain unprepared for the next pandemic. New medical interventions are of no use if they are inaccessible to those who need them; and fine ideas about new interventions are of no use if the right incentives and rewards for development and propagation are not in place. Scientific willingness will always founder on the reef of political and policy complacency, underfunding, and over-cautiousness among international health agencies.

We cannot pretend that this small volume goes very far to solving the problems that face us. Indeed, we cannot be sure that the authors here have even spotted every problem that has to be solved. Nevertheless, what they have done has been to spot *some* of them, and to outline why they are problems, and what kinds of factors would have to be taken into account in any plausible solution. Whether it be from Ebola or influenza, the global public will face another major threat of massive morbidity and mortality sooner or later. Knowing what the obstacles are to an effective defence and response is the first step in overcoming them.

References

Beauchamp T, Childress J (2013) Principles of biomedical ethics. Oxford University Press, Oxford

Brachman P (2003) Infectious diseases—past, present, and future. Int J Epidemiol 32(5):684

GBD 2016 Causes of Death Collaborators (2017) Global, regional, and national age-sex specific mortality for 264 causes of death, 1980–2016: a systematic analysis for the global burden of disease study 2016. The Lancet 390:1151

Hofman M, Au S (eds) (2017) The politics of fear: Médecins sans Frontières and the West African Ebola epidemic. Oxford University Press, Oxford

Katz (2016 Aug 19) The U.N.'s cholera admission and what comes next. New York Times. https://www.nytimes.com/2016/08/19/magazine/the-uns-cholera-admission-and-what-comes-next.html

Mannell et al (2018) UK's role in global health research innovation. The Lancet 391(10122):721

Spellberg B, Taylor-Blake B (2013) On the exoneration of Dr. William H. Stewart: debunking an urban legend. Infect Dis Poverty 2(1):2

Trump DJ (2017) Remarks of President Donald J. Trump—inaugural address, January 20, 2017, Washington D.C. Available at: https://www.whitehouse.gov/briefings-statements/the-inaugural-address/, last accessed 22nd December 2018

UNSC (2000) HIV/AIDS and international peacekeeping operations. S/RES/1308

UNSC (2011) Maintenance of international peace and security. S/RES/1983

World Health Organisation (2014) Antimicrobial resistance: global report on surveillance. Available at: https://apps.who.int/iris/bitstream/handle/10665/112642/?sequence=1, last accessed 22nd December 2018

World Health Organisation (2018) Ebola situation reports: Democratic Republic of the Congo. Available at: https://www.who.int/ebola/situation-reports/drc-2018/en/, last accessed 22nd December 2018

Applying Lessons from the Past in Haiti: Cholera, Scientific Knowledge, and the Longest-Standing Principle of International Health Law

Adam Rainis Houston

Abstract The tragedy of the Haitian cholera epidemic—where a disease brought to the country by United Nations (UN) peacekeepers has killed at least 10,000 people and sickened over 800,000—has propelled a range of complex international law issues into the public eye. The repercussions of the ongoing debate over accountability, and the purposes and limits of UN immunity, are likely to reverberate for years to come. Despite considerable attention from the international law community, however, almost none of the resulting scholarship has focused on the international health law aspects of the case. The international spread of the vast majority of infectious diseases has been the subject matter of international law only since the 2005 revision of the International Health Regulations (IHRs). By contrast, preventing the international transmission of cholera has been the object of multilateral state negotiation for over 160 years, resulting in it becoming the sole subject matter of not merely the first, but the first three binding international health law treaties over a century ago. Since that time, cholera prevention has remained an unbroken thread woven through the history of international health law, from the initial International Sanitary Conventions, through the formation of the World Health Organisation, and into the twenty-first century. The current iteration of the IHRs are today one of the most universally accepted sources of binding international legal obligations of any kind; as the only disease that has appeared in all previous iterations over nearly 125 years, preventing the transnational spread of cholera approaches customary international law status. This chapter builds upon these themes to re-examine the conduct of the United Nations through this lens. It explores UN standards, and actual UN practice, as they relate to medical guidance to peacekeeping missions, preventative measures for peacekeepers such as vaccination and prophylaxis, and treatment of sewage and sanitation. In doing so, it offers valuable lessons from the past and the present on how international law around infectious disease might be effectively implemented, and followed, in the future.

A. R. Houston (✉)
University of Ottawa, Ottawa, Canada
e-mail: ahous062@uottawa.ca

© Springer Nature Switzerland AG 2020
M. Eccleston-Turner and I. Brassington (eds.), *Infectious Diseases in the New Millennium*, International Library of Ethics, Law, and the New Medicine 82, https://doi.org/10.1007/978-3-030-39819-4_2

Keywords International Sanitary Regulations · History · Cholera · United
Nations · Scientific knowledge

1 Introduction (of Cholera)

The tragedy of the Haitian cholera epidemic—where United Nations peacekeepers
introduced a previously unknown disease into the country, causing the most serious
cholera epidemic anywhere in the world in over a century—has propelled a range of
complex international law issues into the public eye.[1] The most prominent among
these have related to UN accountability and justice for the victims of the epidemic.[2]
These issues have been the subject of extensive advocacy efforts, including high-
profile legal proceedings on behalf of the victims.[3] Only after more than six years did
the United Nations finally acknowledge a role in the epidemic and, in a weakly worded
apology, accept its moral, though not its legal, responsibility to address the damage
it caused.[4] In the absence of a binding legal decision, the debate over accountability,
and the point where UN immunity tips into impunity, remains unresolved.

Despite the undeniable importance of these issues, however, they have overshad-
owed the violation of an even longer-standing principle of international law that
remains at the epicentre of the Haitian tragedy: that the international community
shares responsibility for taking measures to prevent certain infectious diseases, and
in particular cholera, from spreading across borders. While the boundaries of this
principle continue to evolve, particularly as new threats emerge ranging from avian
flu to Zika virus, it was preventing the international spread of cholera that first brought
nations together to lay the foundations of international health law over 160 years ago.
Cholera was in turn the sole subject of the first binding multilateral agreement in international health law—indeed, the first three such agreements—and the disease has
remained a constant thread woven throughout the history and development of international health law to the present day. The Haitian epidemic thus serves as a reminder
both of why the international community first came together to address the shared
threat of cholera using the tool of international law, and the deadly consequences of
ignoring this longstanding principle.

Legal measures to prevent the international spread of cholera also offer an intrigu-
ing perspective on the development of international law, as in contrast to other fields,
international health law is necessarily influenced by scientific knowledge alongside
legal theory and state practice. From the very first International Sanitary Conference onwards, national delegations usually comprised both diplomats and scientists.[5]

---

[1] Jenson et al. (2011).

[2] Transnational Development Clinic at Yale Law School, Global Health Justice Partnership of the
Yale Law School and the Yale School of Public Health, and Association Haïtienne de droit de
l'Environnement (2013).

[3] Weinmeyer (2016).

[4] United Nations (2016).

[5] Howard-Jones (1975).

After all, bacteria do not obey legal diktats rooted in abstract concepts such as state sovereignty.[6] Thus, effective rules to prevent the spread of disease must involve what we might now term evidence-based policy.

This being the case, a historical analysis of international health law is complicated by the realisation that what may once have been accepted as scientific fact, and therefore seen as a sensible basis for law and action, may by modern standards seem inadequate or even entirely incorrect. This is readily apparent in the early development of international law around cholera and will be discussed in detail later in this chapter; for the time being, it suffices to say that while acceptance of the principle that evidence-based measures should be taken to prevent the international spread of cholera is widespread and longstanding, the precise measures thought capable of doing so have necessarily evolved alongside changes in scientific knowledge and understanding. The evidentiary aspect has implications not only for what measures might be considered sufficient, but also those that might be deemed excessive; as discussed below, one of the key goals of adopting international standards relating to the spread of cholera has been to avoid undue interference with international trade through overzealous application of measures like quarantines or import bans. As such, adherence to the underlying principle of preventing the international spread of cholera cannot be assessed by determining whether the practice of states or other international law actors is the same as it was a century ago; rather, it must be by whether their practice at any given time has been guided by contemporaneous evidence-based standards in the service of that principle. Nevertheless, while our understanding of the manner in which the international spread of cholera could be prevented has evolved considerably over the last 160 years, certain elements of our knowledge have changed more drastically than others. Some central concepts, such as the importance of clean water and proper sanitation, have long been well understood; others, such as the utility of vaccination as a preventative measure, have fluctuated over time, as new vaccines, and evidence of their efficacy, emerge. Furthermore, collection and sharing of accurate information has also historically been a core component both of the law (particularly in the recording and notification of cases) and of the broader science that informs what measures the law should either require or, in cases where overreaction is a concern, permit, in fulfilment of the principle of preventing the international spread of cholera. Although international health law has expanded over the past 160 years, these core elements, and cholera itself, remain constant. All these elements come into play in what unfolded in Haiti.

2   Cholera Comes to Haiti

Imported diseases have played a crucial role in Haitian history since long before the cholera epidemic. European contact brought diseases like smallpox that devastated the original indigenous inhabitants, removing a source of manual labour for the

---

[6]Aginam (2002).

colonial powers and leading to their replacement with African slaves. In turn, yellow fever first brought from Africa as an inadvertent by-product of this human cargo later took a serious toll on soldiers freshly dispatched from France, playing a valuable supporting role in making Haiti the first and only modern state to gain independence through a successful slave revolt.[7] It has even been suggested that popular perceptions associating Haiti with the emerging HIV epidemic in the early 1980s caused a drastic reduction in American tourists, in turn leading to a drop in income that helped destabilise and eventually topple the Duvalier regime.[8] The bitter irony of these events is that historical records indicate Haiti was one of the few countries to escape the scourge of cholera during the nineteenth century epidemics that propelled the very development of international health law that forms the focus of this chapter.[9]

By the turn of the twenty-first century, Haiti was the poorest country in the Western Hemisphere. Beginning in 2004, it was also home to the United Nations Stabilisation Mission in Haiti, better known by its French acronym MINUSTAH. Then, on January 12, 2010, an earthquake of magnitude 7.0 devastated the country. Estimates of the number of people killed have varied widely, from the official Haitian government figure of over 300,000 to other estimates below 100,000.[10] Hundreds of thousands more were left homeless, and Haiti's already inadequate health and sanitation infrastructure suffered considerable damage.

Despite concerns about the potential for the rapid spread of disease in crowded temporary camps housing displaced victims of the earthquake, it was not until ten months later, in mid-October of 2010, that the first cases of cholera appeared.[11] This unwelcome appearance was not in the capital city of Port-au-Prince, but in the rural area of Mirebalais. It was here that a MINUSTAH base had recently welcomed a contingent of soldiers from Nepal, a cholera-endemic country in the midst of its own outbreak. At least one of these soldiers was carrying *Vibrio cholerae*, the bacterium that causes cholera.[12] Cholera is spread through water contaminated with infected faeces. It causes severe vomiting and diarrhoea, and can cause death by dehydration within as little as a few hours if left untreated. Due to improper sanitation practices, infected faeces from the MINUSTAH base entered the Artibonite river system, which is relied upon by tens of thousands of Haitians for farming, bathing and drinking.[13] The disease spread rapidly throughout the country, and was found in all ten regions of the country by the following month, as well as over the border in the Dominican Republic.[14] It subsequently spread into Cuba and Mexico.[15]

---

[7] Marr and Cathey (2013).
[8] Evans (1988).
[9] Jenson (n 1).
[10] O'Connor (2012).
[11] Alejandro Cravioto et al. (2011).
[12] Transnational Development Clinic (n 2).
[13] Ibid.
[14] 'Haiti Cholera Reaches Dominican Republic' *BBC* (London, 17 November 2010) http://www.bbc.com/news/world-latin-america-11771109, accessed 1 May 2017.
[15] World Health Organisation (2013).

The cholera-naïve population of Haiti had no resistance to the disease, exacerbating its toll. Although the number of new cases decreased considerably following the initial peak of the epidemic, infections continued, with spikes occurring in the wake of further natural disasters such as Hurricane Matthew in 2016.[16] As of early 2017, according to World Health Organisation statistics, the epidemic had killed over 9000 people and sickened close to 800,000 more.[17] There is also evidence that these figures reflect substantial underestimates, particularly during the early months of the epidemic.[18] Sadly, this previously unknown disease now appears to have firmly established itself in Haiti, where it will continue to pose a threat in the absence of access to clean water and sanitation. A combination of basic shoe-leather epidemiological investigation and high-tech genetic analysis of disease samples demonstrates conclusively that the Haitian strain of cholera has its origins in Nepal and arrived via the MINUSTAH base.[19] Had the UN adhered to the longstanding international law principle of preventing the international spread of cholera, this tragedy could have been prevented.

3 The Germ of an Idea: Cholera and the First International Sanitary Conference

Customs and binding rules to prevent the spread of disease have a long history in virtually every culture. The Bible, which influenced the development of the law in many modern states, provides examples of such rules. For instance, Leviticus devotes two chapters to leprosy and how it should be dealt with, coming out in favour of isolation as the preferred recourse: "All the days wherein the plague shall be in him he shall be defiled; he is unclean: he shall dwell alone; without the camp shall his habitation be."[20]

In turn, governments at all levels have long imposed rudimentary legal measures to keep disease from their own territories; the term quarantine itself originates from the Italian "quaranta", referring to the length of the forty-day isolation period imposed on incoming ships by city-states like Venice to prevent the arrival of bubonic plague in the fifteenth century.[21] Historically, however, such efforts focused on protecting the state from outside threats rather than collaboration among states to address mutual interests. It took a new menace to bring nations together to explore novel ways of tackling shared concerns. The menace in question was cholera.

The landmark occasion bringing states together was the first International Sanitary Conference, convened in Paris in 1851. It would be the first of fourteen such

---

[16]Holpuch (2016).

[17]Pan American Health Organisation (2017).

[18]Luquero et al. (2016).

[19]Transnational Development Clinic (n 2).

[20]Leviticus 13:46.

[21]Tognotti (2013).

Conferences spanning a period of nearly ninety years. Today, this first Conference is widely recognised as the origin point of international health law.[22] The Conference occurred at the beginning of a period of rapid change in the development of international law and policy, thus also playing a role in the broader development of modern international relations.[23] To give some perspective, at the time of the first Conference, foundational agreements in international law such as the first Geneva Convention, as well as accords on other issues that underpin the modern diplomatic and legal order such as telegraphs and postal service, were still a decade or more away. The underlying goal of preventing the spread of disease was also an easy place to find common ground; as one later Conference delegate would state, "the only researches made in common by the different governments of Europe were to oppose a barrier in the way of the march of epidemic diseases, and especially of cholera."[24]

Historically found in the Indian Subcontinent, and thus referred to as "Asiatic cholera" in numerous sources, cholera's rapid spread echoed that of globalisation. Although both bubonic plague and yellow fever were also on the agenda of the Conference, it was primarily the initial two cholera pandemics—the first (approx. 1817–24) sweeping across Asia and lapping Europe's eastern boundaries, and the second (approx. 1829–51) penetrating deep into Europe's heart—that provided the impetus for states to come together to address the threat posed by the international spread of disease. Unlike plague and yellow fever, which posed a risk mostly to trade interests and colonial possessions, cholera threatened Europe itself.

Although endemic diseases like tuberculosis exacted a higher toll overall, the trail of a cholera epidemic across the continent was a particularly obvious one, with the arrival of the disease following soon after news of an outbreak in a neighbouring port. Moreover, cholera was especially capable of making an impression: the trappings of death by cholera—profuse vomiting and the characteristic rice-water diarrhoea— were particularly shocking to polite sensibilities, carrying none of the romanticism of wasting away from consumption (TB).[25] Even today, in the era of headline-grabbing diseases like Ebola, it retains the "ignominious distinction of probably being the pathogen that can kill the most number of humans in the shortest period of time", something that would also help stoke fear upon its arrival in Haiti.[26]

Not only was cholera an early priority in developing a shared legal framework, it was also intimately linked with other driving elements of globalisation in the nineteenth century. Such links have continued until the present day.[27] In particular, its spread was tied directly to the increasing size and speed of international trade, which was itself rapidly redefining international relations. In turn, striking the balance between preventing the spread of cholera and minimizing disruption to burgeoning international trade has been a constant theme in the development of the law. Other

---

[22] See for instance, Fidler (2005).

[23] Huber (2006). See also Harrison (2006).

[24] World Health Organisation (1958).

[25] Evans (n 8).

[26] Ryan (2011).

[27] Lee and Dodgson (2000).

conditions in the nineteenth century helped facilitate its spread as well. Unlike many other diseases that increasingly drew the attention of European politicians and scientists in the age of colonial expansion, cholera was readily adaptable to life outside the tropics. It was spread through poor sanitation, meaning it could be passed on as readily, if not more readily, in England or France as in its historical home in the Ganges Delta. Rapid European urbanisation in the era of industrialisation fuelled precisely such conditions; crowded slums with inadequate sanitation proved a fertile breeding ground. Ultimately, as one commentator describes it, "Asiatic cholera has a good claim to be regarded as the classic epidemic disease of the nineteenth century, above all of Europe in the age of industrialisation."[28] Taken altogether, these factors ensured that cholera became the focus of the Conference.

Nonetheless, the International Sanitary Conference of 1851 is notable mostly for its significance as the starting point for international health law. Only twelve states participated in the initial event; in a sign of the very different map of the world in 1851, four of these states would be absorbed into a unified Italy shortly after.[29] Furthermore, although it brought control of disease into the international sphere, its focus was not global collaboration against a mutual threat, but rather regional collaboration to protect Europe from foreign contagion, an approach that from a modern perspective could be charitably described as Eurocentric.[30]

Its tangible outcomes were even less impressive, with no lasting multilateral agreement emerging from the Conference. However, as discussed in detail below, it was not ultimately disagreement over the value of preventing the spread of cholera that created the delay in agreeing upon the concrete and codified steps to address it. Rather, it was lack of understanding of what those measures should be, hindered by the dearth of basic knowledge such as what caused cholera and how it was spread. Interestingly, the balance of the medical and the political was struck in the delegations for each participating country, with each team of two consisting of a diplomat and a physician. As Howard-Jones notes, the voting system at the first Conference allowed these two members to vote separately, even contradictorily.[31] Under such circumstances, it is difficult to know what to make of the knowledge that "[i]n his address at the closure of the first conference, the French Minister of Agriculture and Trade congratulated the participants on their discretion and wisdom in divorcing themselves not only from all questions of politics - but also of science."[32] Ultimately, despite the involvement of an increasingly large and diverse set of countries over subsequent Conferences, a scientific consensus on cholera and its causes was not quickly forthcoming. Nevertheless, Birn argues that the meetings themselves, "far more than the elaboration of the germ theory, the identification of vectors and microorganisms, or the signing of

---

[28] Evans (n 8).

[29] World Health Organisation, *First Ten Years* (n 24).

[30] Huber (n 23). For another interesting perspective, see Ersoy et al. (2011).

[31] Howard-Jones (n 5).

[32] World Health Organisation, *First Ten Years* (n 24).

conventions best characterise success in this initial stage."[33] This is fortunate, given that it would take another six meetings over 41 years before sufficient consensus was found to permit a binding agreement to be reached.

4 The Science of Cholera

It is tempting to look at the history of the health sciences as a linear series of discrete, progressive steps, but the development of the International Sanitary Conferences serves to illustrate that this is certainly not the case. As outlined by Howard-Jones in his masterful exploration of the progression of scientific knowledge over the course of the fourteen Conferences, medical concepts today considered basic facts were bitterly contested or entirely unknown at earlier junctures, making it difficult to take evidence-based action.[34] As was subsequently said of the first Conference, "both diplomats and doctors who participated in these…discussions had in common their total ignorance of the nature and mode of propagation of the three diseases – cholera, plague, and yellow fever – under consideration."[35] And even as science was posited as objective and free of political considerations, the discoveries of eminent scientists— such as the German Robert Koch and Louis Pasteur of France—could also fuel national rivalries.[36]

Consider what is widely agreed to be the seminal moment in the field of epidemiology, which itself stems directly from the cholera epidemics of the nineteenth century. This moment did not even occur until three years after the initial International Sanitary Conference. In 1854, Doctor John Snow mapped cholera cases during an epidemic in London's Soho district. His map allowed him to trace the source of the epidemic back to a well in Broad Street, demonstrating that the disease was transmitted through contaminated water.[37] Despite justified acclaim today, the medical establishment of the era was not so accepting of Snow's theory that cholera was waterborne; for decades afterwards, other theories on the origins of cholera continued to hold sway at the Conferences, ranging from airborne transmission to some unique property of the soil, or to elaborate combinations of such factors. Even after Robert Koch, the founder of modern microbiology, identified the cholera bacterium in 1884, helping advance the germ theory of disease in the process, widespread acceptance of the cause of cholera was not immediate. One of the most influential proponents of alternative theories, the famed German hygienist Max von Pettenkofer, would hold onto them until the end of his career.[38] Indeed, as a further illustration of the fickle integration of scientific discovery into mainstream medical thought, *Vibrio*

---

[33] Birn (2009).

[34] Howard-Jones (n 5).

[35] World Health Organisation, *First Ten Years* (n 24).

[36] Bynum (1993).

[37] For more detail on John Snow, including his other work on cholera, see Halliday (2007).

[38] Morabia (2007).

cholerae had already been isolated and identified as the cause of cholera, to virtually no acclaim, by Filippo Pacini in 1854, the same year that Snow had the handle removed from the Broad Street pump.[39] In the end, unanimous acceptance of cholera as a waterborne disease would not come until the Eleventh Conference in 1903.[40] As a result, the desire to take effective steps to prevent cholera transmission was initially hampered by a lack of scientific knowledge, further exacerbated by the slow mainstream acceptance of new discoveries.

5 The Conventional Approach: The First International Sanitary Conventions

During the course of the six International Sanitary Conferences that took place during the period leading up to the first binding agreement, international interest had increased considerably, with more than thirty countries and territories participating in at least one. Haiti itself would participate in the 1881 International Sanitary Conference in Washington, the only one of the Conferences ever to take place in the Western Hemisphere. This increasing internationalisation was due in large part to the fact cholera itself had become a truly global problem over the same period, affecting almost all corners of the globe. During the latter half of the nineteenth century, the world suffered through the third (approx. 1852–1860) and fourth (approx. 1863–1875) cholera pandemics, and it was in the midst of a fifth (approx. 1881–1896) by the time the first binding multilateral agreement on preventing international transmission of disease was signed at the seventh International Sanitary Conference in Venice.

A landmark agreement in international law, the *International Sanitary Convention* (1892) is the first link in an unbroken chain of international health law agreements that continue to bind countries today. Fourteen nations, including all the major European (and, by extension, colonial) powers, ratified the first Convention.[41] Given global concern about the disease, it is little surprise that the sole subject of the first binding agreement in international health law was cholera. Despite its significance as the first agreement in international health law, the scope of the first International Sanitary Convention is quite limited. Its focus was the Suez Canal, which had shortened the travel time between Europe and the Indian Subcontinent considerably since it opened in 1869. As such, the Convention addressed only westbound shipping through the Suez Canal, in response to concerns about this direct path between the perceived source of the disease and European ports. Once sown, however, the seeds of international health law sprouted quickly. In quick succession, subsequent International Sanitary Conventions yielded the first expansions of the field of international health

---

[39] Lippi and Gotuzzo (2014).

[40] Howard-Jones (n 5).

[41] Protocoles et Procès-verbaux de la Conférence sanitaire internationale de Venise inaugurée le 5 janvier 1892 (Rome: Impr. Nationale de J. Bertero, 1892).

law, or, perhaps more precisely in the earliest years, the field of international cholera law. Measures agreed upon in Dresden (1893) included expanding the geographic scope of the agreement and adding notification provisions.[42] The next agreement, this time in Paris (1894), dealt specifically with the Islamic pilgrimage to Mecca, continuing the emphasis on keeping "Asiatic cholera" out of Europe.[43]

Cholera thus remained the sole topic of international health law throughout the earliest three agreements. Not until 1897 did international health conventions expand to encompass a second disease, with an agreement focusing on bubonic plague.[44] Subsequently, in 1903, the previous agreements were consolidated into a single new agreement, which maintained the focus on cholera and plague, but added reference to yellow fever.[45] The resulting list of three diseases would remain the three constants throughout the subsequent history of international health law, even as later agreements would adjust both the roster of diseases addressed, and the scope of measures countries needed to undertake in order to monitor, prevent and address their spread.

The International Sanitary Conferences would continue until the outbreak of World War II, with further Conferences in 1911 and 1926 before ultimately concluding with the Fourteenth International Sanitary Conference in 1938. Haiti itself participated in the 1926 Conference and was among over 60 countries to be party to the resulting Convention. The 1926 International Sanitary Convention emphasised the importance of mandatory case notification for select diseases including cholera, and highlighted the role of international organisations in the sharing of this information.[46] It also required states to prevent the embarkation onto ships of individuals showing symptoms or people whose relations with the sick placed them at risk, and imposed measures in a range of circumstances regarding the disinfection of human waste where cholera was confirmed or suspected.[47] Public health and national interests remained awkward companions; the US Surgeon General pronounced the agreement "a decided improvement" over the previous conventions, with the caveat that it was still the result of negotiation among states with varying goals conducted "by men of all degrees of intelligence".[48] Meanwhile, the inclusion of the first two diseases considered native to Europe rather than necessarily imported from abroad—smallpox and typhus—was still outweighed by the addition of extensive further regulation around religious pilgrims in the Middle East.[49]

[42] Procès–Verbaux de la Conférence Sanitaire Internationale de de Dresde, 11 mars–15 avril 1893 (Dresde: Impr. B.G. Teubner, 1893).

[43] Conférence Sanitaire Internationale de Paris, 7 février-3 avril 1894: Procès–Verbaux (Paris: Impr. Nationale, 1894).

[44] Conférence Sanitaire Internationale de Venise, 16 février–19 mars 1897: Procès–Verbaux (Rome: Forzani et Cie, Imprimeurs du Sénat, 1897).

[45] International Sanitary Convention (1903) 35 Stat. 1770; Treaty Series 466.

[46] International Sanitary Convention (1926), 45 Stat. 2492; Treaty Series 762.

[47] Ibid.

[48] Cumming (1926).

[49] Fidler (n 22).

Further Conventions emerged from the Conferences, though they were not always completed in the same years; for instance, the *International Sanitary Convention for Aerial Navigation* came into force in 1935. Just as steamships and railways had previously changed the speed with which diseases could disseminate, this Convention highlighted the role new technologies could play in rapidly spreading new diseases, and prescribed special measures for six diseases, including cholera.[50] Cholera, the first disease to be regulated under international law, would thus remain a constant presence throughout the development of international health law within the first century of its development; it would also justify its presence by continuing to pose an international threat to health.

6 Spreading to a New Host: The WHO and the International Health Regulations

By the early twentieth century, international cooperation on public health also led to the development of formal international health bodies, including the Office International d'Hygiène Publique (OHIP) in 1907 and the Health Organisation of the League of Nations in the aftermath of World War I. At times, politics came to the fore; plans to combine the two were undone by objections of the United States, a member of OHIP but not the League.[51] These organisations were complemented by regional bodies like the International Sanitary Bureau, the precursor to the Pan-American Health Organisation (PAHO). This organisation was in fact the oldest of all international health bodies, having been formed in 1902; it would promptly address cholera within its own regional Convention in 1903.[52] Concern for cholera was evident at all levels. For instance, a 1920 report from a League of Nations delegation highlights the role of foreign soldiers—foreshadowing events in Haiti—in spreading cholera from Russia to Poland.[53]

These organisations in turn have a direct lineage to today's World Health Organisation (WHO), which inherited their functions or, in the case of PAHO, absorbed the entire organisation under its umbrella. Since its formation in 1948 as a specialised agency of the United Nations, the WHO has assumed the role of coordinating international public health. In the process, it has moved towards creating a truly global approach to health, shifting away from the Eurocentric viewpoint of the early Conventions towards a more universalist outlook in line with the objectives of the UN system. Furthermore, from its inception, the WHO has had more power than its predecessor organisations. In particular, Article 21 of the WHO's Constitution gives the organisation the authority to create regulations to address "sanitary and quarantine

---

[50] International Sanitary Convention for Aerial Navigation (1935), 49 Stat. 3279; Treaty Series 901.
[51] World Health Organisation, *First Ten Years* (n 24).
[52] 'First General International Sanitary Convention of the American Republics, Held at New Willard Hotel, Washington, D.C., December 2, 3, and 4, 190' (1903) 18 Public Health Reports 233.
[53] Pottevin and Norman White (1920).

requirements and other procedures designed to prevent the international spread of disease".[54] Further enhancing its reach is its "opt-out" model for such regulations, replacing the opt-in nature of traditional treaties such as the International Sanitary Conventions, thus ensuring the near-universal reach of its rules.[55] It is also important to note that in addition to its legal function, the WHO also plays a key role in promoting international standards for cholera prevention and control from a scientific perspective.[56] Although not themselves legally binding, these standards influence national policy and international responses, including around proper measures for the prevention of cross-border spread. These standards thus necessarily inform the legal response.

Even more direct is the lineage of the International Sanitary Conventions themselves; they were inherited by the WHO and adopted by the Fourth World Health Assembly as the International Sanitary Regulations (ISR) in 1951, exactly a century after the initial International Sanitary Conference.[57] At the time of their adoption, they covered six "quarantinable diseases" including cholera. Nonetheless, after the initial adoption of the International Sanitary Regulations, evolution over the next half century would be slow; as Fidler notes, one of the only large-scale changes was to cut back drastically on the number of restrictions governing religious pilgrimages.[58] Still, the ISR were revised and re-christened as the International Health Regulations (IHR) in 1969, at which time typhus and relapsing fever were removed from the list of diseases, leaving only four: cholera, plague and yellow fever, plus smallpox.[59] At this point, improved sanitary standards had largely removed cholera as a concern in the European states that first gathered in 1851, but it remained a threat in many parts of the world.

Indeed, by this time the seventh cholera pandemic was underway, having begun in Indonesia in 1961. Further complicating matters, the strain of cholera responsible, El Tor, posed new challenges for detection and eradication, as it was more both more resilient in the environment and more likely to be carried asymptomatically.[60] Thus, as a serious health concern, cholera remained a focus of the International Health Regulations under the auspices of the WHO, just as it had been the initial impetus for the first Conferences and subsequent Conventions.

However, the threat of the seventh pandemic also demonstrated that the existing IHRs were inadequate to the task of preventing the international spread of cholera. In 1971, the World Health Assembly requested the Director-General of the WHO

---

[54]Constitution of the World Health Organisation (adopted 22 July 1946, entered into force 7 April 1948) 14 UNTC 185, Art. 21.

[55]Fidler (n 22).

[56]See for example, World Health Organisation, WHO guidance on formulation of national policy on the control of cholera (1992) WHO/CDD/SER/92.16 REV.1.

[57]International Sanitary Regulations, 25 May 1951, 175 UNTS 214.

[58]Fidler (n 22).

[59]Choi (2008).

[60]Cvjetanovic and Barua (1972).

"to undertake a study of the implications of the removal of cholera from the International Health Regulations and to report to the next meeting of the Committee on International Surveillance of Communicable Diseases."[61] The central debate at the Twenty-Sixth World Health Assembly (1973) consequently focused around the failure of the IHRs to effectively stop the spread of cholera. In turn, the decision to keep cholera in the IHRs, while modifying the specifics of the response, highlights the international consensus on the importance of maintaining binding legal rules hindering its international spread.[62] At the same time, the resulting modifications reflect how emerging scientific evidence resulted in changes to the measures to be taken to prevent that spread. The biggest modification to the IHRs at the time was to remove requirements around cholera vaccination, including the right of countries to demand a vaccination certificate from incoming travellers. What had once been considered an appropriate action was now judged an overreaction not supported by scientific evidence of its public health efficacy. This is because it was determined that the vaccine then in use was ineffective.[63] As will be seen, this shift in vaccine policy as a result of monitoring the effectiveness of existing tools holds lessons for what would occur in Haiti.

A similar discussion took place around cholera and the concept of "preventive medication in international traffic." The Committee on International Surveillance of Communicable Diseases, tasked with examining the issue, noted that "preventive medication would be justified... provided that the drug used was effective in preventing the spread of the disease when administered orally as a single acceptable dose without adverse effects, and did not cause bacterial resistance."[64] However, the Committee concluded that existing evidence did not suggest any of the drugs under discussion for cholera would meet this standard. This discussion too would gain renewed relevance four decades later.

The interaction of scientific/medical developments and the law is further illustrated by the subsequent revision of the IHRs in response to one of the greatest triumphs of modern medicine: the eradication of smallpox, the first—and at this time only—successful eradication of any human disease. Smallpox was removed from the IHRs in 1981. By contrast, the need to keep cholera within the scope of the International Health Regulations was periodically reinforced, as when it reappeared in Latin America after a century-long absence in 1991, affecting over 330,000 people, and killing more than 3500, across 13 countries in the first nine months alone.[65] As such, its capacity to emerge in new territories, spread rapidly, and cause drastic loss of life was aptly demonstrated nearly 100 years after the first binding agreement designed to prevent its international spread.

---

[61] World Health Assembly Res 24.26 (15 May 1971) WHA24.26.

[62] World Health Assembly Res 26.55, (24 May 1973) WHA26.55.

[63] World Health Assembly, Seventeenth Report of the Committee on International Surveillance of Communicable Diseases (12 March 1973) A26/26.

[64] Ibid., 89.

[65] Tauxe and Blake (1992).

7   Going Global: The Revised International Health Regulations (2005)

The next landmark development for international health law was the dramatic revision and expansion of the International Health Regulations in 2005, and their entry into force in 2007. As outlined in article 3(3) of the revised IHRs, "[t]he implementation of these Regulations shall be guided by the goal of their universal application for the protection of all people of the world from the international spread of disease."[66] To this end, the International Health Regulations of 2005 cover a far broader range of infectious diseases, accommodating new threats from emerging and previously unknown diseases alongside long-standing ones such as cholera. Immediately prior to the revisions, by contrast, the IHRs still focused only on the first three diseases to be tackled by international health law: cholera, plague and yellow fever. The need for such a revision had been debated since the mid-1990s.[67] Nevertheless, the ultimate catalyst for revision was once again a new global threat, much as cholera had been for the first International Sanitary Conference over 150 years earlier.[68]

In this case, the severe acute respiratory syndrome (SARS) epidemic of 2002–3 highlighted numerous barriers to preventing and managing the cross-border spread of disease. Among these was the reticence of China to share information with the rest of the world about this novel disease. Consequently, the revised IHRs expressly require states to develop appropriate surveillance with "the capacity to detect, assess, notify and report" events that, according to a laid-out set of criteria, could be termed "public health emergencies of international concern" rather than relying upon a small and finite list of diseases. Nevertheless, given its intimate connection to the development of the IHRs, and its long-held status as an internationally notifiable disease, cholera can still be thought of as the definitive example of a disease whose spread is a matter of international concern. This status is further supported by the fact that, under the updated IHRs, it remains explicitly identified as a disease for which any incident must always be evaluated using IHR criteria, given cholera has "demonstrated the ability to cause serious public health impact and to spread rapidly internationally".[69]

The current IHRs require states to develop a minimum capacity to address public health emergencies of international concern at airports, ports, and other border crossings. For the first time, the IHRs also make explicit room for third parties, such as non-governmental organisations (NGOs), to provide information where state communication is insufficient; this highlights the role of non-state parties in upholding an important legal principle. Furthermore, in addition to minimum capacities, the IHRs emphasise the need for any additional response measures taken by states to

---

[66] International Health Regulations (adopted 23 May 2005, entered into force 15 June 2007), Article 3(3).
[67] World Health Assembly Res 48.7 (12 May 1995) WHA48.7.
[68] Taylor (2008).
[69] International Health Regulations (2005), Annex 2.

take into account scientific principles, available scientific evidence, and any available guidance or advice from the WHO.[70] Establishing such standards also offers a degree of protection to states that might be reticent to report a disease for fear of disproportionate reprisal by other states. Thus, WHO guidance, and increasing scientific knowledge about a disease like cholera in general, both explicitly inform the steps that must be taken to comply with the IHRs.

The 2005 IHRs are the most recent iteration of a set of rules around the international spread of disease whose development began in 1851. In the often hazy world of international law, where knowing who accepts the rules is as important as the rules themselves, the current IHRs are one of the most widely accepted agreements in existence. Thanks to the WHO's opt-out structure, they are legally binding on 196 states as of 2017—more parties than there are members of the United Nations itself.[71] Certainly, even these revised IHRs have their deficiencies, perhaps most notably the absence of a proper enforcement mechanism. However, these weaknesses do not undo the virtually universal acceptance of the IHRs. To paraphrase an analysis of a previous iteration of the IHRs in the aftermath of the reforms of the early 1970s, despite their imperfections "the present Regulations remain the most acceptable means of trying" to attain their underlying objective.[72] Existing weaknesses also do not negate the underlying goal of preventing the international spread of disease—a principle whose development within international health law began with cholera. As the Haitian tragedy illustrates, adherence to this principle remains as important today as it was in 1851. Furthermore, the IHRs are not the only place where cholera is integrated into international law.

8 The Disease Spreads: Other Treaties and Frameworks

While the WHO is the primary UN body dealing with rules to prevent the international spread of cholera, other international legal instruments can help to further this goal. Some such instruments do so in broad strokes encompassing cholera within their ambit. For instance, the International Covenant on Economic, Social and Cultural Rights obliges states to take steps necessary for the "prevention, treatment and control of epidemic, endemic, occupational and other diseases".[73] At the same time, evolving human rights norms also increasingly implicate cholera; for example, the United Nations now has both a Special Rapporteur on the Right to Health, and a Special Rapporteur on the Rights to Safe Drinking Water and Sanitation. In turn,

---

[70] Ibid., Art. 43.

[71] World Health Organisation (2005).

[72] Delon (1975).

[73] International Covenant on Civil and Political Rights (adopted 16 December 1966, entered into force 23 March 1976) 999 UNTS 171, Art. 12.

international humanitarian law highlights obligations not to destroy or render useless key infrastructure such as drinking water installations and supplies.[74] And the burgeoning field of international environmental law has numerous implications for preventing the spread of cholera. This includes not only rules around clean water and sanitation that would necessarily affect the spread of the disease, but also the emergence of both transboundary responsibility between states and the notion of the precautionary principle.[75]

While these evolving areas of law have serious but indirect implications for cholera, it also remains an explicit consideration in multiple fields of international law outside that of health. Even prior to the formal establishment of the UN, concerns about the international spread of cholera and other diseases found their way into other areas of what would soon become the UN framework. The *Convention on International Civil Aviation* (1944) explicitly highlights the need for each state "to take effective measures to prevent the spread by means of air navigation" of cholera and other designated diseases.[76] Although the Convention, under the auspices of the International Civil Aviation Organisation (ICAO), has gone through eight revisions since that time, this provision remains the same today, and as such is binding on 191 state parties as of 2017. Cholera has also been an explicit consideration in far more recent agreements. For instance, the *International Convention for the Control and Management of Ships' Ballast Water and Sediments*, which entered into force in 2017 under the auspices of the International Maritime Organisation (IMO), explicitly includes cholera as the first of its "indicator microbes, as a human health standard" for ballast water.[77] This is little surprise given that ballast water was a prime suspect in the international spread of cholera in the aftermath of the Peruvian epidemic.[78] Taken together, it is clear that the international spread of cholera has been explicitly considered by states in the context of international law-making on multiple occasions, even outside the auspices of the IHRs.

9 Commerce and Cholera

But it is in the area of international trade that cholera has appeared most often. One novel tool offered by international trade law is that it also supplies enforcement mechanisms largely absent from other areas of international law such as health. As noted earlier, minimizing trade disruption by standardizing measures taken against

---

[74] Jorgensen (2007).

[75] Jones (1999).

[76] *Convention on International Civil Aviation* (adopted 7 December 1944, entered into force 4 April 1947) 15 UNTS 295, Art.14.

[77] *International Convention for the Control and Management of Ships' Ballast Water and Sediments* (adopted 13 February 2004, entered into force 8 September 2017) International Maritime Organisation, Reg D-2(2).

[78] McCarthy and Khambaty (1994).

cholera was a primary goal from the first International Sanitary Conference onwards. This objective was highlighted early in the first Conference by the French Minister of Foreign Affairs, who stated that "the imbalance created in the international system and trade by having separate sanitary regulations has to be eliminated."[79] When Fidler outlines the "classical regime" of the first century of international health law, he describes it as having "two basic parts: obligations on States Parties to (1) notify each other about outbreaks of specified infectious diseases in their territories; and (2) limit disease-prevention measures that restricted international trade and travel to those based on scientific evidence and public health principles."[80] These issues are reflected throughout the development of international health law. For instance, the *International Sanitary Convention* (1903) notes, "No merchandise is capable by itself of transmitting plague or cholera. It only becomes dangerous when contaminated by plague or cholera products."[81] Similar debates around the effectiveness of cholera prevention measures and their impact on trade have surfaced much more recently, particularly in the context of states imposing excessive, scientifically unsupported measures on others to prevent the importation of cholera. The economic consequences can be severe; as one example, it is estimated the 1991 epidemic cost Peru hundreds of millions of dollars in lost trade and tourism.[82] As such, highlighting the need for proportionate, evidence-based responses is important in order to help minimise the possibility states will cover up epidemics for fear of the economic consequences.

Consequently, measures in excess of what is necessary to prevent the international spread of cholera have been the subject of trade disputes. It is important to note that the motivation of preventing the spread of cholera—when exercised in good faith—is not questioned; it is only the character and quality of the measures taken for this purpose that are. Today, the most important agreement governing the question of scientifically appropriate measures for restricting trade in the interests of public health protection is the WTO Agreement on the Application of Sanitary and Phytosanitary Measures.[83] This agreement has underscored the vital importance of scientific knowledge, including the availability of evidence of the efficacy of measures undertaken by countries to avoid cholera.

For instance, in 1998, the WTO Committee on Sanitary and Phytosanitary Measures met to discuss concerns raised by Tanzania over the prohibition placed on fish imports from Tanzania and other East African countries by the European Commission over fears of importing cholera.[84] The meeting makes particular reference to standards set by both the WHO and the Food and Agriculture Organisation (FAO), reinforcing the importance of UN bodies in developing the standards underpinning

---

[79] Ersoy et al. (2011).

[80] Fidler (n 22).

[81] *International Sanitary Convention* (1903), 35 Stat. 1770; Treaty Series 466, Art. 11.

[82] Cash and Narasimhan (2000).

[83] WTO Agreement on the Application of Sanitary and Phytosanitary Measures, 1867 UNTS 493.

[84] World Trade Organisation Committee on Sanitary and Phytosanitary Measures, Summary of the Meeting held on 10–11 June 1998 (17 August 1998) G/SPS/R/11.

law.[85] Once again, it is important to note that while in this case the use of a total embargo on imports is criticised as excessive, the underlying goal of preventing the international transmission of cholera is not. Thus, international trade law highlights how seriously the issue of cholera transmission is taken, as well as the importance of scientific standards in determining which measures are appropriate, and which measures are not, to prevent international transmission.

10   Cholera in Customary International Law

The examples discussed up until this point highlight unremitting attention to the principle of preventing the international spread of cholera not merely in international health law but in international law more broadly. At the same time, it is true that legal commentators have expressed scepticism about the strength of international law as it regards infectious disease.[86] Certainly many of the criticisms frequently raised, particularly in relation to specific rules that have been breached nearly as often as observed, have some validity. Nonetheless, in the case of cholera in particular, states have demonstrated a continuous and consistent pattern of integrating the prevention of its spread into international law. This is not simply a matter of historical inertia; cholera has been inserted explicitly into new agreements in a variety of fields of law, while the need to retain it during the reform of existing instruments has been explicitly debated and its presence reconfirmed. At the same time, ongoing discussion has ensured that both the minimum precautions that need to be taken to prevent the international spread of cholera, and the maximum measures that scientific evidence will support, have evolved over time. At a minimum, the development of international health law over the past century and a half shows a clear recognition by international law actors that the principle of prevention of the international spread of cholera is an important one. Indeed, if any longstanding principle relating to any disease can be thought to have attained the status of customary international law, it is this one. Unfortunately, this would not be reflected in the actions of the United Nations in Haiti.

11   Cholera and the UN

There remains some ambiguity as to precisely where the United Nations fits in under international law. A detailed exploration of this issue is well beyond the scope of this chapter. Nevertheless, given its key role in the development of international law, and promotion of respect for the same, it does not seem credible to suggest the long-established principle of preventing the international spread of cholera should have

---

[85] Ibid.
[86] See for example, Fidler (1997).

no implications for the UN. This is all the more the case given that MINUSTAH's mandate explicitly involves assisting with "the restoration and maintenance of the rule of law, public safety and public order in Haiti".[87] Consider Chang's assertion that

> [a] factor that sets the UN apart from an ordinary public organisation is its role as the guardian of international norms and order. This role not only confers the UN what is commonly referred to as a 'moral authority', but carries with it a special responsibility to discharge duties in a manner that is consistent to the very standards it seeks to promote, thereby demanding an *ethical* sense of accountability higher than those already required in the political, legal or administrative realms.[88]

In turn, the Status of Forces Agreement (SOFA) between the UN and Haiti explicitly establishes that MINUSTAH shall cooperate with the Haitian government "with respect to sanitary services and shall extend to each other the fullest cooperation in matters concerning health, particularly with respect to control of communicable diseases, in accordance with international conventions."[89] Furthermore, although the focus of this chapter is on international law, it is worth noting that were immunity removed from the picture, the UN's actions likely would have violated domestic Haitian law. Haitian laws and regulations prohibit both (a) disposal of human waste in waterways and (b) negligence, including the negligent transmission of a contagious disease.[90]

Given the role of the UN and its specialised agencies not only in developing both binding laws and relevant standards around cholera, but in responding to outbreaks on the ground in vulnerable settings, the UN cannot fail to be aware of what measures might be taken, from open communication to basic sanitation, to uphold the principle of preventing the international spread of cholera. Even if the principle were to be found to fall within the scope of the operational immunity afforded the United Nations, they would still generally be expected to act in accordance with it, particularly in the absence of any justifications for departing from it. Thus, it seems rational to conclude that the UN would be expected to take reasonable steps (and refrain from unreasonable ones) to prevent the international spread of cholera based on scientific and public health principles, while also sharing information about cholera with other international law actors.

Ultimately, the UN's conduct in Haiti, both in the circumstances leading up to the epidemic and after its consequences became clear, fail to demonstrate the respect that this longstanding principle—one predating the UN by nearly a century, and codified over 50 years before its formation—deserves. In 1851, when nations first joined together to recognise the threat posed by cholera, it took over four decades to agree on appropriate measures. As discussed earlier in this chapter, that delay was

---

[87] United Nations Security Council Res 1542 (30 April 2004) UN Doc S/RES/1542.
[88] Chang (2016).
[89] Agreement Between the United Nations and the Government of Haiti Concerning the Status of the United Nations Operation in Haiti (entered into force 9 July 2004) 2271 UNTS 235.
[90] Law No. XV on Rural Hygiene; Civil Code arts. 1168 & 1169(4).

rooted primarily in a lack of scientific knowledge necessary to put the underlying legal principle into effect. The UN in 2010 had no such excuse.

12 Haiti: The Largest Single-Country Cholera Epidemic in a Century

Consequently, an evaluation of what occurred in Haiti must also take the state of scientific knowledge into account. Here, it is clear that the epidemic was entirely foreseeable, particularly for an organisation experienced with post-conflict and post-disaster settings. Although disasters do not automatically result in outbreaks of disease, they are a harbinger of conditions that may fuel such outbreaks. The situation following the earthquake was aptly summed up by the US Centers for Disease Control and Prevention (CDC) in a briefing document nine months before the epidemic began:

> An outbreak of cholera is very unlikely at this time. For a cholera outbreak to occur, two conditions must be met: (1) there must be significant breeches [sic] in the water, sanitation, and hygiene infrastructure used by groups of people, permitting large-scale exposure to food or water contaminated with Vibrio cholera organisms; and (2) cholera must be present in the population. While the current water, sanitation, and hygiene infrastructure in Haiti would certainly facilitate transmission of cholera (and many other illnesses), cholera is not circulating in Haiti, and the risk of cholera introduction to Haiti is low. Most current travelers to Haiti are relief workers from countries without endemic cholera, and they are likely to have access to adequate sanitation and hygiene facilities within Haiti, such that any cholera organisms they import would be safely contained. Similarly, importation of cholera through contaminated food has not been documented in Haiti in decades and is unlikely to become a problem during the relief efforts.[91]

Under such circumstances, and boasting similar expertise, the UN could not fail to be aware that the introduction of the cholera bacterium would be "like throwing a lighted match into a gasoline-filled room."[92] Yet although Nepal is a cholera endemic country, and despite the fact it was itself experiencing an increase in cholera cases at the time, Nepalese peacekeepers were deployed without effective measures to mitigate the possibility they might be bringing a deadly disease with them.[93] Once they arrived, terrible sanitation practices ensured that the local community would soon be exposed.

There are some legitimate questions as to exactly what preventative measures the UN should have taken in 2010; just as the state of knowledge was not the same in 1851 as it was in 1892, so too has it developed in the fallout from the Haitian epidemic. In fact, the epidemic has served as a springboard for new research, and knowledge gleaned in its aftermath will inform future actions. For instance, one review of the genetic evidence establishing the source of the epidemic not only

---

[91] Centers for Disease Control and Prevention (2010).
[92] Sontag (2012).
[93] Maharjan (2010).

proposes that genome sequencing should become a frontline screening method for promptly identifying the origin of infectious agents, but that current barriers limiting such use, such as the absence of a public database of recurring pathogens from different regions, be addressed to make this possible.[94]

However, it is clear that risks arose even before the infected peacekeepers arrived in Haiti. One fundamental problem arises from the fact that at the time the epidemic began, the Medical Manual for UN Peacekeeping then in use focused entirely upon preventing peacekeepers from falling ill, without considering what threats peacekeepers might introduce into the populations they are meant to protect.[95] Much like the Fortress Europe approach of the early International Sanitary Conventions, this is an archaic approach treating disease as a one-way threat emanating from certain populations to menace others. This is despite both hundreds of years of history of soldiers serving as vectors for disease, and the more recent fact that UN peacekeeping presents a unique set of risk factors for introducing outside diseases into vulnerable populations.[96] Recall the CDC briefing document highlighted earlier, which states "[m]ost current travelers to Haiti are relief workers from countries without endemic cholera".[97] By contrast, the current model of UN peacekeeping relies heavily on troops from lower income countries which themselves face higher domestic burdens of infectious disease. In turn, peacekeeping brings these troops into contact with vulnerable populations in interactions that would otherwise be unlikely to occur. Here, trade serves to illustrate the unique international interactions facilitated by United Nations peacekeeping. Given that, according to Nepalese Government statistics, bilateral trade with Haiti in 2010 amounted to roughly US$10,000, peacekeeping appears to have been responsible for creating an interaction that would not have happened outside the auspices of the United Nations.[98] This is not to suggest for a moment that such interactions are undesirable; it is simply to note the importance of ensuring that the accompanying risks are evaluated and addressed. Indeed, as international cooperation between countries of the global south increases outside the UN framework, it is important that the potential health ramifications are considered by both national governments and nongovernmental organisations.

Thus, it is clear that guidance on specific pre-deployment measures to prevent the spread of cholera by UN peacekeepers was lacking. In fact, cholera is mentioned only once in the Manual, and then only in a chart contained in an annex to the document.[99] The obvious inadequacy of the measures in place is underscored by the fact the United Nations sought to untruthfully embellish what actions they had taken. For instance, Edmond Mulet, then Under-Secretary-General in charge of MINUS-TAH, told media that peacekeepers were tested for cholera before deployment to

---

[94] Orata et al. (2014).

[95] United Nations Department of Peacekeeping Operations (1999).

[96] For further discussion, see Houston (2015).

[97] Centers for Disease Control and Prevention (n 94).

[98] Ministry of Foreign Affairs (Nepal) (2013).

[99] United Nations Department of Peacekeeping Operations, Medical Support Manual 1999, (n 96), Annex 9-5.

Haiti, something repeatedly demonstrated to be untrue.[100] The lack of any such pre-deployment measures was confirmed by the Nepalese Army's Chief Medical Officer, among others.[101]

While there is room for some debate over the precise pre-deployment measures that should have been taken based on the state of knowledge in 2010, there is no such ambiguity when it comes to sanitary practices on UN bases. Even once the cholera bacterium was imported, meeting basic sanitary standards—in essence, ensuring that the water source relied upon by tens of thousands of Haitians was not contaminated with human faeces—would almost certainly have prevented the epidemic. As documented both by journalists and epidemiological investigators, sanitary practices at the UN base were deplorable, with leaking pipes and overflowing open-air waste pits on the banks of the river.[102] In confirmation of these views, a leaked UN report reveals that an internal UN investigation had itself revealed serious concerns with sanitation practices at the time of the outbreak.[103]

It is also helpful to examine the actions of the UN following the initial outbreak, and how they conform with the principle of preventing the international spread of cholera. Here, the UN's actions do not reflect the importance of open sharing of information that helped catalyse the reforms leading to the 2005 International Health Regulations. Most immediately, the UN attempted to cover up what had happened, including efforts to hide or repair facilities, while issuing misleading press statements about sanitary standards on the base.[104] They also refused a request by Haitian epidemiologists to examine the MINUSTAH soldiers at the base in the early days of the epidemic.[105] It is hard to justify such actions in the context of the legal principle discussed in this paper, or even of the WHO guidance document on national cholera policies that states "[m]ore detailed information on the sources and routes of transmission of infection should be sought by epidemiological investigation of outbreaks."[106]

The UN's actions have not greatly improved over the longer term. This is most clearly illustrated in their response to the final report of the UN-appointed Independent Panel charged with investigating the epidemic, which made seven recommendations.[107] Although Secretary-General Ban Ki-moon promised a prompt follow-up on these recommendations, such action was not forthcoming.[108] In 2013, two years

---

[100] Le Masurier (2014).

[101] 'Haiti Cholera Outbreak: Nepal Troops Not Tested' *BBC* (London, 8 December 2010) http://www.bbc.co.uk/news/world-south-asia-11949181, accessed 1 May 2017.

[102] Katz (2012).

[103] Clarke and Pilkington (2016).

[104] Katz (n 103).

[105] Frerichs et al. (2012).

[106] World Health Organisation, WHO guidance on formulation of national policy on the control of cholera (1992) WHO/CDD/SER/92.16 REV.1.

[107] Cravioto (n 11).

[108] United Nations Secretary-General, Press Release—Secretary-General, Upon Receiving Experts' Report on Source of Haiti Cholera Outbreak, Announces Intention to Name Follow-up Task Force (4 May 2011) UN Doc SG/SM/13543.

after the report was made public, an NGO report noted that of the seven recommendations made by the Panel, only two had been implemented, and a further two partially implemented.[109] None of the suggested pre-deployment measures—prophylaxis, screening and vaccination—had been acted upon at all. Also not acted upon was the recommendation that UN installations treat faecal waste using on-site systems that inactivate pathogens before disposal.

In 2014, three years after the seven recommendations were made, the UN posted a "Fact Sheet" online outlining their response to them. Notably, it states that the UN accepts the proposal to vaccinate peacekeepers for cholera, an example of how both evolving technology and ongoing evaluation can change policy: consider how cholera vaccination was accepted in the 1920s and rejected in the 1970s. At the same time, it rejects the recommendations on screening and prophylaxis.[110] The fact sheet does not provide the evidence relied upon to support this decision, instead referring to a closed-door PAHO/WHO Expert Consultation on Pharmacological Measures for Prevention of Cholera Introduction in Non-endemic Areas; although a final report was generated in this consultation, it has never been publically released.[111] Thus, while the actual results of the Expert Consultation may indeed be compelling, it is impossible to evaluate them. Concealing from public and expert scrutiny what is presumably an objective evaluation by scientific experts of prospective methods of preventing cholera transmission is not in any way conducive to preventing the international spread of cholera in future. By contrast, where further research has been conducted and shared publically, very different conclusions have been reached. Modelling from Yale University suggests that not only would screening and prophylaxis be effective, but that they would be more cost-effective than vaccination.[112] The UN has yet to directly engage with this study and its implications.

As for the recommendation to treat faecal waste on-site, the Fact Sheet notes "the UN has undertaken substantial actions to improve wastewater management in field missions." However, a subsequent internal audit of waste management in MINUSTAH facilities conducted in 2014 gives a final rating of "unsatisfactory", indicating serious on-going problems even four years after the epidemic began.[113] Such revelations cast doubt on the efforts of the UN to reform its practices. That this audit report was not made public until 2016 does not help their case.

---

[109] Physicians for Haiti, 'Report Card Finds the Most Effective, No-Cost UN Recommendations for Cholera in Haiti Remain Unimplemented Two Years Later' April 23, 2013. http://www.ijdh.org/wp-content/uploads/2013/05/P4H-UN-report-card.pdf, accessed 1 May 2017.

[110] United Nations, 'Fact Sheet United Nations follow-up to the recommendations of the Independent Panel of Experts on the Cholera Outbreak in Haiti', http://www.un.org/News/dh/infocus/haiti/Follow-up-to-Recommendations-of-IPE.pdf, accessed 1 May 2017.

[111] Although it has an official document number (PAHO/HSD/IR/A/00112).

[112] Lewnard et al. (2016).

[113] United Nations Office of Internal Oversight Services, Report 2015/068—Audit of waste management in the United Nations Stabilisation Mission in Haiti (30 June 2015).

This is not to say the UN has not learned anything about the consequences of poor sanitation. For instance, leaked internal documents from the MINUSCA peacekeeping mission in Central African Republic identify health hazards to the local population from a UN dumpsite, and state "[t]he Mission should be highly concerned as this could easily culminate in litigation against MINUSCA which should be avoided taking into account lessons learnt from the Haiti case".[114] Similarly, given the inadequacy of the existing medical guidelines for peacekeeping missions, the United Nations also quietly updated its medical manual for peacekeeping operations five years after the epidemic began. The updated version directly acknowledges the risks that peacekeepers pose to vulnerable populations, noting "the danger inherent in the introduction of diseases into the host country's environment, particularly where such diseases are assumed to be non-existent prior to peacekeeping."[115] It adds: "This is especially important for communicable diseases such as cholera." The revised manual also explicitly includes extensive guidelines for educating peacekeepers about cholera. While these changes are to be welcomed, it remains to be seen how the updated manual will be applied in practice.

Importantly, it must also be noted that the more substantive changes focus heavily on cholera and preventing a repeat of the Haitian scenario, rather than effectively tackling the broader concern of introducing diseases into vulnerable populations. Malaria, for instance, already presents a risk to individual peacekeepers across multiple UN missions, where they are frequently exposed to malaria vectors in the field. In turn, this poses the threat of the introduction, or re-introduction, of malaria into malaria-free areas, or the introduction of drug-resistant strains into areas where those drugs are still effective.[116] This latter scenario is of particular concern given that peacekeepers from countries where resistance to artemisinin-based drugs has emerged are frequently deployed in regions of Africa where the burden of malaria is especially high and those drugs remain a vital public health tool.[117] This is a key example of the need for further practical reforms in the aftermath of Haiti.

Lastly, the Haitian epidemic serves as a reminder of a fundamental concept drawn from the field of medicine applicable not only to the UN but to any states or NGOs engaging in activities that carry a risk of the international transmission of disease: First, do no harm. This should be a primary consideration no matter how well intentioned the intervention, particularly where it affects communities whose circumstances heighten their vulnerability to disease. Only time will tell if the UN, as flagbearer for international cooperation, will belatedly embrace this concept as a result of its experiences in Haiti, along with the related commitments to open communication and evidence-based approaches to disease that have formed part of international health law, particularly in relation to cholera, for well over a century.

---

[114]United Nations Multidimensional Integrated Stabilisation Mission in the Central African Republic, Interoffice Memorandum—MINUSCA Waste Management Status Update and Risks (03 October 2016) UN Doc CSD/025/16.

[115]United Nations Department of Peacekeeping Operations & Department of Field Support (2015).

[116]Fernando et al. (2016) and Juliao et al. (2013).

[117]Houston and Houston (2015).

13 Conclusion

Two centuries after the first pandemic kicked off the globalisation of cholera, it remains both a threat to those who lack access to clean water and sanitation and an important topic under international law. In 2017, controversy over sharing information about cholera erupted within the race for the Directorship-General of the WHO, although allegations that he had covered up cholera outbreaks while serving as Ethiopia's Minister of Health were not enough to derail the eventual winner, Tedros Adhanom Ghebreyesus.[118] At the same time, cholera continues to claim victims around the world, including the massive epidemic in conflict-ridden Yemen that the UN Under-Secretary-General for Humanitarian Affairs has referred to as a "man-made catastrophe" and whose toll could soon eclipse that in Haiti.[119] And in Haiti itself, a once novel disease threatens to become endemic in the absence of concerted action.

As noted at the beginning of this chapter, UN responsibility for the Haitian cholera epidemic touches on a wide range of international law issues. At its core, however, it is a problem that would have been avoided if the UN had only taken steps to adhere to the oldest principle of international health law. With a history stretching back over 160 years, including over a century of binding multilateral obligations, it is evident that preventing the international spread of cholera is a robust and longstanding international legal principle. It is also clear that the UN violated it. It is less clear what the practical implications of this principle and its violation are for the people of Haiti going forward. The term "cholera forcing" was pejoratively coined to refer to the idea that "cholera epidemics, both in the nineteenth century and today, were and can be the key stimulus for procurement of safe water and sanitation."[120] This has not been the experience in Haiti, where the introduction of this previously unknown disease has only exacerbated serious pre-existing problems with access to water and sanitation. As of the time of this writing, a series of plans to address cholera has come and gone, with none of them ever raising even close to the funds required to carry them out.[121] The more recent package accompanying Secretary-General Ban Ki-moon's apology in December of 2016 remains drastically underfunded.[122]

Furthermore, despite the increased prominence of the issue as a result of the epidemic, the precise boundaries between operationally necessary immunity and harmful impunity for the United Nations have still not been delineated; this leaves no legal stick to enforce unfulfilled promises. And while the UN has taken some steps to prevent a similar public health disaster from occurring in the future, it is not

---

[118]McNeil (2017).

[119]Miles (2017).

[120]Hamlin (2009).

[121]Editorial, 'Haiti in the Shadow of Cholera' *The New York Times* (New York, 23 April 2014) https://www.nytimes.com/2014/04/24/opinion/haiti-in-the-shadow-of-cholera.html?emc=edit_tnt_20140423&nlid=47249755&tntemail0=y&_r=1, accessed 1 May 2017.

[122]United Nations, 'UN Haiti Cholera Response Multi-Partner Trust Fund' http://mptf.undp.org/factsheet/fund/CLH00, accessed 14 August 2017.

yet clear if these steps will be sufficient, or indeed whether they are being taken in practice as well as on paper. By contrast, the West African Ebola outbreak, which claimed a similar number of lives but garnered considerably more media coverage, has attracted not only vastly greater sums of money but also drawn far more international attention to failures to implement the IHRs, as well as broader questions about the capacity of the WHO, and the wider international community, to effectively tackle the international spread of disease.[123] The difference in attitude towards the two diseases was hammered home in the midst of the Ebola outbreak, when the UN was quick to suspend the rotation of peacekeepers from the affected countries to MINUSTAH in Haiti.[124] Ebola, perceived as a danger by wealthy and influential countries that have not felt threatened by cholera for decades, may yet direct the course of changes of international law around the transmission of disease. For Haiti, however, a tragic first encounter with cholera, occurring a century and a half after it served as the initial catalyst for states to come together to establish legal measures to prevent the international spread of disease, has resulted in much legal debate but little justice.

Acknowledgements Adam would like to thank his friends and colleagues at the Institute for Justice & Democracy in Haiti (IJDH).

References

Aginam O (2002) International law and communicable diseases. Bull World Health Organ 80:946

Belt R (2014 Oct 16) Haiti: UN troops rotation from Africa suspended to keep Ebola away. Haitian-Caribbean News Network (Port-au-Prince). http://hcnn.ht/en/2014_10/politics/406/Haiti-UN-troops-rotation-from-Africa-suspended-to-keep-Ebola-away.htm, accessed 30 July 2017

Birn A-E (2009) The stages of international (global) health: histories of success or successes of history? Glob Public Health 4:50

Bynum WF (1993) Policing hearts of darkness: aspects of the international sanitary conferences. Hist Philos Life Sci 15:421

Cash RA, Narasimhan V (2000) Impediments to global surveillance of infectious diseases: consequences of open reporting in a global economy. Bull World Health Organ 78:1358

Centers for Disease Control and Prevention (2010 Feb) Acute watery diarrhea and cholera: Haiti pre-decision brief for public health action. http://www.cdc.gov/cholera/haiti/pre-decision-brief.html, (archived) accessed 1 May 2017

Chang KC (2016) When do-gooders do harm: accountability of the United Nations toward third parties in peace operations. J Int Peacekeeping 20:86

Choi KJ (2008) A journey of a thousand leagues: from quarantine to international health regulations and beyond. J Int Law 29:989

---

[123]The Lancet, 'Ebola: What Lessons for the International Health Regulations?' (2014) 384 The Lancet 1321; United Nations General Assembly 'Protecting humanity from future health crises-Report of the High-level Panel on the Global Response to Health Crises' (9 February 2016) UN Doc A/70/723.

[124]Belt (2014).

Clarke JS, Pilkington E (2016 Apr 5) Leaked UN report faults sanitation at Haiti Bases at time of cholera outbreak. The Guardian (London). https://www.theguardian.com/world/2016/apr/05/leaked-un-report-sanitation-haiti-bases-cholera-outbreak, accessed 1 May 2017

Cravioto A et al. (2011) Final report of the independent panel of experts on the cholera outbreak in Haiti. http://www.un.org/News/dh/infocus/haiti/UN-cholera-report-final.pdf, accessed 1 May 2017

Cumming HS (1926) The international sanitary convention. Am J Public Health 16:975

Cvjetanovic B, Barua D (1972) The seventh pandemic of cholera. Nature 239:137

Delon PJ (1975) The international health regulations: a practical guide. World Health Organisation, Geneva

Ersoy N, Gungor Y, Akpinar A (2011) International sanitary conferences from the Ottoman perspective (1851–1938). Hygiea Int 10:54

Evans RJ (1988) Epidemics and revolutions: cholera in nineteenth-century Europe. Past & Present 123

Fernando SD et al. (2016) The risk of imported malaria in security forces personnel returning from overseas missions in the context of prevention of re-introduction of malaria to Sri Lanka. Malar J 15:144

Fidler DP (1997) The role of international law in the control of emerging infectious diseases. Bull Inst Pasteur 95:57

Fidler DP (2005) From international sanitary conventions to global health security: the new international health regulations. Chin J Int Law 4:325

Frerichs RR et al. (2012) Nepalese origin of cholera epidemic in Haiti. Clinic Microbiol Infect 18:E158

Halliday S (2007) The great filth: the war against disease in Victorian England. Sutton Publishing

Hamlin C(2009) "Cholera Forcing". The myth of the good epidemic and the coming of good water. Am J Public Health 99:1946

Harrison M (2006) Disease, diplomacy and international commerce: the origins of international sanitary regulation in the nineteenth century. J Glob Hist 1:197

Holpuch A (2016 Oct 14) Haiti faces fresh cholera outbreak after Hurricane Matthew, aid agencies fear. The Guardian (London). https://www.theguardian.com/world/2016/oct/14/haiti-cholera-hurricane-matthew-aid-agencies, accessed 1 May 2017

Houston A (2015) Peace and pestilence: lessons on peacekeeping and public health from the Haitian cholera epidemic. Foreign Affairs (Tampa, 21 June 2015). https://www.foreignaffairs.com/articles/haiti/2015-06-21/peace-and-pestilence, accessed 1 May 2017

Houston S, Houston A (2015) Screening and treating UN peacekeepers to prevent the introduction of artemisinin-resistant malaria into Africa. PLoS Med 12:e1001822

Howard-Jones N (1975) The scientific background of the International Sanitary Conferences, 1851-1938. World Health Organisation

Huber V (2006) The unification of the globe by disease? The international sanitary conferences on cholera, 1851–1894. Hist J 49:453

Jenson D, Szabo V, the Duke FHI Haiti Humanities Laboratory Student Research Team (2011) Cholera in Haiti and other Caribbean regions, 19th century. Emerg Infect Dis 17:2130

Jones JA (1999) International control of cholera: an environmental perspective to infectious disease control. Indiana Law J 74:1035

Jorgensen N (2007) The protection of freshwater in armed conflict. J Int Law Int Relat 3:57

Juliao PC et al. (2013) Importation of chloroquine-resistant Plasmodium falciparum by Guatemalan peacekeepers returning from the Democratic Republic of the Congo. Malar J 12:344

Katz J (2012) In the time of cholera: how the U.N. created an epidemic—then covered it up. Foreign Policy (Washington, 10 January 2013). http://www.foreignpolicy.com/articles/2013/01/10/in_the_time_of_cholera, accessed 1 May 2017

Le Masurier J (2014) Haiti: injustice in a time of cholera. France24 (Paris, 10 October 2014). http://www.france24.com/en/20141010-reporters-cholera-haiti-earthquake-cholera-united-nations-nepal, accessed 1 May 2017

Lee K, Dodgson R (2000) Globalisation and cholera: implications for global governance. Glob Gov 6:213

Lewnard JA et al. (2016) Strategies to prevent cholera introduction during international personnel deployments: a computational modeling analysis based on the 2010 Haiti outbreak. PLOS Med 13:e1001947

Lippi D, Gotuzzo E (2014) The greatest steps towards the discovery of *Vibrio cholerae*. Clinic Microbiol Infect 20:191

Luquero FJ et al. (2016) Mortality rates during cholera epidemic, Haiti, 2010–2011. Emerg Infect Dis 22:410

Maharjan L (2010 Sept 24) Cholera outbreak looms over capital. The Himalayan Times (Kathmandu). http://www.thehimalayantimes.com/fullNews.php?headline=Cholera+outbreak+looms+over+capital&NewsID=258974, accessed 1 May 2017

Marr JS, Cathey JT (2013) The 1802 Saint-Domingue yellow fever epidemic and the Louisiana purchase. J Public Health Manag Pract 19:77

McCarthy SA, Khambaty FM (1994) International dissemination of epidemic *Vibrio cholerae* by cargo ship ballast and other nonpotable waters. Appl Environ Microbiol 60:2597

McNeil DG Jr (2017 May 13) Candidate to lead the W.H.O. accused of covering up epidemics. The New York Times (New York). https://nyti.ms/2rcHW7Q, accessed 31 July 2017

Miles T (2017 June 22) U.N. blames warring sides for Yemen's "Man-Made" cholera "Catastrophe". Reuters (London). http://www.reuters.com/article/us-yemen-cholera-idUSKBN19D1EX, accessed 31 July 2017

Ministry of Foreign Affairs (Nepal) (2013 Jan) Bilateral relations (Nepal-Haiti). https://web.archive.org/web/20140915115938/, http://www.mofa.gov.np/en/bilateral-relations-nepal-haiti-199.html (archived version), accessed 1 May 2017

Morabia A (2007) Epidemiologic interactions, complexity, and the lonesome death of Max von Pettenkofer. Am J Epidemiol 166:1233

O'Connor MR (2012 Jan 12) Two years later, Haitian earthquake death toll in dispute. Columbia Journal. Rev. New York. http://archives.cjr.org/behind_the_news/one_year_later_haitian_earthqu.php, accessed 1 Aug 2017

Orata FD, Keim PS, Boucher Y (2014) The 2010 cholera outbreak in Haiti: how science solved a controversy. PLoS pathogens 10:e1003967

Pan American Health Organisation (2017 Feb 24) Epidemiological update—Cholera. http://reliefweb.int/sites/reliefweb.int/files/resources/2017-feb-23-phe-epi-update-cholera.pdf, accessed 1 May 2017

Pottevin TM, Norman White R (1920) Typhus and cholera in Poland: the action of the league of nations. The Lancet 196:1159

Ryan ET (2011) The cholera pandemic, still with us after half a century: time to rethink. PLoS Negl Trop Dis 5:e1003

Sontag D (2012 Mar 31) In Haiti, global failures on a cholera epidemic. New York Times (New York). http://www.nytimes.com/2012/04/01/world/americas/haitis-cholera-outraced-the-experts-and-tainted-the-un.html?pagewanted=all&_r=0, accessed 1 May 2017

Tauxe RV, Blake PA (1992) Epidemic cholera in Latin America. JAMA 267:1388

Taylor AL (2008) International law, and public health policy. In: Heggenhougen K, Quah S (eds) International encyclopedia of public health, vol 3. Academic Press

Tognotti E (2013) Lessons from the history of quarantine, from plague to influenza A. Emerg Infect Dis 19:254

Transnational Development Clinic at Yale Law School, Global Health Justice Partnership of the Yale Law School and the Yale School of Public Health, and Association Haïtienne de droit de l'Environnement (2013) Peacekeeping without accountability: The United Nations' responsibility for the Haitian cholera epidemic. https://law.yale.edu/system/files/documents/pdf/Clinics/Haiti_TDC_Final_Report.pdf, accessed 1 May 2017

United Nations (2016 Dec 1) Secretary-General's remarks to the General Assembly on a new approach to address cholera in Haiti. https://www.un.org/sg/en/content/sg/statement/2016-12-01/secretary-generals-remarks-general-assembly-new-approach-address, accessed 1 Aug 2017

United Nations Department of Peacekeeping Operations & Department of Field Support (2015) Medical support manual for United Nations field missions, 3rd edn. United Nations, New York

United Nations Department of Peacekeeping Operations (1999) Medical support manual for United Nations peacekeeping operations, 2nd edn. United Nations, New York

Weinmeyer R (2016) Pursuing justice in Haiti's cholera epidemic. AMA J Ethics 18:718

World Health Organisation (1958) The first ten years of the World Health Organisation. World Health Organisation

World Health Organisation (2005) States Parties to the International Health Regulations. http://www.who.int/ihr/legal_issues/states_parties/en/, accessed 1 May 2017

World Health Organisation (2013 Oct 19) Cholera in Mexico http://www.who.int/csr/don/2013_10_19_cholera/en/, accessed 1 May 2017

Responding to Health Emergencies: The Ethical and Legal Considerations for Militaries

Adam Kamradt-Scott

Abstract The twenty-first century has already witnessed a number of public health emergencies of international concern. Current indications suggest this trend is set to continue. Traditionally, health crises have resulted in a different set of actors responding to the event than if it is declared a humanitarian disaster, and vice versa. The 2014 Ebola outbreak in West Africa blurred these boundaries though, as the event proved to be both a public health crisis as well as a humanitarian disaster. In an unprecedented move, during the outbreak over 5000 foreign military personnel were deployed to assist civilian authorities contain the spread of the virus, build treatment facilities, train health workers, and provide medical care, while domestic military forces were engaged to enforce quarantine, provide protection, and in some instances, assist with burials. The involvement of military personnel in a health emergency has generated concern amongst some communities though that it is yet further evidence of the "militarisation" of humanitarian assistance, while some militaries have since indicated they would be prepared to assist in future health emergencies. This chapter examines the ethical and legal issues arising from the involvement of military personnel in health emergencies. Drawing on work undertaken on civil-military cooperation in humanitarian disaster contexts, the chapter considers the extent to which health crises are qualitatively different from other disasters and what this may mean for the involvement of military personnel and other actors. It explores questions around the types of activities military personnel can be expected to perform and whether these differ between foreign or domestic militaries, how militaries conduct themselves during health emergencies, as well as the limits of military assistance.

Keywords Military assistance · Ebola · Militarisation · Humanitarian assistance

A. Kamradt-Scott (✉)
Centre for International Security Studies, University of Sydney, Sydney, NSW, Australia
e-mail: adam.kamradt-scott@sydney.edu

© Springer Nature Switzerland AG 2020
M. Eccleston-Turner and I. Brassington (eds.), *Infectious Diseases in the New Millennium*, International Library of Ethics, Law, and the New Medicine 82,
https://doi.org/10.1007/978-3-030-39819-4_3

43

1 Introduction

To date, the involvement of military personnel in health-related humanitarian work remains highly controversial. Whereas civil-military cooperation during natural disasters and humanitarian crises has become progressively accepted as a means to help save lives or reduce human suffering, and there is agreement that co-existence is necessary during complex emergencies, health has remained a field of practice in which humanitarian agencies have historically staunchly opposed military participation. This apparently changed in September 2014 when the president of Médecins Sans Frontiéres (MSF), Joanna Liu, called for military intervention to help contain the outbreak of Ebola Virus Disease (EVD) in West Africa. The ensuing deployment of more than 5000 foreign military personnel to the three worst-affected countries of Liberia, Sierra Leone and Guinea has subsequently been interpreted by some as having established a precedent for future health crises.[1] Yet in an international context that has witnessed increased attacks on humanitarian workers—a phenomenon that some have attributed to the 'blurring' of military and humanitarian roles[2]—anxiety remains high amongst humanitarians that military involvement in health-related activities will further diminish the safety and security of humanitarian personnel.[3]

The aim of this chapter is to explore some of the legal and ethical considerations of military assistance in health emergencies. Drawing on work undertaken on civil-military cooperation in humanitarian disaster contexts and the 2014–16 West African Ebola outbreak, it considers the extent to which health crises are qualitatively different from other disasters and what this may mean for the involvement of military personnel and other actors. The chapter explores questions around the types of activities military personnel might be expected to perform and whether these differ between foreign and domestic militaries, how militaries conduct themselves during health emergencies, and the limits of military assistance. The chapter then concludes by considering the implications of future military involvement in health crises.

It is important to appreciate, however, that militaries are as diverse as the countries they were created to serve. Given that military forces are usually divided along functional lines (i.e. army, navy, air force), and each part is then divided further into multiple component parts such as divisions, brigades, and units, each military force is arguably best understood as 'societies of societies' that can have diverse cultures, practices and beliefs.[4] Seen in this light, it is unhelpful to conceptualise or speak of militaries as homogenous entities even within a national context, for while they often have a central purpose of defending the state against external threats, they can be profoundly dissimilar in their ethos and approach to their duties. These differences are understandably further compounded when armed forces personnel are mobilised to help respond to an international humanitarian crisis or natural disaster. Whether deployed as part of a national task force or a multilateral arrangement, it is highly

---

[1] Kamradt-Scott et al. (2015), Sesay (2015).
[2] Burkle (2013).
[3] Frangonikolopoulos (2005).
[4] Barberis (2003).

likely that military personnel will encounter a vast array of different military and civilian organisations—organisations that have their own diverse cultures, principles and approaches—and be expected to work collaboratively and effectively with them.[5] Such complexity can, however, add yet further legal and ethical challenges for the actors involved.

2 Military Health Assistance

As noted above, military assistance in health-related activities is a hotly contested issue, even within the context of humanitarian assistance and disaster relief (HADR) operations. While it is accepted that armed forces have a duty and requirement to care for and provide medical assistance to their own personnel—what is commonly described by defence departments as 'force health protection'[6]—and that militaries have obligations under the Geneva Conventions to care for Prisoners of War and other detained individuals,[7] it is less accepted that militaries have a role to play in rendering health and medical care to civilians. The overriding concern often cited is that militaries are inherently political actors, and accordingly, their involvement in humanitarian activities both infringes and compromises the basic humanitarian principles of neutrality and independence.[8] Correspondingly, any health-related military assistance would be similarly tainted.

Having said this, opposition to military involvement in health activities is not without cause. Aid organisations, for example, have objected to military-led health activity on the grounds it confuses the distinctions between military and humanitarian personnel, thereby increasing the risk that the latter will be targeted by opposition forces as they are perceived to be an extension of the military and/or government. Incidents such as the murder of five MSF staff in Afghanistan after the US military became involved in delivering medical care to local communities would appear to support these concerns.[9] Conversely, military personnel have historically regarded military operations other than war (MOOTWs) poorly on the basis that it is not 'warfighting' and fails to provide a pathway to promotion or significant service recognition.[10] Some armed forces personnel are also sceptical of resources and attention being given to non-warfighting activities, especially when met with defence spending cuts.[11] Others, such as military medical professionals, have pointed to more specific

---

[5]Tong (2004).

[6]Bailey et al. (2016), Trump (2002).

[7]Bricknell and Gadd (2007), Lischer (2007).

[8]Frangonikolopoulos (2005).

[9]Katz and Wright (2004).

[10]Interview with senior US military official, 15 November 2013, Washington, D.C., United States.

[11]Bernard (2013).

limitations, arguing that activities such as Medical Civic Action Programs (MED-CAPs) can be too short-term to have lasting health benefits for the populations they target or may actually adversely affect local health services.[12]

Further compounding the situation is that it is not currently clear when military assistance in health-related matters is considered appropriate. Specifically, while some broad principles for military involvement in humanitarian crises (which may include a health disaster), such as the notion that the military should only ever be called upon as a last resort,[13] have been enshrined in protocols like the Oslo Guidelines, ambiguity remains around the actual meaning of such principles.[14] As a direct result, potential opportunity costs arise (such as in lives lost) while humanitarian organisations or UN agencies wait to cross this decidedly vague threshold. The potential corresponding outcome is thus confusion over when it is appropriate to call on military forces for assistance and the types of health activities they are permitted to perform.

There are, however, at least three analytical distinctions that can be drawn when considering the nature and shape of any military assistance during a health-related crisis. The first is whether a given emergency is 'peaceful' or 'complex'. Since the 1990s, few humanitarian or military organisations would contest that militaries can play an important role in the aftermath of a natural disaster. For example, Russian military aircraft were used to transport humanitarian aid to China following the 2008 Sichuan earthquake.[15] Similarly, the US military airlifted humanitarian aid, healthcare workers, and patients after the 2010 earthquake in Pakistan, and again in 2014 after the Philippine typhoon.[16] The US and Australian militaries also deployed personnel and assets to Indonesia following the 2004 tsunami to provide health-related assistance.[17] In each of these cases, domestic military personnel were already on the ground, and, for many low and middle-income countries, their militaries represent the only emergency services available. Thus, in the context of natural disasters, military medical assistance may even be described as "the backbone of disaster medical relief".[18]

A different set of circumstances arises when the environment may be considered post-conflict or a 'complex emergency' where some form of fighting is underway. Wherever armed forces have previously acted as belligerents, or when the security environment is transitional, civil-military cooperation understandably becomes much more fraught. The risk to humanitarian workers may in turn increase if they are perceived to be associated with armed forces.[19] In these circumstances, rather than

---

[12]Gordon (2010, 2014).

[13]Anderson and Nevin (2016).

[14]Tatham and Rietjens (2016).

[15]Licina (2012).

[16]Lum and Margesson (2014), Madiwale and Virk (2011).

[17]Byleveld et al. (2005).

[18]Liu et al. (2014), p. 33.

[19]Wilson (2009), Winslow (2002).

overt cooperation, an alternative approach may be co-ordination between humanitarian organisations and military forces, where the actors operate independently but regularly liaise to prevent duplication of effort. Yet another, more extreme option is that of co-existence, which is when organisations operate fully independently of each other and accept the potential costs of having little or no communication whatsoever.[20] During complex emergencies, therefore, military and civilian actors usually have less interaction even though they may continue to operate in the same locations.

In addition to the distinctions between natural versus complex emergencies, a second feature to consider is whether the military force(s) involved are foreign or domestic. As discussed below, foreign military assistance (FMA) proved instrumental during the 2014–16 Ebola outbreak in West Africa, especially with regards to an alleged positive psychological impact. The situation in both Liberia and Sierra Leone was, however, a peculiar set of circumstances, principally because the assistance offered by the United States and United Kingdom respectively enjoyed considerable community support. The goodwill extended towards the FMA was as a result of more than a decade of post-conflict reconstruction and bilateral cooperation. Yet this somewhat unique set of circumstances may often not be replicated. It is therefore plausible to assume that FMA can either benefit or detract from the response to health-related emergencies, depending on the relationships and reputations of the militaries involved and the governments they represent.[21]

Equally, civil-military cooperation in health can be greatly swayed by the reputation of domestic military forces. Communities' perceptions of their own armed forces may vary considerably. In countries where military forces have traditionally remained separated from civilian affairs, trust in military integrity is generally high.[22] Even then, political and religious divisions can alter public perceptions.[23] In other countries, even if military involvement or interference in domestic political affairs occurs, it has been observed that the armed forces can still enjoy community support,[24] and this seems to be especially the case where civilian politicians are viewed as corrupt.[25] Conversely, however, the military can also be seen as no less corrupt than civilians (especially where there is limited oversight), exacerbating negative public opinions.[26] Like other security services, the military is not exempt from domestic suspicion and outright distrust.

The third analytical distinction that needs to be drawn pertains to the nature of the health crisis itself. Indeed, the types of activities that militaries may be expected to perform during a 'naturally-occurring' event such as an infectious disease outbreak might vary considerably when compared, for example, to a biological attack or a post-conflict situation entailing infrastructure damage. Likewise, the scale and

---

[20] Heaslip and Barber (2014).

[21] Kamradt-Scott et al. (2015).

[22] Gronke and Feaver (2001).

[23] Narli (2000).

[24] Sarigil (2009).

[25] Lugo and Searing (2014).

[26] Ungar (2013).

scope of the event will have fundamental implications for the size of any military contribution. For instance, in those situations where there is little physical damage to existing infrastructure, it is conceivable the majority of military assistance would be directed towards replacement of services that have been disrupted or were originally unavailable. In such circumstances, unless the crisis is especially large (i.e. regional or global) the level of military assistance is likely to be restricted to military medical personnel and limited logistical support, thus precluding large numbers of troops being deployed. By contrast, in the aftermath of a biological attack or conflict where infrastructure has been damaged or destroyed, it can be predicted that greater numbers of military personnel would be needed to assist in recovery. In these situations, military medical assistance would likely form only a small component of a larger assistance package.

Given these various caveats, it must be acknowledged that—at least for the time being—there is no immediate pathway for military assistance in health emergencies to be automatically sanctioned even if human lives are at risk. Achieving consensus on whether armed forces should be utilised in a health crisis appears remote; and, even more problematically, guidance on what militaries could and should not do in a health crisis is currently very limited. Until this work is undertaken, each event must be weighed carefully to determine whether military assistance is firstly required, and then, ascertain which military assets are the most appropriate to be deployed. In this, regard must to given to the cultural and lived experiences of the affected communities, and how they may view the deployment of domestic and/or foreign military forces. If, for example, the affected community's previous encounter with armed forces personnel was in the context of a civil conflict where violence was used to quell unrest, it is reasonable to assume community members may become fearful observing military convoys entering their community, even if their purpose is to assist halting the spread of an infectious disease. To avoid exacerbating a crisis and ensuring that appropriate consideration is given to the lived experiences of local communities, there is an urgent need for more interdisciplinary collaboration involving multiple professional groups, not simply public health.[27] Without such inter-disciplinary evaluations being conducted as to the appropriateness of military assistance, there is a genuine risk that the crisis may be unintentionally exacerbated. In the event the decision is taken though to engage military actors in a health emergency, there is arguably a number of additional legal and ethical challenges to consider.

3   Legal Considerations of Military Assistance in Health Emergencies

Military forces exist as both an arm of the state—importantly, the only legitimate arm to use lethal force in defence of the state—as well as an important societal institution. Accordingly, functional militaries (as opposed to dysfunctional ones) are governed

---

[27] Venables and Pellecchia (2017).

by strict rules, and in democratic societies are held accountable to the citizenry (via their political leaders) for their behaviour. In addition, when militaries are deployed, whether domestically or abroad, they are expected to comply with certain rules and requirements, such as standard operating procedures (SOPs) and rules of engagement (RoE), that are derived from military doctrine and which have often been developed over decades of praxis, usually in response to previous events that entailed organised violence.[28] Within the armed forces, the RoEs, SOPs, guidelines and regulations contained within military documents usually hold pre-eminent legal status, even—at times—superseding certain civilian legal provisions and freedoms;[29] but following the Nuremberg trials, they are also recognised to hold considerable prominence internationally, enjoying the legal status of customary practice.[30]

In the wake of the cold war, military doctrine (and subsequent documentation to operationalise that doctrine) has been increasingly expanded to incorporate MOOTWs. This has notably included the growing demand for militaries to be involved in HADR operations; but this same trend has witnessed armed forces becoming gradually inculcated into ever diverse, non-warfighting activities—a phenomenon that some have described as the 'militarisation' of foreign policy.[31] In the specific context of the United States, for example, the US Department of Defense (DOD) is authorised—at the request of the US Secretary of State—to provide assistance in humanitarian emergencies in accordance with Title 10, Section 2561, of the Code of Laws of the United States of America, and is held accountable to the US Congress via annual reports.[32] Notably, however, the US Congress "broadly defines humanitarian activities in an effort to enable the US response to be as flexible as possible to adapt to humanitarian needs",[33] granting the US military considerable latitude in the type of activities it performs in fulfilment of any humanitarian operation.

Moreover, particularly since 2005 the utilisation of military assets in HADR environments has been increasingly codified and regulated through the production of international guidelines, as well as through customary practice derived from more than a decade of civil-military cooperation overseen by organisations such as the United Nations' Office for the Coordination of Humanitarian Affairs (OCHA). While detailed guidance on the role of militaries in health emergencies is currently limited (see below), the work undertaken by organisations like OCHA and the United Nations' Inter-Agency Standing Committee (IASC) are legitimately regarded as informing contemporary praxis. Unlike domestic law, however, both the level of awareness and the status of internationally-developed guidelines can be quite limited, allowing for considerable diversity in how they are interpreted and operationalised, if at all.

---

[28] Ansorge and Barkawi (2016), Gabriel (1944).
[29] Cornyn (2008).
[30] Martins (1995), Meron (1996).
[31] Adams and Murray (2014).
[32] Margesson (2013).
[33] Margesson (2013), p. 3.

3.1 IASC Global Health Cluster Provisional Guidelines

Developed in 2011, the single document that deals explicitly with military-led health assistance is the IASC's Global Health Cluster guidelines, *Civil-Military Coordination during Humanitarian Health Action*.[34] Yet, despite the fact that these guidelines were released in 2011, to date their status remains 'provisional'. Moreover, although the document acknowledges the need for divergent approaches to cooperation when confronted with different operational environments (i.e. peacetime; peacekeeping; peace-enforcement; combat) and ranks a limited number of activities from low to high risk, as outlined in the list below the guidelines provide scant detail on the types of health-related activities that military personnel may perform. The IASC has, for instance, identified four broad categories of military health assistance, and cites only a limited number of activities:

Generic Indirect Assistance

- Rehabilitation of infrastructure (e.g. roads, bridges, debris removal)
- Provision of water and sanitation systems
- Construction of camps/provision of shelters
- Transporting relief items.

Health-specific Indirect Assistance

- Preparedness/contingency planning for humanitarian health response
- Health assessment and sharing information/joint health assessment
- Rehabilitation/construction of public health facilities
- Provision of equipment to health facilities/institution.

Direct Health Assistance

- Triage/First Aid/MEDVAC
- Direct patient care (including trauma and non-trauma care)
- Vaccinations and other public health interventions
- Distribution of relief goods
- Health monitoring and surveillance
- Training of health personnel.

Security of Humanitarian Health Actors and Facilities[35]

On account of the fact they were released as 'provisional', the IASC guidelines were clearly never intended to offer a comprehensive account of health-related military assistance. Arguably providing further evidence of this, there is a number of other health-related activities not currently listed in the IASC guidelines that militaries are routinely performing in HADR contexts. These include activities such as the provision of direct medical care through short-term operations involving hospital ships or medical civil-assistance programmes (MEDCAPS), cadaver disposal,

---

[34]IASC (2011a).
[35]IASC (2011a).

and even quarantine. Importantly, however, the IASC guidelines fail to capture or address these types of actions, ensuring that the guidelines—and thus their legal status—remain piecemeal at best. Rather, the IASC Global Health Cluster provisional guidelines were meant to serve as a starting point for subsequent conversations and deliberations; but that dialogue has not transpired. In the absence of such discourse, clarity around the roles and extent of health-related military assistance remains short. For instance, while the IASC has identified that vaccinations may be a permissible activity for military personnel in peacetime, having been categorised as "low risk", no further clarification regarding "other public health interventions" and what this category may entail is provided.[36] Moreover, the international legal standing of guidelines—not to mention provisional guidelines—continues to be highly contested, for while they may inform contemporary practice (and thus enjoy the status of customary law) they can only be regarded as having authority in the event the majority of states accept such practices as law.[37]

Although there was no evidence of an awareness of the IASC guidelines, the range of activities undertaken by FMA and domestic militaries throughout the 2014–16 West African Ebola outbreak were observed to be consistent with the Global Health Cluster's recommendations in broadly aligning with the four core typologies described above. In total, over 5000 foreign military personnel drawn from the United States, United Kingdom, Canada, France, Germany, China, Cuba, and member states of the African Union were deployed to West Africa between August 2014 and April 2015 and were engaged in duties extending from education and training, construction, transport, logistics, and in some instances, the provision of direct patient care. In addition, domestic military forces of Liberia, Sierra Leone and Guinea, the three worst-affected West African countries, also played a key role in maintaining—and in some instances, restoring—law and order, protecting burial teams, and ensuring basic quarantine and isolation[38]; whereas in Liberia, further limited assistance was provided by the United Nations Mission in Liberia (UNMIL) troops.[39] Thus, even though there limited recognition of the existence of international guidelines specific to a health crisis like the Ebola outbreak, military personnel largely *behaved* as though the guidelines applied.

3.2 The Oslo and MCDA Guidelines

Adopted in 1994, the Oslo Guidelines (also known as the *Guidelines on the Use of Foreign Military and Civil Defence Assets in Disaster Relief*) have enshrined the principle that militaries should only ever be used as a last resort, once all civilian means have been exhausted. While the guidelines retain limited legal standing given

---

[36]IASC (2011b).
[37]Cassese (2005).
[38]Kamradt-Scott et al. (2015).
[39]Davies and Rushton (2016).

that they are "non-binding and do not affect the rights, obligations, or responsibilities of states under international humanitarian law",[40] they are nevertheless viewed by many as having established the broad parameters under which military forces can be utilised "in times of peace" such as HADR where there is no recent or ongoing violence.[41] Where there is ongoing or recent violence, additional protocols contained within *The Use of Military and Civil Defence Assets to Support United Nations Humanitarian Activities in Complex Emergencies* (or 'MCDA Guidelines') are considered to apply, specifically that there should not only be the appearance of greater separation between military and humanitarian actors, but also that only humanitarian actors should be seen performing humanitarian activities.[42] Moreover, in contexts of recent or ongoing violence, militaries should not be seen to be providing direct assistance, keeping their activities limited to such measures as transporting supplies or helping secure the wider operational environment—otherwise described as 'indirect assistance'.

In addition to establishing the principle of 'last resort', the Oslo and MCDA Guidelines firmly reinforced the now widely-accepted view that military personnel should not be considered humanitarian actors. As articulated in the Oslo Guidelines' section on Key Concepts, for instance,

> [h]umanitarian work should be performed by humanitarian organisations. Insofar as military organisations have a role to play in supporting humanitarian work, it should, to the extent possible, not encompass direct assistance, in order to retain a clear distinction between the normal functions and roles of humanitarian and military stakeholders.[43]

Similarly, the MCDA Guidelines explicitly note that:

> maintaining a clear distinction between the role and function of humanitarian actors from that of the military is the determining factor in creating an operating environment in which humanitarian organisations can discharge their responsibilities both effectively and safely.[44]

Having said this, it is additionally important to appreciate that the Oslo Guidelines do not apply to domestic military forces or civil defence assets. As clearly stipulated, the aim of the guidelines "is to establish the basic framework for formalising and improving the effectiveness and efficiency of the use of *foreign* military and civil defence assets in disaster relief operations."[45] The Oslo Guidelines thus do not seek to prescribe how governments may choose to utilise their own military during a humanitarian disaster, such as a health emergency. This caveat is critical and not only pays homage to the principle of state sovereignty, but also acknowledges the simple reality that in countries that lack emergency services (e.g. fire, ambulance, coast guard, etc.), military forces are not the last resort: they are the only resort.

---

[40] Madiwale and Virk (2011), p. 1088.
[41] UN (2007).
[42] UN (2006).
[43] UN (2007), p. 9.
[44] UN (2006).
[45] UN (2007).

Crucially, however, neither set of guidelines sufficiently engages with the issue of health and healthcare-related military assistance. Indeed, the single reference to health within the Oslo Guidelines occurs in Annex 1, which states:

> The MCDA operation shall cooperate with the Government of the Affected State with respect to sanitary services and matters concerning health, particularly with respect to the control of communicable diseases, in accordance with international conventions section.[46]

From this, it can be inferred there is a level of acceptance internationally that military personnel may be called upon to assist in restoring basic health services, such as water and sanitation, while also assisting in preventing the spread of infectious diseases; but the extent of such assistance and the types of activities permitted under this authority remains imprecise. The consequence of such obscurity, however, is that armed forces personnel may be asked to perform duties extending from enforcing quarantine and isolation, vaccination, delivering supplies, to engineering and construction intended to repair sanitation services, all without clear parameters and in which they may have not been adequately trained. The scope of activities is vast; but while there remains limited operational guidance on how and under what circumstances military personnel may perform these duties, there remains a strong possibility that actions may be taken that are counterproductive to the wider emergency response effort.

From a legal standpoint, the above distinctions are significant. This is principally because military actors, despite the many challenges surrounding enforcement and/or impeachment where diversions occur, are held to higher standards of conduct under international humanitarian law than humanitarian and non-governmental organisations (NGOs).[47] Put another way, whereas military personnel can conceivably be prosecuted under either military law, the domestic law of their country, or international law, the penalties applied to NGOs and their personnel who engage in poor practices are, by comparison, usually extremely limited. For while NGOs may choose to voluntarily adhere to standards and guidelines, in humanitarian crises "they are not under any legal obligation".[48] Moreover, the 'Good Samaritan' ethic is often put forward as a defence against negligence, offering at least some institutions like the United Nations and its personnel a level of legal immunity.[49] Military actors do not enjoy such latitude though, and can be legally held to account for their behaviour in a humanitarian crisis or disaster.

For example, throughout the 2014–16 West African Ebola outbreak, both the United States and United Kingdom military operations required strict adherence to military directives. Whereas the German military called for volunteers to deploy to the Ebola-affected countries (who were subsequently ordered),[50] US and UK military personnel were commanded to deploy without recourse to refuse.[51] Moreover, US

---

[46]UN (2007), p. 30.

[47]Cassese (1998), Smith (2002).

[48]Crack (2016).

[49]Boon (2016).

[50]Kamradt-Scott et al. (2015).

[51]Bricknell et al. (2015), Robson et al. (2017).

military personnel were under strict orders not to consume alcohol, consume 'bush meat', or fraternise or engage in sexual relations with local community members due to the increased risk of contracting Ebola.[52] Further, while some military forces such as the Chinese, British and Canadians provided clinical care,[53] other forces such as the US military did not, and declined to even transport biological samples suspected of containing Ebola.[54] These variations in behaviour were noted to cause confusion amongst some humanitarian agencies and their personnel.[55]

4 Ethical Considerations of Military Assistance in Health Emergencies

Given the dearth of legal parameters pertaining to military assistance in health emergencies, it is arguably even more important to ensure the potential ethical implications of such aid are taken into account. Fundamentally, ethics is the study of moral convictions about what is right and wrong that informs codes of conduct and social expectations of behaviour.[56] As a field of practice, the humanitarian space has several ethical standards and codes of conduct already in situ, developed by organisations such as the International Committee of the Red Cross and Red Crescent Societies, the United Nations (e.g. The United Nations Office for the Coordination of Humanitarian Affairs), the Sphere Project, and many others. While variations exist between and across different humanitarian organisations, with some choosing to emphasise certain principles above others, there is widespread acceptance that the four humanitarian principles of *humanity*, *neutrality*, *impartiality* and *independence* are the minimum universal standard for humanitarian assistance.

Critically, however, military-led humanitarian assistance is often viewed as incompatible with at least two of the four humanitarian principles. This is principally because, as armed forces serve as an extension of their respective state (and by default, its government), their deployment can be intimately tied to foreign policy objectives and thus military assistance—including military health assistance—is not able to be considered either neutral or independent.[57] This had led a number of humanitarian organisations to argue that it is undesirable for militaries to be involved in providing humanitarian assistance, except as a last resort when there is no civilian alternative. As noted above, this position has been reflected extensively in international guidelines to the extent that military assistance, even in humanitarian disasters, can represent an ethical minefield. In the specific case of health and healthcare-related

---

[52]Robson et al. (2017).
[53]Lu et al. (2016), Marion et al. (2016).
[54]Kamradt-Scott et al. (2015), Robson et al. (2017).
[55]Kamradt-Scott et al. (2015).
[56]Geale (2012).
[57]Chretien (2011).

assistance, however, few humanitarian organisations accept that there is any role for military personnel.[58]

4.1 Do no Harm

Often, one of the core criticisms surrounding the ethics of military health assistance has focused on the role of individual military personnel. Several commentators have, for instance, described what they see as the 'dual loyalty' problem confronting medically-qualified military personnel (and other healthcare professionals), whereby military health professionals may be required to compromise the Hippocratic ideal of 'doing no harm' for military or strategic objectives.[59] Some commentators have even gone so far as to argue that it is "morally unacceptable" for physicians to serve as soldiers.[60] In a similar vein, Anderson and Nevin have suggested that by not providing clinical care throughout the 2014–16 West African Ebola outbreak and deferring to the US Public Health Service Commissioned Corps, the US military established a precedent which, they argue, should serve as model for all future health crises.[61] While such proposals reflect long-held humanitarian opposition to military involvement in all health-related activities, the authors' suggestion nevertheless reflects a typically US-centric worldview that is impracticable for the majority of countries—and notably, militaries—around the world that do not have an equivalent public health corps.

Having said this, particularly in the context of a peace-time health emergency, it is reasonable to expect that military assistance aligns with the principle of doing no harm. Moreover, this principle arguably pertains to all military personnel and activities—not just military medical assistance. Rigidly applying this principle would necessitate that prior to specific interventions being enacted, a series of assessments would be conducted to ensure economic, social, political, physical and psychological harm is avoided, or at the very least, minimised. In the case of the Ebola outbreak, for example, it would have been reasonable to expect that the military assistance would not have unduly harmed the national economies of affected countries further by utilising external resources that could be locally sourced. In the case of US military assistance to Liberia, however, it was later acknowledged that USAFRICOM "did not have an assessment of what materials and commercial-building capabilities were available locally that could be contracted out, contributing to USAFRICOM's underestimation of the indigenous capacity resident in Liberia."[62]

Likewise, given a long-standing criticism of military health assistance has been a tendency to undermine local healthcare systems by providing care in excess of

---

[58] Anderson and Nevin (2016).

[59] Benatar and Upshur (2008), London et al. (2006), Olsthoorn and Bollen (2013).

[60] Sidel and Levy (2003).

[61] Anderson and Nevin (2016).

[62] JCOA (2016).

what is available locally,[63] it would have been reasonable to expect that services and facilities would be scaled to ensure the best possible care for local requirements. In the context of the Ebola outbreak though, while there was a strong commitment across multiple military forces to construct Ebola Treatment Units, significant delays were encountered in constructing buildings to European or North American building codes—causing delays that resulted in treatment beds being unavailable when they were most needed.[64] Accordingly, while it is accepted that conducting assessments to avoid social, political, economic, physical and psychological harm might delay potentially valuable military assistance, avoiding additional harm to a community already adversely affected by a health crisis is an important ethical consideration. Nonetheless, the ethical imperative to avoid unnecessary harm risks creating an ethical conundrum brought about by the need to act—in the example cited above, one that juxtaposes economic considerations against the physical safety, health and well-being of local communities.

4.2   Humanity and Military Motivations

Within this same context, while it is acknowledged that military personnel are not humanitarian actors and thus may not be considered neutral or independent, the two remaining humanitarian principles of humanity and impartiality arguably still apply. As per the United Nations' OCHA, *humanity,* as part of the Humanitarian Principles, is defined as "Human suffering must be addressed wherever it is found. The purpose of humanitarian action is to protect life and health and ensure respect for human rights."[65] Accordingly, where the primary or overriding purpose of military assistance is intended to save human lives or alleviate human suffering, such assistance may be broadly considered to be ethically sound. Further complications potentially do arise, however, if the speed with which actions are taken causes unintended social, political, economic, physical or psychological detriment, which would bring the activities into conflict with the 'do no harm' principle discussed above. Similarly, complications may arise with regards to specific activities that military personnel may perform.

For example, were militaries reconnoitre mobile phone text-messaging to identify potential infectious disease outbreaks in a health crisis, would this be ethically sound given that it is a breach of individuals' privacy? Taken from a public health perspective, the argument may be in the affirmative, for as long as it is accepted—perhaps cautiously—that certain civil liberties (such as the right to privacy) can be temporarily suspended for the benefit of the greater good (i.e. containing a disease outbreak).[66] yet such measures—if they were to become publicly known—would likely cause disquiet amongst humanitarian workers specifically, and potentially the wider public

---

[63]McInnes and Rushton (2014).
[64]Kamradt-Scott et al. (2015).
[65]OCHA (2012).
[66]Kinlaw et al. (2009).

more generally, especially if performed by military personnel. In a health emergency, where lives are at stake, however, it is argued that different ethical standards apply. As Karadag and Hazan note, in pandemics "[i]dentifying and isolating cases for the common good is an accepted feature of communicable disease control".[67] Thus, at least from a public health perspective, the activity—using mobile phone technology to identify new cases of an infectious disease—may reasonably considered to be ethically sound. The issue is thus not the activity itself, but rather the identity of the actor(s) undertaking the activity—in this instance, the military.

Said another way, part of the challenge for military assistance—even in the midst of a health emergency—is the level of mistrust surrounding the motivations of military actors. As one retired US military officer observed, "There's a lot of hesitation to link up with the military side of the house. A lot of people in public health still seem to view us as baby killers."[68] Such perceptions appear to permeate the wider humanitarian movement,[69] even if many humanitarian workers have no direct personal experience of having worked with armed forces personnel in a humanitarian context previously. During the 2014–16 West African Ebola outbreak, for example, an NGO worker observed, "Yes, we've been really surprised working alongside the military. They're actually decent people."[70] In another example, a Red Cross official went on to remark that, as a result of their experience working with military personnel in Liberia, it "has changed my views. I think the hardest issues were at the strategic level. But in my view, we worked well together. Ideally I'd like to take some from the military and some from the Red Cross and put them in a team together."[71] Thus, while practically there may be little difference between the quality of work performed by humanitarian and military personnel, suspicion that military actors may hold secondary motives for engaging in humanitarian work raises ethical questions for many aid workers.

Importantly, however, such attitudes conceivably reflect a double standard. For whereas the motivations of military actors are questioned on the basis that they are a state institution and the troop-contributing country may have secondary foreign policy objectives, very few to no ethical questions are generally raised about the motives of humanitarian organisations. Rather, it is often presumed humanitarians' motivations are purely altruistic.[72] Yet, given most NGOs now derive their finances from governments via official development assistance, grants, or donations from multinational corporations,[73] and that these entities "pay so that something is done, and they pay for the opportunity to be able to say they supported that something was being done",[74] the extent to which there are substantive ethical differences between

[67] Karadag and Hakan (2012), p. 606.

[68] Interview with retired US military officer, 8 November 2013, Atlanta, United States.

[69] Miller (1999).

[70] Interview with Red Cross worker #1, 26 March 2015, Monrovia, Liberia.

[71] Interview with Red Cross worker #2, 26 March 2015, Monrovia, Liberia.

[72] Barnett (2011).

[73] IARAN 2017, Krause (2014).

[74] Krause (2014), p. 48.

military and humanitarian organisations remains debatable: both are enabled by the motivations of others. Indeed, one of the only distinctions that can be drawn is that the military is employed directly by the state, whereas the humanitarian organisations are able to remain partially detached. Most humanitarians would seek to make a further distinction by arguing they voluntarily provide assistance (and are thus morally superior), whereas military personnel may be ordered to render assistance.[75] Having said this, it must be acknowledged the personal motivation of individuals is not intrinsically significant to the principle of humanity.

4.3 Impartiality and Justice

The second humanitarian principle that may be still considered applicable for military assistance during a health emergency is that of *impartiality*. As understood by OCHA, impartiality stipulates that "[h]umanitarian action must be carried out on the basis of need alone, giving priority to the most urgent cases of distress and making no distinctions on the basis of nationality, race, gender, religious belief, class or political opinions".[76] In other words, impartiality "means that relief is given to those in need, not those who we like or who look like us".[77] Whereas concerns persist about military forces' ability to remain impartial during conflict to render care to combatants and civilians alike, raising the 'dual loyalty' problem discussed earlier, during a health crisis like a disease outbreak such distinctions arguably become insignificant. In such circumstances, ideally, where human lives are at stake assistance is the fundamental ethical imperative; the clothing and uniform of those assisting is extraneous.

Throughout the 2014–16 West African Ebola outbreak, however, impartiality was circumvented in a number of instances. Indeed, due to limited FMA medical capabilities, decisions were taken—on a non-medical or triage basis—to prioritise certain groups over others. In Sierra Leone, for instance, while the British military established, operated and staffed a medical unit to care for suspected Ebola patients, access was initially restricted to international (foreign) healthcare workers needing treatment, with provision extended to Sierra Leonean healthcare workers where capacity allowed. Other local patients were only admitted where they might assist,

> to establish procedures and protocols based on actual clinical exposure. This was a careful balance as local patients tended to be admitted in the more severe stages of the disease which is both much more infectious but with a substantially lower chance of survival and consequent higher risk of exposure or healthcare workers employed in the Kerrytown Treatment Unit (KTTU) Red Zone.[78]

---

[75] Winslow (2002).

[76] OCHA (2012), p. 1.

[77] Barnett (2016), p. 13.

[78] Bricknell et al. (2015), p. 172.

In Liberia, US military assistance witnessed the construction of ten Ebola Treatment Units (ETUs) around the country and a 25-bed ETU in Monrovia,[79] but whereas the Monrovia unit was staffed by the US Public Health Service Commissioned Corps,[80] in the other ETUs constructed by the military care was delivered by NGO personnel and local healthcare workers. This situation contributed to the perception that there were differences in the quality of care, and thus prejudice towards local community members even though the decision on who to admit to the ETUs were jointly decided by the US military and the Liberian Public Health Service.[81] As Davies and Rushton note, this overall situation was further compounded with the withdrawal of the limited medical services and some military personnel from the United Nations Mission in Liberia (UNMIL).[82]

Partiality also manifested with regards to the allocation of one particular type of treatment, a trial vaccine. A small number of experimental Ebola treatments were in various stages of development when the West African Ebola outbreak began. Of these, the most promising appeared to be ZMapp™—a vaccine comprising humanised mouse antibodies that had yet to enter clinical human trials.[83] On 12 August 2014, a WHO expert panel authorised the use of this particular experimental vaccine and other medicines on 'compassionate' grounds;[84] yet due to the fact that there were limited supplies of ZMapp™, priority was given to treating patients from high-income countries.[85]

It is important to appreciate the decision to prioritise patients from high-income countries to receive the experimental vaccine was not made by military personnel. Importantly, however, it would not be ethically sound for armed forces personnel to be involved—or perceived to be involved—in making such decisions. This is not only because military personnel are expected to be subservient to civilian authority in HADR contexts,[86] but given past historical atrocities that have contributed to an erosion of trust,[87] it invites unproductive speculation as to the motivations of military actors. There may be cause for senior military officials to argue for increased access to vaccines on the basis of force health protection requirements where treatments are deemed safe; but even here caution must be applied. Certainly, in the context of the Ebola outbreak the decision(s) by civilian authorities to preference those receiving the vaccine added to the overall perception there was favouritism towards Westerners, while those suffering the highest burden of morbidity and mortality—local West Africans—were excluded. Both during and after the West African Ebola outbreak, a number of public health advocates advanced ethical frameworks designed to assist

---

[79]Diehl et al. (2016).

[80]Anderson and Nevin (2016).

[81]Calcagno (2016).

[82]Davies and Rushton (2016).

[83]Fauci (2014), p. 1086.

[84]Sayburn (2014).

[85]Butler (2014), Fauci (2014).

[86]UN (2015).

[87]Schmidt (2013).

in the evaluation of clinical decisions using social justice norms of how, on whom, and when experimental treatments are used.[88] As Asgary and Junck note, however, whereas the principle of clinical justice "argues against resource allocation based on comparative judgement of patients worthiness", they acknowledge the fair and reasonable distribution of scarce resources "can be especially difficult to uphold when triaging patients or resources in [low resource settings] due to differing opinions of fairness and equality."[89] Given, therefore, the ethically fraught nature of making such decisions, it is one area where military personnel would probably be best served by avoiding any and all involvement, particularly given the risk of generating further mistrust that may detract from the wider public health effort.

5   Conclusion

This chapter has sought to examine just some of the legal and ethical challenges confronting military personnel involved in health emergencies. It has revealed that, internationally, there is very little explicit guidance currently available to inform military actors' behaviour in a health crisis. While several broad principles such as 'last resort' and the notion that military actors should be limited to providing indirect assistance enjoy support, the parameters surrounding the type and nature of activities including—notably—the threshold of 'last resort' remain vague and imprecise. Moreover, the provisional guidelines for health emergencies that do exist have yet to move beyond their temporary status, principally as the intellectual and practical work to progress the field went untouched. That is, until the 2014–16 West African Ebola outbreak forced the international community to reconsider the role of militaries in future health crises.

In the absence of clear internationally-agreed precepts, military personnel and humanitarian actors' only recourse is to return to existing humanitarian principles. Importantly, however, as this chapter has shown, not all of the humanitarian principles are ethically applicable to militaries. Of the four universal humanitarian principles, only humanity and impartiality can conceivably apply; but there remain lingering concerns about military actors' motivations for engaging in HADR operations, including health emergencies. Added to this, factors such as the nature of the crisis— whether it is occurring in peacetime or conflict—combined with recipient communities' expectations and previous experiences with military personnel—both foreign and domestic—all conceivably are important considerations in determining whether military assistance is ethical, just and appropriate. Given all indications throughout the first few decades of the twenty-first century suggest that health emergencies like the 2014–16 West African Ebola outbreak are unlikely to lessen, determining the acceptable legal and ethical parameters of military involvement in health emergencies is critical to saving lives, now and into the future.

---

[88]Lane et al. (2016), Rid and Emanuel (2014).

[89]Asgary and Junck (2013), pp. 626–627.

References

Adams G, Murray S (2014) Mission creep: the militarisation of US foreign policy? Georgetown University Press, Washington, DC

Anderson JN, Nevin RL (2016) Prohibiting direct medical care by US military personnel in foreign disaster relief: arguments from the Ebola disaster. Med Confl Surviv 32(1):14–20

Ansorge JT, Barkawi T (2016) Military manuels. In: Salter MB (ed) Making things international 2: Catalysts and reactions. University of Minnesota Press, Minnesota

Asgary R, Junck E (2013) New trends of short-term humanitarian medical volunteerism: professional and ethical considerations. J Med Ethics 39(10):625–631

Bailey M, Beaton K, Bowley D, Eardley W, Hunt P, Johnson S, Round J, Tarmey N, Williams A (2016) Bending the curve: force health protection during the insertion phase of the Ebola outbreak response. J R Army Med Corps 162(3):191–197

Barberis D (2003) In search of an object: organicist sociology and the reality of society in fin-de-siecle Francw. Hist Hum Sci 16(3):51–72

Barnett M (2011) Empire of humanity: a history of humanitarianism. Cornell University Press, Ithaca

Barnett M (2016) The humanitarian act: how humanitarian? Int Soc Sci J 65(215–216):13–24

Benatar SR, Upshur R (2008) Dual loyalty of physicians in the military and in civilian life. Am J Public Health 98(12):2161–2167

Bernard KW (2013) Health and national security: a contemporary collision of cultures. Biosecur Bioterror 11(2):157–162

Boon KE (2016) The United Nations as good samaritan: immunity and responsibility. Chic J Int Law 16(2):341–385

Bricknell MC, Gadd RDM (2007) Roles for international military medical services in stability operations (reconstruction and development). J R Army Med Corps 153(3):160–164

Bricknell MC, Hodgetts T, Beaton K, McCourt A (2015) Operation GRITROCK: the defence medical services' story and emerging lessons from supporting the UK response to the Ebola crisis. J R Army Med Corps 162(3):169–175

Burkle FM (2013) Throwing the baby out with the bathwater: can the military's role in global health crises be redeemed? Prehospital Disaster Med 28(3):197–199

Butler D (2014) Ebola drug trials set to begin amid crisis. Nature 513(7516):13–14

Byleveld PM, Kent M, McCall BJ (2005) Operation Sumatra Assist: post-tsunami environmental and public health response in Banda Aceh. ADF Health 6(October):48–53

Calcagno D (2016) Killing Ebola: the militarisation of US aid to Liberia. J Afr Stud Dev 8(7):88–97

Cassese A (1998) On the current trends towards criminal prosecution of breaches of international humanitarian law. Eur J Int Law 9(1):2–17

Cassese A (2005) International law, 2nd edn. Oxford University Press, Oxford

Chretien J-P (2011) US military global health engagement since 9/11: seeking stability through health. Glob Health Gov 4(2):1–12

Cornyn DK (2008) The military, freedom of speech, and the internet: preserving operational security and service members' right of free speech. Tex Law Rev 87:463–486

Crack A (2016) Reversing the telescope: evaluating NGO peer regulation initiatives. J Int Dev 28(1):40–56

Davies S, Rushton S (2016) Public health emergencies: a new peacekeeping mission? Insights from UNMIL's role in the Liberia Ebola outbreak. Third World Q 37(3):419–435

Diehl G, Bradstreet N, Monahan F (2016) The department of defense at the forefront of a global health emergency response: lessons learned from the Ebola outbreak. Health Secur 14(5):366–374

Fauci A (2014) Ebola—underscoring the global disparities in health care resources. N Engl J Med 371(12):1084–1086

Frangonikolopoulos C (2005) Non-governmental organisations and humanitarian action: the need for a viable change of praxis and ethos. Glob Soc 19(1):49–72

Geale S (2012) The ethics of disaster management. Disaster Prev Manag 21(4):445–462

Gordon S (2010) The United Kingdom's stabilisation model and Afghanistan: the impact on humanitarian actors. Disasters 34(S3):S368–S387

Gordon S (2014) The military physician and contested medical humanitarianism: a dueling identity? Soc Sci Med 120(November):421–429

Gronke P, Feaver PD (2001) Uncertain confidence: civilian and military attitudes about civil-military relations. In: Feaver PD, Kohn RH (eds) Soldiers and civilians: the civil-military gap and American National Security. Belfer Center for Science and International Affairs, Cambridge, MA

Heaslip G, Barber E (2014) Using the military in disaster relief: systemising challenges and opportunities. J Humanit Logist Supply Chain Manag 4(1):60–81

IARAN (2017) The future of aid INGOs in 2030. In: Fraser L (ed) Institut de relations internationales et Stratégiques, Paris

IASC (2011a) Civil-military coordination during humanitarian health action. In: Inter-agency Standing Committee Global Health Cluster. United Nations, Geneva

IASC (2011b) Civil-military coordination during humanitarian health action. In: Inter-agency Standing Committee Global Health Cluster. United Nations, Geneva, p 9

JCOA (2016) Operation united assistance: the DOD response to Ebola in West Africa. Joint and Coalition Operational Analysis, Virginia, p 26

Kamradt-Scott A, Harman S, Wenham C, Smith Frank (2015) Saving lives: the civil-military response to the 2014 Ebola outbreak in West Africa. University of Sydney, Sydney

Karadag O, Hakan K (2012) Ethical dilemmas in disaster medicine. Iran Red Crescent Med J 14(10):602–612

Katz IT, Wright AA (2004) Collateral damage—médecins sans frontières leaves Afghanistan and Iraq. N Engl J Med 351(25):2571–2573

Kinlaw K, Barrett D, Levine R (2009) Ethical guidelines in pandemic influenza: recommendations of the ethics subcommittee of the advisory committee of the director, centers for disease control and prevention. Disaster Med Public Health Prep 3(S2):S185–S192

Krause M (2014) The good project: humanitarian relief NGOs and the fragmentation of reason. University of Chicago Press, Chicago

Lane C, Marston H, Fauci A (2016) Conducting clinical trials in outbreak settings: points to consider. Clin Trials 13(1):92–95

Licina Derek (2012) The military sector's role in global health: historical context and future direction. Glob Health Gov 6(1):1–30

Lischer SK (2007) Military intervention and the humanitarian "force multiplier". Glob Gov 13(1):99–118

Liu Z, Liu Y, Liu X, Kang P, Xue C, Zhang L (2014) The lessons learned from disaster medical relief of Chinese military medical service. Int Rev Armed Forces Med Serv 87(4):33–41

London L, Rubenstein LS, Baldwin-Ragaven L, Van Es A (2006) Dual loyalty among military health professionals: human rights and ethics in times of armed conflict. Camb Q Healthc Ethics 15(4):381–391

Lu Y, Rong G, Yu SP, Sun Z, Duan X, Dong Z, Xia H, Zhan N, Jin C, Ji J, Duan Huijuan (2016) Chinese military medical teams in the Ebola outbreak of Sierra Leone. J R Army Med Corps 162(3):198–202

Lugo K, Searing E (2014) The impact of situational factors on forum choice and criminal justice system development in Bangladesh. Emory Int Law Rev 29(2):327–378

Lum T, Margesson R (2014) Typhoon Haiyan (Yolanda): US and international response to Philippines disaster. Curr Polit Econ South Southeast Cent Asia 23(2):209–246

Madiwale A, Virk K (2011) Civil-military relations in natural disasters: a case study of the 2010 Pakistan floods. Int Rev Red Cross 93(884):1085–1105

Margesson R (2013) International crises and disasters: US humanitarian assistance response mechanisms. Congressional Research Service, Washington, DC

Marion D, Charlebois PB, Kao R (2016) The healthcare workers' clinical skill set requirements for a uniformed international response to the Ebola virus disease outbreak in West Africa: the Canadian perspective. J R Army Med Corps 162(3):207–211

Martins MS (1995) "War Crimes" during operations other than war: military doctrine and law fifty years after Nuremberg—and beyond. Mil Law Rev 149:145–187

McInnes C, Rushton S (2014) Health for health's sake, winning for God's sake: US global health diplomacy and smart power in Iraq and Afghanistan. Rev Int Stud 40(5):835–857

Meron T (1996) The continuing role of custom in the formation of international humanitarian law. Am J Int Law 90(2):238–249

Miller LL (1999) From adversaries to allies: relief workers' attitudes toward the US military. Qual Sociol 22(3):181–197

Narli N (2000) Civil-military relations in Turkey. Turk Stud 1(1):107–127

OCHA (2012) OCHA on message: humanitarian principles. United Nations, New York, p 1

Olsthoorn P, Bollen M (2013) Civilian care in war: lessons from Afghanistan. In: Gross ML, Carrick D (eds) Military medical ethics for the 21st century. Ashgate, Surrey

Ralph G (1944) American experience with military government. Am Hist Rev 49(4):630–643

Rid A, Emanuel E (2014) Ethical considerations of experimental interventions in the Ebola outbreak. Lancet 384(9957):1896–1899

Robson P, Lenze A, Dastoor N, Dickinson J, Rich C (2017) Setting the theater the army service component command way: a humanitarian response to the Ebola epidemic in Liberia. Army Lawyer 2017(2):18–43

Sarigil Z (2009) Deconstructing the Turkish military's popularity. Armed Forces Soc 35(4):709–727

Sayburn A (2014) WHO gives go ahead for experimental treatments to be used in Ebola outbreak. BMJ 349:g5161

Schmidt Ulf (2013) Accidents and experiments: Nazi chemical warfare research and medical ethics during the second World War. In: Gross ML, Carrick D (eds) Military medical ethics for the 21st century. Ashgate, Surrey

Sesay JB (2015) Government to continue building RSLAF's capacity to the highest level of professionalism-VP Foh. In: Shaw IS (ed) ExpoTimes, Bristol

Sidel V, Levy B (2003) Physician-soldier: a moral dilemma. In: Beam TE, Sparacino LR (eds) Military medical ethics, vol 1. TMM Publications, Washington, DC, p 312

Smith T (2002) Moral hazard and humanitarian law: the international criminal court and the limits of legalism. Int Polit 39(2):175–192

Tatham P, Rietjens S (2016) Integrated disaster relief logistics: a stepping stone towards viable civil-military networks? Disasters 40(1):7–25

Tong J (2004) Questionable accountability: MSF and sphere in 2003. Disasters 28(2):176–189

Trump DH (2002) Force health protection: 10 years of lessons learned by the department of defense. Mil Med 167(3):179–185

UN (2006) Guidelines on the use of military and civil defence assets to support united nations humanitarian activities in complex emergencies. United Nations, Geneva, p 3

UN (2007) Oslo guidelines: Guidelines on the use of foreign military and civil defence assets in disaster relief. United Nations, Geneva

UN (2015) UN-CMCoord field handbook. United Nations Office for the Coordination of Humanitarian Affairs, Geneva

Ungar M (2013) The rot within: security and corruption in Latin America. Soc Res: Int Q 80(4):1187–1212

Venables E, Pellecchia U (2017) Introduction: engaging anthropology in an Ebola outbreak: case studies from West Africa. Anthropol Action 24(2):1–8

Wilson RL (2009) Disasters and conflict zones around the world: the roles and relationships of the military and nongovernmental organisations. In: Gaist PA (ed) Igniting the power of community: the role of CBOs and NGOs in global public health. Springer, New York

Winslow D (2002) Strange bedfellows: NGOs and the military in humanitarian crises. Int J Peace Stud 7(2):35–55

The International Red Cross and Red Crescent Movement Response to the West African Ebola Outbreak 2014

Christy Shucksmith-Wesley

Abstract The International Health Regulations 2005 (IHR) are the most up to date international legal rules on the control of infectious diseases and provide a unified code for infectious disease control. The IHR name the International Federation of the Red Cross (IFRC) as one of the international organisations with whom the WHO must cooperate and co-ordinate in implementing the IHR. It was organisations like the IFRC and MSF, that worked to stop the spread of Ebola following the outbreak in 2014. The focus of this chapter is the work of the IFRC during the Ebola outbreak. The IFRC carries out relief operations to assist victims of disasters, and combines this with development work to strengthen the capacities of its member National Societies. The IFRC's work focuses on four core areas: promoting humanitarian values, disaster response, disaster preparedness, and health and community care. Combining a study of the IFRC as an organisation with a legal mandate of its own, elucidated in the Statutes of the International Red Cross and Red Crescent Movement, and the more general international legal framework, this chapter uses international law as a framework to reflect on the limits and effectiveness of legal measures in responding to Ebola. To this end, international law provides a logical and global method to respond to infectious diseases. This chapter finds that the mandate and practice of the IFRC in the response to Ebola provides material to critically analyse each of these parts in light of infectious disease proliferation in 2014–2016. Since outbreak was announced in early 2014 more than 10,000 Red Cross volunteers were trained in Ebola response. IFRC supported emergency operations in Guinea, Liberia, and Sierra Leone have targeted 23 million people.

Keywords Red Cross · Ebola · Humanitarian assistance · WHO · Collaboration · Ebola

C. Shucksmith-Wesley (✉)
University of Nottingham, Nottingham, United Kingdom
e-mail: Christy.shucksmith-wesley@nottingham.ac.uk

© Springer Nature Switzerland AG 2020
M. Eccleston-Turner and I. Brassington (eds.), *Infectious Diseases in the New Millennium*, International Library of Ethics, Law, and the New Medicine 82, https://doi.org/10.1007/978-3-030-39819-4_4

1   Introduction

The purpose of this chapter is to show the legal and practical relationships between the International Federation of the Red Cross (IFRC) and the World Health Organisation (WHO) during the West Africa Ebola outbreak in 2014. Taking Sierra Leone, Liberia and Guinea as examples, this chapter considers the mandate and functions of the International Red Cross and Red Crescent Movement (IRCRCM) and whether its mandate complements, or otherwise competes with, the infectious diseases and international law framework and regulations. The Red Cross mandate includes the provision of health care to civilians and combatants during conflict and disaster situations.[1] This will be described in the first part of the chapter. The Red Cross is not, however, alone in this role. The WHO,[2] MSF,[3] military actors,[4] NGOs and local actors all interlink and, hopefully, coordinate in the preparation for, response to, and rebuilding after the outbreak of an infectious disease.[5] Outbreak response will require medical assistance, possibly the participation of Emergency Medical Teams, and a rapid response in the areas of water, sanitation and hygiene, shelter and food.[6]

Kamradt-Scott et al. argue that the Ebola outbreak in Guinea, Liberia and Sierra Leone proved to be an exceptional outbreak that blurred the lines between health and humanitarian crises. In so doing, it highlighted numerous problems with regard to the coordination of humanitarian disasters that have public health implications of international consequence.[7] In that context, this chapter shows the extensive mandate of the IFRC, and provides a critique of an institution that is widely underappreciated in the literature concerning global health, emergency medicine and humanitarian responses. The Red Cross is a unique humanitarian organisation with an arguably-unparalleled operational mandate to provide essential humanitarian protection and

---

[1] Statutes of the Red Cross and Red Crescent Movement (adopted by the 25th International Conference of the Red Cross at Geneva in 1986, amended in 1995 and 2006), preamble and principle of humanity, art 3(2) National Red Cross and Red Crescent Societies, and art 6(4)(f) IFRC; Resolution 7 of the 31st International Conference of the Red Cross Red Crescent on 'Strengthening normative frameworks and addressing regulatory barriers concerning disaster mitigation, response and recovery' (12 January 2011); Resolution 6 of the 32nd International Conference of the Red Cross Red Crescent on 'Strengthening legal frameworks for disaster response, risk reduction and first aid' (10 December 2015).

[2] Constitution of the World Health Organisation Constitution, reprinted in Basic Documents, Forty-fifth edition, Supplement, October 2006 art 2(a), (b).

[3] Medecins Sans Frontiers mandate, https://www.msf.org.uk/?gclid= EAIaIQobChMIxPyCiLOT2AIVQ7HtCh3RqQtREAAYASAAEgIBxvD_BwE.

[4] Kaplan and Easton-Calabria (2015): MSF, which is a private, international association, has the mandate to 'bring humanitarian medical assistance to victims of conflict, natural disasters, epidemics or healthcare exclusion'.

[5] Research Paper Ross et al. (2017).

[6] WHO and IFRC (2017a).

[7] Kamradt-Scott et al. (2015).

assistance to populations in need. The nature of its operations is described in this chapter. This chapter provides an analysis of the relationship between the WHO and the IRCR. It builds on previous work that showed that the ICRC is an international legal person that has an international legal mandate to protect those in need during armed conflict.[8] That work examined the governance structure of the Movement and showed that the Red Cross and Red Crescent Movement is an institution with power and authority across multiple humanitarian situations, including disasters, armed conflicts, and other situations of violence.[9]

The WHO and IFRC each take their rights and duties from international agreements signed by States, but their working methods make them very different actors. The National Societies of the Red Cross, such as the Liberian Red Cross Society,[10] Red Cross Society of Guinea[11] and the Sierra Leone Red Cross Society,[12] are auxiliaries to governments and are supported by the IFRC. The IFRC works through the existing networks on the ground in the provision of humanitarian aid and protection. The primary role of the WHO is the attainment by all people of the highest possible level of health.[13] In order to achieve this, the functions of the WHO, detailed in Article 2 of the Constitution of the WHO, establish the WHO as the 'directing and co-ordinating authority on international health work'.[14] Article 2 outlines the WHO relationship with States, the United Nations, specialised agencies, governmental health administrations, professional groups and such other organisations as may be deemed appropriate. As with any international organisation, and the Red Cross Movement, the WHO assists Governments at their request and/ or with their consent. Its activities encompass technical support, the provision of aid, and health care (covering emergency assistance and also the overall improvement of international health). If we were to directly compare the WHO with the IFRC, we could say that the key similarity is the human-focused agenda which can only be realised through a State-centric system and is therefore dependent on consent. The key difference is the working method of each entity, as the IFRC is able to mobilise National Societies and support local actors and work towards health goals identified by the citizens, local groups and regional bodies. The WHO is much more hands-off, as it acts as a co-ordinating authority. We can see, therefore, that the WHO and IFRC have the ability to positively affect the ability of States to respond to infectious diseases, but with very different strategies and approaches; how these approaches compliment

---

[8]See Shucksmith (2017).

[9]Ibid.

[10]Liberian Red Cross Society, http://www.ifrc.org/en/what-we-do/where-we-work/africa/liberian-red-cross-society/.

[11]Red Cross of Guinea, http://www.ifrc.org/en/what-we-do/where-we-work/africa/red-cross-society-of-guinea/.

[12]Sierra Leone Red Cross Society, http://www.ifrc.org/en/what-we-do/where-we-work/africa/sierra-leone-red-cross-society/.

[13]For an excellent text on the WHO, see Lee (2009).

[14]Art 2 (a) Constitution of the WHO.

or clash (as the case may be) during a health emergency is the focus of this chapter. With this in mind, this chapter shows the relationship between these two institutions and critically appraises the contribution of the IFRC to the Ebola response in 2014. It examines the coordination role of the WHO and the extent to which the IFRC is coordinated by the WHO and, on the other hand, the areas in which it exercises its autonomy and its own legal mandate.

This chapter critically considers the role of the IFRC in the multi-agency response to Ebola and whether it sits within the response envisaged within the IHR or whether it acts under its own international mandate. The National Societies and the IFRC have local knowledge, expertise and resources to provide a first response to an outbreak. Through its networks, it can coordinate with MSF and other NGOs. However, the WHO is responsible for the overall coordination of all responders.[15] Within this leadership role, I argue, the WHO must respect the international legal mandate of the IFRC and the roles that it has assumed. The WHO has the benefit of acting on the international stage and being able to speak to all actors, but the IFRC is better placed to manage the specific situation on the ground. Overall the chapter will examine what coordination is done by the WHO via the IHR; what is done by the UNGA; and what is done by the RCRCM. It will show the gaps in coordination and critically appraise the independent contribution that the IFRC makes to the response to the outbreak of infectious disease.

2   Red Cross and Red Crescent Mandate

The Red Cross Movement is comprised of the ICRC, IFRC, and National Societies. The ICRC and the IFRC have headquarters in Geneva, whereas the National Societies are based in States. The ICRC is the 'guardian of international humanitarian law', with a mandate, taken from the Four Geneva Conventions, to provide humanitarian protection and assistance during international and non-international armed conflicts.[16]

The ICRC works at the intersection of human needs, state sovereignty and international organisations. It is grounded by its principles and has access to state officials and the local population. It has influence within states and on the international stage, particularly through the International Conference and its observer status at the UN General Assembly.[17] The ICRC can act with legal effect and develop its competences on the international stage. Taken together, the current legal framework and

---

[15]Art 2(a) Constitution of the WHO.

[16]Council of Delegates (ICRC), 'Agreement on the Organisation of the International Activities of the Components of the International Red Cross and Red Crescent Movement—The Seville Agreement' (Council of Delegates, ICRC, 25–27 November 1997). www.icrc.org/eng/resources/documents/misc/57jp4y.htm, preamble (Seville Agreement).

[17]Koenig (1991).

humanitarian protection and assistance strategies allow the ICRC to provide food, healthcare, shelter and water to those in need.

The Red Cross Movement began in 1864 but at the end of the Second World War, with the adoption of the Geneva Conventions I–IV, it truly took on a life of its own. States have consented to the presence of the Red Cross within their sovereign territory through a series of international agreements, including the Geneva Conventions I–IV,[18] Statutes of the Red Cross and Red Crescent Movement, Statutes of the ICRC, and individual Headquarters Agreements drawn up between the ICRC and governments. These international agreements and the governance structure of the Red Cross Movement (from Geneva, to National Societies, to the field) allow the Red Cross to respond to humanitarian situations independently of other actors. This means, for example, that although the WHO may have the power to direct and coordinate activities and policies for global health, the Red Cross can act independently: States can ask for its help directly, it can act through the National Societies of States, and it can establish specific projects through its International Conference, such as the Health Care in Danger project 2011–2015.

The Red Cross was built from a desire to provide health care for wounded soldiers. Henry Dunant envisaged an organisation with volunteer nurses and medics that would help any wounded soldiers, regardless of the side on which they fought. From these beginnings, the Red Cross has continued to develop its health care ambitions and capabilities. In part, its roles are mandated through the international agreements, to which States are parties. These roles of the National Red Cross and Red Crescent Societies include cooperation with public authorities in the prevention of disease, the promotion of health and the mitigation of human suffering.[19] The IFRC is mandated to 'encourage and coordinate the participation of the National Societies in activities for safeguarding public health and the promotion of social welfare in cooperation with their appropriate national authorities'.[20] In addition, the Red Cross is able to act autonomously within States owing to its international legal personality and its existing presence in each State in the guise of the National Societies. This sets it apart from other organisations.

---

[18] Convention (I) for the Amelioration of the Condition of the Wounded and Sick in Armed Forces in the Field. Geneva (adopted 12 August 1949, entered into force 21 October 1950) (Geneva Convention I); Convention (II) for the Amelioration of the Condition of Wounded, Sick and Shipwrecked Members of Armed Forces at Sea. Geneva (adopted 12 August 1949, entered into force 21 October 1950) (Geneva Convention II); Convention (III) relative to the Treatment of Prisoners of War. Geneva (adopted 12 August 1949, entered into force 21 October 1950) (Geneva Convention III); Convention (IV) relative to the Protection of Civilian Persons in Time of War. Geneva (adopted 12 August 1949, entered into force 21 October 1950) (Geneva Convention IV); Statutes of the International Red Cross and Red Crescent Movement 1986 (adopted by the 25th International Conference of the Red Cross at Geneva in 1986 and amended in 1995 by Resolution 7 of the 26th International Conference of the Red Cross and Red Crescent at Geneva and 2006 by Resolution 1 of the 29th International Conference of the Red Cross and Red Crescent at Geneva).

[19] Statutes of the Movement art 3(2) National Red Cross and Red Crescent Societies.

[20] Statutes of the Movement art 6(4)(f).

There are three distinct branches of the Movement; the International Committee of the Red Cross, the International Federation of the Red Cross, and the National Societies.[21] Generally speaking, the IFRC carries out relief operations to assist victims of disasters, and combines this with development work to strengthen the capacities of its member National Societies.[22] The IFRC's work focuses on four core areas: promoting humanitarian values, disaster response, disaster preparedness, and health and community care.[23] Its aim is to inspire, facilitate and promote all humanitarian activities carried out by its member National Societies on behalf of the most vulnerable people. As with all components of the Red Cross, it acts independently, meaning that it is not 'governmental, political, racial or sectarian in character'.[24] The IFRC has access to local knowledge and expertise, through National Societies, which makes it an invaluable responder when there is an outbreak of disease.

Article 6(1) of the IRCRCM Statutes states that

[T]he International Federation of Red Cross and Red Crescent Societies comprises the National Red Cross and Red Crescent Societies. It acts under its own Constitution with all rights and obligations of a corporate body with a legal personality.[25]

Article 6(3) states that the 'general object of the Federation is to inspire, encourage, facilitate and promote at all times all forms of humanitarian activities by the National Societies, with a view to preventing and alleviating human suffering and thereby contributing to the maintenance and the promotion of peace in the world'.[26] Under Article 6(4) (f) IRCRCM Statutes its functions include:

encourag[ing] and coordinat[ing] the participation of the National Societies in activities for safeguarding public health and the promotion of social welfare in cooperation with their appropriate national authorities. Its aim is to inspire, facilitate and promote all humanitarian activities carried out by its member National Societies on behalf of the most vulnerable people. Finally, 'in each country the Federation shall act through or in agreement with the National Society and in conformity with the laws of that country'. The IFRC benefits from the local volunteers of the National Societies. It has access to local knowledge and expertise which makes it an invaluable responder when there is an outbreak of disease.

In order to participate in the IRCRCM, National Societies must first be recognised by the ICRC and then admitted by the International Federation. Article 4 of the IRCRCM Statutes provides ten conditions for recognition as a National Society. Article 4(1) states that National Societies be constituted on the territory of an independent state where the 'Geneva Convention for the Amelioration of the Condition

---

[21] See Shucksmith (n 8).

[22] Art 6(1) of the IRCRCM Statutes.

[23] IFRC, 'Constitution: Revised and Adopted by the 16th Session of the General Assembly' (IFRC, Geneva, Switzerland, 20–22 November 2007). www.ifrc.org/Global/Governance/Statutory/Constitution_revised-en.pdf.

[24] IRCRCM Statutes, Art 6(2).

[25] IFRC, 'Constitution: Revised and Adopted by the 16th Session of the General Assembly' (IFRC, Geneva, Switzerland, 20–22 November 2007). www.ifrc.org/Global/Governance/Statutory/Constitution_revised-en.pdf.

[26] IRCRCM Statutes, Art 6(3).

of the Wounded and Sick in Armed Forces in the Field' is in force. In addition, under Article 4(3), a National Society must be duly recognised by the legal government of its country based on the Geneva Conventions I, II, III and IV 1949 and of the national legislation as a voluntary aid society, auxiliary to the public authorities in the humanitarian field.

National Societies are made up of staff and volunteers from the community. They design and deliver humanitarian projects based on the needs of the local population. Guinea,[27] Liberia[28] and Sierra Leone[29] each has a National Society. The benefit of the National Societies is their unparalleled local knowledge and the fact that they are staffed by local people and volunteers who can best represent and support their communities. Thus, the three constituent components of the Red Cross are 'responders' to humanitarian crises, including infectious diseases. It is theoretically possible to look at the Red Cross response to Ebola in isolation, but international organisations do not act in a vacuum. It is one thing to describe the mandate and activities of one entity, it is another thing entirely to understand how multiple actors interact, coordinate and respond to the outbreak of infectious diseases. This chapter provides an initial overview of the extent to which the WHO, tasked with coordination of response, can 'dictate' to a humanitarian organisation, which existed prior to its conception.

3   Ebola Outbreak 2014

Ebola is an infectious disease that originates in bush meat and then spreads from person to person. Once a person is infected, the disease can spread through sweat, tears, mucus, saliva, vomit, diarrhoea, breast milk, urine, blood, and through sexual intercourse.[30] The 2014 West African outbreak of the disease was the worst to date, culminating in Public Health Emergency of International Concern being declared in August 2014.[31] The outbreak began in remote rural districts of Guinea and was later reported in Liberia and Sierra Leone.

Some incidences of illness had been reported in November and December 2013, and in late January 2014, local health officials in Guinea investigated unexplained deaths, suspecting cholera. Three days later, a larger investigatory team, including MSF and regional WHO, began work. As the infection spread, it also led to cases

---

[27] http://www.ifrc.org/en/news-and-media/news-stories/africa/guinea/.

[28] http://www.ifrc.org/en/what-we-do/where-we-work/africa/liberian-red-cross-society/.

[29] http://www.ifrc.org/en/what-we-do/where-we-work/africa/sierra-leone-red-cross-society/.

[30] Stein (2015).

[31] World Health Organisation, 'WHO Statement on the Meeting of the International Health Regulations Emergency Committee Regarding the 2014 Ebola Outbreak in West Africa', http://www.who.int/mediacentre/news/statements/2014/ebola-20140808/en/; for a more detailed timeline see: Mark Eccleston-Turner & Scarlett McArdle, 'The Law of Responsibility and the World Health Organisation: A Case Study on the West African Ebola Outbreak' [—].

in cities, where the risk of the spread of infection was much higher.[32] By the 1st February, the infection had spread into Conakry, Guinea's capital and largest city. It was not until the 13th March that the Ministry of Health in Guinea issued its first alert, followed by an investigation from 14 to 25 March. It was during this time, on the 21 March 2014, that the disease was identified as Ebola. Cases were reported in Liberia on 22 March 2014, and it was at this point that the infection could have been deemed to be an *international* epidemic.

Guinea, Liberia, and Sierra Leone struggled to stop the spread of disease, in part because of resource limitations, lack of knowledge and understanding, cultural practices that facilitated the spread of disease, and in part, as noted above, because of the porous borders. One limitation to the initial response by the state itself is that public health systems in Guinea, Liberia, and Sierra Leone were 'already weakened by protracted conflicts, [and were] struggling to implement measures to contain the virus'.[33] In addition, as Alasan Senghore writes,

> West Africa's cultural, political and geographical context, with porous borders and a mobile population, [had] much to do with the unprecedented scale of [the epidemic]. So has the parlous state of health systems, some in countries not long emerged from conflict. Community distrust—of institutions and agencies—has certainly had an impact. As a consequence, health information campaigns have struggled.[34]

In brief, state health care systems were not ready for Ebola, and health workers lacked specialised equipment and training. Some succumbed to the disease, while others refused to work for fear of infection.[35] A lack of available national healthcare facilities, especially primary care services, is an issue for many post-conflict states.[36] In situations like this, the response of the international community and actors is critical to prevent the spread of the infection. The outbreak required international cooperation to treat those already infected and prevent the spread of infection further. As the WHO and IFRC stated,

> [t]he high mortality rates (over 70% among untreated patients), the exponential escalation of cases in Guinea, Liberia, and Sierra Leone and the potential for the epidemic to spread globally through international travel resulted in a massively scaled and coordinated international response from Emergency Medical Teams.[37]

---

[32]Campbell (2017).

[33]Murray et al. (2014).

[34]Foreword by Alasan Senghore (IFRC Africa Regional Director) in IFRC (2015a).

[35]Ibid.

[36]Concluding Observations of the Committee on Economic, Social and Cultural Rights: Croatia (5 December 2001) UN Doc E/C.12/1/Add.73, para 34; Serbia and Montenegro (23 June 2005) UN Doc E/C.12/1/Add.108, paras 33–36, 60–63; Cambodia (12 June 2009) UN Doc E/C.12/KHM/CO/1, paras 32–33; Democratic Republic of Congo (16 December 2009) UN Doc E/C.12/COD/CO/4, para 34; Afghanistan (7 June 2010) UN Doc E/C.12/AFG/CO/2-4, paras 40–42; CESCR, 'Concluding Observations on the Second to Fourth Periodic Report of Rwanda, adopted by the Committee at its Fiftieth Session (29 April–17 May 2013)' (10 June 2013) UN Doc E/C.12/RWA/CO/2-4, para 25.

[37]WHO and IFRC (2017b).

The speed of response was much faster in Nigeria, where the first case was confirmed in July 2014; health officials immediately repurposed technologies and infrastructures from the WHO and other partners to find and track potential chains of transmission of Ebola.[38] The end of transmission in Liberia, and the 'effective end of the outbreak in West Africa', was marked on the 14th January 2016.[39]

4 The Role of the WHO in Coordinating a Medical Humanitarian Response

Infectious diseases did not come within the normative confines of international law until the mid-nineteenth century.[40] International law is a consensual system whereby states agree to be bound by treaties or customs that they freely enter into with other states.[41] There are two inherent weaknesses in international law when it comes to infectious diseases. The first is consent by states to external actors being present; the second is that, as infectious diseases do not respect state borders, states and organisations must collaborate and cooperate to prevent, respond to and recover from infection. Sovereignty is paramount to states and therefore any global intervention must be consented to by the state.[42]

The International Sanitary Conferences were convened to meet the need for agreeing quarantine procedures to prevent the spread of diseases, particularly cholera, without unduly disrupting rapidly growing international trade.[43] In 1903, the first international organisation dedicated to health was created. Fidler argues that, at the time, the international legal regime had three pillars: (1) duties to notify other States of outbreaks of specified diseases, (2) limits on the measures other states could take against ships and aircraft coming from states experiencing disease outbreaks, and (3) involvement of an international organisation dedicated to health.[44] The international legal framework that facilitates the provision of healthcare during outbreaks of disease is complex and refers to a multitude of actors that can enter into partnerships, forge relationships to oversee certain activities, or coordinate response on the ground.

In the aftermath of the Second World War, the focus of the UN was peace and security. The foundation of the WHO in 1948 recognised the transboundary nature of disease and envisaged an international support system for the prevention of the spread of disease coordinated by the WHO. The Red Cross, at the same time, was drafting

---

[38] See WHO Media Centre; Brookings Edu (2014).

[39] WHO, http://www.who.int/mediacentre/news/releases/2016/ebola-zero-liberia/en/.

[40] Aginam (2002).

[41] Art 38 (1) Statutes of the ICJ; See also International Sanitary Convention 1851, 1859, 1866, 1874, 1881, 1885, 1892, 1893, 1894 and 1897. Four treaties 1892, 1893, 1894 and 1897. See Howard-Jones (1950) in Fidler (1997).

[42] Harman (2012) 28.

[43] Clift (2013a).

[44] Fidler (2000).

the Geneva Conventions, which foresaw conflict and insecurity across boundaries and, to a lesser extent, within sovereign states. Nevertheless, the mandate provided to the Red Cross by the Geneva Conventions envisaged a humanitarian presence at the consent of sovereign states and, furthermore, created a system whereby there was a potentially permanent Red Cross presence in every state. Official relations were established between the WHO and the League of Red Cross Societies, the previous name of the IFRC, in 1948.[45]

What these parallel systems mean today is that it is unclear which actor has the ultimate authority. Can the WHO, as a specialised agency of the UN, coordinate an international institution with its own mandate provided by international agreement?[46] It is all very well to think about the relationship between the WHO and NGOs active in health and humanitarianism, but the Red Cross is different from such entities. What is the more nuanced relationship between the WHO and the Red Cross? Is it possible to determine the power and authority of each in the provision of health care and the prevention of the spread of infectious disease?

In 1951, the WHO adopted the International Sanitary Regulations, which became the International Health Regulations in 1969. The IHRs represent the 'only international health agreement on communicable diseases that is binding on Member States [of the WHO]'.[47] The World Health Assembly adopted the revised IHRs on 23 May 2005 at a time when 'public health, security, and democracy became intertwined'.[48] States recognised that they needed to act together to stop the spread of infectious diseases, as 'states could better protect their populations through early detection of health hazards and containment at their source'.[49] Presently, the 2005 International Health Regulations are the most up to date international legal rules on the control of infectious diseases, and provide a unified code for infectious disease control.

The overall purposes of the IHRs are to prevent, protect against, control and provide a public health response to the international spread of disease... commensurate with and restricted to public health risks, and which avoid unnecessary interference with international traffic and trade,[50] and to 'ensure maximum protection against the international spread of disease with minimum interference with world traffic.'[51] The IHRs have 'universal application for the protection of all people of the world'.[52] They are coordinated by the World Health Organisation (WHO); the Constitution sets out twenty-two functions for the WHO, which cover almost every conceivable activity linked to the promotion of health,[53] and states that the WHO is a 'directing

---

[45] XVIIth International Red Cross Conference, Report by the Director-General (7 September 1948, EB2/38).
[46] See Art 14(2) International Health Regulations 2005.
[47] WHO (1996).
[48] Gostin (2014).
[49] Ibid.
[50] Art 2 IHR 2005.
[51] WHO (1983).
[52] Art 3 IHR 2005.
[53] Clift (2013b).

and coordinating authority for health within the United Nations system'.[54] These words are key to our understanding and analysis of the WHO and the response to the West Africa Ebola outbreak.

The IHRs stipulate that health measures must be applied in a transparent and non-discriminatory manner.[55] States must consider a quarantined individual's gender, as well as sociocultural, ethnic, or religious concerns, and provide adequate food, water, accommodation, baggage protection, medical treatment, and communication.[56] Fidler states that 'although the IHR are technically binding rules, most States view them as merely recommendations rather than real obligations'.[57] Nevertheless, in some ways soft law, argues Dupuy, can be 'seen not only as a description of a type of norm but also a process that seeks to build cooperation and consensus in achieving certain objectives'.[58] States bordering the 'infected' State will want to stop the spread of disease, so there are questions over who or what should support the intervention by third States, international organisations, or NGOs. In a global age, however, the perceived threat and potential responders go beyond neighbouring states. Globalisation and increased travel and trade within and between countries have resulted in the rapid spread of disease. This was typified by the rapid spread of Severe Acute Respiratory Syndrome (SARS) across three continents within weeks in 2003[59] and by pandemic 2009-H1N1 influenza.[60] There is, therefore, an international legal framework including the Constitution of the WHO and the IHRs that seeks to provide an adequate response to outbreaks of infectious diseases. Overall, the IHRs aim to provide global health security but this relies on informational and communication channels being utilised to pass correct information from local healthcare providers to national bodies and then on to the WHO.

Despite the clear role and mandate of the WHO, it is a frequently-criticised entity. Its internal governance structures are argued to be in need of reform. It has been argued that the Ebola outbreak of 2014 served to highlight the inadequacies of the WHO.[61] Harman, for example, criticised the WHO for failing to keep up with the 'mission creep' of other institutions. She argued that the WHO needed to build partnerships with other institutions as 'partnerships are integral to its operations', but highlighted

---

[54] Clift (2013c).

[55] Art 42 IHR 2005.

[56] Art 32 IHR 2005; See also Arts 23 and 45 IHR 2005.

[57] Fidler (n 41) 63.

[58] Dupuy (1991) in Fidler (n 41) 63.

[59] Skowronski et al. (2005).

[60] Bajardi et al. (2011).

[61] Mackey (2016); WHO Interim Assessment panel established by the WHO Executive Board (Interim Panel), Report of the Ebola Interim Assessment Panel, http://www.who.int/csr/resources/publications/ebola/report-by-panel.pdf; Moon et al. (2015); Commission on a Global Health Risk Framework for the Future (CGHRF) convened by the U.S. National Academy of Medicine (formerly the Institute of Medicine) 'The Neglected Dimension of Global Security: A framework to counter infectious disease crises' (the National Academies Press 2016); Report of the High-Level Panel on the Global Response to Health Crises, 'Protecting Humanity from Future Health Crises' (25 January 2016).

the fact that the WHO has focused on working with States and other UN agencies[62]: 'Institutions such as the ICRC have greater presence within the meetings of the WHO than governments from small developing countries'.[63]

The criticisms levied echo many made over the past 15 years, whereby a number of infectious disease outbreaks have highlighted the limitations of the WHO mandate and practice, including SARS 2002, H1N1 2009, MERS 2013, H5N1 2005, and, most recently, the 2014 West African Ebola outbreak.[64] Moreover, if we think about the UN approach as one that is now securitising the idea of global health, then this is an extension of the idea that health is a 'global public good'.[65] Indeed, global health has, for a long time, been linked to 'wider processes of international politics' and 'political economy'.[66] The problem with this, argued Harman, is that the WHO might be thwarted by 'member state sovereignty and the trumping of economic issues such as trade over global health concerns'.[67] If we consider the above critique of the WHO, then the West African Ebola outbreak was a pivotal episode. It was an opportunity to demonstrate is capabilities and response to a transnational disease outbreak.

5   WHO and Ebola 2014–2016

'On 25 March, 2014 the WHO Global Emergency Management Team had graded the outbreak as a Level 2 emergency and were coordinating daily conferences on risk assessment, operational planning and review between Ministry of Health officials in of Guinea, Sierra Leone, and Liberia, the WHO country offices, the WHO Inter-country support teams (IST) of West Africa, WHO headquarters and the WHO African regional office (WHO AFRO)'.[68] The WHO declared the Ebola outbreak a 'public health emergency of international concern' (PHEIC) under the IHR on the 8th August 2014.[69] The WHO published materials on the evolution of the Ebola outbreak, then it chronicled its spread from earlier than 8th August.[70] It suggested, in its 'Statement on the 1st Meeting of the IHR Emergency Committee on the 2014 Ebola outbreak in west Africa', increasing oversight and support at the requests of the presidents of Guinea, Sierra Leone, and Liberia, culminating in the WHO

[62] Harman (n 42) 40.

[63] Harman (n 42) 56.

[64] Wibulpolprasert and Chowdhury (2016), Mackey and Liang (2012), Baker and Fidler (2006), Siedner (2015), Gostin (2015), Garrett (2015), Kupferschmidt (2015), and Checchi et al. (2016).

[65] Harman (n 42) 33.

[66] Harman (n 42) 34.

[67] Harman (n 42) 38.

[68] WHO and IFRC (2017c).

[69] Art 12 IHR gives WHO Director-General the authority to determine whether an event constitutes PHEIC.

[70] See the Ebola Response Modelling Tool designed by Centers for Disease Control and Prevention which estimated the potential number of future Ebola cases, https://www.cdc.gov/media/releases/2014/s0923-ebola-model-factsheet.html (23 September 2014).

PHEIC of 8th August.[71] It could be suggested that that this delay is indicative of a weak international framework for the response to international epidemics, but the alternative argument is that the WHO was involved through its regional organs. In addition, indeed, 'the WHO's coordinating role in developing the Ebola vaccine also highlights one of its unique benefits—no other body has the convening power of this intergovernmental agency, which can rapidly bring together scientists, industry, regulators and national public-health officials when needed'.[72]

Though '[o]nly the government of [an] affected country can make the decision whether to accept or reject EMTs (Emergency Medical Teams) in non-conflict disasters',[73] it is recognised, however, that there is a multitude of complex reasons as to why the treatment delivered during a pandemic may not be the highest standard available, most notably that many states who bear the greatest burden of infectious diseases are the least well positioned to respond to outbreaks.[74] In its joint 2017 publication, 'The Regulation and Management of International Emergency Medical Teams', the WHO and IFRC noted that

> [t]he tasking of teams responding to the EVD outbreak followed a 4-step process. Firstly, teams either stepped forward and offered their assistance (very few actually did this), or were directly approached by the WHO EMT initiative. Secondly, local needs were assessed and as far as possible met by the WHO and its partners. Thirdly, the WHO helped channel the offers of assistance to the respective Ministries of Health. Fourthly, tasking to an ETC location was undertaken by the Ministry of Health with support from the WHO EMT coordination cell. Importantly, this process could only begin once there were sufficient numbers of EMTs offering their assistance; therefore the majority of steps 3 and 4 did not take place until November and December 2014. The complexity of a three-country response to Ebola was further compounded when individual donor countries supported specific countries that were affected, rather than all three (e.g. the US supported Liberia, the UK supported Sierra Leone, and France supported Guinea).[75]

If we consider the importance of travel and trade to many developing economies, disease emergence can have a catastrophic effect. Gostin suggests that in the past, this has led to 'a vicious cycle of disease emergence, failure to report, and economic ramifications'.[76] It doesn't appear from the existing literature and reports concerning Ebola that the lack of reporting in Guinea was down to fear of economic ramifications, but rather owing to incorrect diagnosis and insufficient public health infrastructure.[77]

---

[71] WHO Statement, 'Statement on the 1st meeting of the IHR Emergency Committee on the 2014 Ebola outbreak in West Africa' (8 August 2014), http://www.who.int/mediacentre/news/statements/2014/ebola-20140808/en/.

[72] https://www.nature.com/news/the-time-is-ripe-to-reform-the-world-health-organisation-1.21394.

[73] WHO and IFRC (2017d).

[74] Wilson et al. (2010); Report by the Director-General, 'Report of the Review Committee on the Functioning of the International Health Regulations (2005) in relation to Pandemic (H1N1) 2009: Implementation of the International Health Regulations (2005)' 64th World Health Assembly A64/10, 11 May 2011.

[75] WHO and IFRC (2017e).

[76] Gostin (n 48)178.

[77] Shoman et al. (2017).

The more critical comments were levied at the delay by the WHO responding to Ebola. It took over eight months from the first case to the WHO declaration. The Director-General of WHO called for UN full capacity to help with the response.[78]

On the 18th September 2014, the UN Security Council, for the first time, declared a disease outbreak as a threat to international peace and security. This was the first time they had used 'declaratory' language.[79] The securitisation of disease at the UNSC is not without precedent—the Security Council concerned itself with AIDS, although this took 19 years, and Article 39 of the UN Charter was not used.[80] Perhaps what is more critical when looking at this gap between identification of the disease and UN response is the context. In the context of this paper, I would contend that the addition of other UN agencies, beyond WHO, makes the coordination and response even more confusing. In addition to the coordination role of the WHO, the UN has other mechanisms to respond to global health crises.

On 20 September UN Secretary-General Ban Ki-Moon established the UN Mission for Ebola Emergency Response (UNMEER).[81] The mission ran between 19 September 2014 and 31 July 2015, after which the WHO took the lead of the oversight of the UN's emergency response. Security Council Resolution 2177 'represents the most cogent recognition to date of a "non-traditional threat to international peace and security"'.[82] The UN Secretary-General deployed the UN Emergency Health Mission to 'harness the capabilities and competences of all relevant United Nations actors under a unified operational structure'.[83] Critically for this paper, Security Council Resolution 2177 refers to the IFRC as a first line responder.[84]

---

[78] WHO (2015).

[79] United Nations Security Council resolution 1308, adopted unanimously on 17 July 2000, was the first resolution to address the impact of HIV/AIDS worldwide. The UNSC stated that 'the HIV/AIDS pandemic, if unchecked, may pose a risk to stability and security' and held a meeting in 2000 on "The situation in Africa: the impact of AIDS on peace and security in Africa".

[80] On 5 June 1981, the US Centers for Disease Control and Prevention (CDC) published a Morbidity and Mortality Weekly Report (MMWR). It described cases of a rare lung infection, Pneumocystis carinii pneumonia (PCP), in five young, previously healthy, gay men in Los Angeles. It is the first official reporting of what became known as the AIDS epidemic.

[81] General Assembly Resolution 69/1 (2014); Security Council Resolution 2177 (2014).

[82] UN Secretary General, Statement by Secretary-General on the establishment of the United Nations Mission for Ebola Emergency Response (UNMEER) (19 September 2014); Security Council Resolution 2177 (18 September 2014); United Nations General Assembly Resolution 69/1 (2014); see also 'Introductory Note to WHO and UN Documents on the Ebola Outbreak in West Africa' (2015) 54 International Legal Materials 535–560.

[83] UN Secretary General, 'Identical Letters Dated 17 September 2014 from the Secretary-General Addressed to the President of the General Assembly and the President of the Security Council' UN Doc A/69/389- S/2014/679 (18 September 2014) 2.

[84] Security Council Resolution 2177 (18 September 2014) preamble.

6 The UN Relationship with Other Actors, Including the IFRC

There are several actors on the international stage with their own legal mandate to respond to infectious disease outbreaks. The WHO, UNMEER, and the Red Cross undertook several actions, established working groups and committees, and coordinated on the ground to try to stop the spread of infection and to treat those who had already succumbed. They relied on partnerships with each other and the governments of each state. The working relationships were essential as the outbreak was too large in scale for one organisation, state or local community to respond to alone. The necessity of expertise, resources, technical assistance, and personnel required a coordinated and sustained approach.

The international legal framework that facilitates the provision of healthcare during outbreaks of disease is complex and involves a multitude of actors that can enter into partnerships, forge relationships to oversee certain activities, or coordinate response on the ground. The IFRC is a 'partner' of the WHO in disaster response and has established 'formal agreements' in several contexts to facilitate its presence and role in specific situations on the ground.[85] It also has an active agreement, a Memorandum of Understanding, with the South-East Asia Regional Office of the World Health Organisation (SEARO).[86]

The IHRs do not specifically mention the National Red Cross and Red Crescent Societies but the IFRC is named as one of the international organisations with which the WHO must co-operate in implementing the IHRs.[87] The IFRC and National Societies work with governments on humanitarian protection and assistance issues and it is one of the aims of the IFRC to help governments prepare its legislation and resources for disaster situations. In fact, part of the role of the National Societies is to make the governments aware of changes in legislation that may be necessary to implement the IHR. At the national level, therefore, the National Societies can help to improve pandemic preparedness and response, which in turn can prevent the spread of disease, thus protecting international public health.

Importantly, in addition to the roles prescribed by its own mandate, and its direct relationship with the WHO, the IFRC has a standing invitation to participate in the Inter-Agency Standing Committee (IASC) Health Cluster under the leadership of WHO. The role of the IASC is to 'empower humanitarian country teams to better

---

[85]The IFRC has a working agreement with the WHO for disaster response and it also has an agreement with WHO and South-East Asia Regional Office. See also IFRC, 'Setting up a national disaster preparedness and response mechanism'. www.ifrc.org/Files/160282/175200_Setting-up-national-dpr-mechanism_EN.pdf.

[86]Memorandum of Understanding (MoU) with the South-East Asia Regional Office of the World Health Organisation (SEARO): covers public health, non-remunerated blood donation, health in disaster preparedness and emergency response, and collaboration in other health related areas. Countries covered are Bangladesh, Bhutan, DPRK, India, Indonesia, Maldives, Myanmar, Nepal, Sri Lanka, Thailand and Timor-Leste.

[87]Art 14(1) IHR 2005.

address the health aspects and crises'.[88] The IASC was established in June 1992 following General Assembly Resolution 46/182. Its role is to 'serve as the primary mechanism for inter-agency coordination relating to humanitarian assistance in response
to complex and major emergencies under the leadership of the Emergency Relief
Coordinator'. The Red Cross is a standalone humanitarian organisation and partner
of the WHO/ IASC at the international level. It can interpret its own mandate and
support or be called upon to support the work of other international actors. In addition, its National Societies provide it with an existing local presence, which aids in
the provision of humanitarian relief during times of conflict and in the event of a
disaster. Nevertheless, overall, the picture is quite confusing as to who is lead agent,
whether the IFRC is an autonomous actor, and whether the IFRC coordinates successfully with other agencies. The Red Cross, in some ways, escapes the political
and economic hindrances of the international stage and can respond to outbreaks of
disease from the 'bottom-up'. The mandate of the IFRC allows it to respond to public
health emergencies and it also has a separate role in disaster relief and disaster risk
reduction.

The WHO is meant to coordinate, but given the range of global health NGOs on
the international stage, there are many other actors with the mandate and resources
to react to the outbreak of disease. The UN is not the only organisation that States
will form agreements with, as actors such as the Red Cross have the capacity to
negotiate and enter into agreements too. Moreover, the UN does not always have
the operational capacity to respond adequately. The dilemma facing responders is
whether there should be one central coordinating body for the entire response, perhaps
the WHO, or whether they are each within their rights to do what they want and help
whom they want. In this light, the IHRs might, by necessity, have to be renegotiated
to include specific mention of a wider set of institutions. However, perhaps doing so
might put more operational pressure on NGOs to respond to all outbreaks of disease
rather than making choices.

The overall argument in this chapter, taking this all into account, is that there
are more actors ready and willing to respond to international health issues than are
within the ability of the WHO to coordinate presently. That said, it is not the sole
purpose of this chapter to criticise the WHO; its purpose is to add to the literature
to show that the Red Cross has an international legal mandate to provide health care
during the outbreak of infectious disease. In addition, although, in some instances,
it might make sense for the IFRC and National Societies to work with the WHO,
on its own terms, they cannot and will not wholly subjected to WHO coordination.
The Red Cross, critically, also has the scope through its organisational structure and
International Conference to increase its competences over time to continue its ability
to respond to health crises.

---

[88] IASC, https://interagencystandingcommittee.org/.

7 The IFRC Response

As stated above, the IFRC is one of the actors involved in the response to infectious diseases. The IFRC was founded in 1919 in Paris after the First World War to help National Societies.[89] Its first objective was to improve the health of people who had suffered during the four years of the war. The Red Cross provides a counterpart to the more state interest focused international system, which includes the WHO and IHR. The Red Cross was created to provide humanitarian protection and assistance directly to those in need. The Red Cross has an international mandate to provide health care to civilians and combatants during conflict and disaster situations.[90] Critically, the Red Cross was designed to reach communities and people in need. It is still subject to the consent of states, whether that is through the Geneva Conventions, Statutes of the Red Cross and Red Crescent Movement, and Headquarters agreements. However, its principles mean that is stays in favour with governments and is able to stay in countries for long periods of time. The ICRC, for example, often maintains a presence long after an identifiable armed conflict has ended. In this way, its reputation and humanitarian mandate set is apart from other organisations and NGOs. In circumstances where, for whatever reason, states decide that they no longer wish for the Red Cross to work within its territory, states might, should they be so inclined, refuse to grant visas to delegates, or perhaps even revoke visas, but this is unlikely. The Red Cross is renowned for its discretion and states trust that the organisation will work without exposing its inability to provide for its own population.

The IFRC is well placed to understand and respond directly to the needs of the people on the ground without being swayed by the economic, trade and tourist considerations that may preclude the state reporting to the WHO. Its principle of confidentiality, working with National Societies that understand the local context, and working on the ground to help and support those in need, keeps it in favour with both the government and local population. However, this did not prevent local fears and cultural requirements stopping the IFRC from doing its work during the 2014 West African Ebola outbreak.

The IFRC response was coordinated from late March 2014 when the Ministry of Health in Guinea had raised the alarm, even though the WHO did not declare a PHEIC until the 8th August the same year. For the Red Cross, it meant training 10,000 volunteers in Ebola response; the IFRC also supported emergency operations in Guinea, Liberia, and Sierra Leone, which targeted 23 million people.[91] As argued above, the IFRC has the mandate to provide health care to citizens and is well placed on the ground to do so quickly. It is, however, undertaking such action within a multi-agency response, including WHO via the IHRs, MSF, and the military and so

---

[89]The original organisation was called the League of Red Cross Societies until 1983 when it became the League of Red Cross and Red Crescent Societies until 1991. Since 1991 it has been called the International Federation of the Red Cross.

[90]Statutes of the Red Cross and Red Crescent Movement, preamble, principle of humanity, art 3(2) National Red Cross and Red Crescent Societies, and art 6(4)(f) IFRC.

[91]Senghore (n 34).

on. This chapter shows that the IFRC is simultaneously a leader, and directed by other entities, in its response to infectious disease.

The IFRC deployed a Field Assessment Coordination Team to Guinea that included an infectious disease specialist from the French Red Cross Society and a psychosocial support delegate. The IFRC was already on the ground in Guinea working through a cholera epidemic and measles outbreak.[92] However, as symptoms of Ebola are similar to cholera, it was difficult for the IFRC to recognise and, therefore, announce that Ebola was spreading. Ebola outbreaks have occurred previously but the IFRC documented that this outbreak presented several unique challenges. Firstly, it affected communities and governments that were 'new to the disease' and did not have the appropriate equipment, facilities and procedures in place. Secondly, in some areas people believed that the people spraying disinfectant were the ones spreading the disease, which caused violent, sometimes deadly, reactions. In addition, some cultural practices, including burial practices, facilitated the spread of the disease.[93] Finally, the outbreak occurred in an area where three states—Guinea, Sierra Leone and Liberia—have borders, and 'the porous nature of the borders of the countries involved, regional trade, interconnectedness of families and fluid population movement both within and between the affected countries [was] key to the geographical spread'.[94]

In terms of the IFRC response to Ebola, Alasan Senghore stated that

[t]he Red Cross and Red Crescent is community-based. Our people were there before the outbreak and they will remain there when it is over and most of the other responders have gone. It is what we have always been about, and our volunteers will continue to support communities as they recover, not only in relation to Ebola but also the parallel health and humanitarian challenges.[95]

The specifics of the IFRC response to the 2014 West African Ebola outbreak show how a humanitarian organisation with a local base can act quickly in response to an infection. During the outbreak of Ebola, the IFRC suggested that the Ebola outbreak was an instance of a public health response within its disaster management systems.[96] Usually when there is a disaster the situation on the ground improves from day one. The teams respond, assess and produce a plan of action for relief, recovery and build back better.[97] However, with Ebola, the situation worsened over time.[98]

---

[92] IFRC (2014d).

[93] Tiffany et al. (2017).

[94] IFRC (2015b).

[95] Senghore (n 34).

[96] International Red Cross and Red Crescent Movement, 'Ebola Strategic Framework' (January 2015).

[97] Build Back Better is defined as "The use of the recovery, rehabilitation and reconstruction phases after a disaster to increase the resilience of nations and communities through integrating disaster risk reduction measures into the restoration of physical infrastructure and societal systems, and into the revitalisation of livelihoods, economies and the environment." See United Nations Office for Disaster Risk Reduction (UNISDR), 'Build Back Better in recovery, rehabilitation and reconstruction' (2017 Consultative Version). http://www.unisdr.org/files/53213_bbb.pdf.

[98] IFRC (2015c).

The political and cultural resistance by states to acknowledging the outbreak delayed official recognition.[99] In this situation, the IFRC was an essential organisation on the ground, not least because of its local volunteers who possessed the local knowledge and expertise necessary to work with the local communities, as 'no other organisation has such a resource and harnessing it is key'.[100] This is part of the uniqueness of the IFRC. In addition, it is clear that the IFRC is an essential institution on the ground. Its mandate, reputation and operations capability set it apart from the WHO, which focuses on coordination. The IFRC is able to coordinate from Geneva to the state level and then reach individual communities through its network of National Societies. This infrastructure is unique to the IRCRCM, and critical for an effective response to an infectious disease outbreak.

The international community recognised Ebola as a threat to international peace and security through UN Security Council resolution 2177 and the WHO used its most extreme category for the outbreak; but for the most part the international community was slow to act. The IFRC, however, mobilised quickly and effectively. The IFRC was guided by several humanitarian policy guidelines to ensure that the Ebola emergency response met the necessary standards.[101] The Red Cross focused on education and awareness raising, providing psychosocial support and safe burial practices.[102]

The IFRC response was built on five pillars including surveillance and contact tracing, community engagement, safe and dignified burials and disinfection, psychosocial report, and case management.[103] The IFRC launched six emergency appeals to respond to Ebola outbreaks in Guinea, Liberia, Sierra Leone, Nigeria, and Senegal.[104] Smaller preparedness and response operations were financed by the IFRC Disaster Response Emergency Fund (DREF) in Mali, Cote d'Ivoire, Cameroon, Togo, Benin, Central African Republic, Chad, Gambia, Kenya, Guinea Bissau and Ethiopia.[105] There were an anticipated five outcomes of the IFRC Ebola Strategic Framework, including stopping the epidemic; ensuring that the National Societies have better Ebola preparedness and stronger long-term capacities; ensuring the good coordination of IFRC operations; facilitating safe and dignified burials by all actors; and the recovery of community life and livelihoods.[106] 'The overall IFRC response [was] coordinated from the IFRC Ebola coordination centre in Conakry, Guinea where

---

[99] Senghore (n 34).

[100] IFRC, 'Ending Ebola' 8; See also IFRC (2017).

[101] Principles and Rules for Red Cross and Red Crescent Humanitarian Assistance (IFRC 2013), http://www.ifrc.org/Global/Documents/Secretariat/Accountability/Principles%20Rules%20for%20Red%20Cross%20Red%20Crescent%20Humanitarian%20Assistance.pdf; IFRC Disaster Preparedness Policy, http://www.ifrc.org/Global/Governance/Policies/disaster-policy-en.pdf; Emergency Response Policy and Sphere Standards, The Sphere Hanbook (New edn 6 November 2018), http://www.spherestandards.org/.

[102] American Red Cross (2014).

[103] See the IFRC Emergency Appeals for Guinea, Sierra Leone and Liberia.

[104] See www.ifrc.org.

[105] See IFRC (2015c).

[106] International Red Cross and Red Crescent Movement, 'Ebola Strategic Framework' (January 2015).

the IFRC head of emergency operation leads a programme support team in order to maintain a coordinated response in multiple countries following the same response strategy but adapted to specific contexts and National Society capacity, role and mandate'.[107] The IFRC Africa Regional Director stated that:

> What the world must understand is that West Africa's epidemic has been about more than Ebola itself. It has shown how weak health systems with insufficient health workers unable to respond to emerging needs can spiral into a severe humanitarian crisis, especially when international response is slow. Whether it be in Ebola affected areas or anywhere else, support for health and community systems is central to ensuring universal health access, and that is the cornerstone of resilient communities and sustainable development.[108]

Critically, Guinea, Sierra Leone and Liberia are places where governments cannot deliver basic services to most of their population. Across Guinea, Liberia and Sierra Leone, the IFRC works to implement the five pillars, taking the lead on Safe and Dignified Burials. They partner with the Ministry of Health, WHO, World Food Programme, UNICEF, MSF and other regional and international organisations to deliver the five pillars. Other organisations and departments take the lead on other pillars, but with support from the IFRC. It is beyond the scope of this chapter to describe each partnership and 'hierarchy' in the Ebola response, but, as we know from its relationships with other institutions described above, the IFRC does not act alone. The IFRC is well placed to engage with the local communities and the reports from Guinea, Sierra Leone and Liberia show the importance of such engagement. It was noted early in this chapter that superstition and fear prevented a number of infected people from coming forward, made communities suspicious of external actors, and in many cases actually quickened the spread of disease through failure to take the proper steps to prevent the spread of disease.

If we look at the three key states responding to the Ebola outbreak as the number of cases and geographical spread of Ebola increased in Guinea, the IFRC reported that

> [t]he major factors that continue to quicken the spread of the virus include: poor understanding of the disease; inadequate communication; misconceptions and fear among affected communities; lack of adherence to strict protocols by healthcare workers dealing with [Ebola]; and limited responding capacities.[109]

These factors were present, as noted above, in other states affected by Ebola. The IFRC does not have a representation in Guinea but it does participate in all national and other coordination meetings with the Guinea Red Cross (GRC). The IFRC established an Ebola Management Unit in Conakry. The GRC is focused on four of the five pillars identified above, including social mobilisation, safe and dignified burials and disinfection of houses, psychosocial support, and case management and treatment.[110]

---

[107] IFRC, 'Emergency Appeal Sierra Leone: Ebola Virus Disease', http://www.ifrc.org/en/publications-and-reports/appeals/?p=43&zo=SP1.

[108] Senghore (n 34).

[109] IFRC (2014a).

[110] Ibid.

The IFRC accepted a request by the United Nations Mission for Ebola Emergency Response (UNMEER) to take a leading role in the safe and dignified burials, disinfection of households and contaminated areas, as well as the transportation of sick patients in certain regions.

In Liberia, the Liberia Red Cross Society, with support of the IFRC operations team, increased the number of volunteers active. Its focus, as in Guinea, was the safe and dignified burials of those who were suspected to have died of Ebola— a key task required in order to reduce transmission.[111] In Sierra Leone, the first announcement of cases were accompanied by reports that six of the initial eight suspected and confirmed cases had refused to be placed in isolation and had gone into hiding. There were also reports that Ministry of Health and Sanitation officials had been subjected to aggression in the communities they visited. As a result, early attempts to control the outbreak were unsuccessful.[112] Finally, the IFRC established a field base of operations in Sierra Leone after the outbreak. It coordinates the same projects as in Guinea, namely social mobilisation, surveillance and contact tracing, psychosocial support, dead body management, coordination, and case management.

8 Conclusion

Almost 20 years ago, Fidler remarked that disease needs a complete international legal regime, as 'infectious diseases render borders impotent and undermine a government's ability to protect public health'.[113] It is common sense that an infectious disease will spread amongst communities and populations, regardless of state borders. When people succumb to disease, they need access to health care that will cure them or, at the very least, ease their suffering. States have the primary obligation to provide such through national health care systems, but there is no universal standard for this. When an infectious disease affects the human population and the State is unable to stop its spread, there is a number of actors on the international stage with the mandate to react and protect people. To this end, international law provides a global legal framework to regulate and coordinate the international response to infectious diseases, including through the mandate of the International Red Cross and Red Crescent Movement (IRCRCM) and the Constitution of the WHO. Of course, any response to infectious disease needs to be bespoke to the disease but there exist a number of international laws and international institutions to provide global mechanisms by which external actors, States and organisations, can support States threatened by the spread of disease.

---

[111] IFRC (2014b).
[112] IFRC (2014c).
[113] Fidler (1999).

Despite international efforts to coordinate humanitarian responses, whether in relation to armed conflicts or disasters, the United Nations Secretary-General's decision to convene a High-Level Panel on the Global Response to Health Crises suggests that new ground needs to be broken in the future coordination of humanitarian responses to infectious diseases.[114] Similarly, Strategic Aim 1 of the IFRC's Strategy 2020 is to "save lives, protect livelihoods, and strengthen recovery from disasters and crises"[115]; and the WHO's objective of "the attainment by all people of the highest possible level of health"[116] as well as its objective in disasters and emergencies to "reduce the consequences the event may have on world health and its social and economic implications", shows the ambition of the WHO to respond better to infectious disease in the future.

Ultimately, this chapter has shown the nuanced and complex relationship between the Red Cross Movement and the WHO. As two actors with international mandates concerning health, they have very different roles. The international community should not be aiming for an ultimate coordinating body to oversee the entire response as organisations have grown up independently of one another and have unique and established relationships with the states and communities that they may serve. Of course, on the international stage, delegates may converse, build relationships, discuss operations, but that it not to say that the best practice would come from an ultimate authority dictating the actions of all possible responders. This is particularly the case with the IFRC and National Societies which have built and nurtured relationships with States and each other for decades in order to develop institutional best practice. The autonomy of the Red Cross to react to an outbreak should be respected and, where beneficial to both the WHO and the Red Cross, it may be part of a multi-institutional operation or response.

References

Aginam O (2002) International law and communicable diseases. Bull World Health Organ 80:946

American Red Cross (2014) American Red Cross supports Ebola response in West Africa, 19 Aug 2014. http://www.redcross.org/news/press-release/American-Red-Cross-SupportsEbola-Response-in-West-Africa. Accessed 23 Jul 2015

Bajardi P et al (2011) Human mobility networks, travel restrictions, and the global spread of 2009 H1N1 pandemic. PLoS ONE 6(1):e16591

Baker MG, Fidler D (2006) Global public health surveillance under new international health regulations. Emerg Infect Dis 12:1058–1065

---

[114] Report of the High-level Panel on the Global Response to Health Crises, 'Protecting Humanity from Future Health Crises' (25 January 2016).

[115] See Resolution 7 of the 31st International Conference of the Red Cross Red Crescent on 'Strengthening normative frameworks and addressing regulatory barriers concerning disaster mitigation, response and recovery' (2011); Resolution 6 of the 32nd International Conference of the Red Cross Red Crescent on 'Strengthening legal frameworks for disaster response, risk reduction and first aid' (2015), available online at www.ifrc.org/dl.

[116] See the Constitution of the World Health Organisation (1946).

Brookings Edu (2014) Understanding the economic effects of the 2014 Ebola outbreak in West Africa, Oct 2014

Campbell L (2017) Learning from the Ebola response in cities: population movement. ALNAP working paper

Checchi F et al (2016) World Health Organisation and emergency health: if not now, when? BMJ 352:i469

Clift C (2013a) The role of the World Health Organisation in the international system. Chatham House, Centre on Global Health Security Working Group Papers, p 6, Feb 2013

Clift C (2013b) The role of the World Health Organisation in the international system. Chatham House, Centre on Global Health Security Working Group Papers, p 7, Feb 2013

Clift C (2013c) The role of the World Health Organisation in the international system. Chatham House, Centre on Global Health Security Working Group Papers, Feb 2013. Executive summary

Dupuy P-M (1991) Soft law and the international law of the environment. Mich J Int Law 12:420–435

Fidler DP (1997) The role of international law in the control of emerging infectious diseases. Bull Inst Pasteur 95:57, 59

Fidler D (1999) International law and infectious diseases. Clarendon, Oxford, p 5

Fidler D (2000) The role of international law in the control of emerging infectious diseases. In: Whitman J (ed) The politics of emergent and resurgent infectious diseases. Palgrave Macmillan, London, United Kingdom, p 65

Garrett L (2015) Ebola's lessons. Foreign Aff 94:80–107

Gostin LO (ed) (2014) Global health law. Harvard University Press, Cambridge, MA, p 177

Gostin LO (2015) Reforming the World Health Organisation after Ebola. JAMA 14:1407–1408

Harman S (2012) Global health governance. Routledge, New York, p 28

Howard-Jones N (1950) Origins of international health work. Br Med J 1:1032–1037

IFRC (2014a) Emergency Plan of Action (EPoA) update Guinea: Ebola virus disease, 18 Nov 2014

IFRC (2014b) Emergency Plan of Action (EPoA) revision Liberia: Ebola virus disease, 9 Apr 2014

IFRC (2014c) Emergency Plan of Action (EPoA) Sierra Leone: Ebola virus disease, 9 Sept 2014

IFRC (2014d) Red Cross responds to Ebola outbreak in Guinea, 25 March 2014. www.ifrc.org/en/ .../guinea/red-cross-responds-to-ebola-outbreak-in-guinea--65316/

IFRC (2015a) Beyond Ebola: from dignified response to dignified recovery. IFRC

IFRC (2015b) Terms of reference for real time evaluation of the IFRC response to the Ebola virus disease outbreak. In: Ebola real time evaluation report, 25 Jan 2015

IFRC (2015c) Terms of reference for real time evaluation of the IFRC response to the Ebola virus disease outbreak. In: Ebola real time evaluation report, p 3, 25 Jan 2015

IFRC (2017) Closer to communities means better response to health crises, 23 May 2017. https:// media.ifrc.org/ifrc/2017/05/23/closer-to-communities-means-better-response-to-health-crises/

Kamradt-Scott A, Harman S, Wenham C, Smith F III (2015) Saving lives: the civil-military response to the 2014 Ebola outbreak in West Africa, October 2015. http://sydney.edu.au/arts/ ciss/downloads/SavingLivesPDF.pdf

Kaplan J, Easton-Calabria E (2015) Military medical innovation and the Ebola response: a unique space for humanitarian civil-military engagement. Humanitarian Practice Network, June 2015. http://odihpn.org/magazine/military-medical-innovation-and-the-ebola-response-a-unique-space-for-humanitarian-civil-military-engagement/

Koenig C (1991) Observer status for the International Committee of the Red Cross at the United Nations: a legal viewpoint. IRRC 280:47

Kupferschmidt K (2015) Global health: report prescribes strong medicine for WHO. Science 349:223–224

Lee K (2009) The World Health Organisation (WHO). Routledge

Mackey T (2016) The Ebola outbreak: catalyzing a "shift" in global health governance? BMC Infect Dis 16:699

Mackey T, Liang BA (2012) Lessons from SARS and H1N1/A: employing a WHO/WTO forum to promote optimal economic-public health pandemic response. J Public Health Policy 33:119–130

Moon S et al (2015) Will Ebola change the game? Ten essential reforms before the next pandemic. The report of the Harvard-LSHTM Independent Panel on the Global Response to Ebola. Lancet 386:2204–2221

Murray A, Majwa P, Roberton T, Burnham G (2014) Inception report: real time evaluation of the IFRC response to the Ebola virus disease outbreak, 30 Nov 2014. In: Ebola real time evaluation report. IFRC, p 11, 25 Jan 2015

Ross E, Welch GH, Angelides P (2017) Sierra Leone's response to the Ebola outbreak management strategies and key responder experiences. Centre on Global Health Security, March 2017

Shoman H, Karafillakis E, Rawaf S (2017) The link between the West African Ebola outbreak and health systems in Guinea, Liberia and Sierra Leone: a systematic review. Global Health 13:1–22

Shucksmith C (2017) The International Committee of the Red Cross and its mandate to protect and assist: law and practice. Hart

Siedner MJ (2015) Strengthening the detection of and early response to public health emergencies: lessons from the West African Ebola epidemic. PLoS Med 12:e1001804

Skowronski DM et al (2005) Severe acute respiratory syndrome (SARS): a year in review. Annu Rev Med 56:357–381

Stein RA (2015) What is Ebola? Int J Clin Pract 69(1):49–58

Tiffany A et al (2017) Estimating the number of secondary Ebola cases resulting from an unsafe burial and risk factors for transmission during the West Africa Ebola epidemic. PLoS Negl Trop Dis 11(6):e0005491

WHO (1996) Division of emerging and other communicable diseases surveillance and control. Emerging and other communicable diseases strategic plan 1996–2000. WHO/EMC/96.1, Geneva, Switzerland

WHO (2015) The role of WHO within the United Nations mission for Ebola emergency response: report of the secretariat, April 2015

WHO, IFRC (2017a) The Regulation and Management of International Emergency Medical Teams, June 2017

WHO, IFRC (2017b) The Regulation and Management of International Emergency Medical Teams, pp 9–10, June 2017

WHO, IFRC (2017c) The Regulation and Management of International Emergency Medical Teams, p 19. IFRC and WHO, June 2017

WHO, IFRC (2017d) The Regulation and Management of International Emergency Medical Teams, p 25. IFRC and WHO, June 2017

WHO, IFRC (2017e) The Regulation and Management of International Emergency Medical Teams, pp 37–38. IFRC and WHO, June 2017

Wibulpolprasert S, Chowdhury M (2016) World Health Organisation: overhaul or dismantle? Am J Public Health 106:1910–1911

Wilson K, Brownstein J, Fidler DP (2010) Strengthening the international health regulations: lessons from the H1N1 pandemic. Health Policy Plan 25(6):505–509

The Law of Responsibility and the World Health Organisation: A Case Study on the West African Ebola Outbreak

Mark Eccleston-Turner and Scarlett McArdle

Abstract The delay between the WHO being made aware of the 2014 Ebola epidemic in West Africa and declaring it a Public Health Emergency of International Concern (PHEIC) has been the subject of some considerable criticism in the literature, as well as in the Report of the Ebola Interim Assessment Panel commissioned by the WHO, which stated that that 'significant and unjustifiable delays occurred in the declaration of a Public Health Emergency of International Concern (PHEIC) by WHO.' This paper examines this late declaration of a PHEIC for Ebola through the lens of the law of responsibility, arguing that the WHO incurs responsibility for this delay. The law of responsibility is long standing in international law as the framework for providing redress for breaches of law. It gives rise to an obligation to provide redress and ensures some form of culpability for a breach of international law. In this paper we argue that the WHO does not merely have the power to declare a PHEIC via the International Health Regulations (2005), but also has a legal obligation to do so when the criteria are met. An obligation which we argue, they breached in failing to declare the recent Ebola outbreak in West Africa a PHEIC in a timely manner. This breach should then engage the law of responsibility for the consequences of the delay. The paper argues, however, that there exist substantial issues with the application of the principles of responsibility to international organizations.

Keywords WHO · Ebola · Responsibility · Legal personhood · PHEIC · International Organisations

M. Eccleston-Turner (✉)
Keele University, Newcastle-under-Lyme, England, UK
e-mail: m.r.eccleston-turner@keele.ac.uk

Fondation Brocher, Geneva, Switzerland

S. McArdle
University of Lincoln, Lincoln, England, UK

© Springer Nature Switzerland AG 2020
M. Eccleston-Turner and I. Brassington (eds.), *Infectious Diseases in the New Millennium*, International Library of Ethics, Law, and the New Medicine 82,
https://doi.org/10.1007/978-3-030-39819-4_5

1   Introduction

The law of responsibility establishes consequences and redress for breaches of international law; it is a longstanding element of public international law.[1] At its most basic, responsibility in international law ensures some form of culpability for an international wrongful act and gives rise to an obligation for the wrongdoer to provide redress. The key principles in the law of responsibility establish that responsibility will arise when an internationally wrongful act has been committed, which constitutes a breach of international law, and which is attributable to the international actor concerned.[2] In this chapter we apply the principles of the law of responsibility to the 2014 West African Ebola epidemic, arguing that legal responsibility can be established at an international level on the part of the World Health Organisation (WHO) for their delayed action in respect of the West African Ebola response.

The West African Ebola epidemic began in Guinea during December 2013,[3] and the WHO was officially notified of the outbreak on the 23rd of March, 2014.[4] The WHO did not declare the outbreak to be a 'Public Health Emergency of International Concern'[5] (PHEIC) until August 8th that year.[6] By this time there were 1779 confirmed and suspected cases of Ebola, nearly a thousand of which were confirmed or suspected to have resulted in death.[7] This delay between the WHO being made aware of the epidemic and declaring it a PHEIC has been the subject of considerable criticism in the literature.[8] Further criticism came via the Report of the Ebola Interim Assessment Panel commissioned by the WHO, which stated that 'significant and unjustifiable delays occurred in the declaration of a PHEIC by the WHO.'[9]

The International Health Regulations (IHRs) empower the Director-General of the WHO to declare an event a PHEIC.[10] The IHRs were passed by the World Health Assembly in 2005, as an update to the 1969 Regulations, and serve as the primary set of rules that govern state conduct in the build up to and during infectious disease outbreaks. The overarching goal of the Regulations is to prevent, detect and respond to the international spread of infectious diseases and other public health

---

[1] Grotius (2005), Ch XVII, para. 1 (vol II, 884); and see the Prolegomena, para. 8 (vol. 1, 86), in Pellet (2010), at p. 5.

[2] Articles 1 and 2 Articles on the Responsibility of States for Internationally Wrongful Acts; Articles 3 and 4 Articles on the Responsibility of International Organisations.

[3] Briand et al. (2014).

[4] The WHO Ebola Response Team (2014).

[5] The WHO has the power to declare a PHEIC via the WHO, International Health Regulations (2005).

[6] World Health Organisation (2015a).

[7] WHO (2016).

[8] Gostin and Friedman (2014), Gostin (2015), Siedner et al. (2015) and Kekulé (2015).

[9] World Health Organisation (2015b).

[10] Article 12, ibid.

emergencies,[11] whilst at the same time attempting to prevent unnecessary restrictions being placed upon trade and travel to affected states.[12] The Regulations define a PHEIC as an extraordinary event which is determined: (i) to constitute a public health risk to other States through the international spread of disease and (ii) to potentially require a coordinated international response.[13]

The ability to declare an event a Public Health Emergency of International Concern provides the WHO with significant power and influence over international health affairs. First, such a declaration directs international attention and resources to the public health emergency[14]; this is intended to ensure a fast, coordinated global response to the outbreak. There is, however, a second, negative, element to this influence with the potentia significant impact on travel and trade that a PHEIC can give rise to.[15]

As Adam Rainis Houston identifies in his chapter, the concept of a declaring a disease as a PHEIC on the basis of characteristics did not properly exist before the 2005 revisions to the International Health Regulations; rather, only specific diseases (cholera, plague and yellow fever, and smallpox) were considered notifiable under the 1969 IHR.[16] Since 2005 the WHO's mechanisms for determining if an event constituted a PHEIC have been tested on a number of occasions, resulting in a declaration in 2009 for H1N1 pandemic influenza, in 2014 for Polio, in 2016 for Ebola, and in 2016 for Zika, 2018 for Ebola in the DRC and 2019 for Covid-19. Other events—MERS in 2013 and yellow fever in 2016—have been considered potential PHEICs, but have not resulted in declarations. The seemingly inconsistent approach the WHO takes to declaring, or not declaring, an event a PHEIC has resulted in some considerable criticism of the Organisation and its decision-making processes in this area.[17] While the focus of this chapter is on the 2014 West African Ebola outbreak, as this is arguably the most controversial use of the WHO's PHEIC powers in the new millennium, it is important to note that our arguments in respect of Ebola are generalisable to other PHEICs. We return to this later in the chapter.

In the meantime, we present four claims: first, that the WHO is a distinct legal actor on the international stage capable of incurring responsibility for its actions; second, that the WHO does not merely have the *power* to declare a PHEIC, but also

---

[11] See 'Foreword' and Article 2 World Health Organisation, 'International Health Regulations' (2005).

[12] Article 12, ibid.

[13] Article 12, ibid.

[14] Lawrence Gostin & Eric Friedman, (n 5).

[15] A PHEIC being declared empowers the WHO to make a number of recommendations regarding the movement of persons, baggage, cargo, containers, conveyances, goods and/or postal parcels to states involved in, or at risk from, the outbreak. These recommendations to states can include the closing of borders between states; requiring vaccinations within the state or to gain entry; implement quarantine for those suspected of being affected; isolation for those affected; and implement entry or exit screening on persons from affected regions, and are designed to minimise or control the public health threat. See: Reinalda and Verbeek (2011).

[16] P. [—].

[17] Andrus et al. (2010), Gostin and Lucey (2015) and Lucey and Gostin (2016).

has a *legal obligation* to do so and to do so in a timely manner; third, that the WHO failed to discharge this legal obligation in failing to declare the recent Ebola outbreak in West Africa a PHEIC in a timely manner; and fourth, that the failure to declare a PHEIC in a timely manner gives rise to legal responsibility at the international level for the consequences of the delay.

2 The WHO, Accountability and the Need for Responsibility

As we have noted elsewhere, the WHO is substantially lacking in appropriate accountability mechanisms, particularly in respect of the actions of the Organisation during a PHEIC.[18] We have also suggested appropriate mechanisms by which the WHO could improve its accountability mechanisms.[19] Accountability and responsibility are inextricably linked: while reform of the accountability system would be of great benefit to the WHO and the international system as a whole, this should be done in combination with development of the international law of responsibility to enable greater redress for wrongful acts when they occur. The law of responsibility enables legal action to be brought against a responsible actor at the international level.[20] As Hafner stated, "accountability seems to reflect primarily the need to attribute certain activities under international law to such actors as a precondition for imposing on them responsibility under international law."[21]

Responsibility in international law originally developed in the context of the traditional nature of international law being focused around bilateral state relations and the importance of state sovereignty. If an international legal obligation had been breached then this offended the wronged state's sovereign rights and, consequently, such state should have the ability to reinforce and uphold its rights. Consequently, the law of responsibility was the law of state responsibility.[22] In spite of this early limitation, the ability to apply this law beyond the state was soon being called for.[23] These calls largely arose in response to the growth of international organisations,

---

[18]Eccleston-Turner and McArdle (2017).

[19]ibid.

[20]See for example Articles 1 and 31 Articles on Responsibility of states for Internationally Wrongful Acts, with commentaries 2001, Yearbook of the International Law Commission 2001, 2001, vol. II, Part Two and Articles 3 and 31 Articles on the Responsibility of International Organisations, with Commentaries, 2011, *Yearbook of the International Law Commission, 2011,* vol. II, Part Two.

[21]Hafner (2003), at 237.

[22]Articles on the Responsibility of States for Internationally Wrongful Acts, General Assembly Resolution 56/83 of 12 December 2001; Report of the ILC, 53rd Session, *ILC Yearbook 2001,* Vol. II(2), 25.

[23]First Report by El Erian (1963) at p. 184; Report by Ago (1963) at p. 234; *Exchange of Letters Constituting an Agreement relating to the Settlement of Claims filed against the United Nations in the Congo by Belgian nationals New York, 20 February 1965,* No. 7780 (1965) *Recueil des Traités* p. 198; Kent (2005); The Secretary'General, Investigation by the Office of Internal Oversight

both in terms of number and powers. This eventually led in 2009 to the International Law Commission (ILC) developing the Articles on the Responsibility of International Organisations (ARIO).[24] In spite of the established differences in nature and powers of states and international organisations,[25] the ARIO largely mirror the ILC's earlier Articles on State Responsibility,[26] which are well established within international law. While the principles may largely still be in their infancy in respect of international organisations, there exists a breadth of state-based practice to assist in the interpretation and application of such principles.

In order for the actions of the WHO to be addressed by the ARIO, and in order for the WHO's delay in declaring a PHEIC to be addressed by the law of responsibility, two factors must be established. First, the WHO must be accepted as a distinct legal actor at the international level. Second, the ability to declare a PHEIC in a timely fashion must be considered to not just be a power of the WHO, but a legal obligation as well. We argue below that these two factors can be established. From this it will be clear that there exists an international obligation on the part of an autonomous international actor, which was not upheld in this situation.

3 The WHO as an Autonomous International Actor: A Capacity for Responsibility?

The first thing that must be considered is the nature of the WHO as an autonomous subject of international law, as only subjects of international law are capable of possessing the sort of legal personality required in order to be subject to the law of responsibility. The broad concept of autonomy is a complex one. In existing in this distinct manner, it is only autonomous institutions with this separate will that are capable of incurring legal responsibility.[27]

While the overarching idea of autonomy can be a useful one, it is quite broad. A more concrete idea can be found in legal personality, which identifies subjects of international law capable of possessing rights, duties, powers and, crucially, obligations and liabilities of their own accord, and distinct from those of its Member States.[28] This firmer legal concept can be aligned with the idea of identifying a separate will of an organisation; in addressing autonomy and the idea of a distinct

---

Services into Allegations of Sexual Exploitation and Abuse in the United Nations Organisation Mission in the Dem. Rep. Congo, U.N. Doc. A/59/661 (Jan. 5, 2005).

[24]Report of the ILC, 61st Session, 2009, A/64/10, 13–178.

[25]Reparation for injuries suffered in the service of the Nations, Advisory Opinion, [1949] ICJ Rep 174, ICGJ 232.

[26]Articles on the Responsibility of States for Internationally Wrongful Acts, General Assembly Resolution 56/83 of 12 December 2001; Report of the ILC, 53rd Session, *ILC Yearbook 2001*, Vol. II(2), 25.

[27]Klabbers (2011), at p. 122; Sari (2011).

[28]White (2005), at p. 31.

will, many commentators focus on the presence (or absence) of legal personality.[29] Personality is important not only in identifying a distinct identity on the part of the organisation, but it also in establishing whether an organisation has the capacity to incur responsibility as a distinct actor on the international stage. In spite of personality being slightly more concrete than the overarching idea of autonomy, there does not exist a clear definition of personality in international law. International law is largely state-centric, and states are presumed to have legal personality by their very nature; but the expansion of personality beyond the state has not led to a clear definition.

Institutions were first accepted as having the capacity for legal personality by the International Court of Justice in *"Reparations"* in relation to the United Nations in 1949:

> In the opinion of the Court, the Organisation was intended to exercise and enjoy, and is in fact exercising and enjoying functions and rights which can only be explained on the basis of the possession of a large measure of international personality and the capacity to operate upon an international plane.[30]

In spite of this acceptance, identifying personality continues to be complex. The above statement, while utilised by many as a definition, has long been criticised,[31] both in terms of its mention of a 'degree' of personality when such a concept is a discrete one, and also in terms of its circularity. This criticism has given rise to continued debate as to precisely how to establish personality.[32] In spite of the criticism, an engagement with the concepts in the statement, while somewhat difficult, becomes almost inevitable. The important consideration begins with the intentions of member states, primarily those intentions explicitly mentioned but also, building from this, implicitly derived through the actions, powers and organs of the institution in an attempt to identify this broad notion of a 'distinct will'.

Ensuring the intentions of the member states may be a useful starting point, but this approach is limited when applied to multi-layered, multi-faceted supraorganisations such as the UN or the WHO; the intentions of the member states very often are not stated or are unclear. Indeed, the role, functions, and powers of such organisations are organic in nature: they grow, shift and develop over time without a conscious statement of the intentions of the member states that are enabling this growth and development. Many organisations now differ substantially in role, functions, and powers from those which were created in the post-war era, with much of this development having been unconscious and evolutionary as opposed to explicit member state reform. The consequence is that, to identify personality, intentions are inferred from considering aspects of the institution: such as a degree of permanency and distinct purposes and powers, the existence of organs within the institution with the

---

[29] White (2005), at p. 30.

[30] *Reparations for injuries suffered in the service of the United Nations, Advisory Opinion ICJ Reports,* 1949, p. 179.

[31] Brölmann (2007), at p. 78; White (2005), at p. 44.

[32] Seyersted (1964), Klabbers (1998), see in particular, 243–249; Klabbers and Wallendahl (2011).

capacity for decision making, and the exercise of powers, without the prior approval of the member states.[33]

Determining the WHO's personality is slightly more complex than with some other institutions due to its existence as a specialised agency of the UN.[34] As with most other international organisations, there is no definitive statement on personality in its founding documents, meaning there was no distinct conferral of personality on the WHO from the Member States at the time of its creation. The *Reparations* statement then directs us to consider a more implicit conferral of personality from the Member States; when considering the powers and capacities given to an institution, personality can be identified.

The Constitution of the WHO considers its "legal capacity, privileges and immunities", which are to be determined by the WHO in "consultation" with the Secretary-General of the United Nations and concluded between the Members of the WHO.[35] While this statement does not state much about personality and capacity, it can be interpreted to show the WHO to have "legal capacity, privileges and immunities", which could go some way towards establishing personality. It is significant that such capacity is to be "determined" by the organisation itself.[36] This is an important element. The power to develop its own capacity, even to a small degree, shows a significant element of 'separate will' from its members on the part of the institution.

Moreover, it is interesting that some mention of personality is made in the Convention on the Privileges and Immunities of the Specialised Agencies, concluded by the UN General Assembly.[37] This Convention, which does apply to the WHO, makes explicit reference to the institution possessing 'juridical personality', and defines this as the capacity "(a) to contract, (b) to acquire and dispose of immovable and movable property, [and] (c) to institute legal proceedings".[38] In explicitly recognising an aspect of legal personality and in attempting to delimit it in a specific way, the Convention recognises that the organisation has the ability to act in a manner that is distinct from its Member States. There is an identification of the WHO as being separate from its Members, not just broadly in terms of its actions but in far more legal terms.

The considerable expansion of the role, functions, and powers of the WHO since they were first articulated in 1946 only strengthens the case for establishing legal personality and determining the WHO as an autonomous institution. The Member States have allowed the role, functions and powers of the WHO to move its personality beyond that which was initially envisaged in the founding of the organisation. In the

---

[33] White (2005), at pp. 30–32.

[34] Article 69, Constitution of the World Health Organisation.

[35] Article 68, Constitution of the World Health Organisation.

[36] ibid.

[37] Adopted by the First World Health Assembly on 17 July 1948 (*Off. Rec. Wld Hlth Org.*, **13**, 97, 332).

[38] Adopted by the First World Health Assembly on 17 July 1948 (*Off. Rec. Wld Hlth Org.*, **13**, 97, 332), Section 3.

words of the ICJ opinion in *Reparations* this can only be explained by the possession of international personality, and a capacity to operate upon an international plane.[39]

While some progress on this argument can be made in relation to the initial idea of will and powers, further support can be found in the institutional structure of the WHO: it possesses its own organs. Under its auspices exist the World Health Assembly, the Executive Board, and the Secretariat, each of which has a number of distinct powers to act on behalf of the WHO. The Assembly, for example, determines policies and adopts regulations, which can be seen as akin to a legislative process. It is also able to adopt conventions with respect to the objectives of the WHO. The Executive Board exists as an executive organ of the Health Assembly, although it must be noted that it has some degree of independence from the Assembly, and thereby from the Member States that make up the Assembly. For instance, while membership of the Board is elected by the Assembly, the Board does not need to reflect the national membership of the Assembly,[40] implying that the Board members are acting in a manner that is institutionally distinct from the Assembly and the Member States. Moreover, the Board elects its own Chair and sets its own rules and procedures,[41] addresses any questions within its competence,[42] sets the agenda for the Assembly,[43] and proposes the general programme of work for the Assembly to vote upon.[44] Each of these powers and duties of the Board implies that it is distinct from the Assembly and the decision-making powers of the Member States that make up the Assembly. Most notably in this regard however, is the fact that the Board has the power to take emergency measures within the functions and financial resources of the Organisation to deal with events requiring immediate action. In particular it may authorise the Director-General to take the necessary steps to combat epidemics, to participate in the organisation of health relief to victims of a calamity and to undertake studies and research the urgency of which has been drawn to the attention of the Board by any Member or by the Director-General.[45]

While the Board typically exists to work in harmony with the Assembly, and the Member States that comprise it, it is clear that it has some degree of independence, particularly when responding to epidemics and calamities such as Ebola. The existence of distinct organs in this fashion begins to give further credence to the existence of personality on the part of the WHO. While the existence of organs in themselves may not be a determining factor, their *distinct* identity as providing much more than a simple discussion forum for Member States can contribute towards the argument of an institution possessing personality. When considering the WHO's organs, they exist as part of the institution and, most particularly, do so during epidemics the

---

[39]*Reparations for injuries suffered in the service of the United Nations, Advisory Opinion ICJ Reports*, 1949, p. 179.

[40] Article 25, Constitution of the World Health Organisation.

[41] Article 27, Constitution of the World Health Organisation.

[42] Article 28(h), Constitution of the World Health Organisation.

[43] Article 28(f), Constitution of the World Health Organisation.

[44] Article 28(g), Constitution of the World Health Organisation.

[45] Article 28(i), Constitution of the World Health Organisation.

management and prevention of which is one of the key functions of the Organisation itself.[46]

When considering further powers of the WHO, its ability to accede to international treaties also gives particular credence to an existence of legal personality. It is particularly telling that the WHO acceded to the Vienna Convention on the Law of Treaties in spite of the existing accession of many of its Member States.[47] The report of the Secretariat of the Executive Board on the Participation by the WHO to the Vienna Convention is interesting in this respect.[48] In this Report, drafted by the Secretariat, the Executive Board of the WHO advises the WHA to authorise the Director-General of the WHO to sign the Convention. This Report clearly discusses the WHO as an actor distinct from its Member States. Indeed, many Member States of the WHA were already signatories to the Convention by this stage, the implication being that the membership of its Member States was insufficient to bind the WHO to the Convention, and accession by the WHO as a distinct legal actor was required. This led to the WHO signing the Convention in 1987 and giving formal confirmation of its intention to be bound, without reservations, in 2000.[49]

All of these points show that the WHO has the capacity to act in a distinct fashion that is beyond the sum of its parts; it is more than simply a collective of its Member States. In existing in this distinct manner and having certain rights, powers and obligations as this distinct actor, it clearly possesses legal personality. The WHO's legal personality gives it both the capacity to act in certain areas within its remit, but also makes it 'subject to international law', giving rise to the need to provide redress for any issues arising from its actions, or omissions, in the areas within its competence. It has the capacity for legal responsibility arising from its powers. In order to consider any possibility of legal responsibility, however, the existence of obligations over and above powers to act must first of all be found.

The identification of obligations on the part of institutions, rather than simply powers to act, has been a difficult one to determine in relation to international organisations. The traditional state-centric international system recognises two main sources of international law: customary principles, and international treaties. How these sources of international law apply to institutions, such as the WHO, has long been questioned. While the ICJ has often stated that obligations exist on the part of institutions,[50] a clear identification of such obligations, or even the source of such obligation, is rare.

We argue that such a legal obligation does exist on the part of the WHO in the requirement to declare an extraordinary event a PHEIC in a timely manner. While this is not stated in explicit terms, we draw upon a number of sources below in more detail to argue this. It must first of all be noted that when examining the IHR and the obligation to declare a PHEIC, that the language used is not that of the discretionary

---

[46] Article 2(g), Constitution of the World Health Organisation.

[47] United Nations, Vienna Convention on the Law of Treaties (1969).

[48] World Health Organisation (1999).

[49] United Nations (2016a).

[50] ICJ Reports 1980, pp. 89–90, para. 37.

'may', but of the obligatory 'shall'. As noted above, a PHEIC can only be declared by the Director-General,[51] on the advice of an Emergency Committee, which is convened by the Director-General.[52] The decision to declare (or not to declare, as the case may be) an event a PHEIC is one that has significant repercussions for affected states. While the International Health Regulations provides the Director-General with the *power* to declare an extraordinary event a PHEIC, we argue that the Director-General actually has a legal obligation to declare an event a PHEIC and to do so in a timely manner. The first element of this obligation to declare may have been eventually fulfilled but (as we will argue in a moment), the failure to declare the 2014 West African Ebola outbreak a PHEIC in a timely fashion was not, and therefore constitutes an internationally wrongful act, for which responsibility ought to arise on the part of the Organisation.

The finalised articles on the Responsibility of International Organisations establish that in order for responsibility to be established, an internationally wrongful act must be identified.[53] There are two key elements that constitute an internationally wrongful act: a breach of an international obligation, and attribution of that breach to the responsible international actor.[54] Could the delay in the declaration of a PHEIC by the Director-General, on behalf of the WHO, be a breach of an international legal obligation that can be attributed to the institution, resulting in legal responsibility? Arguably, it could.

In identifying a breach of international law, the commentaries to the ILC's articles provide some guidance as to what will be sufficient; they consider that any source of international law applicable to the organisation will suffice.[55] The ILC elaborates further with reference to the International Court of Justice (ICJ) advisory opinion on the *Interpretation of the Agreement of 25 March 1951 between the WHO and Egypt*, stating that international organisations are bound by any obligations incumbent upon them under general rules of international law, under their constitutions or under international agreements to which they are parties.[56]

The legal obligation to declare a PHEIC is not explicitly identified as an obligation in and of itself within the relevant core documents of the WHO. Rather, numerous obligations are identified within the Constitution of the World Health Organisation, in particular Articles 2(v), (a) and (g) of the Functions, and an external agreement with the African Congress, which when taken together would create the legal obligation pursuant upon the WHO to declare the West African Ebola outbreak PHEIC and, secondly, to do so in a timely fashion. We explore these obligations below.

---

[51] Article 12, International Health Regulations.
[52] Article 12(4), International Health Regulations.
[53] Articles 3 and 4, Articles of the Responsibility of International Organisations.
[54] Article 4, Articles of the Responsibility of International Organisations.
[55] Commentary to Article 4, para. 2, p. 14.
[56] ICJ Reports 1980, pp. 89–90, para. 37.

4   The Timely Declaration of a PHEIC as a Legal Obligation

The Constitution of the World Health Organisation is the founding document of the Organisation and was adopted by the International Health Conference, a meeting of the Economic and Social Council of the United Nations, in 1946.[57] Despite the fact that it has been amended four times,[58] the Objective and Functions of the World Health Organisation remain largely unchanged from the original text that was approved in 1946. The simple, if somewhat lofty, objective of the World Health Organisation is 'the attainment by all peoples of the highest possible level of health.'[59] The Constitution of the WHO also outlines the manner in which the WHO intends to meet this objective and ensure all peoples attain the highest possible level of health via the 'Functions' provided at Article 2 of the Constitution. Within the Functions of the Constitution there is no explicit obligation to make a timely declaration of a PHEIC: indeed, there is no reference to the notion of a PHEIC in the Constitution at all. However, there are obligations pursuant upon the WHO set out at the Functions of the Constitution that give rise to an obligation to make a timely declaration of a PHEIC.

The first relevant Function that gives rise to an obligation on the WHO to make a timely declaration of a PHEIC is contained within Article 2 of the WHO Constitution, and requires the WHO 'generally to take all necessary action to attain the objective of the Organisation'.[60] Clearly a prompt and effective global response to an epidemic, a response which is instigated by the declaration of a PHEIC by the WHO, is needed to ensure all affected, or at risk, persons can attain the highest possible level of health. While this is a broad Function of the Organisation, and in and of itself it cannot be said to confer upon the WHO specific and particular obligations in respect of declaring a PHEIC in a timely manner, when taken in combination with the two further Functions outlined below, a compelling case can be made that there *is* an obligation binding upon the WHO to declare a PHEIC, and to do so in a timely manner. The first additional relevant function outlined at 2(a) of the Constitution outlines that the WHO is 'to act as the directing and coordinating' authority on international health work'.[61] The WHO's role as directing and coordinating authority during a major outbreak such as Ebola is typically triggered by a declaration of a PHEIC by the WHO. Article 13 of the IHR states that a PHEIC Declaration being made triggers the following response from WHO:

---

[57] For an interesting historical perspective on the development of the Constitution see: Grad (2002).

[58] World Health Assembly, Resolution WHA26.37 'Amendments to articles 34 and 55 of the Constitution' (1973), World Health Assembly, WHA29.38 'Amendments to articles 24 and 25 of the Constitution' (1976); World Health Assembly, WHA39.6 'Amendments to articles 24 and 25 of the Constitution' (1986); World Health Assembly, WHA51.23 'Amendments to articles 24 and 25 of the Constitution' (1998).

[59] Article 1, International Health Regulations.

[60] Article 2(v), International Health Regulations.

[61] Article 2(a), International Health Regulations.

At the request of a State Party, WHO shall collaborate in the response to public health risks and other events by providing technical guidance and assistance and by assessing the effectiveness of the control measures in place, including the mobilisation[sic] of international teams of experts for on-site assistance, when necessary.[62]

Further, if the WHO considers that a PHEIC is occurring it can assess the severity of the event, the adequacy of support, and offer additional assistance: Such collaboration may include the offer to mobilise[sic] international assistance in order to support the national authorities in conducting and coordinating on-site assessments.[63]

This process of having the WHO coordinate and direct the response to an outbreak is crucial in ensuring an effective response from the affected states and the wider international community. A PHEIC declaration triggers the mechanisms of the WHO into action, and also directs international attention and resources to the outbreak. A consequence of this is that any PHEIC declaration must be done in a timely fashion. A PHEIC works to direct and coordinate action in response to an outbreak, and so a failure to act in a timely fashion will affect the ability to respond to a crisis. This can be seen with comments by the Report of the Ebola Interim Assessment Panel that during the Ebola outbreak the 'WHO not only coordinates the health cluster, but is also responsible for the coordination of specific technical activities such as surveillance. In the Ebola crisis, WHO should have had a key role to play in coordination, but it took a long time to get this started.'[64]

The second relevant function of the WHO that could give rise to there being an obligation to declare a PHEIC in a timely fashion is 'to stimulate and advance work to eradicate epidemic, endemic and other diseases'.[65] Clearly this cannot be adequately achieved without the timely declaration of a PHEIC by the Director-General. As noted above, a PHEIC declaration not only triggers the mechanisms of the WHO, but also directs international attention and resources to the outbreak—resources that are key to controlling or eradicating disease.

These Functions, which are binding upon the WHO through its Constitution, give rise to international obligations, which in turn are binding upon the WHO itself. When these obligations are taken together, the natural consequence is an obligation to declare a PHEIC when the appropriate circumstances arise, and to make said declaration in a timely fashion. The WHO is the coordinating authority on global health and, from its Constitution, possesses obligations to work towards the eradication of disease and to pursue the highest possible level of health. These obligations cannot be satisfied without the timely declaration of a PHEIC.

Hence, it would appear that the internal obligations stemming from the Constitution of the WHO are sufficient to create a legal obligation pursuant upon the WHO to declare a PHEIC in a timely fashion when it appears right to do so. Moreover, this legal obligation stemming from the Constitution is not limited to the 2014 West African Ebola outbreak, but any other extraordinary event that meets the criteria to be

---

[62] Article 13(3), International Health Regulations.

[63] Article 13(4), International Health Regulations.

[64] World Health Organisation, (n 9).

[65] Article 2(g), International Health Regulations.

declared a public health emergency of international concern. This obligation may be bolstered by external agreements to which the WHO is a party as part of its external relations.

In the case of the 2014 West African Ebola outbreak, in addition to the internal obligation stemming from the Constitution, there was an external obligation on the WHO to make a timely declaration of a PHEIC. This is derivable from the membership of the African Union of Sierra Leone, Guinea, and Liberia, the states that were most seriously impacted by the outbreak, with which the WHO signed an agreement in 2012. The WHO's agreement with the Commission of the African Union includes an obligation "to contain [...] crises and outbreaks of disease, and impart [...] knowledge and skills".[66] The declaration of a PHEIC is envisaged to address "a public health risk to other States through the international spread of disease" and, consequently, an obligation to contain crises and outbreaks of disease ought naturally to give rise to an obligation to utilise any legal tools that may assist with this. A PHEIC declaration is clearly a central tool through which this obligation is fulfilled. Not only is there a general obligation to declare a PHEIC when appropriate in a timely fashion, but the WHO-AU Agreement created an obligation upon the WHO to do as much as possible to contain disease outbreaks in African Union Member States which would clearly include declaring a PHEIC where appropriate. This is an obligation that was clearly not fulfilled in respect of the 2014 West African Ebola outbreak.

The central aspect of a PHEIC is the actions that may arise from it. A PHEIC declaration not only triggers the mechanisms of the WHO outlined above, but also directs international attention and resources to the outbreak—resources that are key to the control or eradication of disease. In the case of the 2014 Ebola epidemic, the PHEIC declaration did not occur until August 8th, over six weeks after Médecins Sans Frontières had warned that Ebola was 'out of control', and had called for a 'massive deployment of resources'.[67] Senior staff at the WHO had also raised the prospect of declaring a PHEIC, but it was resisted.[68] As Gostin and Friedman noted, international donations, technical assistance and military assistance finally began to flow to the region only after the PHEIC was declared.[69] This was despite the fact that the WHO had briefed the international community on the seriousness of the outbreak from 8th April, with increasing emphasis being placed on the severity of the outbreak up to the point a PHEIC was declared.[70] It is clear that a PHEIC declaration was appropriate in this instance. As such, the appropriate and timely declaration of a PHEIC is central in ensuring the obligations for preventing crises and spread of disease mentioned both generally within the WHO Constitution, and specifically in

---

[66] World Health Assembly, "Agreements with intergovernmental organisations: agreement between the Commissions of the African Union and the World Health Organisation" (2012) A65/42.

[67] Médecins Sans Frontières (2015).

[68] Cheng and Satter (2015).

[69] Lawrence Gostin & Eric Friedman, (n 5).

[70] World Health Organisation (2015c) at 'Chapter 7—Key events in the WHO response to the Ebola outbreak'.

the particular agreement between the WHO and the AU. The failure to declare a PHEIC in a timely fashion is capable, therefore, of giving rise to responsibility and the specific legal principles on this will now be considered.

5 Determining Responsibility for the Delay Responding to Ebola

While the WHO did declare a PHEIC in relation to the West African Ebola outbreak, thereby satisfying the first stage of their legal obligation, that declaration was not timely, and therefore did not satisfy the second stage of the obligation. Timely in this context should be flexible in its application to individual circumstances—a set period of time cannot be attached to it, but rather reasonableness with regard to all the circumstances should be the guiding principle. The period between the criteria for declaring a PHEIC having been met and a declaration being made ought to be as short as possible and with no unjustifiable delay. Ultimately, questions of timeliness will be resolved by determining if the Director-General could have acted more quickly in declaring a PHEIC once the criteria for doing so had been satisfied. In relation to Ebola the declaration of a PHEIC was not timely, inasmuch as that there were no justifiable reasons for this delay.

The WHO was originally notified of the outbreak on 23rd March 2014 but, as we have seen, it was not until 8th August that a PHEIC was declared. By the time a PHEIC was declared there were 1779 confirmed and suspected cases of Ebola, nearly a thousand of which were confirmed or suspected to have resulted in death.[71] The Ebola Interim Assessment Panel, set up by the WHO itself, stated that there were "significant and unjustifiable delays" in the declaration of a PHEIC by the WHO.[72] Furthermore, when examining the communications about the Ebola situation, it is clear that in the time between the WHO being made aware of the Ebola crisis and its decision to declare a PHEIC, numerous individuals and bodies with expertise in this area were arguing that the situation was a severe one that required further action and attention from the WHO. Internal WHO communications show clear concerns about the severity of the outbreak and the lack of action on the part of the WHO, including the virus spread being worse than the data implied and continued pleas for assistance from staff on the ground not being answered, as well as refusals to consider convening an Emergency Committee, which would begin the process of declaring a PHEIC.[73] These communications show that there was a two-month delay from the WHO having become aware of the severity of the outbreak in West Africa to

---

[71] WHO (2016).

[72] World Health Organisation, (n 9).

[73] Associated Press, "Emails Show WHO Resisted Declaring Ebola an Emergency," *NBC News* (NBC News), March 20, 2015, Accessed May 15, 2017. http://www.nbcnews.com/storyline/ebola-virus-outbreak/emails-un-health-agency-resisted-declaring-ebola-emergency-n326956.

an Emergency Committee being convened.[74] Taking two months to begin to move towards the process of declaring a PHEIC is not plausibly timely, especially when taken together with the knowledge of how severe the outbreak was becoming.

In order for responsibility to be established, any breach of international law must be attributed to the international actor concerned. It is the requirement of attribution that is often problematic when considering international organisations. The transparent nature of institutions means that it is often difficult to determine with certainty the action as being that of the institution. Action is often carried out by Member States on behalf of the institution and determining that an action is that of the institution as opposed to the state is complex. The declaration of a PHEIC is, arguably, an exception to this difficulty.

The basic rule of attribution in the ARIO is that all actions of an organ or agent of the institution are attributed to that institution.[75] A substantial critique of the ARIO has been that this is limited in its application as institutions often depend upon their member states to carry out their actions and obligations. When considering the actions of the WHO in these circumstances, however, it is clear that it is the 'pure' institutional organs and agents that are being considered. The decision to declare a PHEIC is one that lies with the Director-General of the WHO. As the Director-General is clearly an agent of the WHO and not acting on behalf of a Member State of the organisation, any failure to declare a PHEIC in a timely fashion will be attributed to the WHO through agency. With the elements of breach and attribution being satisfied in respect of the failure to declare the 2014 West African Ebola outbreak a PHEIC in a timely fashion, there exists an internationally wrongful act, attributable to the WHO through an agent of the organisation, for which responsibility on the international stage can be established.

6 The Practical Limitations of Responsibility

In spite of the clear ability to determine responsibility in this regard, it should be noted that enforcing this is far from straightforward. There are numerous practical limitations to finding and giving effect to any determination of responsibility in relation to an international organisation like the WHO. Not only is there a question about a lack of judicial fora before which cases on breach of international law by international organisations could be brought, but there is also the question of practical consequences arising from actions before such courts, if one with appropriate jurisdiction could be identified. A determination of responsibility gives rise to an obligation to make reparation.[76] The extent to which this is possible in the present case, both in terms of enforcement, and of where any money would be drawn from in order to make such reparation, is highly questionable.

---

[74]ibid.

[75]Article 6 Articles of the Responsibility of International Organisations.

[76]Article 31, ARIO.

Regarding enforcement, there does not exist an identifiable court before which the WHO could be taken by a state, or indeed an individual or institution affected by the WHO's omissions in the present case, to enforce the determination of responsibility. This is one of the fundamental weaknesses of responsibility in relation to international organisations; there are few, if any, possibilities in terms of judicial fora. When considering the case law that has discussed the principles contained in the ARIO, it is notable that all of them return to the responsibility of a state, after engaging with the ARIO principles in respect of the relevant institutions in order to 'discount' the institution concerned, return to the responsibility of the states concerned.[77] It is difficult to conceive of a case where the responsibility of an institution could be explicitly determined and later enforced. This is all before considering the difficult question of immunity, which is a principle that has continued to block numerous cases considering the responsibility of the United Nations.[78]

While there are questions about the existence and nature of institutions' immunity, including discussions about whether they are absolute or limited, most consider the UN to possess an absolute immunity from prosecution in line with Article 105(1) of the UN Charter, together with section two of the Convention on Privileges and Immunities of the United Nations (1946), which states:

> The United Nations, its property and assets wherever located and by whomsoever held, shall enjoy immunity from every form of legal process except insofar as in any particular case it has expressly waived its immunity.[79]

While it was established early on that such prosecution was in relation to national law and did not preclude international responsibility,[80] the lack of an international judicial system has necessarily meant that these questions arise in national courts. With the questions arising in relation to national law, immunity arises time and again. Furthermore, the WHO constitution states that

> [t]he Organisation shall enjoy in the territory of each Member such privileges and immunities as may be necessary for the fulfillment of its objective and for the exercise of its functions.[81]

---

[77] Behrami and Behrami v France and Saramati v France, Germany and Norway App no 71412/01 and 78166/01 (ECtHR 2 May 2007); R (on the application of Al-Jedda) v Secretary of State for Defence, [2008] 1 AC 332; Case of Al Jedda v the United Kingdom App no. 27021/08 (ECtHR, 7 July 2011); Netherlands (Ministry of Defence and Ministry of Foreign Affairs) v Nuhanović, Final appeal judgment, ECLI/NL/HR/2013/BZ9225, ILDC 2061 (NL 2013), 12/03324, Supreme Court (6 Sept 2013); Claimant 1 et al. and the Mothers of Srebrenica v the State of the Netherlands and the United Nations Case Number C/09/295247/ HA ZA 07-2973, Judgment of The Hague District Court (16 July 2014).

[78] See, for example, Netherlands (Ministry of Defence and Ministry of Foreign Affairs) v Nuhanović, Final appeal judgment, ECLI/NL/HR/2013/BZ9225, ILDC 2061 (NL 2013), 12/03324, Supreme Court (6 Sept 2013); Claimant 1 et al. and the Mothers of Srebrenica v the State of the Netherlands and the United Nations Case Number C/09/295247/ HA ZA 07-2973, Judgment of The Hague District Court (16 July 2014).

[79] Article 2, United Nations, 'Convention on Privileges and Immunities of the United Nations' (1946).

[80] Difference Relating to Immunity from Legal Process of a Special Rapporteur of the Commission on Human Rights, Advisory Opinion [1999] ICJ Reports p. 62 at p. 88.

[81] Article 67(a), Constitution of the World Health Organisation.

The UN General Assembly concluded the Convention on the Privileges and Immunities of the Specialised Agencies that explicitly included the WHO within its remit.[82] Although the International Court of Justice is seemingly given some remit for action by the Constitution of the WHO, and also specifically within the Convention on Privileges and Immunities, this is substantially limited when read together with provisions of the Statute of the ICJ. Only states are able to be parties to adversarial proceedings before that Court.[83] Any proceedings involving international organisations can only be heard by the Court in the remit of an advisory opinion, in respect of interpreting international law, not enforcing it. Overall, it appears that the ability to establish responsibility judicially is highly limited; the remit of the ICJ is restricted and all attempts to bring cases in national courts have resulted in immunity preventing any action proceeding against the international organisation. While there have been some limited examples of litigants looking beyond immunity where not to do so would lead to a 'denial of justice',[84] this appears to be a highly limited approach largely addressing private law cases; cases beyond this in the sphere of public law have seen continual deference to immunity, in particular in relation to the United Nations.[85] In the present case, the WHO is privilege to the same immunity and protection from legal action as the UN.

The funding of reparation is a more complex issue that returns, again, to the difficult nature of the identity of an international organisation. Institutions are dependent for their budget upon their member states, and a call for reparation raises a number of difficulties. It must be considered whether the institution would pay for such reparations out of its general budget, or whether it would be feasible for it to call upon member states to contribute to a special fund in order to fulfill its reparation obligations. The difficulties surrounding this can be seen with the issues arising from the outbreak of cholera in Haiti, and the attempt by the UN to set up a compensation fund in response to the outbreak[86]: there continues to be uncertainty surrounding how this fund will be paid for. The UN has sought to address two main parts within this fund, one aspect being compensation for the victims and another being about eradication and prevention. There is a target for $200 million for each of these parts.[87] However, it was initially unclear whether this should be funded from the general budget or from member state contributions. The approach eventually taken by the UN was to rely upon voluntary donations from member states. The consequence of this was that the

---

[82] Adopted by the First World Health Assembly on 17 July 1948 (*Off. Rec. Wld Hlth Org.*, **13**, 97, 332), Section 1(ii)(g).

[83] Article 34, United Nations, Statute of the International Court of Justice (1946).

[84] Application no. 26083/94, judgment of February 18, 1999 and Application no. 28934/95, Judgment of February 18, 1999.

[85] See, for example, *Claimant 1* et al. *and the Mothers of Srebrenica v the State of the Netherlands and the United Nations* Case Number C/09/295247/HA ZA 07-2973, Judgement of The Hague District Court (16 July 2014).

[86] United Nations (2016b).

[87] Gladstone (2017).

fund never reached anywhere near $400 million, and is currently at risk of running out completely.[88]

While it is important to ensure that the WHO follows its international obligations, it is questionable whether the imposition of legal responsibility, without immunity, would be effective in encouraging the WHO to engage in its role at the global level. If there arises a concern that its actions may result in determinations of responsibility, this may result in a more cautious approach by the WHO out of fear of liability being imposed through the law of responsibility. This may end up amounting to a disincentive on the part of the institution to act and develop. Even where an institution has developed a significant amount of autonomy, it remains dependent upon its Member States for expansion and development. If the consequence of developing an institution has been that Member States have been subjected to greater requirements for payment and effective obligations for reparations then this will only discourage the development here. There are huge potential benefits in the development of institutional frameworks and the ability that they have to address global issues, such as that of global health and, in this circumstance, epidemic and pandemic emergencies. It has to be asked whether a framework that may prove a disincentive on the part of states to act and enable global action is really the best approach here. Not only did the practical limitations to imposing liability on the WHO for the mismanagement of the PHEIC declaration during the West African Ebola outbreak serve to shut down any discussion of legal restitution from the WHO, but an opportunity to acknowledge the situation and make a step towards remedying it was lost.

7   Conclusion

The WHO has developed significantly since its inception in 1948. Its role and powers are far beyond what was originally envisaged. As the Organisation has evolved it has become increasingly distinct from its Member States, meaning that it now possesses a substantial degree of autonomy to act in an independent manner. Furthermore, the WHO has developed to face a number of obligations, as well as powers. However, this development has not been accompanied with any development of the WHO's internal accountability mechanisms,[89] nor any meaningful engagement with external accountability and responsibility mechanisms. Since the 2005 revisions to the International Health Regulations, the manner in which the WHO has responded to a number of PHEICs, and potential PHEICs, has been subject to considerable criticism from member states and the academic literature.[90] It is our contention that on at least one occasion the WHO, in responding to an extraordinary event that likely constitutes a PHEIC, has breached its legal obligations to declare such an event a PHEIC in a

---

[88] See: United Nations (2017).
[89] Eccleston-Turner and McArdle (2017).
[90] see (n 8).

timely manner. This has been demonstrated most clearly with the WHO's delayed response to the Ebola outbreak in West Africa during the 2014 outbreak.

The argument we have presented in respect of the timely declaration of a PHEIC being a legal obligation of the WHO is not limited to Ebola. It applies equally to any other extraordinary event where the criteria for declaring a PHEIC have been met. This area becomes further complicated when we consider not only the timely declaration of a PHEIC as being an international legal obligation for which responsibility can be attributed to the WHO, but also the appropriate, timely downgrading of a PHEIC's status once the extraordinary event no longer meets the criteria to be considered a PHEIC. This again, is a decision that is delegated to the Director-General via the IHR, and one that has been subject to criticism for its usage.[91] It is arguable that not only is the timely declaration of a PHEIC a legal obligation binding upon the WHO, but also that the timely and appropriate downgrading of a PHEIC amounts to a legal obligation binding upon the WHO (though the full development of that point is beyond the scope of this chapter).

In spite of the ability to make a legal determination of responsibility, this is highly unlikely to result in any sort of legal consequences. There is a substantial number of practical barriers that stand in the way of determining legal responsibility of an international organisation, from lack of judicial fora, to the principle of immunity and the difficult question of how to fund claims for reparation. A legal determination of responsibility in a judicial setting remains highly unlikely. Therefore, a productive move forward would be a clear and unequivocal acknowledgement of wrongdoing on the part of WHO when mistakes are made and the further development of accountability mechanisms. While this is highly limited, and the examples that do exist of institutions acknowledging wrongdoing have a number of substantial flaws,[92] the possibility exists for institutions such as the WHO to develop internal mechanisms that work and allow some redress. Overall this will only improve the WHO's position in the global community and its work with its member states to develop better responses to disease outbreaks.

References

Ago R (1963) Chairman of the Sub Committee on State Responsibility, 16 January 1963, Document A/CN.4/152, in Yearbook of the International Law Commission 1963, vol 2, p 227 UN Doc/A/CN.4/SER.A/1963/Add. 1

Andrus JK et al (2010) Global health security and the International Health Regulations. BMC Public Health 10(1):S2

Briand S et al (2014) The international Ebola emergency. New Engl J Med 371:1180

Brölmann C (2007) The institutional veil in public international law: international organisations and the law of treaties. Hart, Oxford

---

[91] Most notably the 2014 Yellow Fever PHEIC in which the WHO faced considerable criticism for its early downgrading of Yellow Fever from a PHEIC.

[92] See above discussion on the UN, Cholera and Haiti at p[...].

Cheng M, Satter R (2015) Emails: UN Health Agency resisted declaring ebola emergency. Associated Press. http://bigstory.ap.org/article/ea7199795faa48989449131404b7043e/emails-un-health-agency-resisted-declaring-ebola-emergency. Accessed 21 Oct 2015

Eccleston-Turner M, McArdle S (2017) Accountability, international law, and the World Health Organisation: a need for reform? Global Health Gov XI(1):27–40

El Erian A (1963) Special Rapporteur, relations between states and inter governmental organisations, Document A/CN.4/161 and Add. 1, contained in ILC yearbook, vol II, A/CN.4/SER.A/1963/ADD.1, p 159

Gladstone (2017) After bringing cholera to Haiti, U.N. can't raise money to fight it. New York Times, New York, 19 Mar 2017. Available at: https://www.nytimes.com/2017/03/19/world/americas/cholera-haiti-united-nations.html

Gostin L (2015) The future of the World Health Organisation: lessons learned from Ebola. Milbank Q 93:475

Gostin L, Friedman E (2014) Ebola: a crisis in global health leadership. Lancet 384:1323

Gostin L, Lucey D (2015) Middle east respiratory syndrome: a global health challenge. JAMA 314(8):771–772

Grad F (2002) The preamble of the constitution of the World Health Organisation. Bull World Health Org 981

Grotius H (2005) The rights of war and peace. In: Tuck R, Barbeyrac J (eds) 1625. Liberty Fund, Indianapolis

Hafner G (2003) Accountability of international organisations. In: Proceedings of the annual meeting (American Society of International Law), vol 97, pp 236–240

Kekulé AS (2015) Learning from Ebola virus: how to prevent future epidemics. Viruses 7:3789

Kent VL (2005) Peacekeepers as perpetrators of abuse. examining the UN's plans to eliminate and address cases of sexual exploitation and abuse in peacekeeping operations. Afr Secur Rev 14

Klabbers J (1998) Presumptive personality: the European UNION in international law. In: Koskenniemi M (ed) International legal aspects of the European Union. The Hague, Kluwer

Klabbers J (2011) Autonomy, constitutionalism and virtue in international institutional law. In: Collins R, White N (eds) International Organisations and the Idea of Autonomy: Institutional Independence in the International Legal Order. Routledge, p 120

Klabbers J, Wallendahl Å (eds) (2011) Research handbook on the law of international organisations. Edward Elgar, Cheltenham, p 36

Lucey D, Gostin L (2016) The emerging Zika pandemic: enhancing preparedness. JAMA 315(9):865–866

Médecins Sans Frontières (2015) Ebola in West Africa: epidemic requires massive deployment of resources. http://www.msf.org/article/ebola-west-africa-epidemic-requires-massive-deployment-resources. Accessed 21 Oct 2015

Pellet A (2010) The definition of responsibility in international law. In: Crawford J, Pellet A, Olleson S (eds) The law of international responsibility. Oxford University Press, Oxford

Reinalda B, Verbeek B (2011) Policy autonomy of intergovernmental organisations: a challenge to international relations theory? In: Collins R, White N (eds) International Organisations and the Idea of Autonomy: Institutional Independence in the International Legal Order. Routledge

Sari A (2011) Autonomy, Attribution and Accountability. Reflections on the *Behrami* case. In: Collins R, White N (eds) International Organisations and the Idea of Autonomy: Institutional Independence in the International Legal Order. Routledge, p 257

Seyersted F (1964) International personality of international organisations: do their capacities really depend upon their constitutions? Indian J Int Law 4(1)

Siedner MJ et al (2015) Strengthening the detection of and early response to public health emergencies: lessons from the West African Ebola epidemic. PLOS Med 12:e1001804

The WHO Ebola Response Team (2014) Ebola virus disease in West Africa—The first 9 months of the epidemic and forward projections. New Engl J Med 371:1481

United Nations (2016a) United Nations treaty collections: Vienna convention on the law of treaties between states and international organisations or between international organisations. https://treaties.un.org/Pages/ViewDetails.aspx?src=TREATY&mtdsg_no=XXIII-3&chapter=23&lang=en. Accessed 21 Mar 2017

United Nations (2016b) United Nations United Nations Haiti Cholera response multi-partner trust fund launched. New York. 14 Oct 2016. Available at: http://mptf.undp.org/factsheet/fund/CLH00

United Nations (2017) UN Haiti Cholera Response Multi-Partner Trust Fund. United Nations, Geneva. Available at: http://mptf.undp.org/factsheet/fund/CLH00

White N (2005) The law of international organisations, 2nd edn. Manchester University Press, Manchester

WHO (2016) Ebola data and statistics: situation summary, World Health Organisation. http://apps.who.int/gho/data/view.ebola-sitrep.ebola-summary-20150807?lang=en.World. Accessed 7 Aug 2015–24 Oct 2016

World Health Organisation (1999) World Health Organisation Executive Board EB105/30 105th session participation by WHO in the 1986 Vienna convention on the law of treaties between states and international organisations or between international organisations. http://apps.who.int/gb/archive/pdf_files/EB105/ee30.pdf. Accessed 21 Mar 2016

World Health Organisation (2015) WHO statement on the meeting of the International Health Regulations Emergency committee regarding the 2014 Ebola outbreak in West Africa. http://www.who.int/mediacentre/news/statements/2014/ebola-20140808/en/. Accessed 7 Oct 2015

World Health Organisation (2015) Report of the Ebola Interim assessment panel. http://www.who.int/csr/resources/publications/ebola/report-by-panel.pdf. Accessed 14 Oct 2015

World Health Organisation (2015) Key events in the WHO response to the Ebola outbreak. http://www.who.int/csr/disease/ebola/one-year-report/who-response/en/. Accessed 22 Oct 2015

Rules and Tools in the Battle Against Superbugs—A Call for Integrated Strategies and Enhanced International Collaboration to Promote Antimicrobial Drug Development

Timo Minssen and Ana Nordberg

Abstract The lack of treatments during the recent Ebola and Zika outbreaks dramatically exposed the vulnerability of the global health system and the dire consequences of that vulnerability. But even where therapies against infectious diseases had been available, an additional threat has gained world-wide attention: antimicrobial resistance (AMR). A growing number of microbial organisms are becoming resistant to available drugs with increasingly diverse risks for a rapid global spreading of infections. Unfortunately, the traditional intellectual property (IP)-based innovation system and regulatory frameworks do not provide sufficient incentives to invest in the development of new antimicrobials. Hence, there are few new treatments in the pipeline to replace a growing number of ineffective drugs or problematic drug combinations. Repairing these broken economic incentives, improving access to and sustaining the effectiveness of antimicrobials is among the most important challenges in the health and life sciences. In this paper we emphasise that this goal can only be achieved through integrated strategies and a better global coordination of interdisciplinary multi-sector responses.

Keywords Sustainable incentives · Regulation · IPRs · Antimicrobials · Antibiotics · Resistance

---

This chapter could only consider developments until March 2018.

T. Minssen (✉)
Faculty of Law, Centre for Advanced Studies in Biomedical Innovation Law (CeBIL), University of Copenhagen, Copenhagen, Denmark
e-mail: timo.minssen@jur.ku.dk

A. Nordberg
Law Faculty, Lund University, Lund, Sweden

© Springer Nature Switzerland AG 2020
M. Eccleston-Turner and I. Brassington (eds.), *Infectious Diseases in the New Millennium*, International Library of Ethics, Law, and the New Medicine 82, https://doi.org/10.1007/978-3-030-39819-4_6

1   Introduction: Antimicrobial Resistance a Global Public Health Concern

The absence of therapeutic options to cure viral diseases such as SARS, Ebola and Zika amidst the recent and deadliest outbreaks in the diseases' history has dramatically highlighted a significant global public health emergency: developing life-saving cures for those who need them the most. In a rapid response, both the European Medicines Agency (EMA) and the U.S. Food and Drug Administration (FDA) have implemented a variety of measures, speeding up the approval procedure, facilitating clinical trials and rewarding specific orphan drug status.[1] In addition, both the EU and the US orphan drug legislation provides powerful market exclusivities for the development of treatments against *rare* and *neglected diseases*.[2] However, despite these incentives, drug manufacturers often do not have strong enough economic incentives to devote resources to making drugs against a wide variety of such diseases. According to World Health Organisation (WHO) estimates, conditions classified as neglected tropical diseases affect more than 1.4 billion people in low-income countries.[3] The high cost of developing drugs, combined with an inability of the patient population to afford them, has resulted in a tremendous public health challenge. In the EU, a disease is considered rare if life-threatening or chronically debilitating and when it affects fewer than 5 in 10,000 persons in the European population.[4] There are between 5000 and 8000 rare diseases[5]; most have a genetic basis, but others are caused by microbes: viruses (for example, SARS, Ebola and Zika), bacteria, or fungi.

A growing number of microbial organisms are becoming resistant to available drugs. If new treatments are not developed, humanity's ability to fight bacterial, fungal and viral infections successfully may decline significantly. This has prompted the WHO to classify AMR as a serious actual threat that has the potential to affect

---

[1] See e.g. the summary of different EMA initiatives and actions on "Public Health Threats", available at: http://www.ema.europa.eu/ema/index.jsp?curl=pages/news_and_events/general/general_content_000788.jsp&mid=WC0b01ac05809db683 (accessed 10 August 2017). Cf. the FDA Medical Countermeasures Initiative with a summary of special initiatives and actions, available at: https://www.fda.gov/EmergencyPreparedness/Counterterrorism/MedicalCountermeasures/AboutMCMi/ucm262925.htm (accessed 10 August 2017).

[2] See e.g. the EMA's overview on "Marketing authorisation and market exclusivity", available at: http://www.ema.europa.eu/ema/index.jsp?curl=pages/regulation/general/general_content_000392.jsp&; as for the U.S. cf. FDA, Economic Assistance and Incentives for Drug Development, available at: https://www.fda.gov/drugs/developmentapprovalprocess/smallbusinessassistance/ucm069929.htm (both accessed 10 August 2017).

[3] Ibid.

[4] Article 3(1) (a), Regulation (EC) No 141/2000 of the European Parliament and of the Council of 16 December 1999 on orphan medicinal products (Orphan Drugs Regulation).

[5] EURORDIS. What is a rare disease?, available at http://www.eurordis.org/about-rare-diseases (accessed 29 June 2017); However, the European portal Orphanet lists 21,503 entries. Source: http://www.orpha.net/consor/cgi-bin/Disease_Search_List.php?lng=EN&TAG=S (accessed 29 June 2017).

anyone, of any age, in any country.[6] The need to shape an international agenda to tackle these issues has also been recognised at a recent United Nations high-level meeting on AMR.[7]

Increased mobility of persons and populations, natural disasters, climate change, mass migrations, expansion of international commercial trade in foodstuffs and medicinal biological products, rapid urbanisation, and deforestation are a common global reality. Adding to this development, the ability of microorganisms to adapt rapidly has enabled the return of communicable diseases nearly eradicated in affluent regions, and the emergence of new ones; this is the reality of AMR. AMR means that the available overall therapeutic options for a wide range of parasitic, bacterial and viral infections have become less effective. Consequently, communicable diseases, including rare and neglected diseases, are not a problem exclusive to the developing world. They present a global public health emergency.[8]

Whereas each category of the different microbial diseases poses both common and distinct problems, the decreasing effectiveness of antibiotics is emblematic for the resistance challenge: antibiotics are the central pillar of contemporary medicine. Antibiotics are used to kill bacteria that cause serious infectious disease, but also enable a wide array of vital medical procedures. Without antibiotics, the risk of infection from surgery or implanted medical devises would render them untenable options. Unfortunately, when an antibiotic is used frequently, bacterial populations can acquire resistance to it, generating what is known as "superbugs", or bacteria that are resistant to many different antibiotics. The most infamous superbug is methicillin-resistant *Staphylococcus aureus* (MRSA), which is increasingly present in hospitals. This creates a paradox of hospital infections: patients seeking medical care risk contracting an antibiotic-resistant bacterial infection that may prove fatal. Even more frightening, in late spring 2016, U.S. authorities announced the discovery of bacteria resistant to colistin, the crucial antibiotic of last resort.[9]

Hence the world is in dire need of new antibiotics and of an innovation system that incentives and supports the process of developing such drugs. In the following we will argue that to be most effective, the development process should engage a broad variety of stakeholders, including public entities and private companies. However, while considerable investments have been made to enhance the development of new antibiotics through the establishment public-private partnerships,[10] the traditional IP-based innovation system does not provide sufficient incentives and regulatory support for pharmaceutical companies to invest in new antibiotic drugs, and there are few

---

[6]*WHO Fact Sheet on AMR*, available at: http://www.who.int/mediacentre/factsheets/fs194/en/ (accessed 10 July 2017).

[7]WHO update, United Nations high-level meeting on AMR, available at: http://www.who.int/ antimicrobial-resistance/events/UNGA-meeting-amr-sept2016/en/ (accessed 20 August 2017).

[8]*WHO Fact Sheet on Global infectious disease surveillance*, available at: http://www.who.int/ mediacentre/factsheets/fs200/en/ (accessed 10 July 2017).

[9]Sun and Dennis (2016).

[10]For a good overview on current public funding see e.g. Eichberg (2015). Regarding public-private partnerships in the U.S. and the EU see e.g.: Goldman et al. (2013).

new antibiotics in the development pipeline to replace the increasingly ineffective drugs. An important task is to fix these broken economic incentives.

Taking the broader challenge posed by AMR as a starting point, this chapter will focus on incentives for the developments of antibiotics and intellectual property issues. But it will also touch upon related regulatory challenges. We describe and discuss the legal implications of a number of "push" and "pull" mechanisms—or combinations of these—to tackle the challenges of providing sufficient incentives for the developments of antibiotic treatments. Section 2 of this paper will begin with a brief description of the biology and causes of AMR in order to explain why the current public policies and regulatory frameworks lead to market failures with insufficient incentives for the development of antibiotics. Section 3 will explain in more detail why the patent system alone is not capable to address these problems in this crucial area. Section 4 will then describe how a wide variety of interventions have been initiated or proposed to enhance the development of new antimicrobials and antibiotics. These include additional push and pull incentives or innovative combinations thereof. The suitability of these proposals and initiatives, as well as future perspectives will be discussed in Sect. 5, which will allow us to draw some conclusions in Sect. 6.

2   The Causes and Implications of AMR

Infectious microbial organisms are becoming progressively resistant to the available drugs. AMR increases with antimicrobials' use, due to the natural evolutionary process of adaptation. Antimicrobials include antibiotics, antivirals, antifungals and antiprotozoals. These consist of active substances of synthetic or natural origin that kill or inhibit the growth of microorganisms. They are used in everyday medicine and are vital to preventing and treating infections in humans and animals.[11] AMR occurs when microorganisms change after being exposed to antimicrobial drugs.[12] Bacteria and other microorganisms adapt to resist an antimicrobial, so that different medicines will be necessary to treat the infection.[13] AMR becomes a problem when microorganisms become resistant to many or all of the existing a drugs, until few or none can effectively treat the infections. Microorganisms that succeed in acquiring AMR are popularly known as "superbugs".

In the case of bacteria resistance occurs naturally over time. But several factors are known contributors to accelerating the process: deficient clinical use of antibiotics (underuse and overuse), use of antibiotics in animal breeding for food production,

---

[11] European Commission (2017).

[12] *WHO Fact Sheet on AMR*, available at: http://www.who.int/mediacentre/factsheets/fs194/en/ (accessed 10 July 2017).

[13] Ibid.

and environmental contamination through release of manufacturing waste.[14] Microbial evolution generates a constant need to research and develop new antibiotics. The problem is that antibiotic resistance is happening faster than new antibiotics are being developed. Since the late 1980s there has been a decrease in antibiotic innovation, with no new classes of antibiotics reaching the market.[15] All antibiotics currently available on the market belong to a class discovered between the early 1900s and 1984.[16] This is a well-known global phenomenon.[17] Development of bacterial resistance is outpacing our global capacity for antibiotic discovery: over the past fifty years, only two new classes of antibiotics reached the market.[18]

AMR, including antibiotic resistance, is not a theoretical probability; it is a very real and immediate threat, now beginning to be recognised as such and starting to garner much-needed global attention, as exemplified by recent UN meetings and proclamations.[19] Such global responses are crucial, since resistance mechanisms are emerging and spreading rapidly globally due to increased mobility of the global population. This directly and indirectly threatens modern medicine's ability to treat common infectious diseases, resulting in prolonged illness, disability, and death. As indicated above, antimicrobials—and in particular antibiotics—are also essential for prevention and treatment of infections in a variety of medical situations; without them medical procedures such as organ transplantation, cancer chemotherapy, diabetes management and routinely performed surgeries (for example, caesarean sections) would become very high-risk procedures.[20]

Thus, AMR already presents a serious social and economic burden. Every year approximately 25,000 deaths in the EU,[21] and 700,000 worldwide,[22] can be attributed to multidrug-resistant infections. In the absence of urgent and coordinated global action, projections point to a global annual death toll of millions: AMR might cause more deaths than cancer by 2050.[23] Without an urgent and coordinated global effort, we run the very real risk of falling into a post-antimicrobial and antibiotic era in which surgeries and treatments that depress the immune system, such as chemotherapy, are too dangerous to perform, and minor injuries can kill again. On top of the

---

[14]Holmes et al. (2016).

[15]Laxminarayan (2014) and Silver (2011a).

[16]Silver (2011b).

[17]Boucher et al. (2009), Mossialos et al. (2009), and WHO (2012).

[18]Dr. Margaret Chan, Director-General of the World Health Organisation, Address to the UN General Assembly on AMR, New York, USA, 21 September 2016. http://www.who.int/dg/speeches/2016/unga-antimicrobial-resistance/en/ (accessed 09 June 2017).

[19]See Ban Ki-moon, Secretary-General's remarks to High-Level Meeting on AMR (as delivered on 21 September 2016), available at: https://www.un.org/sg/en/content/sg/statement/2016-09-21/secretary-generals-remarks-high-level-meeting-antimicrobial (accessed 16 June 2017).

[20]WHO fact sheet on Anitimicrobial resistance, available at http://www.who.int/mediacentre/factsheets/fs194/en/ (accessed 20 August 2018).

[21]EMA Annual Report 2015, available at http://www.ema.europa.eu/docs/en_GB/document_library/Annual_report/2016/05/WC500206482.pdf, at 20 (accessed 18 August 2017).

[22]O'Neill et al. (2016).

[23]Ibid.

human suffering, AMR increases cost of treatment and implies loss of productivity due to illness. In the EU alone that cost is estimated at €1.5 billion annually.[24] The World Bank has warned that, by 2050, drug-resistant infections could cause a global economic crisis comparable to the 2008 financial crisis.[25] During her tenure as WHO Director-General Dr. Margaret Chan compared AMR to a slow motion tsunami for development goals, affecting the health sector in particular.[26] AMR threatens the realisation of several of the United Nations' Sustainable Development Goals, especially goal number 3: good health and well-being.[27] Because AMR is a natural evolutionary process, public policy strategies to fight AMR include conservation policies and guidelines.

The area of antibiotic drug development illustrates these dynamics very well: antibiotics should be used as cautiously as possible. Newer antibiotics should be placed on reserve and only used when older drugs are inefficient. Moreover, the WHO has highlighted the need for regulations on the optimal use of antimicrobial medicines in human and animal health, so that the right antibiotics are being chosen, in the optimal amount and at the right time of the infection.[28] The WHO also emphasised that antibiotics should also be inexpensive in order to be accessible to low income populations.[29]

Companies shy away from the antibiotics market, where the high cost of development and the low rate of return do not leave much room for profit. The antibiotics market is characterised by specific elements that make them financially less attractive to companies.[30] The low profitability of antibiotics is due to limits on sales imposed by national conservation plans, the existence of a strong generic market functioning as substitute products, the fact that health regulations and reimbursement procedures encourage the use of the less expensive drug, and the short duration of treatment. Regulatory frameworks for market approval in major revenue markets, such as the USA and the EU, are perceived by companies as a source of uncertainty due to

---

[24]Technical report by the ECDC/EMEA Joint Working Group, available at https://ecdc.europa.eu/sites/portal/files/media/en/publications/Publications/0909_TER_The_Bacterial_Challenge_Time_to_React.pdf (accessed 10 August 2017).

[25]World Bank (2016).

[26]Dr. Margaret Chan, Director-General of the World Health Organisation interviewed by UN News Centre, https://www.youtube.com/watch?v=_SmkvAeq1R4 (accessed 10 June 2017).

[27]On Sept. 25th 2015, countries adopted a set of goals to end poverty, protect the planet, and ensure prosperity for all as part of a new sustainable development agenda. Each goal has specific targets to be achieved over the next 15 years, see: United Nations Sustainable Development Goals, available at: http://www.un.org/sustainabledevelopment/sustainable-development-goals (accessed 09 June 2017).

[28]See e.g. the WHO News Release: WHO updates Essential Medicines List with new advice on use of antibiotics, and adds medicines for hepatitis C, HIV, tuberculosis and cancer, available at: http://www.who.int/mediacentre/news/releases/2017/essential-medicines-list/en/ (accessed 10 August 2017).

[29]Ibid.

[30]Renwick et al. (2016a).

regulatory gaps[31] and frequent changes in legislation.[32] The success rate for clinical drug development in this area is low: only 1 in 5 infectious disease products that enter phase 1 clinical trials will go on to receive regulatory approval.[33] As of March 2016, only an estimated 37 new antibiotics with the potential to treat serious bacterial infections were undergoing clinical development for the U.S. market.[34]

The combination of high costs, low success rate, and the substantial complexity and severity of the scientific challenges is a factor that weighs heavily in companies' reluctance to invest in crucial areas of AMR-related drug development.[35] For example, an area where new solutions are urgently needed is antibiotics capable of fighting Gram-negative bacteria. There has not been any new antibiotic class approved to treat Gram-negative infections in nearly 50 years. Here scientific barriers are important: the specific characteristics of the outer membrane of Gram-negative bacteria protect them against many of the currently available antibiotics and makes them generally less vulnerable to antibiotics than Gram-positive bacteria.

In summary, proposals for incentives to antibiotic research must simultaneously account for the need to ensure compliance with conservation best practices, and ideally to incentivise conservation strategies. These also need to address the need to incentivise collaborative multidisciplinary research in basic science to overcome scientific barriers and provide academia and industry with a solid foundation for antibiotic innovation.

3 Why the Patent System Alone Won't Do the Job

For many years, the role of the patent system in enhancing (bio)-pharmaceutical innovation has been hailed as a major success story.[36] However, whereas patents remain crucial to the pharmaceutical industry, so-called innovation inefficiencies have been detected (or predicted) in several areas of drug development and biomedical innovation. The existence of a market failure is particularly evident in the area of antimicrobial research and drug development and is reflected in the declining numbers of truly new approved drugs and the absence of novel antibiotic classes. It appears that the general incentives to innovation supplied by intellectual property

---

[31]Rex et al. (2013) at p. 269; see also Echols (2011) and Payne et al. (2007).

[32]Renwick et al. (2016b) at p. 73; see also Projan (2003).

[33]Hay et al. (2014).

[34]The PEW Charitable Foundation (2016).

[35]The Pew Charitable Foundation report, 'A Scientific Roadmap for Antibiotic Discovery: A sustained and robust pipeline of new antibacterial drugs and therapies is critical to preserve public health' 2016, available at http://www.pewtrusts.org/en/research-and-analysis/reports/2016/05/a-scientific-roadmap-for-antibiotic-discovery (accessed 10 June 2017).

[36]Roin (2009).

rights have decreased efficiency in this market, due to a number of factors intrinsic to the characteristics of the market. In the following sections, we will focus on analysing different types of cumulative and alternative incentives.

The patent system is insufficient for certain research and development activities, including the development of products with small commercial market potential, precommercial research and development, research outcomes that due to legal changes can no longer be successfully patented, monopolised and monetised, and particularly risky development projects.[37] The patent system provides 'one size-fits-all' incentives, which in the case of antibiotic innovation provide an example of how patent incentives can be poorly aligned with social benefits of innovation. The story of antibiotic development, antibiotic resistance, and patent incentives is highly complex.

First, patents are not available to all innovation, due to limitations imposed by eligibility and patentability rules, e.g. for new drug combinations that the patent system would regard as obvious. Second, even if patentability is possible, the incentive provided is insufficient, because the available market for antibiotics suffers from restrictions and does not fully reflect their social value. Antibiotics have had historically low prices, and are only prescribed for acute disease episodes, rather than long-term for chronic conditions, reducing the number of sales.[38] Market sales are further reduced both by conservation policies establishing that newer drugs should only be used as last resort to save them from bacterial resistance, and health regulations favouring the prescription of generics over newer patented antibiotics which are typically more expensive.

Additional factors make patents on new antibiotics somewhat less attractive, including the idea that developing resistance over time decreases the ability to manage the drug over its life-cycle.[39] Thus, the social value of new antibiotics represented in having further lines of defence against aggressive bacterial infections, and emergency drugs available when needed, does not sufficiently correspond to the value of the patent-appropriable market.

These tangled dynamics result in additional problems because patents not only provide relatively low incentives to develop new antibiotics, but may also hamper conservation and stewardship efforts to govern and control the use of those that do come to market. Patents' incentive mechanisms are based on enabling the patent owner to appropriate much of the market demand for the patented invention. In turn, such appropriation requires that the patented invention is actually sold (or licensed) and—presumably—used. Either way, patentees do not profit financially merely by developing or patenting a drug; for monetisation to occur the drug has to be manufactured and sold. Pharmaceutical companies have, therefore, a strong

---

[37] WIPO Committee, Study on Alternatives to the Patent System that are Used to Support R&D Efforts, Including both Push and Pull Mechanisms, Special Focus on Innovation-Inducement Prizes and Open Source Development Models, Fourteenth Session Geneva, November 2014, available at: http://www.wipo.int/edocs/mdocs/mdocs/en/cdip_14/cdip_14_inf_12.pdf (accessed 10 June 2017).

[38] Kesselheim and Outterson (2011).

[39] Power (2006); cf. Outterson (2009a) (on limitations of this potential dynamic).

incentive to sell as much antibiotics as possible.[40] This incentive goes directly against the ongoing global efforts of stewardship, which promote developing new antibiotics to be kept in reserve and used sparingly to prolong as long as possible their efficacy. Such a strategy would make most patents' value diminish considerably and creates a paradox: considering the limited lifespan of patents—20 years—if stewardship efforts are successful, any patents on a new antibiotic may well expire before the antibiotic becomes widely used. Once the patents lapse and generics enter the market and prices tumble, chances to recoup investment and make large profits become fewer and more unpredictable.

4 Additional Incentives to Push the Development of New Antimicrobials

For the reasons discussed above, it can be assumed that the patent system needs to be complemented with targeted "push" and "pull" initiatives to bridge the incentives gap in areas where traditional mechanisms are deficient or less efficient. Only then it will be possible to ensure a sustainable innovation ecosystem capable of continually delivering new antibiotics over time.

Mechanisms that are alternative and/or complementary to patents have been proposed and defended as potentially more effective to foster antibiotic innovation. These include various "push" mechanisms (e.g. public subsidies of biomedical research and clinical trials, public-private partnerships etc.) and "pull" mechanisms (e.g. impact-based and royalty-based rewards for new drugs), or combinations of these.[41]

In the following we will give a short overview on the various push and pull mechanism that are typically being debated and applied to enhance and incentivise the development of antimicrobial therapies.

4.1 Pull Incentives

Pull incentives are intended to pull more economic actors into the market, e.g. through impact-based and royalty-based rewards for new drugs.[42] These are outcome-based rewards, such as monetary prices and advanced market commitments. They can manifest in regulatory policies for extended market exclusivity rights, increased reimbursement prices, but also in incentives with combined pull and push effects, including faster regulatory market approval procedures as described below. Typical

---

[40] Kesselheim, A. S. & Outterson, K., supra n. 39.

[41] Kremer and Williams (2010), Stiglitz and Jayadev (2010), and Pogge (2012).

[42] Kremer and Williams (2010), Stiglitz and Jayadev (2010), and Pogge (2012).

examples of pull incentives that might help drive and sustain antibiotic innovation include de-linkage, market-exclusivity vouchers, and value based-reimbursement.

The concept of "delinkage" implies decoupling a company's income from the number of antibiotic doses it sells. Under the general IP-based incentive structure, a company's return on investment is normally linked to the number of product units it sells. Patents typically create a limited market exclusivity to sell a product, and thereby the ability to recover research and development (R&D) costs and to make profits. This is normally linked to the quantity of sales of that product. De-linkage strategies are based on the premise that the link between product sales and income should be severed or attenuated because it is plagued by market failure and hinders antibiotic conservation efforts.[43] Instead, the argument goes, incentive policies should focus on mechanisms that allow companies to receive one or more lump-sum payments upon reaching pre-determined milestones, such as product marketing approval. This would simultaneously create a financial incentive to invest in antibiotic research and market approval, while compensating companies for marketing constraints and antibiotic conservation efforts for public health reasons.

Delinkage solutions have been advocated as a solution to access to medicines in poor countries by NGOs[44] and international organisations.[45] Delinkage is currently on the international relations agenda with UN High Level Panel on Access to Medicines calling for negotiations on establishing an R&D treaty.[46] Yet the idea has been regarded by some as hostile to the patent system instead of complementary.[47] As a result it was generally opposed by the industry and has not gathered much governmental support among European nations.[48] However, while delinkage strategies remain for good reasons very controversial for many areas of drug development, there seems at least to be an increasing support for such strategies with regard to selected areas of drug development, such as AMR-related treatments.

In 2015, a review on AMR commissioned by the UK Government and the Wellcome Trust proposed a system by which a global organisation is established with the

---

[43] Outterson et al. (2016).

[44] See for example https://www.keionline.org/delinkage (accessed 10 September 2017) and https://keionline.org/endorsedelinkage (accessed 10 September 2017). Generally see: Love and Hubbard (2007) and Love (2014, 2016).

[45] See World Health Organisation, the World Intellectual Property Organisation and the World Trade Organisation (2013); See World Health Organisation Assembly resolution WHA69.23 on 'Follow-up of the report of the Consultative Expert Working Group on Research and Development: Financing and Coordination' at para 9 to 11, available at: http://apps.who.int/gb/ebwha/pdf_files/WHA69/A69_R23-en.pdf (accessed 10 May 2017).

[46] See: Dreifuss and Mogae (2016).

[47] Stevens (2017).

[48] See European Parliament resolution of 19 May 2015 on safer healthcare in Europe: improving patient safety and fighting AMR (2014/2207(INI)), Article 62 'Calls on the Member States and the Commission to start a reflection process to develop a new economic model, that de-links the volume of sales from the reward paid for a new antibiotic, which would reflect the societal value of a new antibiotic and allow for sufficient return on investment for the company, while the purchaser would gain the right to use the product and have full control over volumes'.

authority and resources to commit lump-sum payments to successful drug developers.[49] This Review and the measures approved in its wake demonstrates that political support for solutions based on de-linkage is also emerging and growing in countries with a strong innovative pharmaceutical industry. Although officially the report represents only the opinion of its chair and other participants, the Review was published with institutional support and some of its proposals begun to be implemented even before the final version of the Report was published. The Report also proposes the establishment of a "Global Innovation Fund" for early-stage and non-commercial R&D into new antimicrobials and other related products such as vaccines and diagnostics. This new institution, led by governments and research funding organisations, could be built on existing bilateral and multilateral arrangements for pooling and coordinating the spending of research funds.[50] As for financing, the report proposes three alternatives: (a) the allocation of a very small percentage of G20 countries' existing healthcare spending to tackle AMR; (b) the reallocation of a fraction of global funding from international institutions to AMR; and/or (c) new funding streams, including options as establishment of "an antibiotic investment charge" for pharmaceutical companies selling pharmaceutical and healthcare products or devices, "which could be levied as a percentage of their sales and charged as a condition for accessing the health markets",[51] a tax on antibiotics,[52] and a system of 'Exchangeable "vouchers" to reward new antibiotics'.[53] As an incentive mechanism, the Report proposes a system of lump sum payments, or "market entry rewards", granted to companies if they successfully develop a drug meeting specified criteria (to be further developed). Companies would transmit their rights completely, with the Global Innovation Fund managing the international supply of the product.[54] Under a second and the authors' preferred option (called 'hybrid'), companies could retain marketing control and receive a lower market entry reward in exchange for accepting a number of restrictions on pricing and distribution devised to promote both conservation and access.[55] A more thorough analysis and debate of these proposals transcends the scope of the current chapter, however these are interesting proposals deserving further consideration and critical evaluation elsewhere (see also Sect. 5).

Market-Exclusivity Vouchers are a type of market exclusivity mechanism, and are based on a similar economic arguments and rationale that sustain other mechanisms such as the Patent Term Extension (US) or Supplementary Patent Certificate (Europe).[56] These are justified by the need to compensate the pharmaceutical industry for lengthy regulatory market approval procedures, which can delay market entry

---

[49]O'Neill (2015).
[50]Ibid.
[51]Ibid., p. 67.
[52]Ibid.
[53]Ibid., p. 68.
[54]Ibid., p. 63.
[55]Pages 54–58; see also O'Neil (2015), supra n. 56.
[56]See generally: Rai et al. (2008) and Kesselheim (2010).

for several years and severely reduce the time range of the market exclusivity period provided by patents.

An example of market exclusivity vouchers can be found in the "FDA priority review vouchers". In September 2008, the USA launched a new federal programme to promote R&D of pharmaceutical products for neglected diseases, based on providing companies developing drugs targeting neglected diseases with a "voucher" entitling the company to obtain expedited FDA review of a new drug application and usable on any other product (including 'blockbuster' drugs).[57]

In relation to antibiotics the basic idea is similar: in order to compensate for the different type of regulatory restriction on the marketing of the product, i.e. stewardship initiatives and measures, pharmaceutical companies would be provided with a voucher that would extend market exclusivity for a newly approved antibiotic. The grant of these vouchers would necessarily be subject to strict eligibility criteria, including that the new antibacterial is truly innovative and addresses an unmet medical need.

It has also been suggested that the granted market exclusivity should not be completely linked to the product where it was earned. The recipient of the voucher could use it on any drug on their portfolio or sell it to another company. Thus it would be possible to use it to extend or create market exclusivity on any off-patent product, even potentially blockbuster drugs. Proponents of this suggestion back increasing the duration of patent protection directly, so that patentees are able to capture more value over the useful life of the antibiotic and will thus avoid socially "wasting" the product by flooding the market prior to patent expiration, and driving resistance accordingly.[58]

Patent protection extension, however, will have effect only at the end of the patent's life, which from an economic perspective will not influence present value calculations, and thus will have little bearing in shifting the strategy planning for pharmaceutical companies' long term investment in research and development.[59] Corporate decisions take into consideration prospects for future income, but also their correlated level of uncertainty. In the case of patent term extensions the uncertainty level is high, because the income is both deferred to the future (and therefore has a lower net present value), and depends on assumptions about future pharmaceutical spending (and is thus uncertain).[60] Indeed, some commentators even challenge the use of intellectual property as a principal tool to drive antibiotic innovation and stewardship.[61]

Value-Based Reimbursement proposals focus on establishing value-based pricing policies and mechanisms. Outterson and Kesselheim, for instance, recommend

---

[57]Title XI, Food and Drug Administration (FDA) Amendments Act of 2007.

[58]Kades (2005).

[59]See Kesselheim objections to FDA review vouchers, in Kesselheim (2008).

[60]Outterson et al. (2007).

[61]Outterson (2009a).

reform of payer-reimbursement systems to capture the social value of new antibiotics more accurately and to encourage stewardship of existing antibiotics.[62] Public and private health insurance systems and subsystems influence to a great extent the behaviour and mechanics of pharmaceutical markets. There are complex regulations and negotiations procedures where different factors intersect. Reimbursement structures and mechanisms are a major de facto determinant in setting the final consumer prices of products and thus the profit margin of companies.

The proposal for pricing products according to their value for patients and based on a health-technology assessment would allow reinforcing incentive to innovation in areas from which society can benefit most. Ideally, price should be set in close correspondence with the social value of innovation. Pricing mechanisms should be put in place to better reflect the lifesaving and societal value of these medicines, including the chance for revaluation of reimbursement rates to adapt to and reflect to changes in antibiotic effectiveness. Any resulting price increase could also minimise the inappropriate use of antibiotics.

4.2 Push Incentives

Push incentives, as the language indicates, are mechanisms intended to push new drugs into the market,[63] and seek to make investments in drugs development financially more appealing. Push incentives primary focus on either reducing costs or compensating investments in the process of researching and developing new drugs, being that such investments may originate both from public and private sources (including venture capital or large philanthropic donors). Accordingly, push incentives comprise, for example, regulatory approval accelerators (i.e. mechanisms intended to diminish the time length of regulatory procedures and accelerate the regulatory decision making process), additional funding in the form of public subsidies for biomedical research and clinical trials, and public-private partnerships.

Renwick, Brogan and Mossialos conducted a systematic review on 47 proposed incentive strategies.[64] These strategies comprised both single incentives and policies and business models combining multiple incentives, policies and conservation mechanisms. Among the push mechanisms reviewed they found: (1) funding for open access to research; (2) grants for training and development of scientific staff; (3) direct funding/subsidies for R&D of novel antibiotics; (4) conditional grants tied to conservation strategies in the event of market approval; (5) funding translational

---

[62] Kesselheim and Outterson (2011).

[63] The characterisation of an incentive mechanism as either push or pull mechanism may be uncertain at times and should be understood as indicative of the intended objectives of the measure in concrete circumstances. Meaning that the same mechanism, depending on the optic of analysis, may be at times considered a pull or a push mechanism or even both.

[64] Renwich et al., above at n 33, p. 2.

research; (6) tax incentives such as tax credits, allowances, or deferral and refundable tax credits; and (7) product development partnerships.[65]

These push mechanisms reduce barriers to enter the market and therefore produce a larger impact in small and medium size enterprises (SMEs). These SMEs are very active in drug development in preclinical research phases, but lack the financial means to translate their research into the clinical trial phases. Because antibiotics compared to other drugs typically register higher success rates in the later stages of development, early push incentives are more likely to help those SMEs to move to later R&D phases and actually create new antibiotics. The timing of financial incentives also plays an important role, since early stage funding is more valuable than the same amount paid at a later date.[66] In this regard, there is research suggesting that funding at an early phase of research could be as much as 95% smaller than an equally effective future reward.[67] It has also been claimed that policy subsidies may be attributed selectively to a given stage of R&D or to a particular type of drug, in order to induce alignment between public policy priorities and company internal strategies for product development.[68]

Other solutions have been proposed to address the problem of incentives for antibiotic development.[69] These include both stewardship initiatives and regulatory incentives.[70] These can be characterised by focusing on reducing regulatory hurdles and improving legal mechanisms, instead of providing direct monetary incentives. These incentive mechanisms seek to push antibiotics into the marked by streamlining procedures in order to reduce the time necessary to achieve regulatory approval. The drug discovery and development process implies significant expenses and financial risk, therefore one option to stimulate R&D is to improve the regulatory process. For a long time, stakeholders in the antibiotic field have argued that regulatory processes are too expensive and require streamlining to foster innovation.[71] Options for developing regulatory frameworks to foster innovation could include accelerating the development process by adopting less onerous regulatory requirements, speeding up the decision process regarding market authorisation, and diminished liability measures.[72]

Such initiatives have surfaced most prominently in the USA, where the Generating Antibiotic Incentives Now (GAIN) Act creates an additional period of FDA-mediated regulatory exclusivity for qualifying antibiotics, essentially augmenting patent protection with regulatory protection. Passed in 2012, the GAIN Act provides an accelerated approval pathway and a five-year regulatory extension of exclusivity

[65]Mossialos et al. (2010), Morel and Mossialos (2010), Sharma and Towse (2011), and Infectious Diseases Society of America (2011).
[66]Renwich et al., above at n 33, p. 3.
[67]Spellberg et al. (2012).
[68]Morel and Mossialos (2010).
[69]Gould and Lawes (2016).
[70]Mossialos et al., above at n. 74, p. 100 et seq.
[71]Finch and Hunter (2006).
[72]Mossialos et al., above at n. 74, p. 101.

for novel antibiotics that address serious or life-threatening infections. This legislative measure is accompanied by the twenty-first Century Cures (or Cures) Act, enacted in December 2016.[73] The Cures Act is not specifically designed to provide mechanisms to incentivise the creation of new antibiotics, but it does establish a new FDA-limited population-approval pathway for antibiotics that treat serious or life-threatening infections with unmet medical needs. The Cures Act provides a streamlined regulatory process for medicines treating rare illnesses for which there are few or no available alternative treatments, which is the case of antimicrobials capable of killing 'super bugs'.

The United States Government Accountability Office (GAO) has recently reported that "GAIN has not been in place long enough yet to have been a factor in motivating any drug sponsors to develop and submit an application to FDA to market a new antibiotic".[74] In compliance with GAIN provisions of the Food and Drug Administration Safety and Innovation Act of 2012, the FDA released updated or new guidance for antibiotic development, and used the qualified infectious disease products (QIDP) designation to encourage the development of new antibiotics. As of August 2016, the FDA had coordinated the release of 14 updated or new guidance documents on antibiotic development; however, half of these guidance documents remain in draft form. Industry stakeholders expressed concerns over legal uncertainty: they were either uncertain whether they could rely on the FDA's draft guidance, or were concerned about the lack of guidance describing the QIDP designation and its requirements.[75] Although these initiatives are positive, there is still much work to be done in terms of improving legal certainty, such as clarifying the role of the FDA's draft guidance and further development of written guidance on the QIDP designation to help drug sponsors better understand the designation and its associated incentives.[76]

In the EU, the Innovative Medicines Initiative (IMI) has been established. This is a Public-Private partnership (PPP) between the European Union and the European pharmaceutical industry. IMI objective is to facilitate open collaboration in research, in order to advance the development of, and accelerate patient access to, personalised medicines for the health and wellbeing of all, especially in areas of unmet medical need.[77] The IMI works by providing funding and facilitating collaboration between key players involved in healthcare research, including universities and research institutions, the health and pharma industry (including small and SME's active in the sector), patient organisations, and medicines regulators. Objectives are

---

[73] See. H.R. 6, 21ST CENTURY CURES ACT, available at: http://docs.house.gov/billsthisweek/20150706/CPRT-114-HPRT-RU00-HR6.pdf (accessed 10 October 2017).

[74] United States Government Accountability Office (GAO) (2017).

[75] United States Government Accountability Office (GAO) (2017).

[76] Ibid.

[77] For further information, see the webpage of the European Innovative Medicine Initiative, available at: http://www.imi.europa.eu/about-imi/how-imi-works (accessed 17 October 2017).

set out in the IMI1 and IMI2 legislation,[78] and the Strategic Research Agenda[79] sets the guidelines for the choice of topics for calls for proposals and, ultimately, to the selection of projects.

The European Medicines agency (EMA) has introduced an accelerated review procedure in order to reduce the length of time spent making regulatory decisions.[80] Accelerated assessment reduces the timeframe for the EMA's Committee for Medicinal Products for Human Use (CHMP) to review a marketing-authorisation application. The accelerated review procedure aims to provide a regulatory decision 150 days from date of submission, down from 210 days (excluding clock stops). Products may be eligible for accelerated assessment if they are considered of major interest for public health and therapeutic innovation by a CHMP decision.[81] In addition, there are two other EMA procedures aimed at facilitating regulatory procedures: conditional approval (similar to the FDA's accelerated approvals) and approval for exceptional circumstances. In parallel, the EMA launched the so-called Priority Medicines scheme (PRIME). This is a voluntary scheme that builds upon the existing regulatory framework and tools already available such as scientific advice and accelerated assessment.[82] PRIME aims to enhance support for the development of medicines that target an unmet medical need. The main idea is to foster dialogue between the regulatory authorities and industry at early stages, aiming at improving clinical trial designs so that the data generated is suitable and meets regulatory standards and requirements. Early dialogue and EMA scientific advice[83] are also intended to improve efficient use of limited resources and ensure that patients only participate in trials designed to provide the data necessary for a marketing introduction application.

As indicated above, the incentives explored in this section do not necessarily have to substitute the traditional incentives provided by intellectual property rights. Typically they offer instead complementary incentives and options for public policy implementation in areas of strategic need such as antibiotic innovation. In the next

---

[78]EU's 2nd Innovative Medicine Initiative (IMI 2), available at: http://www.imi.europa.eu/content/imi-2 (accessed 10 October 2017).

[79]The right prevention and treatment for the right patient at the right time Strategic Research Agenda for Innovative Medicines Initiative 2, available at http://www.imi.europa.eu/sites/default/files/uploads/documents/About-IMI/research-agenda/IMI2_SRA_March2014.pdf (accessed 17 October 2017).

[80]Guideline on the scientific application and the practical arrangements necessary to implement the procedure for accelerated assessment pursuant to Article 14(9) of Regulation (EC) No. 726/2004, available at: http://www.ema.europa.eu/ema/index.jsp?curl=pages/regulation/general/general_content_001788.jsp&mid= (accessed 17 October 2017).

[81]See: http://www.ema.europa.eu/ema/index.jsp?curl=pages/regulation/general/general_content_000955.jsp&mid=WC0b01ac05809f843a (accessed 16 October 2017).

[82]See: http://www.ema.europa.eu/ema/index.jsp?curl=pages/regulation/general/general_content_000660.jsp&mid=WC0b01ac05809f8439 (accessed 17 October 2017).

[83]European Medicines Agency guidance for applicants seeking scientific advice and protocol assistance, 30 June 2017 EMA/4260/2001 Rev. 9, available at: http://www.ema.europa.eu/docs/en_GB/document_library/Regulatory_and_procedural_guideline/2009/10/WC500004089.pdf (accessed 17 October 2017).

section we will discuss what needs to be considered for the future in order to pursue these different options most effectively.

5 Discussion: A Call for Integrated Strategies and Improved International Collaboration

Rapid progress in many scientific areas such as gene editing, pharmacogenomics, artificial intelligence and big data-driven precision medicine, introduces substantial changes to the eco-system for biomedical innovation. There is no doubt that these new technologies hold great promise for the development of new diagnostics, more effective therapies and better drug development in many therapeutic disciplines, including antimicrobials. Yet the total number of truly new and innovative drugs receiving market authorisation remains unsatisfactory, and some of the more innovative therapies that actually could reach patients have become extremely expensive or ethically problematic.

While the incentives provided by patents and other intellectual property rights continue to be pivotal to the pharmaceutical industry, innovation deficits and market failures have emerged in important areas of pharmaceutical innovation. These problems can be detected not only in antimicrobial drug development,[84] but also in precision medicine,[85] orphan drug development,[86] new medical uses,[87] biologics,[88] and innovative pharmaceutical manufacturing methods.[89] A great variety of complex factors may contribute to these innovation deficits, ranging from problems associated with patent mechanics (such as acquisition, examination and enforcement) and patent-related market failures (such as differential ability to pay, payment distortions and non-additive value). All of these deficits require careful academic studies, as well as national and international responses.

As discussed above, the phenomenon of AMR and its underlying biological processes adds additional problems to the debate. One of the specific AMR challenges can be found in the discrepancy between patent incentives, which promote widespread use, and the goal of avoiding antibiotic resistance, which requires use-limitations and careful stewardship.[90] Given the growing number of deaths every year attributed to superbugs, it is an increasingly important task to develop new solutions to improve and adapt economic incentives. It is evident that "to create sustainable future solutions for just access and appropriate use of antibiotics interventions need

---

[84]Cf. Kesselheim, A. S. & Outterson, K., supra n. 39; Outterson (2014).

[85]Cf. Minssen and Nilsson (2012), Price (2015), and Sachs (2016).

[86]Cf. Millman (2014).

[87]Roin (2013).

[88]Minssen (2012) and Budish et al. (2015).

[89]Cf. Price (2014).

[90]Outterson (2009b) and Kesselheim and Outterson (2011).

to reflect the complex adaptive system of antibiotic use and availability."[91] Hence pull and push incentives will have to be combined within the framework of models that take this complexity into consideration. Kevin Outterson summarises matters eloquently:

Any solution must overcome at least three obstacles simultaneously: (1) inadequate market incentives for companies to invest in antibiotic R&D; (2) inadequate market incentive to protect these valuable resources from overuse and premature resistance; (3) inadequate market incentives to ensure global access to life-saving antibiotics. Creating new drugs achieves no lasting success if the underlying incentives for inappropriate use are not addressed, or if the drugs do not reach patients in need.[92]

Due to the immediate threats of AMR, considerable economic and health science research has now been devoted to this problem. A typical finding stemming from such research clearly indicates that the interdependent and interconnected problems of AMR have to be met with integrated solutions. There also appears to be a widespread consensus that to tackle the biological phenomenon of AMR effectively and sustainably, the rewards and return on investment in antimicrobial drug-development should not generally depend on the price and quantity of drugs sold.

This has resulted in the proposals noted above and in initiatives for alternative and complementary forms of incentives to pharmaceutical innovation. These include financial incentives, such as specific IP protection and market exclusivities, health impact funds, crowd-funded open innovation initiatives, pre-competitive collaborations, public-private partnerships (PPPs) (including between academia and industry), and other innovative alternatives, such as "integrated" strategies based on prizes administered by reimbursement systems requiring compliance with conservation targets. As demonstrated above, this has more recently led to the adoption of new legislation and initiatives on both the national and international level.[93]

Our summary of these developments revealed that the innovation system has many weapons in the arsenal to improve the availability of delinked incentives for antimicrobial drug R&D. However, revised regulatory frameworks and procedures encompassing non-patent incentives imply complex interactions with the general national and international legal system, as well as repercussions with the economic and political realities. It is also often still unclear whether or how these proposed alternatives—either alone or in combination—could be integrated into the current systems of drug safety and efficacy regulation, insurance, and patent treaties.[94] Hence

---

[91] Merrett et al. (2016).

[92] Outterson (2014).

[93] Such as Regulation (EC) No 141/2000 of the European Parliament and the Council on orphan medical products, OJ L 18/2000, pp. 1–5; the US-Orphan Drug Act of 1983 and US-Orphan Drug Regulations (21 CFR 316) (recently revised). Cf. the EU's 2nd Innovative Medicine Initiative (IMI 2), available at: http://www.imi.europa.eu/content/imi-2 (accessed 10 June 2017), or the US Generating Antibiotics Incentives Now (GAIN) ACT. See. H.R. 6, 21ST CENTURY CURES ACT, available at: http://docs.house.gov/billsthisweek/20150706/CPRT-114-HPRT-RU00-HR6.pdf (accessed 10 June 2017).

[94] Grootendorst et al. (2011).

much work still needs to be done in improving and coordinating curtailed and sustainable delinkage strategies that detach innovation rewards from unit-based sales incomes.

Moreover, it should be emphasised that new combinations of incentives form just one part of the solution. The societal effects of antibiotic use requires that broader safeguards are in place ensuring that antimicrobials are accessed, prescribed, dispensed and used appropriately and accurately based on robust scientific evidence.[95] When considering the multi-tiered system of AMR within the broader epidemiological and ecological contexts, the potential areas for synergy and the potential unintended consequences need to be considered very carefully in a deliberative process reflecting the complexity of the issue.[96] This will require coordination, communication and control of stakeholder activities and multisector responses involving new kinds of partnerships within the health care, health science, agriculture, and veterinary sectors.[97]

Further, it will be important to support and regulate the opportunities that new technologies provide for gaining scientific evidence or for developing precautionary measures, control mechanisms, diagnostics and new treatments. For example, phage therapy, gene editing (including CRISPR/Cas 9 and gene-drives), as well as artificial intelligence and big data-driven technologies, should be carefully considered and employed to develop and improve our arsenal in the battle against AMR. These new technologies could be used to enhance (1) access, (2) R&D strategies, (3) measures to ensure the quality of antibiotics, (4) measures to encourage just and sustainable decision making and help-seeking, (5) effective therapeutic and dosing strategies and (6) the use of accurate diagnostics; and (7) the speed of reacting to pandemics and new disease outbreaks.[98]

The European IMI initiative takes into account and addresses some of these factors in its AMR-related projects. But recently, more specialised accelerators have taken shape. These accelerators have received dedicated funding and an efficient institutional set-up, which allows them to effectively pool a wide variety of international key stakeholders with key capabilities and competences in antibiotic drug development. A good example is the Combating Antibiotic Resistant Bacteria Biopharmaceutical Accelerator (CARB-X), which is headquartered at Boston University School of Law. It arose from President Obama's 2015 Combating Antibiotic Resistant Bacteria (CARB) initiative and brings together and impressive association of leaders in industry, philanthropy, government, and academia. CARB-X aims to revitalise the antimicrobial pipeline for the next 25 years by addressing several goals laid out in the US Federal CARB National Action Plan.[99] CARB-X is headed by executive director

---

[95] Merrett et al. (2016).

[96] Ibid.

[97] Årdal et al. (2016).

[98] Ibid.

[99] See homepage of the Boston University School of Law, CARB-X GLOBAL PARTNERSHIP, available at: https://www.bu.edu/law/faculty-scholarship/carb-x/). For further information see also

and principal investigator Kevin Outterson, who is a law professor at Boston University (BU). According to BU's homepage, the CARB-X partners will pool their broad scientific, technical, business and legal expertise to help grantees navigate the maze of regulatory steps, studies, and data collection required for new drugs and other products to gain approval by US and/or European regulators. CARB-X aims to deliver a growing portfolio of promising new antibiotics, diagnostics, and vaccines to tackle the threat posed by untreatable bacterial infections.[100]

The US/UK partnership, which includes the Biomedical Advanced Research and Development Authority (BARDA) (U.S.), the Wellcome Trust (U.K.), the AMR Centre (U.K.), Boston University School of Law (U.S.), the National Institutes of Health's National Institute of Allergy and Infectious Disease (NIAID) (U.S.), Mass-Bio (U.S.), California Life Sciences Institute (U.S.), The Broad Institute of MIT and Harvard (U.S.), and RTI International (U.S.), will support a suite of products through early preclinical development to a stage where they can be taken forward by private or public investment.[101]

While the recent U.S. and European initiatives are indeed impressive, it is clear that the public also plays a critical role in preventing and stopping post-antibiotic crises. It therefore important to involve not only stakeholders from different sectors, but also citizens on a global scale and to develop codes of conduct and best practice on matters such as use-limitation, precautionary measures, and non-antibiotic disinfection. A coherent and globally enforceable framework of regulations, education and use limitations will be crucial to tackle the AMR challenge effectively. Fortunately, and as discussed and demonstrated in more detail by Christine Årdal et al.,[102] the WHO Member States have endorsed WHO's global action plan to combat AMR, and regional and international collaborations are also progressing:

The USA has launched a national strategy and an action plan to address antibiotic resistance, which awaits Congressional action. The Transatlantic Task Force on AMR between the USA and the European Union has put forward a series of recommendations for joint action. South Africa has agreed to an AMR national strategy framework. The UK has initiated an independent review on AMR, which stated that development of ten new highly effective drugs in the next decade would cost less than US$25 billion (or 0.03% of global gross domestic product [GDP]). A recent report

---

the CARB-X webpage, which is available at http://www.carb-x.org/ (both accessed 10 September 2017).

[100]Ibid.

[101]Ibid. (adding more information on the funding: "The Biomedical Advanced Research Authority (BARDA), within HHS' Office of the Assistant Secretary for Preparedness and Response, will provide $30 million in research and development funding through CARB-X during the first year and up to $250 million over five years. The AMR Centre, a public-private initiative formed in 2016 to drive the development of new antibiotics and diagnostics, aims to provide $14 million to support CARB-X projects in year one and up to $100 million over five years. The Wellcome Trust, a global charitable foundation focused on biomedical research, will contribute further funding and its expertise in overseeing projects of this kind.").

[102]Christine Årdal, Kevin Outterson, Steven J Hoffman et al. supra n. 97.

to the Nordic Council of Ministers recommended a global investment of 0.005% of annual global GDP over a 5-year period.[103]

But it is also pointed out by Årdal et al. that the national endorsement of the WHO's action plans and the implementation of regional international collaboration alone will not be sufficient to drive, monitor and organise the necessary multi-sector responses. A powerful and institutionalised global coordination will be necessary, and it needs to involve national and international institutions with sufficient financing mechanisms, mandates, authority, resources, and power. This underlines the importance of ensuring that these issues are also regulated and codified in enforceable global treaties, which requires further negotiations and a committed engagement from international organisations.

Fortunately, this appears to be happening now. During a meeting of the United Nations in September 2016, the General Assembly reaffirmed a commitment to creating or strengthening national action plans to counter AMR. In his speech, then-UN Secretary-General Ban Ki-moon classified antibiotic resistance as 'a fundamental, long-term threat to human health, sustainable food production, and development.'[104] For the first time, Heads of States represented at the UN collectively committed to taking a broad, coordinated approach to address the root causes of AMR across multiple sectors, especially human health, animal health and agriculture.[105] In a joint statement issued during the UN General Assembly meeting in 2016, the general directors for WHO, FAO and OIE pointed out that common and life-threatening infections like pneumonia, gonorrhoea, and post-operative infections, as well as HIV, tuberculosis and malaria, are increasingly becoming untreatable because of AMR: 'Left unchecked, AMR is predicted to have significant social, health security, and economic repercussions that will seriously undermine the development of countries.'[106]

This indicates that the challenges of AMR appear to have finally gained worldwide public, scientific, and political attention. As set out above, many issues require urgent attention and demand robust interventions on a global level.[107] It is therefore fortunate and crucial that we can expect more concrete and diverse global action. It will now be more important than ever that policy makers consistently support, improve, authorise, and fund new global institutional set-ups that could monitor, review and enforce vigorous implementations and determined collaborative interventions.[108]

---

[103] Ibid.

[104] See Ban Ki-moon, Secretary-General's remarks to High-Level Meeting on AMR (as delivered on 21 September 2016), available at: https://www.un.org/sg/en/content/sg/statement/2016-09-21/secretary-generals-remarks-high-level-meeting-antimicrobial (accessed 16 June 2017).

[105] At UN, global leaders commit to act on AMR', 21 September 2016, United Nation News Centre, http://www.un.org/apps/news/story.asp?NewsID=55011#.WVjUyYiGM2w (accessed 18 July 2016).

[106] ibid.

[107] Thomas (2014), Minssen (2014), and Saez (2016).

[108] Cf. Årdal et al. (2016).

6 Conclusion

The world is in dire need of new antibiotics and of an innovation system that incentivises and supports the process of developing such drugs. To be most effective, the development process must engage a broad variety of stakeholders, including patients, hospitals, public entities and private companies in various sectors. However, while considerable investments are being made to enhance the development of new antibiotics through the establishment public-private partnerships, the traditional IP-based innovation system has so far not provided sufficient incentives and regulatory support for the relevant stakeholders to invest in new antibiotics drugs. As a consequence, there are still too few new antimicrobials in the development pipeline to replace the increasingly ineffective drugs. It is an important task to repair these broken economic incentives and to promote carefully regulated access to these drugs.

Fortunately, this challenge has gained the attention of policy-makers and legislators. Recent initiatives and regulatory interventions provide special market-based incentives and additional regulatory support for the testing and approval of antimicrobial drugs and therapies. But to tackle the biological phenomenon of AMR effectively and sustainably, the rewards and return of investment in antimicrobial drug-development should not generally depend on the price and quantity of drugs sold. Hence much work still needs to be done in improving and coordinating curtailed and sustainable delinkage strategies that detach innovation rewards from unit-based sales income.

In that regard, it has become clear that devising effective incentives for the development of antimicrobials is not enough to fight and treat the complex, interconnected and interdependent challenges of antibiotic resistance. An effective and sustainable response demands solutions that combine access to effective antimicrobials with infection prevention, reduction of inappropriate use of existing antimicrobials, surveillance, and innovation.[109] It is thus important to study, support and regulate the opportunities that new technologies, such as gene editing, phage therapies, AI and big-data driven innovation provide in the battle against AMR. This does not only require further interdisciplinary research that should involve a wide range of specialised expertise spanning from the natural sciences to the social and economic sciences. It also demands political determination and a committed implementation of well-coordinated actions that must be *enforceable* across all sectors, including, agriculture, animal farming, public health and trade.[110]

Last but not least, it is crucial that these responses are agreed upon, implemented and orchestrated at global level. Committed international collaboration and effective public education will be the key to battling the worldwide dangers of AMR. Multiresistant microbes exist, prevail and evolve every day and in every region of the world. Lethal pathogens do not stop at borders, and neither should our responses.

---

[109] Ibid.
[110] Ibid.

Acknowledgements Denmark. CeBIL's research is supported by a Novo Nordisk Foundation grant for a Collaborative Research Programme (grant agreement number NNF17SA0027784).

References

Årdal C, Outterson K, Hoffman SJ et al (2016) International cooperation to improve access to and sustain effectiveness of antimicrobials. Lancet 387:296–307. https://doi.org/10.1016/S0140-6736(15)00470-5

Boucher HW, Talbot GH, Bradley JS et al (2009) Bad bugs, no drugs: no ESKAPE! An update from the Infectious Diseases Society of America. Clin Infect Dis 48:1–12

Dreifuss R, Mogae FG (co-chairs) (2016) The United Nations Secretary-General's high level panel on access to medicines report promoting innovation and access to health technologies, pp 31–32. Available at: https://static1.squarespace.com/static/562094dee4b0d00c1a3ef761/t/57d9c6ebf5e231b2f02cd3d4/1473890031320/UNSG+HLP+Report+FINAL+12+Sept+2016.pdf. Accessed 10 Jun 2017

Echols RM (2011) Understanding the regulatory hurdles for antibacterial drug development in the post-Ketek world. Ann N Y Acad Sci 1241:153–161

Eichberg MJ (2015) Public funding of clinical-stage antibiotic development in the United States and European Union. Health Secur 13(3):156–165. https://doi.org/10.1089/hs.2014.0081. Available at: https://www.ncbi.nlm.nih.gov/pmc/articles/PMC4486734/

E Budish, Roin BN, William H (2015) Do firms underinvest in long-term research? Evidence from cancer clinical trials. Am Econ Rev 105(7):2044–2085

European Commission (2017) European one health action plan against AMR. Available at: https://ec.europa.eu/health/amr/sites/amr/files/amr_action_plan_2017_en.pdf. Accessed 10 Jul 2017

Finch R, Hunter P (2006) Antibiotic resistance—action to promote new technologies: report of an EU Intergovernmental Conference held in Birmingham, UK, 12–13 Dec 2005. J Antimicrob Chemother 58:3–22

Goldman M, Compton C, Mittleman BB (2013) Public-private partnerships as driving forces in the quest for innovative medicines. Clin Transl Med 2:2. https://doi.org/10.1186/2001-1326-2-2. Available at: https://www.ncbi.nlm.nih.gov/pmc/articles/PMC3564715/. Accessed 18 Sept 2017

Gould IM, Lawes T (2016) Antibiotic stewardship: prescribing social norms. Lancet 387:1699

Grootendorst P et al (2011) New approaches to rewarding pharmaceutical innovation. CMAJ 6:183

Hay M et al (2014) Clinical development success rates for investigational drugs. Nat Biotechnol 32(1):40–51. https://doi.org/10.1038/nbt.2786. Accessed 10 Jul 2017

Holmes AH, Moore LS, Sundsfjord A et al (2016) Understanding the mechanisms and drivers of AMR. Lancet 387(10014):176–187

Infectious Diseases Society of America (2011) Combating AMR: policy recommendations to save lives. Clin Infect Dis 52(Suppl 5):S397–S428

Kades E (2005) Preserving a precious resource: rationalizing the use of antibiotics. NW Univ Law Rev 99:611

Kesselheim AS (2008) Drug development for neglected diseases—the trouble with FDA review vouchers. N Engl J Med 359:1981. Available at: http://dx.doi.org/10.1056/NEJMp0806684. Accessed 10 Jun 2017

Kesselheim AS (2010) Using market-exclusivity incentives to promote pharmaceutical innovation. N Engl J Med 363:1855. Available at: http://www.nejm.org/doi/abs/10.1056/NEJMhle1002961. Accessed 15 Aug 2017

Kesselheim AS, Outterson K (2011) Improving antibiotic markets for long-term sustainability. Yale J Health Policy Law Ethics 11:101

Kremer M, Williams H (2010) Incentivizing innovation: adding to the tool kit. In: Lerner J, Stern S (eds) Innovation policy and the economy, vol 10. University of Chicago Press, Chicago, IL, pp 1–17

Laxminarayan R (2014) Antibiotic effectiveness: balancing conservation against innovation. Science 345(6202):1299–1301

Love J (2014) Alternatives to the patent system that are used to support R&D efforts, including both push and pull mechanisms, with a special focus on innovation-inducement prizes and open source development models. World Intellectual Property Organisation, CDIP/14/INF/12

Love J (2016) Discussion paper: an economic perspective on delinking the cost of R&D from the price of medicines. UNITAID

Love J, Hubbard T (2007) The big idea: prizes to stimulate R&D for new medicines. Chic-Kent Law Rev 82(3)

Merrett et al (2016) Towards the just and sustainable use of antibiotics. J Pharm Policy Pract 9:31. https://doi.org/10.1186/s40545-016-0083-5

Millman J (2014) Why the drug industry hasn't come up with an Ebola cure. The Washington Post, 13 Aug 2014. Available at: http://www.washingtonpost.com/blogs/wonkblog/wp/2014/08/13/why-the-drug-industry-hasnt-come-up-with-an-ebola-cure/. Accessed 10 May 2017

Minssen T (2012) Assessing the inventiveness of biopharmaceutical under EU & US patent law. INEKO, Lund

Minssen T (2014) European responses to the Ebola crisis. Part I: Initiatives at the European Medicines Agency. Available at: http://blogs.law.harvard.edu/billofhealth/2014/11/12/european-responses-to-the-ebola-crisis-part-i-initiatives-at-the-european-medicines-agency-ema/. Accessed 13 Jul 2017

Minssen T, Nilsson David (2012) The US Supreme Court in Mayo v Prometheus—taking the fire from or to biotechnology and personalized medicine? QMJIP 376:383

Morel C, Mossialos E (2010) Stoking the antibiotic pipeline. BMJ 340:c2115. https://doi.org/10.1136/bmj.c2115

Mossialos EM et al (2010) Policies and incentives for promoting innovation in antibiotic research. European Observatory on Health Systems and Policies. http://www.euro.who.int/__data/assets/pdf_file/0011/120143/E94241.pdf. Accessed 3 Oct 2017

Mossialos E, Morel C, Edwards S, Berenson J, Gemmill-Toyama M, Brogan D (2009) Policies and incentives for promoting innovation in antibiotic research. European Observatory on Health Systems and Policies. Available at: http://www.euro.who.int/__data/assets/pdf_file/0011/120143/E94241.pdf. Accessed 6 Dec 2012

O'Neill J (2015) Securing new drugs for future generations: the pipeline of antibiotics. Review on AMR, Wellcome Trust and UK Government, p 23. Available at: https://amr-review.org/sites/default/files/160525_Final%20paper_with%20cover.pdf. Accessed 10 Jun 2017

O'Neill J et al (2016) The review on AMR: final report and recommendations, at 1. Available at: https://amr-review.org/sites/default/files/160525_Final%20paper_with%20cover.pdf. Accessed 10 Sept 2017

Outterson K (2009a) Legal ecology of resistance: the role of antibiotic resistance in pharmaceutical innovation. Cardozo Rev 31:613

Outterson K (2009b) The legal ecology of resistance: the role of antibiotic resistance in pharmaceutical innovation. Cardozo Rev 31:1

Outterson K (2014) New business models for sustainable antibiotics. Center on Global Health Security Working Group Papers, Chatham House (The Royal Institute of International Affairs), Working Groups on AMR, Paper 1

Outterson K, Samora B, Keller-Cuda K (2007) Will longer antimicrobial patents improve global public health? Lancet Infect Dis 7:559

Outterson K, Gopinathan U, Clift C, So AD, Morel CM, Røttingen J-A (2016) Delinking investment in antibiotic research and development from sales revenues: the challenges of transforming a promising idea into reality. PLoS Med 13(6):e1002043. https://doi.org/10.1371/journal.pmed.1002043 Accessed 10 May 2017

Payne DJ, Gwynn MN, Holmes DJ, Pompliano DL (2007) Drugs for bad bugs: confronting the challenges of antibacterial discovery. Nat Rev Drug Discov 6:29–40

Pogge T (2012) The health impact fund: enhancing justice and efficiency in global health. J Hum Dev Capab 13(4):537–559

Power E (2006) Impact of antibiotic restrictions: the pharmaceutical perspective. Clin Microbiol Infect 12:25. Available at http://dx.doi.org/10.1111/j.1469-0691.2006.01528.x. Accessed 10 Sept 2017

Price WN (2014) Making do in making drugs: innovation policy and pharmaceutical manufacturing. BCL Rev 55:491

Price WN (2015) Black-box medicine. HARV J Law Technol 28:419

Projan SJ (2003) Why big pharma getting out of antibacterial drug discovery? Curr Opin Microbiol 6:427–430

Rai AK, Reichman JH, Uhlir PF, Crossman C (2008) Pathways across the valley of death: novel intellectual property strategies for accelerated drug discovery. Yale J Health Policy Law Ethics 8:1–36

Renwick MJ, Brogan DM, Mossialos E (2016a) A systematic review and critical assessment of incentive strategies for discovery and development of novel antibiotics. J Anthibiotics 69(2):73. Available at: http://dx.doi.org/10.1038/ja.2015.98. Accessed 10 Sept 2017

Renwick MJ, Brogan DM, Mossialos E (2016b) A systematic review and critical assessment of incentive strategies for discovery and development of novel antibiotics. J Anthibiotics 69(2):73–88 at p. 73. Available at: http://dx.doi.org/10.1038/ja.2015.98. Accessed 10 Jun 17

Rex JH et al (2013) A comprehensive regulatory framework to address the unmet need for new antibacterial treatments. Lancet Infect Dis 13(3):269–275

Roin BN (2009) Unpatentable drugs and the standards of patentability. Texas Law Rev 87:503–570. Available at SSRN: http://ssrn.com/abstract=1127742. Accessed 10 Sept 2017

Roin BN (2013) Solving the problem of new uses. Available at SSRN: http://ssrn.com/abstract=2337821 or http://dx.doi.org/10.2139/ssrn.2337821. Accessed 10 Jun 2017

Sachs R (2016) Preserving the future of personalized medicine. UC Davis L Rev 49

Saez C (2016) AMR, regulatory systems high on pharma industry 2016 agenda. IP Watch. Available at: http://www.ip-watch.org/2016/02/17/ifpma-interview-antimicrobial-resistance-regulatory-systems-high-on-pharma-industry-2016-agenda/. Accessed 10 May 2017

Sharma P, Towse A (2011) New drugs to tackle AMR: analysis of EU policy options. Office of Health Economics. https://www.ohe.org/publications/newdrugstackleantimicrobialresistanceanalysiseupolicyoptions. Accessed 17 Oct 2017

Silver LL (2011a) Challenges of antibacterial discovery. Clin Microbiol Rev 24(1):71–109

Silver LL (2011b) Challenges of antibacterial discovery. Clin Microbiol Rev 24(1):71–109. http://doi.org/10.1128/CMR.00030-10. Accessed 10 Jun 2017

Spellberg B, Sharma P, Rex JH (2012) The critical impact of time discounting on economic incentives to overcome the antibiotic market failure. Nat Rev Drug Discov 11(2). https://doi.org/10.1038/nrd3560-c1

Stevens P (2017) Delinkage: can prizes replace patents for medicine innovation? Available at: https://geneva-network.com/article/delinkage-2-2/. Accessed 20 Dec 2017

Stiglitz JE, Jayadev A (2010) Medicine for tomorrow: some alternative proposals to promote socially beneficial research and development in pharmaceuticals. J Generic Med 7:217–226. https://doi.org/10.1057/jgm.2010.21

Sun LH, Dennis B (2016) The superbug that doctors have been dreading just reached the U.S. The Washington Post. Available at: https://www.washingtonpost.com/news/to-your-health/wp/2016/05/26/the-superbug-that-doctors-have-been-dreading-just-reached-the-u-s/?utm_term=.8158c3d51b54. Accessed 13 Jul 2017

The PEW Charitable Foundation (2016) Antibiotics currently in clinical development, May 2016. http://www.pewtrusts.org/~/media/assets/2016/05/antibiotics-currently-in-clinical-development.pdf?la=en. Accessed 16 Sept 2017

Thomas JR (2014) Toward a theory of regulatory exclusivities. In: Okediji RL, Bagley MA (eds) Patent law in global perspective. Oxford University Press, New York, pp 345–376

United States Government Accountability Office (GAO) (2017) Report to congressional requesters: antibiotics. Available at: http://www.gao.gov/products/GAO-17-189. Accessed 17 Oct 2017

WHO (2012) The evolving threat of AMR. Options for action. World Health Organisation, Geneva. Available at: http://apps.who.int/iris/bitstream/10665/44812/1/9789241503181_eng.pdf. Accessed 10 Jun 2017

World Bank (2016) Drug-resistant infections: a threat to our economic future. Washington, DC

World Health Organisation, the World Intellectual Property Organisation, the World Trade Organisation (2013) Promoting access to medical technologies and innovation intersections between public health, intellectual property and trade. Available at: https://www.wto.org/english/res_e/publications_e/who-wipo-wto_2013_e.htm

R&D for Emerging Infectious Diseases of Epidemic Potential: Sharing Risks and Benefits Through a New Coalition

Unni Gopinathan, Elizabeth Peacocke, Dimitrios Gouglas, Trygve Ottersen, and John-Arne Røttingen

Abstract The lack of effective vaccines for emerging infectious diseases (EID) of limited market potential, such as Chikungunya and Zika, poses a serious threat to human life and prosperity. Research and development (R&D) for new vaccines for EIDs faces two major challenges. The first is R&D preparedness: that is, to advance EID vaccine candidates to the latest R&D stage possible during non-epidemic times, on the basis of any feasible safety or efficacy data. The second is R&D response: that is, to test the clinical efficacy of vaccine candidates rapidly once an outbreak erupts. To overcome these challenges, the Coalition for Epidemic Preparedness Innovations (CEPI) was established in August 2016. Here, we explore why the realisation of CEPI's mission—preventing outbreaks of emerging infectious diseases from becoming humanitarian crises—is a global public good, and the crucial role R&D preparedness and R&D response play in providing this good. We next examine why providing this global public good requires incentivising involvement and sharing risks with the private sector. Finally, we explore the potential for CEPI to be an agent mobilising shared responsibilities, including key factors that must be addressed in order for CEPI to demonstrate to governments that collective action is the preferred strategy for preventing future epidemics and strengthening global health security.

Keywords Research and development · CEPI · Neglected diseases · Intellectual property · Access to medicines

1 Introduction

In 2014–15 the world experienced the most severe Ebola epidemic in history. The epidemic hit the three West African states—Guinea, Liberia, and Sierra Leone—the hardest. In addition, Ebola was transmitted to several neighbouring states and, unlike in previous outbreaks, the world also observed the first confirmed cases of Ebola transmission outside Africa. The outbreak was unprecedented in length and

U. Gopinathan (✉) · E. Peacocke · D. Gouglas · T. Ottersen · J.-A. Røttingen
University of Oslo, Oslo, Norway
e-mail: unni.gopinathan@gmail.com

© The Author(s) 2020
M. Eccleston-Turner and I. Brassington (eds.), *Infectious Diseases in the New Millennium*, International Library of Ethics, Law, and the New Medicine 82,
https://doi.org/10.1007/978-3-030-39819-4_7

137

size, and affected more people and more states than any other previous outbreaks of Ebola (Box 1). It is now widely accepted that the affected states and the global health system was unprepared for an Ebola epidemic of this magnitude. Assessments after the Ebola outbreak highlighted a number of factors affecting the response to the outbreak.[1]

Of these, we can highlight four major ones. Firstly, health systems in Guinea, Liberia, and Sierra Leone had never before encountered sustained transmission of Ebola, so health workers, communities, and policymakers had little or no experience dealing with the virus. A second major factor was that Guinea, Liberia, and Sierra Leone are all post-conflict states. As a consequence, these states had fragile and poorly-resourced health systems that were quickly overburdened by the epidemic, and low level of trust between the public and the governments when interventions to reduce the spread of Ebola had to be implemented. The third crucial factor was the slow and inefficient international response. The World Health Organisation (WHO) in particular was criticised for not declaring more quickly that the outbreak represented a public health emergency of international concern.[2] Finally, a fourth area which received considerable attention was the lack of effective vaccines, therapeutics, and diagnostics to prevent the spread of Ebola.[3] During and after the epidemic, it was recognised that R&D of effective biomedical tools were lacking for Ebola, as well as for other emerging infectious diseases (EIDs) with the potential to cause epidemics at a scale similar to Ebola. A consensus among post-Ebola assessments was the need for a more concerted global effort to strengthen R&D for these diseases—with an emphasis on vaccines as an effective countermeasure against future epidemics.[4]

In response to these concerns, a new global health initiative—the Coalition for Epidemic Preparedness Innovations (CEPI)—was formally announced at the World Economic Forum in January 2017.[5] The founding members of CEPI are the governments of Norway and India, the Gates Foundation, the Wellcome Trust, and the World Economic Forum. Motivating CEPI's establishment is the fact that clinical testing of Ebola vaccines proved successful during the epidemic, which in turn inspired the vision that "vaccines can prevent outbreaks of emerging infectious diseases from becoming humanitarian crises".[6] CEPI's corresponding mission is to "stimulate, finance, and co-ordinate vaccine development against emerging infectious diseases with epidemic potential, especially in cases where market incentives alone do not achieve this".[7]

In this chapter, we begin by examining whether the prevention of future epidemics of EIDs, which is CEPI's vision, represents a global public good. We then identify the main factors preventing the realisation of this good, and the rationale for establishing

---

[1]Gostin et al. (2016), Moon et al. (2017a).

[2]Kamradt-Scott (2016).

[3]Plotkin et al. (2015), Perkins et al. (2017), Bixler et al. (2017).

[4]Gostin and others (n 1); Plotkin, Mahmoud and Farrar, ibid.

[5]Brende et al. (2017).

[6]Røttingen et al. (2017).

[7]Ibid.

CEPI. Next, we explore how CEPI will engage with private actors as part of its efforts to generate a global public good. We end by examining the potential for CEPI to demonstrate that collective action is the preferred strategy for preventing future epidemics.

Box 1. The 2014–15 Ebola outbreak

Retrospective identification of cases in this outbreak traced the index patient to be a 2-year old toddler in Guinea infected in December 2013. It took until March 2014 before an outbreak of Ebola was declared by national health authorities. Shortly after, Ebola was detected in neighbouring Liberia. On May 2016, Ebola had reached Sierra Leone, and over the next month the number of new cases per week escalated. Late in June, Doctors Without Borders called for increased international support—declaring that the epidemic was getting "out of control". In July, two infected US aid workers were evacuated from Liberia, Ebola was detected in Lagos in a patient who had travelled by air from Liberia, and Sierra Leone declared a state of emergency in order to quarantine the epicentres of the disease. This series of events ultimately compelled the WHO to declare the Ebola outbreak to be a public health emergency of international concern. An international response was triggered, which included an increased influx of financial resources and health personnel, building of treatment centres in Guinea, Liberia, and Sierra Leone, and the establishment of the UN Mission for Ebola Emergency Response (UNMEER).

Since its discovery in 1976, there had been twenty Ebola outbreaks prior to 2014. Previous outbreaks were confined to remote rural areas and contained within months, with the largest outbreak, in Uganda in 2000–01, having 425 cases and causing 223 deaths. In comparison, the 2014–15 outbreak spread to urban centres and the capital cities, lasted for over two years, and ultimately resulted in 28,616 cases (numbers from WHO's situation report as of June 10, 2016, including confirmed, probable, and reported cases) and 11,310 deaths— more than all previous outbreaks combined.

---

2 Vaccines Against EIDs: A New Approach Needed to Provide a Global Public Good

The classical, technical definition of a public good is a good that is both non-excludable and non-rivalrous.[8] A good is non-excludable when people cannot be prevented from enjoying its benefits once the good becomes available. When a good

---

[8]Samuelson (1954, 1955).

is non-rival, the consumption of the good does not diminish the quantity available to others. Classic examples are the benefits of clean air and traffic lights.

What then qualifies as a global public good is interpreted differently in the vast literature on the subject.[9] Discussing these differences in great detail is beyond the scope of this chapter. However, it is worth noting that a strict interpretation would only qualify goods that at all times, without exceptions, exhibit non-rivalry and non-excludability.[10] An even stricter interpretation would additionally demand that everybody derive the same level of utility from the good. Successfully eradicating polio is a clear example of a good that is non-rivalrous and non-excludable. However, while eradication of polio eliminates the risk to everybody, it is reasonable to imply that populations living closer to sites of ongoing wild polio transmission (Afghanistan, Nigeria, and Pakistan) would value this good more than populations living in states where polio has long been eliminated.

More relaxed, and perhaps more useful, interpretations of what constitute global public goods can take two main forms. One where goods qualify as a global public good if the benefits *in principle* could reach populations across all states, without necessarily demanding that everyone derive the same measurable benefits.[11] A second which includes goods that are subject to either excludability or rivalry, but where there is potential for specific policies to secure that these goods are non-rival and non-excludable. For example, as a result of patents, copyright, and paywalls, knowledge becomes excludable, and accordingly, knowledge is only a global public good insofar such restrictions are removed. Goods that incompletely exhibit non-rivalry or non-excludability are also referred to as impure public goods.[12]

It is also useful to be aware that a global public "good" refers both to directly providing utility, such as the benefits of making knowledge globally accessible, and reducing disutility by reducing harmful, cross-border spillover effects. The aforementioned examples of smallpox and polio eradication underscore the latter point. Other relevant examples are the effects of greenhouse gas emissions on climate change, or air pollution on clean air. The costs and harms of inaction on these issues exhibit both non-rivalry and non-excludability. It is also useful to distinguish between whether one considers the global public good to be the actual benefits (for example the prevention of future epidemics), or the infrastructure or systems put in place to produce these benefits (for example the International Health Regulations to reduce the cross-border risks of infectious diseases). In the context of this chapter, we consider the realisation of CEPI's mission—preventing outbreaks of emerging infectious diseases from becoming humanitarian crises—as the global public good. Numerous previous epidemics have demonstrated that if lack of capacity, resources or other reasons prevent a state from acting in time, the harms of an infectious disease may quickly be distributed to neighbouring states or to a different corner of the world— demonstrating the non-excludable and non-rivalrous nature of the good. The Ebola

---

[9]Ress (2013), Kaul (2012), Morrissey et al. (2002).

[10]Morrissey, Willem te Velde and Hewitt, ibid.

[11]Kaul (n 9); Morrissey, Willem te Velde and Hewitt (n 9).

[12]Kaul (n 9); Morrissey, Willem te Velde and Hewitt (n 9).

outbreak that started in 2014 is one example. Another striking example is the SARS outbreak in 2003–04. After emerging as an unknown disease in Guangdong in China in 2002, SARS had by May 2003 taken 41 lives in Canada (the only state outside Asia with fatal cases of SARS).

A different term applied to describe the global public good of mitigating the risk of infectious diseases is "global health security"—a term recognising that national borders do not stop the spread of infectious diseases, and that populations in all states can potentially be exposed to the risk if the spread in one part of the world is not prevented or controlled.[13] In this context, vaccines play a crucial role. Vaccines can protect entire communities and states—either by reducing the incidence or eliminating an infectious disease from one part of the world, or as in the case of smallpox, eradicating it completely. Developing vaccines is a complex, costly, lengthy, and risky process. It is estimated that, on average, developing a vaccine from preclinical research requires over 10 years, with less than 10% probability of entering the market.[14] Due to limited availability of publicly available data, precise estimates of vaccine development costs do not exist, but is suggested to be somewhere between $200 m and $500 m.[15] Depending on the complexity of the vaccine technology developed, the cost could be greater. Since vaccines are deployed to protect healthy individuals, strict regulatory requirements must be met to ensure safety, including continued monitoring for adverse effects once the vaccine has been introduced in immunisation programmes. In some cases, additional clinical trials are needed to disprove side effects.[16] To recover the cost of constructing and maintaining vaccine and production facilities, vaccine manufacturers need to rely on economies of scale. For these reasons, large and predictable financial returns on investment are needed to attract pharmaceutical companies to invest in R&D of vaccines.[17] The market potential has been the main motivating factor for developing new vaccines (such as more recently developed vaccines against pneumonia and rotavirus) that protect against diseases also affecting populations in high-income states. Hence the *lack* of market potential is the main reason explaining why vaccines against EIDs are lacking.

At least two major factors explain why EIDs do not present themselves as an attractive investment. First, the emergence and re-emergence of these diseases is highly sporadic and confined to limited geographic areas in most cases. For example, prior to the Ebola outbreak in 2014–15, eleven of thirteen recent outbreaks had been confined to rural areas in either Uganda or the Democratic Republic of the Congo.[18] Another example is SARS. Starting first in South-China, it spread to Singapore, Taiwan, and Canada, with 774 deaths reported globally.[19] After China was declared free of SARS in May 2004, no new outbreaks have been detected.

---

[13]Commission on a Global Health Risk Framework for the Future (2016).
[14]Pronker et al. (2013).
[15]Serdobova and Kieny (2006).
[16]Offit (2005).
[17]Ibid.
[18]CDC (2017).
[19]WHO (2017c).

The sporadic epidemiology of these diseases creates uncertainty about how the vaccines will be used. Introduction into a state's routine immunisation programme or frequent use in mass vaccination campaigns are the most lucrative incentives for vaccine manufacturers to invest in R&D of new vaccines; but for most EIDs, vaccines are unlikely (with a few potential exceptions) to be used in these ways. Instead, it is expected that vaccines will be stockpiled and reserved for emergency use or deployed in a few limited "hot zones". At the time of investments, uncertainty exists about volumes needed to stockpile and replenish a certain vaccine, and meeting stockpiling needs may be insufficient to recoup R&D investments and earn profits.

A second important factor deterring participation in R&D of EIDs is that clinical testing of a vaccine must be initiated in response to an outbreak of the disease. The risk exists that during an outbreak, clinical trials are delayed so much that an epidemic might be waning by the time the trials are initiated. If an insufficient number of events is observed, clinical trials will be unable to demonstrate conclusive evidence for efficacy. For example, in the midst of the Ebola outbreak in 2014–15, three phase III trials were initiated in Liberia, Sierra, and Guinea. Only one of these trials—the *Ebola Ça Suffit!* ring vaccination trial in Guinea—was able to successfully demonstrate efficacy (Box 2). The other two trials—the PREVAIL trial in Liberia and the STRIVE trial in Sierra Leone—were unable to determine vaccine efficacy due to a rapid decline in number of cases in these states.[20]

Reducing the time from the beginning of an outbreak until a safe vaccine is available for clinical evaluation requires, in addition to an available vaccine, agreement on scientifically sound, feasible, and ethically acceptable ways of testing vaccines during a public health emergency.[21] The planning and execution of already expensive clinical trials therefore becomes more complicated, and implementation must occur under challenging conditions.

These factors explain why an effective vaccine for Ebola was unavailable prior to the 2015 epidemic, despite seven vaccines having been tested in monkeys with encouraging results prior to the epidemic.[22] It is worth noting that the rVSV-ZEBOV Ebola vaccine was invented by researchers from the Public Health Agency of Canada in 2003, and had very promising animal results already in 2005.[23] The vaccine was later licensed to the biopharmaceutical company NewLink Genetics in 2010. Due to the lack of commercial incentives, further development and testing in healthy humans was not initiated until after the Ebola outbreak had intensified and high-income countries had begun to fly back health workers infected with Ebola.[24]

---

[20] Kennedy et al. (2016), CDC (2016).

[21] Folayan et al. (2016).

[22] Marzi and Feldmann (2014).

[23] Jones et al. (2005).

[24] Attaran and Nickerson (2014).

Box 2. Successful testing of an Ebola vaccine in Guinea

During the WHO's first high-level Ebola vaccine meeting in October 2014, plans were drawn to test Ebola vaccine candidates in Sierra Leone and Liberia. Guinea, where the outbreak began, was initially thought to be too challenging a setting for assessing a vaccine. However, Guinea asked to be part of the Ebola vaccine development effort, and options for clinical trials designs for Guinea were discussed during an informal side meeting. Informed by data on safety, induction of potentially protective immune response, and availability of vaccine doses, the recombinant vesicular stomatitis virus Ebola vaccine (rVSV-ZEBOV) was selected as the vaccine candidate. This vaccine was originally developed by the Public Health Agency of Canada, and licensed to NewLink Genetics. To develop, manufacture, and distribute the vaccine candidate, Merck entered into an exclusive licensing arrangement with NewLink Genetics in November 2014. A consortium of the WHO, the Ministry of Health in Guinea, the Norwegian Institute of Public Health, and Médecins sans Frontières (MSF) lead the implementation of the trial, which also involved a trial team with representatives from a number of academic institutions. Phase 1 testing of the rVSV-ZEBOV vaccine candidate was planned prior to the October vaccine meeting, and was undertaken in Germany, Kenya, Gabon, and Switzerland over the next months. By January 2015, funding for an efficacy trial in Guinea was secured from a number of sources.

A novel clinical trial design—the 'ring vaccination trial'—was adopted. Under this design, direct contacts of a person newly diagnosed with Ebola, as well as contacts of contacts, constitute an epidemiologically defined ring. This ring is randomised to either an intervention group receiving immediate vaccination or a control group receiving delayed vaccination after 21 days (the incubation period in which 95% of EVD cases arise). The ring vaccination trial is based on smallpox eradication strategy. The efficacy trial in Guinea began already four months after the first discussions about a potential trial had been held. In July 2015, the consortium released results from an interim analysis demonstrating 100% vaccine efficacy. Final results published 1.5 years later confirmed these results. No cases of Ebola cases were recorded 10 days or more after vaccination among the 5837 people who received the vaccine. In comparison, there were 23 cases 10 days or more after vaccination among those who did not receive the vaccine.

Ultimately, the successful testing of this vaccine gave rise to two major lessons. Firstly, if phase 1 and phase 2 trials of the Ebola vaccine had been conducted prior to the epidemic, the vaccine could have been tested more quickly, probably as much as six months earlier, and even contributed to halting the spread of the epidemic.[25] It was

---

[25]Røttingen and Godal (2015).

therefore recognised that R&D preparedness—understood as innovation, advancement, and production of vaccine candidates that are stockpiled and ready for testing
prior to an epidemic—needs strengthening. Secondly, testing of vaccines in response
to an outbreak requires clarity in advance about issues such as manufacturing capacity to meet the needs of an epidemic, feasibility, scientific value, ethical acceptability
of clinical trial designs, and a clear regulatory pathway towards approval. In other
words, the R&D response too needed to be strengthened (Box 3). Together, R&D
preparedness and R&D response represent areas that must be addressed to provide
the global public good of preventing future epidemics.

> **Box 3. R&D response—accelerating R&D and clinical evaluation
> of a vaccine in an outbreak**
> Since phase 3 trials testing vaccine efficacy only can be initiated during an
> EID outbreak, CEPI will have to be part of a concerted effort with various
> stakeholders—including the WHO, governments, vaccine manufacturers, and
> global vaccine purchasers such as GAVI—to establish vaccine stockpiles that
> can be maintained and ready for potential emergency use. Even if stockpiles
> are established, the risk exists that clinical trials are delayed so much that an
> epidemic might be waning and almost over by the time the trials are initiated.
> As a consequence, clinical trials may not be able to demonstrate statistically
> significant effects. For example, during the recent Ebola outbreak, several vac-
> cine trials were not completed due to the declining number of new Ebola cases
> at the time when trials were initiated. Reducing the time from the beginning
> of an outbreak until a safe vaccine is available for clinical evaluation there-
> fore requires clarity on a number issues, such as agreement on manufacturing
> capacity, agreement on scientifically sound, feasible, and ethically acceptable
> ways of testing vaccines, a clear regulatory pathway in the states in which
> the vaccines are to be tested, and agreement on how clinical trials are to be
> coordinated and how data is to be shared.

What then explains the world's inability to achieve this? Part of the explanation is
provided by the lack of market potential for EIDs, as described above. Fully explaining why no Ebola vaccine was available prior to 2015, or vaccines for other EIDs for
that matter, requires also examining the public good characteristics of the benefits
of R&D preparedness and R&D response. The classic challenge encountered by all
public goods is that they are under-supplied since their two key properties—non-
rivalry and non-excludability—prevent actors from capturing the full benefits from
investing in them. Market mechanisms therefore frequently fail to provide public
goods. A collective failure to provide the good results if no actor is willing to bear
the costs of providing them. At the national level, governments and public authorities
may use policies such as taxation, statutes, and regulations to provide public goods
that are undersupplied by market forces. At the global level, no institutions exist to
coerce national governments to contribute to the supply of global public goods, and

nor does there exist a single global institution that is entrusted authority and financial resources to provide for such goods.

To fill this vacuum, a number of institutions has been established at the global level to organise and work out the details of international cooperation around specific issues such as environmental change, financial regulation, and global health R&D—issues that exceed the capacity of national governments to address alone, and which require coordination and collaboration between public and private actors.[26] The establishment of CEPI is born out of this recognition—that there is a need for a global institution to operate in the space between public and private actors in order to strengthen collaboration, coordination, and the sharing of risks. In the following two sections, we will examine how CEPI may mobilise and engage with these two groups of actors in order to strengthen R&D preparedness and R&D response.

3   Incentivising the Private Sector to Strengthen Global Health Security

Public goods and global public goods have in general been linked to the state as a provider and public financing as the main strategy for increasing provision.[27] However, in many fields the private sector may play a crucial role for the provision of public goods given the right incentives from governments. In R&D, factors necessitating the involvement of the private sector include their existing intellectual property and know-how, R&D capabilities, manufacturing capacity, and systems for distributing vaccines. Incentivising private innovators to participate in partnerships to develop vaccines against EIDs will therefore prove vital to strengthening global health security. CEPI will fill a gap in the vaccine development pipeline (Fig. 1), and channel increased public and philanthropic financing in order to share the risk of R&D.

Attracting private innovators to CEPI's public mission will require attention to two factors. Firstly, private innovators must perceive an acceptable level of risk of engaging in vaccine development against EIDs.[28] CEPI's main risk-sharing strategy will be to invest directly in projects that move candidate vaccines from preclinical research through phase I and II trials, and thereby substantially reduce the total R&D cost to private innovators. Secondly, private innovators can be incentivised to engage if there is commercial potential in addition to the public objectives. For some EIDs, a commercial market may exist for the vaccine in high-income states. For example, a vaccine may become profitable in the travel vaccines market in addition to protecting populations in states where an epidemic most likely will strike. Vaccine manufacturers may also see an opportunity to receive funding to develop vaccines on new platforms that may be later applied to develop vaccines with commercial

---

[26] Kaul (2013), Ötker-Robe (2014).

[27] Inge Kaul, 'Public Goods: Taking the Concept to the twenty-first Century' http://www.yorku.ca/drache/talks/pdf/apd_kaulfin.pdf.

[28] Kettler and Towse (2002).

Fig. 1 CEPI's gap-filling role in vaccine development for EIDs

potential, in addition to the public objective funded by CEPI. In other cases where similar market opportunities are non-existent, a return on investment will depend on global financing bodies such as GAVI stepping in and procuring the vaccines at prices above the marginal cost of production.

From the public's point of view, investing public funds to reduce private innovators' economic risk of R&D risks spending scarce public resources on unsuccessful projects. A complementary strategy for CEPI is therefore to implement some incentives that enhance the value of the EID vaccine market without exposing public funds to the risk of failure. This could be achieved by implementing "pull" incentives that reward outputs of R&D instead of paying for R&D inputs.[29] One example is the milestone premium where innovators are rewarded for successfully completing predefined scientific milestones. At the time of writing, CEPI plans to implement a strategy where it only will provide additional funding for the next phase of vaccine development if milestones are met. If a project fails, no further investments are made and the project is discontinued.

In theory, CEPI could also experiment with larger milestone and end-stage prizes to motivate vaccine development. Such prizes have the benefit of making publicly financed incentives accessible for a broader range of actors without specifying the scientific route to success, which may be an advantage for vaccines in early-stage development. Over time, it can be expected that CEPI—in coordination with other funding entities—will implement a broader range of innovation incentives to motivate private investment in EID vaccines.

It should be recognised that CEPI plans in addition to make non-financial contributions to reduce uncertainties in EID vaccine development. This includes working with stakeholders to achieve a more predictable regulatory pathway, optimising coordination and data sharing, and facilitating interaction with regulatory authorities of states where the vaccines are likely to be tested. Over the past 15 years, a number of

---

[29]Kremer and Glennerster (2016).

different public-private partnerships such as the Drugs for Neglected Disease initiative and the Medicines for Malaria Venture have been established to address market failures affecting R&D for neglected diseases.[30] These too have pooled private and public resources to pursue publicly defined objectives, and to achieve mutually beneficial goals.[31] Examining the experience and lessons from these initiatives suggest three broader areas where CEPI could make valuable contributions.

The first is diversifying the range of actors engaged with vaccine development against EIDs, and strengthening global R&D capacity in this area. By implementing the incentives described above, it is reasonable to expect that multinational vaccine manufacturers will bring crucial know-how, manufacturing facilities, and platform technologies to the table. Leading multinational vaccine manufacturers have already actively been engaged as part of CEPI's establishment.[32] Three additional groups could potentially add value to CEPI's mission. The first group is small to medium-sized commercial vaccine companies, biotechs and contract manufacturing organisations (CMOs). The second group is the members of the vaccine-industry alliance The Developing Countries Vaccine Manufacturers' Network (DCVMN), who have an increasingly important role in meeting the global demand for vaccines as well as developing novel ones.[33] A testament to their role is that of 2.4 billion doses of vaccines procured by UNICEF in 2015, 60% were sourced from DCVM.[34] Finally, CEPI can also work with existing government-run and publicly funded non-profit organisations that have know-how and expertise on vaccine development and manufacturing capabilities. These have traditionally been set up to focus on meeting national public health needs. By engaging with CEPI, their expertise could be leveraged to meet global needs. One concrete example is the Centers for Innovation in Advanced Development and Manufacturing. This centre was set up as a private-public private partnership with the U.S. Department of Health and Human Services Biomedical Advances Research and Development Authority (BARDA). It is part of the US national strategy to strengthen manufacturing capacity to respond to various biological threats including novel and previously unrecognised infectious diseases, as well as chemical, biological, radiological and nuclear threats.[35] BARDA suggested during the establishment of CEPI that it could work with CEPI's partners to produce vaccines using vaccine platforms supported by the Center.[36]

A second area where CEPI can meaningfully contribute is in demonstrating that coordination and collaboration between public and private actors motivated by a public objective can optimise the use of available knowledge and intellectual property, reduce duplication and waste and deliver R&D at costs lower than has been observed for vaccine development under a commercial model. It has for long been considered

---

[30]DNDi (2014), MMV (1999).

[31]DNDi (2014).

[32]CEPI (2017–2021).

[33]Pagliusi et al. (2017).

[34]Ibid.

[35]Ravi and Adalja (2017).

[36]CEPI (n 32).

that the public sector's role in R&D is primarily in preclinical research and early-stage discovery, and that know-how, resources and skills to translate these findings to biomedical products are the prerogative of private innovators. However, public-private partnerships (PPPs) established to address the market failure for neglected diseases have demonstrated otherwise. For example, between 2003 and 2016, DNDi drove R&D and marketing approval of six drugs targeting neglected diseases (sleeping sickness, malaria, Chagas's disease, and kala-azar), and has estimated that on average it can develop drugs for between \$110 million and \$170 million.[37] This is around one tenth of the average cost of developing a drug according to estimates based on proprietary data from pharmaceutical companies, though it should be noted that these estimates are controversial.[38] Another example is the MenAfriVac vaccine against meningitis, which cost \$50 million to develop—again much lower than the cost usually required to bring a new vaccine to market.[39]

Finally, a third area where CEPI can contribute both intellectually and through action is in advancing the debate on how to maximise public benefits of publicly-funded research. One specific issue concerns norms guiding decisions to transfer intellectual property and know-how of publicly-funded vaccines and other health technologies to private innovators. A recent example reigniting this debate is the decision by the US Department of Defense to grant an exclusive licence of a Zika vaccine to the pharmaceutical company Sanofi Pasteur.[40] This vaccine was originally developed with public funding by scientists at the Walter Reed Army Institute of Research.[41] In this case, the major objection raised by Médecins Sans Frontières (MSF) and other civil society organisations is that the license has been issued without conditions that secure affordability and access to the vaccine.[42] One concern is that the patent monopol can be abused to charge prices that drive vaccines out of reach for populations who need them. Another concern is that exclusive licensing may unnecessarily delay the entry of competitive suppliers that can manufacture and distribute the vaccine to geographic regions with unmet needs. Finally, exclusive licensing can be a barrier to accessing intellectual property and know-how in order to enhance the characteristics of the vaccine so as to make these more effective in low-resource settings (such as developing more heat-stable versions). Non-governmental organisations, such as MSF and Knowledge Ecology International, have consistently claimed that exclusive licenses are unnecessary, and that the development of vaccines and other publicly funded research could be concluded by public and private actors by sharing the costs of finalising R&D.[43]

CEPI will operate along the lines of such a model. Governments and philanthropic foundations will originally have financed many promising vaccine candidates CEPI

---

[37]Maxmen (2016).

[38]DiMasi et al. (2016), Maxmen (2016).

[39]WHO (2010).

[40]Doctors Without Borders (2017a).

[41]Barbero et al. (2017).

[42]Doctors Without Borders (2017b).

[43]Doctors Without Borders (2017c), Knowledge Ecology International (2017).

decides to invest in. Public and philanthropic investments channelled through CEPI can move these vaccines from preclinical research and early-stage discovery through phase 1 and phase 2 trials. It is expected that phase 3 trials, too, will be financed by public and philanthropic actors. In these cases, there exist fair arguments for setting conditions for affordability and access at the time when CEPI invests in them, and that these conditions follow the vaccine through its development stages. In some cases, CEPI and other funders could together make a claim for vaccines being priced close to the marginal cost of production.

CEPI's policy on equitable access—approved for a one-year trial period and released in February 2017 after several months of discussions internally as well as with other PDPs, universities, civil society organisations, and private innovators[44]—considers many of these issues, and sets out a number of guiding principles for managing them.[45] One key principle is that intellectual property will be managed as a strategic tool to ensure that vaccines are made affordable and available, while maintaining the incentives for private innovators to participate. This is similar to approaches taken by other PDPs.[46] A second principle is that CEPI, while recognising that an affordable price range may not be possible to determine at an early stage when there are uncertainties around the vaccine development process, still will work with partners to establish a transparent and agreed method for determining the price. This includes considering different sources of information, including information about public and philanthropic contributions to vaccine development costs, cost of goods, expected scale of production, price of existing comparable products, cost of maintaining manufacturing capacity, and procurement agreements. A major concern is ensuring that public and philanthropic investments in R&D is reflected in the final price of the vaccine. A third principle is that knowledge generated through CEPI's investments should be considered global public goods, and accordingly, CEPI should therefore promote and encourage open access to knowledge and sharing of data in publicly available databases.

More than 80 organisations and over 200 individuals collaborated to create CEPI.[47] It is expected that CEPI over time will engage with many more public and private actors. DNDi, for example, engaged in over 350 collaborations in 43 states over its first ten years, including over 50 universities and research institutes.[48] A crucial role played by CEPI is that of an "honest broker", in the form of a neutral, central entity that build trust and foster collaboration between the public and private actors.[49] Legal and operational independence from collaborating partners and independent decision-making processes will therefore be crucial to act in the interest of its public mission, and to strengthen legitimacy as a global mechanism for

---

[44] It is worth noting that after this chapter was written, CEPI has initiated a process to review and if necessary revise its equitable access policy, based on lessons learned from the one-year trial period.

[45] CEPI (2017).

[46] Kettler and Towse (2002).

[47] Røttingen and others (n 3).

[48] DNDi (n 21).

[49] Goldman (2012).

ensuring global health security. A crucial role will have to be played by national governments—a topic to which we turn next.

4 CEPI—An Agent for Mobilising Shared Responsibilities for Global Health Security?

As of September 2017, a group of high-income states—Australia, Belgium, Canada, Germany, Japan, and Norway—have committed to fund CEPI together with the major philanthropic foundations the Wellcome Trust and the Gates Foundation. The European Commission has committed to using its own funding instruments to invest in joint efforts with CEPI. In addition, The Government of India—one of CEPI's founding partners—is finalising its level of commitment.

Most other PDPs and global R&D organisations have until now relied on financial contributions from OECD states and philanthropic foundations. For example, DNDi's list of public institutional donors includes nine OECD states, and public funding from only two non-OECD states, Brazil and South Africa.[50] Similarly, MMV lists nine OECD states as funders, and not a single non-OECD state.[51] UNITAID, which focus on market-interventions to increase access to drugs for HIV/AIDS, malaria and tuberculosis, has broader support, with low- and middle-income countries (LMICs) contributing with financial resources generated by an airline levy. However, analysis of financial streams to UNITAID between 2006 and 2011 has shown that high-income states and the Gates Foundation were responsible for 95.8% of UNITAID's funding.[52] The beneficiaries of these initiatives are primarily populations in LMICs, although it can be argued that increasing the availability of treatments for neglected diseases also brings benefits to populations in high-income states. It is, however, not unreasonable to argue that the main motivation for these initiatives has been to meet humanitarian needs in LMICs.

In contrast, CEPI explicitly frames its mission as a shared interest for all states. At present, it may be fair to view CEPI as a step initiated by a smaller group of participants, with the aim of mobilising greater support.[53] For CEPI to be successful over the longer term, there are several reasons why a vigorous effort to broaden the scope of participation—including mobilising participation from LMICs—will be vital. The first is legitimacy: moving towards greater or full participation strengthens CEPI's legitimacy as global mechanism for joint-decision making. The second is sustainability: greater participation avoids the supply of a global public good from depending on a small group of states, and so avoids the political risks associated with such an arrangement. Increasing the number of states investing in CEPI can have a catalytic effect by incentivising contributions from other states from the same

---

[50]DNDi (2017).

[51]MMV (2017).

[52]Center for Global Development (2013).

[53]Ötker-Robe (n 18).

region. In addition, involving LMICs may avoid CEPI's mission being framed as only a responsibility of bilateral development agencies and official development assistance (ODA), or only a health security issue for high-income states. There are two reasons why the latter may be beneficial. One is to avoid limiting the sources and channels of funding from which CEPI's mission could be financed. The second is that allocating the responsibility for financing CEPI's mission to ODA funds alone can risk diverting resources from other pressing priorities in LMICs.[54]

Broadening the scope of states depends on the willingness of national governments to share the responsibility for investing in a global institutional response. To achieve this objective, a number of factors affecting this willingness needs to be addressed. First of all, CEPI will—similarly to other international institutions set up to address global public goods—face the temptation of states to freeride on the contributions of others. If a small group of states invests in CEPI to develop vaccines, other states may benefit from the prevention of epidemics without incurring any costs. Some proposals for overcoming collective action failures, such as the club mechanism for climate change proposed by William Nordhaus, argue in favour of a voluntary group to cooperate to derive mutual benefits from sharing the costs of producing a global public good, and that non-participants are penalised in the form of trade or financial sanctions.[55] However, most proposals operate with voluntary participation as a precondition for cooperation between sovereign actors, and CEPI too follows this path. The large number of environmental treaties negotiated by the UN system indicates willingness on part of sovereign states to share the costs of international cooperation.

Remote and uncertain benefits generate another prominent factor explaining why willingness may be low. This is especially a challenge for CEPI. Investing in vaccines against EIDs is, with a few exceptions, a matter of mitigating future risks. We do not know when the next epidemic will strike, and if vaccines developed through CEPI's investments actually will be put to use. In addition, the burden of disease directly attributable to EID outbreaks is low. Many other health challenges—child and maternal health, HIV/AIDS, and non-communicable diseases—cause continuous concern to policymakers and health professionals in all states. Politicians may therefore be unwilling to prioritise upfront expenditures to address uncertain future risks amidst other pressing challenges, especially if there are political risks associated with redirecting resources. Yet studies of previous epidemics suggest that the disruptive effect of epidemics on communities and states leads to total costs that exceed the cost of mitigation. In addition, the health impact of an outbreak may go well beyond the burden of disease directly attributable to the actual pathogen (Box 4). In their assessment of the international response to the Ebola outbreak, Save the Children identified the amount committed by external donors to fight Ebola in Sierra Leone, Guinea, and Liberia to be fifteen times the annual national health budgets of the three states combined, and three times the cost of ensuring essential

---

[54]Guillamount (2002).
[55]Nordhaus (2015).

healthcare for the populations in these states.[56] Overall, there is sound evidence for investing in epidemic preparedness to prevent future risks, and accordingly, CEPI has been framed as an insurance policy to protect against the human and financial risks of future epidemics.[57]

The concern for equity bolsters the case for making upfront investments. Mortality and morbidity from epidemics and pandemics tend to be distributed unequally, both between states (as observed for Ebola and Zika), and within states, including high-income states.[58]

Box 4. Disruption, aversion behaviour and the economic and health impact of the 2014–15 West African Ebola outbreak

In the context of an epidemic, aversion behaviour refers to behaviour resulting from the fear of being exposed to the pathogen. Reduced economic activity, cautious investors, and closure of businesses may be the result of individuals avoiding exposure to the disease. Governments often also exercise aversion behaviour by overestimating risks and imposing unwarranted restrictions on travel and trade. The World Bank estimated the foregone short-term economic output in 2014 due to Ebola in Guinea, Liberia, and Sierra Leone to be over US$300 million. The cost of health care, forgone productivity of people directly affected by the epidemic, and the behaviour of other actors—such as trading partners—were suggested to be the main explanatory factors. The loss in GDP in 2015 was estimated to be US$1.6 billion in the three most affected states. Neighbouring states, too, were reported by the World Bank to experience adverse economic impacts of the epidemic. Moreover, the disease can cause disruption of health care systems—often in already fragile and low-resourced settings—and reduce access to diagnostic services and treatments for other healthcare conditions in affected areas. Modelling based on cross-sectional surveys, interviews, and malaria indicators between 2011 and 2014 suggested that Ebola-affected areas observed a greater number of malaria deaths. The same areas also observed growing risk of outbreaks of vaccine-preventable diseases such as measles and pertussis due to childhood vaccinations being disrupted during the Ebola outbreak. Studies have also observed 20% nation-wide drop in in-hospital deliveries and C-sections during the Ebola outbreak, indicating a likely indirect impact of the epidemic on maternal mortality.

In addition, a case for CEPI can be made from intergenerational equity—a general concept of fairness between generations, which frequently has been invoked in response to climate change and environmental degradation to argue that the present

---

[56] Save the Children (2015).

[57] Yamey et al. (2017); Brende and others (n 5).

[58] Mamelund (2006), Grantz et al. (2016).

generation has a moral responsibility for protecting future generations from disproportionately experiencing the harmful consequences.[59] Invoking the concept for epidemic preparedness and protection against infectious diseases would make the case that present generation has benefited from vaccines developed by the previous generation, and accordingly, the present generation should do the same for future generations. Moreover, since vaccine development takes a long time, and the present generation has experienced the consequences of outbreaks and acquired knowledge about the value of vaccines in preventing such outbreaks, the present generation should be compelled to invest today for the sake of preventing human suffering in the future.

Even when the costs and benefits of mitigating a future risk is well understood, uncertainty about the benefits of the proposed policy response, namely cooperation through an international institution, may be a factor impeding collective action.[60] CEPI will therefore have to make a convincing case to states that the benefits of investing in R&D together, and entrusting CEPI with the authority to manage and allocate these resources will yield more benefit and be less costly than investments made by states on their own. The benefits will have to be clearly and quickly demonstrated in the form of vaccines developed and stockpiled over the next five years, and contributions to an effective response if a pathogen targeted by CEPI becomes the cause of an epidemic.

CEPI must also ensure that its decision-making processes are fair and that it grants all investors as well as other states at high risk of epidemics an effective voice, and truly represents an instrument for joint decision-making.[61] CEPI may gain over the longer term from early and active involvement of states that have not yet invested in its mission, since participation may increase exchange of information about the benefits of cooperation, and over time incentivise contributions from non-participants. To this end, CEPI's governance bodies are composed of not only representatives from states that have committed financially during its establishment, but also have allocated seats for states that will be crucial for local manufacturing, surveillance, implementing clinical trials, and other areas of R&D preparedness and response. On an operational level, CEPI is also engaging with the states that are likely to be most affected by outbreaks of the prioritised diseases, and has sought input on how to improve vaccine development projects giving due consideration to implementation, engagement, and partnership needs in affected states.

The factors described above can be considered equally relevant for all states. Two additional factors are important for CEPI consider with respect to participation from LMICs. One is the ability to demonstrate that CEPI's mission is fully aligned with the interests and priorities of LMICs, and not driven by the interests of high-income states. A danger with the concept of "global health security" is that, instead of being associated with a concern for the collective security of people across all nations, it is understood as an agenda prioritising interventions (such as vaccines) to protect

---

[59] Beckerman (1997).

[60] Ötker-Robe (n 18); Kaul, 'Global Public Goods: Explaining Their Underprovision' (n 8).

[61] Kaul, *Global Public Goods* (n 18).

high-income states from diseases that emerge from LMICs.[62] It may therefore be strategically valuable for CEPI to align its notion of global health security with "human security"—a concept placing emphasis on people over states with a particular concern for the most vulnerable populations.[63] There may also be a concern that an emphasis on vaccines alone displaces attention and resources from strengthening public health capacities, general health services, and the push towards universal health coverage. While it is not part of CEPI's mission to engage in these areas, CEPI can still contribute to strengthening capacity for vaccine development, testing and manufacturing in LMICs. For LMICs, efforts that boost technical know-how and vaccine manufacturing capacity reduce the dependence and vulnerability of relying on multinational manufacturers for availability and accessibility of vaccines. Moreover, increasing vaccine manufacturing capacity in LMICs contributes towards increasing overall global production capacity in the event of a future epidemic or pandemic. When different partnership models were reviewed prior to the establishment of CEPI, it was noted that achieving equitable distribution of benefits would require broadening the base of vaccine manufacturers across LMICs and increasing their capacity for scale-up manufacturing, including implementing appropriate arrangements for technology transfer. CEPI has publicly signalled an intent to work with LMICs and to be a mechanism for transfer of knowledge and expertise for strengthening capacity for vaccine development and testing.[64] CEPI has also actively engaged with the DCVMN, including being present at their annual general meeting in 2016.[65] Moreover, CEPI's policy on securing equitable access to vaccines stipulates that CEPI will seek to reach agreement on arrangements up-front for sub-licensing intellectual property related to the vaccine candidate and accessing know-how, trade secrets and other undisclosed knowledge in order to achieve equitable access obligations.[66] At the time of writing, CEPI has not more specifically described how it will move forward with respect to setting up technology transfer arrangements. It is expected that arrangements will develop over time as CEPI gains experience negotiating individual contracts with its grantees.

To inform such arrangements, experience from previous models for technology transfer of vaccine technologies is worth noting.[67] The International Technology Platform for Influenza Vaccines was established in 2008 with support from WHO and hosted by the Netherlands Vaccine Institute both to provide training in influenza vaccine development and manufacturing to inexperienced grantees from LMICs, and to facilitate technology transfer.[68] The hub was set up as part of implementing the 2006 WHO Global Action Plan for Influenza Vaccines, which included the objective

---

[62]Rushton (2011).

[63]Labonté (2014).

[64]Hatchett (2017).

[65]Pagliusi et al. (2017).

[66]CEPI (2017).

[67]WHO (2011).

[68]Hendriks et al. (2011), Grohmann et al. (2016).

of transferring influenza vaccine production technology to manufacturers and governments in LMIC in order to reduce the overreliance of vaccine manufacturers in high-income states, and strengthen the capacity needed to protect the global population in the event of a pandemic. CEPI is unlikely to hold similar levels of in-house capacity needed to serve as a technology transfer "hub" by its own, but could pool the knowledge and expertise on vaccine-related technologies and processes of its coalition partners.

Two other models could also be explored. The first would involve CEPI being a facilitator for technology transfer, similar to how WHO and PATH facilitated technology transfer through funding and technical support to Serum Institute of India to develop the MenAfriVac vaccine.[69] The second would involve setting up shared technology platforms where the facilitating entity involves a range of partners to facilitate technology transfer to multiple recipients. Such a platform was set up by PATH to facilitate technology transfer to vaccine manufacturers from Brazil, China, and India for developing new rotavirus vaccines.[70] Finally, it is worth noting that technology transfer should not be seen as something occurring solely between donors in high-income states and recipients in LMICs. With increasing capacity for vaccine R&D and manufacturing among LMICs, CEPI could facilitate technology transfers *between* these states to strengthen epidemic preparedness globally.

A second important factor for mobilising participation from LMICs is to ensure that the benefits of investing in CEPI are equitably shared. Participation may be affected negatively if it has not been duly considered how to secure equitable benefit sharing among states. A telling example is the global influenza network system that operated under the WHO. In 2007, Indonesia objected to sharing virus samples of avian flu and cooperating with the international network, arguing that insufficient attention had been paid to equitable access to the benefits of cooperating (Box 5).[71] As already described, CEPI has paid attention to a number of crucial issues that address concerns for access to vaccines and data sharing.

Box 5. The Pandemic Influenza Preparedness framework: sharing the benefits of international cooperation
An example of a case where the lack of specific mechanisms for benefit-sharing acted as a disincentive to international cooperation is the Global Influenza Surveillance and Response System (GISR, formerly known as the Global Influenza Surveillance Network) coordinated by the WHO. The objectives of this network are to characterise influenza viruses circulating in humans globally, to monitor the evolution of influenza viruses, and to detect and obtain isolates of new influenza viruses infecting humans, paying special attention to

---

[69]Tiffay et al. (2015).

[70]Préaud (2010).

[71]Fidler and Gostin (2011).

viruses with pandemic potential. Through this system, many low- and middle-income states had been sharing influenza viruses with designated laboratories in the US, Australia, the UK, and Japan. It became known that these laboratories had shared viruses with private companies in order for these to develop vaccines without the permission from the states that had provided the samples. The crux of the problem was that these vaccines were later sold at prices unaffordable to many low- and middle-income states. As a consequence, LMICs questioned why they should contribute to sample sharing if their own populations weren't secured access to the benefits of sharing viruses—that is, vaccines at an affordable price. During the emergence of avian influenza (also known as influenza A virus subtype H5N1), Indonesia took the step of not sharing virus specimens with the WHO, and called for greater equity and access to the benefits of sharing influenza viruses with the international network. In response to these concerns and after multilateral negotiations, a new framework for sharing viruses and access to vaccines, the Pandemic Influenza Preparedness (PIP) framework, was established. The framework seeks to ensure that all states benefit equally from sharing influenza virus specimens. In addition, 50% of the running costs of the WHO GISR are covered by influenza vaccine manufacturers that benefit from the use of WHO's surveillance and response network.

While full participation of states may be the long-term objective, it may be unreasonable to expect this over the short term. A meaningful exercise is therefore to consider whether some states should carry a greater responsibility for investing in CEPI, and what norms should guide such contributions. Criteria and norms to guide contributions are relatively underexplored in the field of global public goods in general and global public goods for health in particular. A useful starting point for advancing this discussion is to draw upon insight from the rich literature specifying ethical principles for informing burden- and benefit-sharing arrangements for mitigation and adaptation to climate change.[72] It may particularly be useful to examine the application of the principle of "common but differentiated responsibilities" (CBDR) (Box 6), the burden-sharing norms that follow from this principle, and the appropriateness of these norms to CEPI's mission.[73]

Box 6. Common but differentiated responsibilities

The principle of CBDR was formalised in international environmental law at the United Nations Conference on Environment and Development in 1992. When the principle was originally devised, the burden-sharing framework that followed apportioned limited responsibility to low- and middle-income states, most notably observed by the differentiation between the high-income states

---

[72]Ringius et al. (2002), Méjean et al. (2015), Page (2008).
[73]Pauw et al. (2014).

listed as "Annex 1" parties, and the LMICs listed as "non-Annex 1" parties. This was mainly due to the emphasis placed on the historical contribution to the problem. The proffered justification for differentiating responsibilities this way was that high-income states both contributed more greatly to the problem and benefited economically from higher levels of greenhouse gas emissions in the past, and therefore should bear greater responsibility for addressing the problem. Over time, and with the economic growth and increasing levels of greenhouse gas emissions in LMICs (particularly in China and India), it has become clear that mitigation efforts by high-income states alone will be insufficient to reach global targets, and recent attempts have therefore been made to identify how CBDR can become a more meaningful guiding principle for global climate change agreements. The recent Paris Agreement recognises the principle of CBDR and that high-income states must continue to take the lead in mitigating climate change, but for the first time establishes that all states have the obligation to contribute to mitigating and adapting to climate change.

In connection with climate change, the principle of CBDR recognises two dimensions of the challenge. The first is that the challenge is of concern to all states, and accordingly, the "widest possible cooperation by all states is needed to combat climate change and the adverse effects thereof".[74] The second is that responsibility for addressing this shared challenge should be "differentiated"; that is, some states should bear greater responsibility due to differences in historical contribution to the problem, ability to address the problem, and specific development needs. Global drivers for future epidemics include climate change, international travel, population growth, and urbanisation.[75] The extent to which states contribute to these drivers differ; for the sake of argument, it will be assumed that future epidemics cannot be attributed directly to any form of historical activity by states. We can therefore concentrate on the latter two aspects, which offer more relevant inputs to a potential burden-sharing framework for epidemic preparedness.

An alternative way of thinking about the ability to address the problem is to translate it into a principle of "capacity to pay", which implies two things: firstly, that all states should be considered as potential contributors, but that richer states should pay to address the common challenge based on a principle of solidarity; and secondly, that no state should bear unacceptably high costs, thereby indicating the need to broaden the base of contributors in order to share responsibilities.[76] The second aspect—a concern for development needs—is also relevant to consider in the context of R&D preparedness. LMICs face many pressing challenges which needs to be taken into account, and perhaps adjusted for, when clarifying the expectation for contributions from these states.

---

[74]Ibid.

[75]Bloom et al. (2017).

[76]Ibid., Dellink et al. (2009).

Calls for shared responsibility have also been made in relation to financing of global health R&D. Most notably, the WHO Consultative Expert Working Group (CEWG) on Research and Development concluded in 2012 that all states should commit at least 0.01% of GDP on government-funded health technology-related R&D to meet the specific health needs of LMICs.[77] Relevant to the context of CEPI are the three main arguments that formed the basis of this recommendation. The first was that R&D to meet neglected health needs is not "just a responsibility of development aid or indeed donors", but that there is a need to "reframe the issue away from development assistance".[78] Accordingly, the same target was set for states from all income groups. The second was that R&D efforts should be related to GDP, since this represents the best available measure of ability to pay. The target—0.01% of GDP—was set to increase total public sector R&D spending on health needs of LMICs to US$ 6 billion globally, which at the time would be 0.01% of global GDP.

The CEWG, while calling for participation from all states, did not examine different criteria that indicate the ability to pay in detail, nor how these criteria should relate to other considerations, such as health and development needs. For this purpose, it may be useful to consider contributions from the recent literature examining allocation criteria and contribution norms for financial resources and in-kind contributions for activities aimed at improving health in low- and middle-income states, also known as development assistance for health (DAH).[79] Allocation and eligibility criteria that guide the allocation of DAH are focused on states, and attempt to establish which states have the greatest need for DAH and in which states the allocation of DAH will yield the greatest developmental gains. In the context of CEPI and global public goods, the beneficiaries are not individual states, but the global population. Considering allocation criteria in the same way is therefore not relevant.

With respect to contribution norms, two broad categories may be considered: benefit-related norms, and capacity-related norms.[80] Benefit-related norms indicate that contributions should increase according to the extent to which the contributor benefits from investing in the specific arrangement. The WHO has developed a priority list of EIDs with potential to generate a public health emergency, and for which insufficient or no preventive or curative solutions exist. The latest list, updated in February 2018, includes priority diseases where low- and middle-income states will carry the greatest risk of outbreaks and a disproportionately heavy disease burden, as well as economic burden.[81] Accordingly, these states stand to benefit the most from vaccines against EIDs (assuming that these are available and accessible to populations regardless of ability to pay). Thus, benefit-related norms strengthen the case for contributions from LMICs. However, benefit-related norms must be considered together with capacity-related norms.

---

[77]Røttingen and Chamas (2012).

[78]WHO (2012).

[79]Ottersen et al. (2014, 2017).

[80]Ottersen and others (n 79).

[81]WHO (2017a).

The main capacity-related norm that may guide contributions to DAH, and plausibly also global public goods, is gross national income per capita (GNIpc), where higher GNIpc indicate greater capacity to contribute. In connection with DAH, this criterion has been interpreted as an indicator for the domestic capacity to address health needs without external support.[82] Many low-income states have limited domestic capacity and large health needs for which they rely on external support. Moon has estimated that DAH comprised 31.7% of total health spending in low-income states in 2013, compared with 3.1% in lower-middle-income states, and 0.3% in upper-middle-income states.[83] It may therefore be fair not to expect contributions from low-income states over the short term, but rather expect increased domestic financing to strengthen things like laboratory capacity, surveillance, and other core public health capacities—efforts which also contribute to global health security and CEPI's mission of preventing the spread of epidemics.

Therefore, and in tune with the emerging literature debating the role of middle-income countries (MICs) as funders and/or recipients of DAH, we may focus on the role of these states as potential contributors.[84] According to the World Bank classification, and at the time of writing, there are 108 middle-income states. For many MICs, their mid-level GNIpc indicates some internal capacity to respond to domestic health needs. However, many MICs have also large unmet health needs (almost 70% of the global disease burden), are home to a large proportion of the people living in poverty (over 75%), and have large inequalities in health between income groups. In the context of CEPI and epidemic preparedness, the crux of the matter is to consider whether it is reasonable that these states are called upon to pull weight for vaccine development to secure global health security, or whether it is reasonable that their resources are fully devoted to ensuring priority health services for their own populations first. It here paramount to recognise that MICs represent a heterogeneous group of states which differ widely in capacity to pay and health needs. A starting point for identifying states that should contribute financially to epidemic preparedness can therefore be to identify those states with a GNIpc which indicate ineligibility for DAH. In the case of DAH, it has been argued that a transition zone is needed whereby states gradually move from being ineligible for DAH to becoming funders.[85] This may equally apply to the identification of funders for epidemic preparedness (and other global public goods). The major reason for why such a transition zone can be useful is that one may want to consider mobilising financing only from states with domestic capacity to ensure priority health services for their populations.[86] Directing resources towards CEPI's mission should not introduce harms or impede progress on other areas, referring back to the discussion about how CEPI's mission to strengthen global health security should avoid impeding broader efforts to strengthen general health services, but instead should reinforce these efforts.

---

[82] Ottersen, Moon and Røttingen (n 79).

[83] Moon et al. (2017b).

[84] Ottersen, Moon and Røttingen (n 79); Verbeke and Renard (2011).

[85] Ottersen, Moon and Røttingen (n 79).

[86] Ibid.

Overall, a provisional conclusion may be that CEPI over the short term should expect contributions from high-income states and most upper middle-income states. A strategic choice to be made is whether or not CEPI should operate with an inclusion threshold, above which states should be expected to invest in CEPI's mission. A source of arguments for there being no threshold is maintenance of a focus on CEPI's mission being a shared responsibility for all states.

Moreover, an inclusion threshold based on GNIpc alone will not precisely reflect the significant contributions specific states below a threshold could make, and the benefits these states could get in return. The Government of India is among CEPI's founding members and is expected to contribute financially to CEPI's mission. India's GNIpc of US$1570 in 2015 corresponds to a classification as a lower-middle-income state, placing it well below thresholds that identify upper-middle-income states as funders of DAH.[87] However, India is also an economic powerhouse and emerging donor of development assistance.[88] Through its vaccine industry, India has a significant impact on the global vaccine market, including leading the development of vaccines for meningitis and rotavirus.[89] In addition to financial contributions, India is therefore well positioned to make significant non-financial contributions through the transfer of knowledge and R&D capabilities. India could also expect to benefit domestically, both through the involvement of its vaccine industry, and through the development of vaccines that meet its own public health needs, for example vaccines that protect against Chingunkunya—a virus which caused a large outbreak in New Delhi in 2016.[90] India's investment in CEPI could operate as a benchmark against with other states with similar and higher levels of GNIpc may consider their own contributions.

Finally, a crucial part of discussing whether CEPI can represent a legitimate global response to a shared challenge is discussing how CEPI fits into the broader global health architecture, and above all, how it will relate to the WHO. Similarly to the critique of other global health initiates, it may be argued that CEPI, voluntarily funded by a small group of donor states to focus on a specific problem in global health, draws attention away from strengthening poorly resourced health systems.[91] Moreover, it may be argued that establishing a new institution to strengthen epidemic preparedness challenges the central role of WHO as the world's directing and coordinating authority for health.

Some arguments can be made in defence of CEPI. Historically, the WHO has had a limited role in the financing R&D, but it has played a crucial role as a convenor of partnerships to address underprioritised health needs. Two examples have already been mentioned: the MenAfriVac and Ebola vaccines, where WHO played crucial roles.[92] Another example is the Special Programme for Research and Training in

[87]Ibid.
[88]Piccio (2014).
[89]Kaddar et al. (2014), Bhan et al. (2014).
[90]Donald (2016).
[91]Clinton and Sridhar (2017).
[92]Tiffay and others (n 69).

Tropical Diseases (TDR), which is hosted by WHO (and sponsored by the United Nations Children's Fund (UNICEF), the United Nations Development Programme (UNDP), and the World Bank).[93]

The WHO was closely involved in the establishment of CEPI. The idea of establishing CEPI came, among other processes, out of a consultation meeting on the financing work stream of a WHO process to develop a R&D blueprint for action to prevent epidemics.[94] To ensure a sustained strong relationship between CEPI and WHO, a memorandum of understanding (MoU) was developed and approved by both institutions to clarify the respective roles of each institutions.[95] Importantly, it is expected that CEPI will rely on and be responsive to the WHO's normative functions and leadership, for example on norms for data and sample sharing, liability, and scientifically sound and ethically acceptable clinical trial designs. WHO and its member states have prioritised the issue of R&D against EIDs by approving the R&D blueprint for action to prevent epidemics at the World Health Assembly in 2016.[96] CEPI can therefore also be viewed as an implementation mechanism through which states may act on a priority set by the multilateral system.

5 Conclusion

In this chapter, we have explained the rationale for establishing a new global health institution to generate the global public good of preventing future epidemics from becoming humanitarian crises. CEPI can be considered to add to an evolving global institutional framework for international cooperation to address shared challenges. It is being established at a time when various forms of international cooperation and agreements is facing greater uncertainty. It is therefore crucial that CEPI manages the trust placed in it by demonstrating the value of investing together to address a shared challenge. Over the next 5–10 years, it is hoped that CEPI will have successfully demonstrated to governments, private actors, and civil society organisations that collective action is the preferred strategy for preventing future epidemics and strengthening global health security.

References

Attaran A, Nickerson JW (2014) Is Canada patent deal obstructing Ebola vaccine development? Lancet 384:e61 (London, England)

---

[93] Ridley and Fletcher (2008).

[94] WHO (2016, 2017b).

[95] Memorandum of Understanding between the World Health Organisation and the Coalition for Epidemic Preparedness Innovations (2017).

[96] WHO, 'An R&D Blueprint for Action to Prevent Epidemics. Plan of Action.' (n 94).

Barbero CJ et al (2017) Zika virus purification. Google Patents. https://encrypted.google.com/patents/WO2017109227A1?cl=pt

Beckerman W (1997) Debate: intergenerational equity and the environment. J Polit Phil 5:392

Bhan MK et al (2014) Team science and the creation of a novel rotavirus vaccine in India: a new framework for vaccine development. Lancet 383:2180 (London, England)

Bixler SL, Duplantier AJ, Bavari S (2017) Discovering drugs for the treatment of Ebola virus. Curr Treat Opt Infect Dis 9:299

Bloom DE, Black S, Rappuoli R (2017) Emerging infectious diseases: a proactive approach. Proc Natl Acad Sci U S A 114:4055

Brende B et al (2017) CEPI—a new global R&D organisation for epidemic preparedness and response. Lancet 389:233 (London, England)

CDC (2016) Sierra Leone trial to introduce a vaccine against Ebola (STRIVE) Q&A, 20 Apr 2016. https://www.cdc.gov/vhf/ebola/strive/qa.html. Accessed 10 Oct 2017

CDC (2017) Outbreaks chronology: Ebola virus disease. https://www.cdc.gov/vhf/ebola/outbreaks/history/chronology.html

Center for Global Development (2013) UNITAID. Background paper prepared for the working group on value for money: an agenda for global health funding agencies. https://www.cgdev.org/doc/Silverman_UNITAID_Background.pdf

CEPI (2017–2021) Preliminary Business Plan 2017–2021. http://cepi.net/sites/default/files/CEPI%20Preliminary%20Business%20Plan%20011116.pdf

CEPI (2017) CEPI policy documentation. http://cepi.net/sites/default/files/CEPI%20Policy%20Documentation.pdf

Clinton C, Sridhar D (2017) Who pays for cooperation in global health? A comparative analysis of WHO, the World Bank, the global fund to fight HIV/AIDS, Tuberculosis and Malaria, and Gavi, the vaccine alliance. Lancet (London, England)

Commission on a Global Health Risk Framework for the Future (2016) The neglected dimension of global security: a framework to counter infectious disease crises. http://nam.edu/GHRFreport. Accessed 1 Feb 2016

Dellink R et al (2009) Sharing the burden of financing adaptation to climate change. Glob Environ Change 19:411

DiMasi JA, Grabowski HG, Hansen RW (2016) Innovation in the pharmaceutical industry: new estimates of R&D costs. J Health Econ 47:20

DNDi (2014) An innovative approach to R&D for neglected patients ten years of experience & lessons learned by DNDi. https://www.dndi.org/wp-content/uploads/2009/03/DNDi_Modelpaper_2013.pdf

DNDi (2017) Donors. https://www.dndi.org/donors/donors/. Accessed 10 May 2017

Doctors Without Borders (2017a) US department of defense announces decision to give pharmaceutical corporation exclusive rights on taxpayer-funded Zika vaccine, failing to ensure affordable and sustainable access. http://www.doctorswithoutborders.org/article/us-department-defense-announces-decision-give-pharmaceutical-corporation-exclusive-rights

Doctors Without Borders (2017b) Appeal to the department of defense decision to grant an exclusive license for U.S. Government-Owned Patents on Zika Vaccine Candidate. https://www.doctorswithoutborders.org/sites/usa/files/appeal_dod_zika_vaccine_may_19.pdf

Doctors Without Borders (2017c) Doctors without borders/Médecins Sans Frontières (MSF) comments to the department of defense notice of grant intent to an exclusive license of U.S. government-owned patents on Zika vaccine. https://www.doctorswithoutborders.org/sites/usa/files/msf_comments_to_fr_notice_re_zika_vaccine_candidate_licensing.pdf

Donald C (2016) Delhi has been hit by a Chikungunya epidemic—what is this disease? The conversation, 19 Sept 2016. https://theconversation.com/delhi-has-been-hit-by-a-chikungunya-epidemic-what-is-this-disease-65592. Accessed 10 Oct 2017

Fidler DP, Gostin LO (2011) The WHO pandemic influenza preparedness framework: a milestone in global governance for health. JAMA 306:200

Folayan MO et al (2016) Ebola vaccine development plan: ethics, concerns and proposed measures. BMC Med Ethics 17:10

Goldman M (2012) Public-private partnerships need honest brokering. Nat Med 18:341

Gostin LO et al (2016) Toward a common secure future: four global commissions in the wake of Ebola. PLoS Med 13:e1002042

Grantz KH et al (2016) Disparities in influenza mortality and transmission related to sociodemographic factors within Chicago in the pandemic of 1918. Proc Natl Acad Sci U S A 113:13839

Grohmann G et al (2016) Challenges and successes for the grantees and the technical advisory group of WHO's influenza vaccine technology transfer initiative. Vaccine 34:5420

Guillamount P (2002) Linkages between official development assistance and global public goods. https://pdfs.semanticscholar.org/d8ab/e2b314b7f15b118ca55deb3b15e304fcfec5.pdf. Accessed 13 May 2017

Hatchett R (2017) Op-Ed: Africa needs an insurance policy against future epidemics. CNBC Africa. https://www.cnbcafrica.com/insights/world-economic-forum/wef-africa-2017/2017/05/05/africa-vaccines/. Accessed 5 Oct 2017

Hendriks J et al (2011) An international technology platform for influenza vaccines. Vaccine 29(Suppl 1):A8

Jones SM et al (2005) Live attenuated recombinant vaccine protects nonhuman primates against Ebola and Marburg viruses. Nat Med 11:786

Kaddar M, Milstien J, Schmitt S (2014) Impact of BRICS' investment in vaccine development on the global vaccine market. Bull World Health Organ 92:436

Kamradt-Scott A (2016) WHO's to Blame? The World Health Organisation and the 2014 Ebola Outbreak in West Africa. Third World Q 37:401

Kaul I (2012) Global public goods: explaining their underprovision. J Int Econ Law 15:729

Kaul I (2013) Global public goods: a concept for framing the post-2015 Agenda? Dt Inst für Entwicklungspolitik

Kennedy SB et al (2016) Implementation of an Ebola virus disease vaccine clinical trial during the Ebola epidemic in Liberia: design, procedures, and challenges. Clin Trials 13:49 (London, England)

Kettler H, Towse A (2002) Public private partnerships for research and development: medicines and vaccines for diseases of poverty. Office of Health Economics. https://www.ohe.org/publications/public-private-partnerships-research-and-development-medicines-and-vaccines-diseases. Accessed 13 May 2017

Knowledge Ecology International (2017) KEI/MSF comments to NIH on licensing of patents on attenuated respiratory syncytial virus (RSV) vaccines. https://www.keionline.org/node/2445. Accessed 1 Oct 2017

Kremer M, Glennerster R (2016) Strong medicine. Creating incentives for pharmaceutical research on neglected diseases. Princeton University Press, Princeton

Labonté R (2014) Health in all (foreign) policy: challenges in achieving coherence. Health Promot Int 29(Suppl 1):i48

Mamelund S-E (2006) A socially neutral disease? Individual social class, household wealth and mortality from Spanish Influenza in two socially contrasting parishes in Kristiania 1918–19. Soc Sci Med 62:923

Marzi A, Feldmann H (2014) Ebola virus vaccines: an overview of current approaches. Expert Rev Vaccines 13:521

Maxmen A (2016) Busting the billion-dollar myth: how to slash the cost of drug development. Nature 536:388

Méjean A, Lecocq F, Mulugetta Y (2015) Equity, burden sharing and development pathways: reframing international climate negotiations. Int Environ Agreem Polit Law Econom 15:387

Memorandum of Understanding between the World Health Organisation and the Coalition for Epidemic Preparedness Innovations. http://www.dcvmn.org/IMG/pdf/mou_cepi_-_who.pdf. Accessed 10 Oct 2017

MMV (2017) Our donors. https://www.mmv.org/partnering/our-donors. Accessed 10 May 2017

MMV: New Medicines for Malaria Venture (1999) TDR News 2

Moon S et al (2017a) Post-Ebola Reforms: ample analysis, inadequate action. BMJ (Clin Res ed) 356:j280

Moon S, Røttingen J-A, Frenk J (2017b) Global public goods for health: weaknesses and opportunities in the global health system. Health Econ Policy Law 12:195

Morrissey O, te Velde DW, Hewitt A (2002) Defining international public goods. In: Ferroni M, Mody A (eds) International public goods: incentives, measurement, and financing. Springer, Berlin. https://doi.org/10.1007/978-1-4615-0979-0_2

Nordhaus W (2015) Climate clubs: overcoming free-riding in international climate policy. Am Econ Rev 105:1339

Offit PA (2005) Why are pharmaceutical companies gradually abandoning vaccines? Health Affairs (Proj Hope) 24:622

Ötker-Robe İ (2014) Global risks and collective action failures: what can the international community do? IMF Working Paper. International Monetary Fund

Ottersen T et al (2014) Development assistance for health: quantitative allocation criteria and contribution norms. The Royal Institute of International Affairs. https://www.chathamhouse.org/sites/files/chathamhouse/field/field_document/20140901DevelopmentAssistanceHealthQuantitativeOttersenKamathMoonRottingenRevised.pdf. Accessed 13 May 2017

Ottersen T, Moon S, Røttingen J-A (2017) The challenge of middle-income countries to development assistance for health: recipients, funders, both or neither? Health Econ Policy Law 12:265

Page EA (2008) Distributing the burdens of climate change. Environ Polit 17:556

Pagliusi S et al (2017) Vaccines: shaping global health. Vaccine 35:1579

Pauw P et al (eds) (2014) Different perspectives on differentiated responsibilities: a state-of-the-art review of the notion of common but differentiated responsibilities in international negotiations. Dt Inst für Entwicklungspolitik

Perkins MD et al (2017) Diagnostic preparedness for infectious disease outbreaks. Lancet (London, England)

Piccio L (2014) In latest Indian budget, aid spending dwarfs aid receipts, devex, 24 Feb 2014. https://www.devex.com/news/top-donors-to-india-85708. Accessed 10 Oct 2017

Plotkin SA, Mahmoud AAF, Farrar J (2015) Establishing a global vaccine-development fund. N Engl J Med 373:297

Préaud J-M (2010) ARVAC project: the "enabling platform" model, Nov 2010. http://www.who.int/phi/news/Presentation8.pdf. Accessed 10 Oct 2017

Pronker ES et al (2013) Risk in vaccine research and development quantified. PLoS ONE 8:e57755

Ravi S, Adalja AA (2017) Strengthening the US medical countermeasure enterprise for biological threats. Health Secur 15:12

Ress MA (2013) Global public goods, transnational public goods: some definitions. Knowledge Ecology International. https://www.keionline.org/node/1790. Accessed 6 Oct 2017

Ridley RG, Fletcher ER (2008) Making a difference: 30 years of TDR. Nat Rev Microbiol 6:401

Ringius L, Torvanger A, Underdal A (2002) Burden sharing and fairness principles in international climate policy. Int Environ Agreem 2:1

Røttingen J-A, Chamas C (2012) A new deal for global health R&D? The recommendations of the consultative expert working group on research and development (CEWG). PLoS Med 9:e1001219

Røttingen J-A, Godal T (2015) Speeding up epidemic emergency response. Science 350:170 (New York, NY)

Røttingen J-A et al (2017) New vaccines against epidemic infectious diseases. N Engl J Med 376:610

Rushton S (2011) Global health security: security for whom? Security from what? Polit Stud 59:779

Samuelson PA (1954) The pure theory of public expenditure. Rev Econ Stat 36:387

Samuelson PA (1955) Diagrammatic exposition of a theory of public expenditure. Rev Econ Stat 37:350

Save the Children (2015) A wake-up call. Lessons from Ebola for the World's Health Systems. https://www.savethechildren.net/sites/default/files/libraries/WAKE%20UP% 20CALL%20REPORT%20PDF.pdf. Accessed 5 Oct 2017

Serdobova I, Kieny M-P (2006) Assembling a global vaccine development pipeline for infectious diseases in the developing world. Am J Public Health 96:1554

Tiffay K et al (2015) The evolution of the meningitis vaccine project. Clini Infect Dis Off Publ Infect Dis Soc Am 61(Suppl 5):S396

Verbeke K, Renard R (2011) Development cooperation with middle-income countries. Institute of Development Policy and Management, University of Antwerp. https://ideas.repec.org/p/iob/ wpaper/2011011.html. Accessed 13 May 2011

WHO (2010) Revolutionary new meningitis vaccine set to wipe out deadly epidemics in Africa. http://www.who.int/mediacentre/news/releases/2010/meningitis_20101206/en/

WHO (2011) Increasing access to vaccines through technology transfer and local production. World Health Organisation

WHO (2012) Research and development to meet health needs in developing countries: strengthening global financing and coordination. World Health Organisation

WHO (2016) An R&D blueprint for action to prevent epidemics. Plan of action. World Health Organisation. http://www.who.int/csr/research-and-development/WHO-R_D-Final10.pdf. Accessed 9 May 2017

WHO (2017a) Annual review of the list of priority diseases for the WHO R&D blueprint, Jan 2017. http://www.who.int/emergencies/diseases/2018prioritisation-report.pdf?ua=1. Accessed 27 Sept 2018

WHO (2017b) Outcome document: financing of R&D preparedness and response to epidemic emergencies. http://www.who.int/medicines/ebola-treatment/Outcome.pdf. Accessed 10 Oct 2017

WHO (2017c) Summary of probable SARS cases with onset of illness from 1 November 2002 to 31 July 2003. http://www.who.int/csr/sars/country/table2004_04_21/en/. Accessed 10 Oct 2017

Yamey G et al (2017) Financing of international collective action for epidemic and pandemic preparedness. Lancet Glob Health

Restricting Access to Pathogen Samples and Epidemiological Data: A Not-So-Brief History of "Viral Sovereignty" and the Mark It Left on the World

Michelle F. Rourke

Abstract In 2007 the Indonesian government claimed sovereignty over the H5N1 influenza virus samples isolated within Indonesia's territories, refusing to share those samples with the World Health Organisation. Indonesia's sovereignty claims conflicted with the decades-long practice of sharing influenza samples with the WHO, and was seen as an affront to scientific norms of cooperation and openness. The conflict was ostensibly resolved in 2011 with the introduction of the WHO's Pandemic Influenza Preparedness Framework (PIP Framework), which was intended to secure access to influenza viruses from around the world and effect a fairer distribution of vaccines and other benefits associated with the use of pandemic influenza samples. The problem is, the PIP Framework did not resolve the issues created with the concept of viral sovereignty. In fact, by recognising the sovereign rights of states over this subset of pathogens, the PIP Framework legitimised viral sovereignty as a broader legal norm. Instead of resisting this concept, the WHO quietly acceded to it and reinforced a set of perverse incentives for countries to restrict access to pathogens precisely when those pathogens embody the greatest value: during a public health emergency. This chapter demonstrates that the concept of viral sovereignty did not begin with Indonesia in 2007, and more importantly, it did not end with the PIP Framework in 2011. Despite the term "viral sovereignty" fading into relative obscurity, the concept itself is now an established legal norm that could delay efforts to save lives during epidemics and pandemics.

Keywords Viral sovereignty · Biopiracy · PIP Framework · Virus sharing

M. F. Rourke (✉)
Griffith University Law School, Brisbane, Australia
e-mail: m.rourke@griffith.edu.au

© Springer Nature Switzerland AG 2020
M. Eccleston-Turner and I. Brassington (eds.), *Infectious Diseases in the New Millennium*, International Library of Ethics, Law, and the New Medicine 82, https://doi.org/10.1007/978-3-030-39819-4_8

167

1 Introduction

Viral sovereignty is the concept that virus samples isolated from within the territorial boundaries of a nation state are the sovereign property of that state. The history of viral sovereignty as a concept in international law is always told in the classic three-act narrative structure: the setup, the confrontation, and the resolution. The first act plays out across the latter half of the twentieth century, with the development of the World Health Organisation's (WHO) global network of more than 100 influenza laboratories. The system that became known as the Global Influenza Surveillance Network (GISN)[1] and now known as the Global Influenza Surveillance and Response System (GISRS), depended on the open sharing of influenza viruses from around the world to monitor the spread of seasonal influenza and detect the emergence of novel pandemic strains. The second act is the confrontation, set in 2007 when the Indonesian Health Minister refused to share H5N1 influenza viruses with the GISN, troubled by the fact that the WHO was giving their virus strains to pharmaceutical companies who used them to develop vaccines that were unaffordable to Indonesia and other lower and middle-income countries (LMICs).[2] The Indonesians cited an environmental conservation treaty as the legal basis for claiming sovereignty over the viruses isolated within their territorial borders. This is the time at which the notion of viral sovereignty first entered the public discourse.[3] The standoff between Indonesia and the WHO split global opinion along the old North-South political divide: developed countries were indignant at such a "morally reprehensible" move on Indonesia's part,[4] and developing countries were largely sympathetic to Indonesia's claim.[5] The third and final act is neatly wrapped up by 2011 with the adoption of the WHO's *Pandemic Influenza Preparedness Framework* (PIP Framework). Indonesia was apparently placated and access to influenza viruses with pandemic potential was secured by this "innovative" and "enforceable" international agreement.[6] Viral sovereignty as a concept in law was seen as nothing but a blip on the international radar; a problem both created and resolved in less than five years.[7]

It is a compelling tale, but it is not the whole story. This chapter will provide both a prequel and a sequel to the standard three-act viral sovereignty story. It will demonstrate that while Indonesia was the first to invoke the United Nations' *Convention on Biological Diversity* (CBD) to claim sovereignty over its viruses, it was not the first country to deny the WHO access to influenza viruses. Nor was Indonesia the first to raise the types of distributive justice issues that they framed as access and

---

[1] After the adoption of the *Pandemic Influenza Preparedness Framework* in 2011, the GISN was renamed the Global Influenza Surveillance and Response System (GISRS).

[2] Sedyaningsih et al. (2008).

[3] It appears that the term "viral sovereignty" was originally coined by Holbrooke and Garrett (2008).

[4] Ibid.

[5] See Lange (2012).

[6] Gostin et al. (1918).

[7] For examples of this portrayal of the viral sovereignty tale, see Vezzani (2010).

benefit-sharing (ABS), using the language of the CBD.[8] Furthermore, this chapter will outline some of the viral sovereignty disputes that have played out since the introduction of the PIP Framework in 2011. Far from being the legal resolution to a problem posed by Indonesia in 2007, the PIP Framework is responsible for legitimising the concept of viral sovereignty as a legal norm. The only thing that has really changed since 2011 is the language that the WHO and the rest of the international community uses to discuss viral sovereignty. "Access" to viruses (or other pathogens) is now usually referred to as "sample sharing" or "material transfer". "Benefit-sharing" contracts are now referred to almost exclusively as "material transfer agreements". The term "sovereignty" has fallen out of use altogether, despite becoming an entrenched conceptual norm.

Despite the abundant praise for the PIP Framework, the problem of viral sovereignty remains entirely unresolved. This is not news for anyone working in the realm of pandemic preparedness or involved in responding to international public health emergencies. But the typical three-act portrayal of this saga means that the viral sovereignty issue is depicted as having been settled by the PIP Framework. This is not the case. It should be clearly stated that there is absolutely nothing about or contained within the PIP Framework that could stop a repeat performance of the 2007 viral sovereignty episode today.[9] Meanwhile, the PIP Framework explicitly "recognise[d] the sovereign right of states over their biological resources", making it very difficult for the WHO to fight for a future exemption to this notion for any pathogens that pose a threat to global health. Their reinforcement of sovereign rights over pathogens actually strengthens the incentives for countries to restrict access to dangerous pathogens with the hopes of trading access for related benefits, potentially delaying the global health response to infectious disease outbreaks. Furthermore, the WHO has now extended this notion to data and information related to pathogens, stating that "epidemiologic data belong to the countries where they are generated".[10] Without constant access to up-to-date pathogen samples and epidemiological data, the international public health community is working blindfolded. This chapter aims to demonstrate that viral sovereignty did not start with Indonesia in 2007, and it certainly did not end with the PIP Framework in 2011. The intention is to reinvigorate the conversation about viral sovereignty and the effects that this international legal concept continues to have on infectious disease preparedness and response.

2   The Prequel to Viral Sovereignty

Indonesia's claim of viral sovereignty in 2007 is usually represented as being an unprecedented move on Indonesia's part. What has been lost is that the incident occurred in a contemporary context where nation states had already been exercising

---

[8]Convention on Biological Diversity 1992, Art. 1.
[9]Smith (2012), Bollinger (2015).
[10]World Health Organisation (2015a).

a level of authority over virus samples for years.[11] This first appears in the media coverage about the outbreak of Severe Acute Respiratory Syndrome (SARS) in 2003. One news story published in *Nature* in April 2003 stated that after 23 probable cases of SARS arose in Taiwan, Taiwanese epidemiologists requested Chinese SARS virus samples and related information from the WHO and were reportedly told to instead approach the People's Republic of China.[12] Given the political sensitivities surrounding the relationship between China and Taiwan, it is understandable that the WHO may not have wanted to act as an intermediary to this transfer. This is despite the WHO having the samples in its possession and the supposed custom of free and open sharing of viruses that was said to have existed prior to Indonesia's sovereignty claim in 2007. Thus, there was an implicit acknowledgement that the viruses belonged to China, not the WHO.[13]

In September 2003, Russian news agency Tass reported that "Russian and Chinese Public Health Ministries agreed to share virus samples with each other to study infectious diseases, including SARS" as part of a broader programme "for cooperation in education, culture, public health and sport".[14] Again, this indicates that viruses like SARS were already thought of as belonging to the nation state from which they originated as early as 2003. While the media coverage of virus transfers during the SARS outbreak did not yet embody any notion of sovereign rights over those viruses, there was still an implicit recognition that the originating nations had a level of functional control over their movement and use. In the example between China and Taiwan, this control also extended to the information that was associated with the SARS viruses, not just the physical virus samples themselves.

In April 2004, Japanese scientists reported delays in accessing South Korean samples of influenza viruses.[15] The *Yomiuri Shimbun* story out of Tokyo headlined "DISPUTE OVER OWNERSHIP OF VIRUS COULD COST LIVES" refers to viruses as

---

[11]It is also worth noting the geographical link that is created through the naming conventions for human viruses. Marburg virus, Lassa fever, Ebola, Ross River virus, Barmah Forest virus, Middle Eastern Respiratory Syndrome virus, and Crimean-Congo haemorrhagic fever to name but a few, are all named after the places where the first cases appeared, or the virus was initially isolated. In recent times this has been identified as a "stigmatizing" practice that can result in reputational damage to the virus' namesake (see World Health Organisation, "WHO issues best practices for naming new human infectious diseases" 2015 at http://www.who.int/mediacentre/news/notes/2015/naming-new-diseases/en/) but it does demonstrate the connection of geographical location to virus samples that has existed well before the acknowledgement of sovereign rights over viruses.

[12]Cyranoski (2003).

[13]As an aside, the media coverage of the Human Immunodeficiency Virus (HIV) discovery controversy between Robert Gallo (USA) and Luc Montagnier (France) in the mid to late-1980 sometimes referred French or U.S. virus samples, but this was really just shorthand for what were considered the samples belonging to the French or U.S. research teams. There is no sense from the literature or news reports from the time that these were considered the sovereign property of any nation state. It was, however, a matter of national pride, which did result in both French and U.S. government leaders holding meetings over the dispute. For more information on the Gallo and Montagnier HIV sample dispute, see Ranga (2009) and Singer (1989).

[14]'Russia, China Cooperate in Fighting Infections-Karelova' *ITAR-TASS Information Telegraph Agency of Russia*, 17 September 2003.

[15]Yasuda (2004).

valuable "assets", mentions the "tacit agreement in the world of researchers that a disease agent belongs to whoever found it first", and concludes with the following:

> There currently are no international rules on the exchange of viruses. If researchers cannot work out the common ownership issue themselves, governments will be forced to step in. Negotiations between nations on the matter are expected to be conducted under the auspices of the World Health Organization. Even so, international dialogue between scientists will be an essential part of finding a solution.[16]

In May 2005 another news story in *Nature* stated that it had been "nearly eight months since the [WHO] last saw data on [H5N1 avian influenza virus] isolates from infected poultry in Asia".[17] The article states:

> Affected countries are failing, or refusing, to share their human samples with the WHO's influenza programme in Geneva. The UN Food and Agricultural Organization (FAO) set up a network of labs to collect animal samples last year, but it has not received any for months.[18]

The article did not directly accuse any particular Asian nation of not providing samples, although it did imply that Vietnam was withholding data and samples because it was concerned about "losing control over information".[19] Vietnamese government officials contested the article, stating that they had been sharing information with the WHO since the outbreak of bird flu.[20] The WHO also released a statement about the *Nature* article stating that "[t]here is no refusal to share human samples by Vietnam or any country with avian influenza cases".[21] It is not clear whether the *Nature* article, Vietnamese government officials and the WHO are talking about the same things here. The *Nature* article mentions both human and animal-derived influenza virus samples, the Vietnamese statement refers to information, and the WHO statement refers to human samples. What is clear though, is that there are influenza virus ownership disputes involving multiple countries and UN agencies (WHO and FAO) well before 2007.

The WHO had also published numerous documents referring to virus sharing in the years before 2007. In 2005 the WHO released "Guidance for the timely sharing of influenza viruses/specimens with potential to cause human influenza pandemics".[22] The guideline document included "[p]rinciples for sharing influenza viruses/specimens with the WHO Global Influenza Programme", one of which stated

---

[16] Ibid.

[17] Butler (2005).

[18] Ibid.

[19] Ibid.

[20] Vietnam News Agency (2005).

[21] Ibid.

[22] This document was originally available online at http://www.who.int/csr/disease/avian_influenza/ guidelines/Guidance_sharing_viruses_specimens/en/index.html however, since the dispute with Indonesia in 2007, the document is no longer accessible. See Sedyaningsih et al., above n 2, 21. The Third World Network reproduced the guidance document in Annex 1 to their briefing paper issued in May 2007 "Sharing of Avian Influenza Viruses" which can be accessed at https://web.archive.org/web/20120822191210/, http://www.twnside.org.sg/title2/avian.flu/papers/ avian.flu.twn.briefing.paper.may2007.doc.

that "designated WHO Reference Laboratories will seek permission from the originating country/laboratory to co-author and/or publish results obtained from the analyses of relevant viruses/samples".[23] Another principle stated that "[t]here will be no further distribution of viruses/specimens outside the network of WHO Reference Laboratories without permission from the originating country/laboratory".[24]

In 2005, the 58th World Health Assembly (WHA) adopted Resolution 58.5, urging member states "to facilitate the rapid sharing of clinical specimens and viruses through the WHO Global Influenza Surveillance Network".[25] Then in 2006, the 59th WHA adopted Resolution 59.2 on the application of the International Health Regulations (2005) (IHR 2005). It urged member states to disseminate to WHO collaborating centres information and relevant biological materials related to highly pathogenic avian influenza and other novel influenza strains in a timely and consistent manner.[26]

Clearly this issue was on the radar of the WHO before Indonesia made its move in 2007, only it was not yet labelled viral sovereignty. Furthermore, upon her appointment as Director General of the WHO in 2006, Margaret Chan was asked about the issue of China not sharing influenza samples with the WHO.[27] Chan responded, "I will definitely speak out and urge China to share specimens and information".[28] China resumed sharing viruses with the WHO (via the United States' Center for Disease Control and Prevention) shortly thereafter.[29]

This demonstrates that Indonesia's claim of viral sovereignty in 2007 was not unprecedented. It occurred in a diplomatic context in which many other nation states had exercised control over the viruses isolated from within their territories. Not only that, the arguments that these nations proffered in defence of withholding samples often related to the attribution of credit for their research: credit they felt was unfairly assumed by scientists from other nations using *their* virus isolates.[30] This was nominally addressed by the abovementioned WHO guidelines[31] but was still a major point of contention for the Indonesians in 2007.[32] There was already a growing sense of unease about the informal and unfair sharing practices of the WHO's GISN well before the Indonesians forced the WHO and the rest of the international community to grapple with that unfairness in spectacular fashion.

---

[23] Third World Network (2007, p 17).

[24] Ibid.

[25] World Health Organisation (2005a).

[26] World Health Organisation (2006).

[27] Nebehay (2006).

[28] Ibid. It is interesting to note that in this same news report, Indonesian Health Minister (2004–2009) Dr. Siti Fadilah Supari, spoke positively about Chan's appointment.

[29] Beck (2006).

[30] Butler, above n 17.

[31] Third World Network, above n 23.

[32] Sedyaningsih et al., above n 2, 485.

3 Indonesia's Viral Sovereignty Claim

The WHO's GISN laboratories operate to monitor the spread of seasonal influenza, the background against which the emergence of potentially pandemic strains can be detected. The network relies on the provision of clinical specimens and virus isolates from countries around the world to create risk assessments and recommend candidate vaccine virus strains to vaccine manufacturers.[33] These surveillance activities began in 1952[34] and the WHO had never developed any formal protocols or legal agreements for the sharing of virus samples.[35] The viral inputs to the system had little value to the countries that were contributing the virus samples, whereas the value to the world in having a continuous influenza monitoring system was clearly very high.

The calculus changed for Indonesia in 2006 when the epidemiological situation saw the value of their influenza viruses appreciate. Indonesia had been reporting clusters of human influenza A (H5N1) infections since July 2005.[36] In 2006 the number of new cases spiked to 55 infections, up from 19 the year before.[37] The case fatality rate had also risen to 80.4% from 63.2% in 2005, and in 18% of cases it was unclear if the patient had interacted with sick or dead poultry.[38] These trends were extremely concerning: the data were indicative of the emergence of a more virulent form of H5N1 and the start of human-to-human transmission of a virus that was previously transmitted to humans only through close contact with infected birds.

This is when Indonesia made its move. In December 2006, Indonesian Health Minister, Dr. Siti Fadilah Supari announced that Indonesia was withdrawing its support from the GISN. It would no longer be sharing its virus samples until it could be guaranteed fairer access to the vaccines and antivirals created using them.[39] The Indonesians cited the CBD as the basis for their argument, claiming sovereign control over the influenza viruses isolated within their territory.[40] Since ratifying the CBD in the mid-1990s, Indonesian domestic law required that international transfers of biological materials occurred under material transfer agreements (MTAs), but Indonesia had apparently "made a dispensation and had faithfully shared the specimens to the WHO system".[41] Indonesia highlighted what it saw as the unfair practices of the GISN: expecting individual nations to freely provide the raw materials required by pharmaceutical companies to produce vaccines and antivirals, that were then patented and sold at a profit to those provider nations.[42]

---

[33] Fidler (2008).

[34] World Health Organisation (2015b, p. 1).

[35] Fidler, above n 33, 90.

[36] Sedyaningsih et al., above n 2, 484.

[37] Ibid.

[38] Ibid.

[39] Sedyaningsih et al., above n 2.

[40] Ibid., 485.

[41] Ibid., 487.

[42] The factors that led to Indonesia's withdrawal of support for the GISN have been discussed at length elsewhere. See, for instance, Sedyaningsih et al., Hameiri (2014).

As stated, Indonesia's refusal to share its influenza viruses was not quite as out of the blue as most accounts portray it to have been. What was different this time was that the epidemiological data pointed to Indonesia being the probable emergence site of the next influenza pandemic strain. The thing that could inflict great devastation for Indonesia's people was also the thing that gave the Indonesian government enough leverage to negotiate with the WHO and put them on a better footing to deal with that very possibility. At the time, Indonesia's actions were described as "a form of moral blackmail"[43] and denounced as "morally reprehensible".[44] However, such condemnation failed to acknowledge that domestic governments can be claimed to have "a moral obligation to provide for the health and wellbeing of its citizens".[45]

One other point of difference was the framing of Indonesia's argument. The invocation of the CBD to claim sovereign authority over their virus samples meant that this issue and the ensuing discussions about this issue were couched in the access and benefit-sharing (ABS) language of the CBD. This was significant because the CBD provided a very clear statement about the sovereign rights of nation states over their genetic resources.[46]

4 Viruses and the CBD

The United Nations' CBD was signed at the Rio Earth Summit in 1992 and now has 196 State Parties.[47] It is an environmental conservation treaty with three objectives:

> the conservation of biological diversity, the sustainable use of its components and the fair and equitable sharing of the benefits arising out of the utilization of genetic resources.[48]

It is this third objective, which has been abbreviated to "access and benefit-sharing" (ABS) that was at the core of the Indonesians' sovereignty claims. In order to ensure the "fair and equitable sharing of the benefits arising out of the utilization of genetic resources", the CBD reaffirms "the sovereign rights of states over their natural resources", and clearly states that "the authority to determine access to genetic resources rests with the national governments".[49] In controlling the terms

---

[43] Caplan and Curry (2007). Note that Caplan and Curry also say that Indonesia's "strategy can be seen as innovative, perhaps even courageous".

[44] Holbrooke and Garrett, above n 3.

[45] Bagley (2018). Bagley's article was referring to a separate issue (compulsory licensing) but it is cited here because it so elegantly details the moral obligation of domestic governments to provide for the health of its own citizens.

[46] Indonesia's claim in 2007 might even be considered completely predictable in the context of the ABS discussions underway at other UN bodies (the United Nations Environment Programme and the Food and Agriculture Organisation).

[47] Convention on Biological Diversity, *List of Parties* (2016). https://www.cbd.int/information/parties.shtml.

[48] Convention on Biological Diversity 1992, Art. 1.

[49] Ibid., Art. 15(1).

of access to their genetic resources, countries are able to demand a quid pro quo. This was supposed to address (or perhaps redress) the market failure of conservation, capturing the genetic resources in the sovereign domain of the nation state so that access to those resources could be traded for money or other benefits, ultimately creating an economic incentive to conserve them. This then delivered on the CBD's other objective of sustainable development.

The GISN's continued operation after the adoption and entry into force of the CBD was an implicit statement by the WHO that it did not consider viruses to be within the remit of the CBD.[50] That the GISN informally transferred influenza viruses to privately owned and operated pharmaceutical companies was a further reiteration of this position. Viruses are unequivocally "genetic resources" within the remit of the CBD.[51] But this does not necessarily mean that they should be.[52] The CBD, and its supplementary Nagoya Protocol on Access to Genetic Resources and the Fair and Equitable Sharing of Benefits Arising from their Utilisation (Nagoya Protocol)[53] prescribes a default bilateral ABS system. That is, the party that wants to utilise genetic resources (whether for commercial or non-commercial purposes, including research and development) must obtain "prior informed consent"[54] from the originating nation state[55] and negotiate "mutually agreed terms"[56] for the sharing of associated benefits. This bilateral mode of ABS is cumbersome as it requires parties to negotiate terms anew every time a user party requires access to genetic resources; the process is slow and the transaction costs are high. It is evidently ill-suited to the rapid sharing of ever-evolving pathogens, particularly highly variable RNA viruses like influenza. While the Nagoya Protocol does ask parties to "[p]ay due regard to cases of present or imminent emergencies that threaten or damage human, animal or plant health" this provision on special considerations merely calls for ABS to be "expedited" in such situations; it cannot be ignored.[57] The Nagoya

---

[50]Fidler noted that "State practice under CBD supports the conclusion that CBD does not apply to avian influenza virus. States parties to CBD have addressed avian influenza, not as a biological resource subject to CBD but as a threat to biological diversity". Fidler, above n 33, 91.

[51]Rourke (2017).

[52]In 1995 the COP to the CBD "reaffirm[ed]" that human genetic resources are outside the scope of the CBD, despite neatly fitting the definition of the term provided by the CBD. It reaffirmed this position at the adoption of the Nagoya Protocol in 2010. Convention on Biological Diversity, *Report of the Second Meeting of the Conference of the Parties to the Convention on Biological Diversity* (1995) UNEP/CBD/COP/2/19 Decision II/11, Access to Genetic Resources (para 2); Convention on Biological Diversity, *Report of the Tenth Meeting of the Conference of the Parties to the Convention on Biological Diversity* (2010) UNEP/CBD/COP/10/27 Decision X/1, Access to genetic resources and the fair and equitable sharing of benefits arising from their utilisation (para 5).

[53]The Nagoya Protocol is a voluntary and legally-binding supplementary agreement to the CBD. It was adopted by the Conference of the Parties to the CBD in 2010 and entered into force on 12 October 2014. It currently has 107 parties. See https://www.cbd.int/abs/nagoya-protocol/signatories/default.shtml (accessed 12 October 2018).

[54]Convention on Biological Diversity 1992, Art. 15(5); Nagoya Protocol 2010, Art. 6(1).

[55]Convention on Biological Diversity 1992, Art. 15(3); Nagoya Protocol 2010, Art. 6(1).

[56]Convention on Biological Diversity 1992, Art. 15(4); Nagoya Protocol 2010, Art. 5(1).

[57]Nagoya Protocol, 2010, Art. 8(b).

Protocol also recognises that alternative modes of ABS might be more appropriate for certain subsets of genetic resources,[58] and allows for the adoption of specialised international ABS instruments "that [are] consistent with, and [do] not run counter to the objectives of the [CBD] and [Nagoya] Protocol".[59] This is likely where the PIP Framework is situated within the international regime of ABS created by the CBD and Nagoya Protocol, and as such, the PIP Framework might be a specialised instrument.

5   The PIP Framework as a Specialised ABS Instrument?

The PIP Framework does not mention the CBD but its recognition of the sovereign rights of states over the biological resources in the preamble of the PIP Framework represents an implicit recognition that states do have sovereign rights over all other pathogens. The 2016 review of the PIP Framework stated that "[t]he PIP Framework is a multilateral access and benefit sharing instrument that appears to be consistent with the objectives of the Nagoya Protocol" and recommended that it be officially recognised as such.[60] The review also noted that there was no formal mechanism through which this might be achieved,[61] but it is evident that the international community has accepted that the PIP Framework is a specialised ABS agreement governing the transfer of influenza viruses with human pandemic potential. That is, when sharing pandemic influenza viruses with and through the WHO (noting that the PIP Framework does not include within its scope seasonal influenza viruses), the international community chooses to do so under the terms of the PIP Framework, and not the CBD or Nagoya Protocol. By acknowledging that it is a specialised multilateral ABS instrument consistent with the Nagoya Protocol, the WHO's review of the PIP Framework becomes an overt recognition that states have sovereign rights over all other pathogens. It also demonstrates that if the PIP Framework did not exist, the transfer of influenza viruses with human pandemic potential would "require bilateral agreements on a case-by-case basis" as per the terms of the CBD and Nagoya Protocol,[62] should provider countries wish to exercise their right do so. In the ten years since Indonesia made the first claim of viral sovereignty using the language of the CBD, the WHO has, as a matter of practice, embraced and codified this concept as a new legal norm.

---

[58] See, e.g., Nagoya Protocol 2010, Art. 10 "Global Multilateral Benefit-Sharing Mechanism".

[59] Nagoya Protocol 2010, Art. 4(4).

[60] Seventieth World Health Assembly (2017, 22–23).

[61] Ibid., 22.

[62] Ibid., 23.

6 The Sequel to Viral Sovereignty

During the dispute with Indonesia in 2007, some commentators stated that the Indonesians had contravened the newly negotiated International Health Regulations (2005) [IHR (2005)].[63] Indeed, this was the official position of the United States:

> The United States wishes to be clear that our view is that withholding influenza viruses from the Global Influenza Surveillance Network greatly threatens global public health, and will violate the legal obligations we have all agreed to undertake through our adherence to the IHRs.[64]

The IHR (2005) were adopted by the 58th WHA on 23 May 2005, but did not enter into force until 15 June 2007,[65] around six months after Indonesia had claimed viral sovereignty. Even if the IHR (2005) were in force at that time, there are no provisions in this treaty that mandate the sharing of virus samples.[66] Indonesia was not, in any technical sense, in violation of the newly negotiated IHR (2005). The fact is that if the IHR (2005) adequately addressed the virus sharing issue, there would have been no need to negotiate an entirely new agreement in the PIP Framework. The IHR (2005) does not provide a solution to the problem of viral sovereignty or virus ABS. There is just the PIP Framework, a highly specific (and imperfect) framework for the sharing of pandemic influenza viruses, and everything else is left, by default, within the domain of the CBD and Nagoya Protocol.

As noted by Fidler, "[w]hen possession is cloaked in the principle of sovereignty, those who require access to the property have to come to terms with the need to bargain for it".[67] Fidler wrote those words a decade ago, and events since then have proven that the international public health community has not yet come to terms with issue of viral sovereignty. This is clearly "a major gap in global health governance".[68] As illustrated in the following examples, we are still taking a decidedly ad hoc approach to accessing viruses during public health emergencies, sometimes with disastrous consequences.

---

[63] Hurlbut (2017).

[64] U.S. Mission to the United Nations in Geneva, 'U.S. Statement on Pandemic-Influenza Preparedness: Sharing of Influenza Vaccines and Access to Vaccines and Other Benefits' Press Release 23 May 2007. https://web.archive.org/web/20090504014606/, http://geneva.usmission.gov/press2007/0523whabirdflu.html.

[65] World Health Organisation (2005b, 1).

[66] Fidler, above n 33. Fidler provides a comprehensive legal analysis of the possible interpretations of related provisions of the IHR (2005) and how these may or may not have applied to the Indonesian viral sovereignty claim.

[67] Ibid., 93.

[68] Gostin (2014, 101).

7   Middle East Respiratory Syndrome (MERS) Coronavirus

In September 2012, a report on ProMED-mail alerted the world to the emergence of a novel coronavirus isolated from a patient in Saudi Arabia.[69] Human infections with the Middle East Respiratory Syndrome coronavirus (MERS-CoV) presented in much the same way as the genetically-related SARS coronavirus,[70] which had killed almost 800 people in 2003.[71] Since its discovery, there have been 2200 confirmed cases of MERS-CoV and nearly 800 deaths across 27 countries.[72] The largest outbreak outside of the syndrome occurred in 2015 in South Korea, with 186 confirmed cases and 38 deaths.[73] The virus is still causing sporadic outbreaks in the Middle East and, six years after its discovery, there is still a great deal that is not yet known about the virus and its transmission cycle.[74]

The outbreak of MERS-CoV in 2012 was the first incident after the introduction of the PIP Framework that demonstrated the broader and longer-lasting effects of Indonesia's viral sovereignty claim. Coming hot on the heels of the PIP Framework, the discussion about sovereign rights over pathogens was still raw for many in the global health community. The situation surrounding the discovery of the MERS coronavirus was controversial. Working from a hospital in Jeddah, Egyptian microbiologist Dr. Mohammed Ali Zaki was unable to determine the causative agent of his patient's pneumonia. He sent a specimen to Dutch virologists at Erasmus Medical Center (EMC), apparently without the consent of the Saudi Ministry of Health. The researchers at Erasmus were able to isolate the virus and sequence its genome. Just days after Dr. Zaki posted the discovery on ProMED-mail, the research team at EMC, together with Dr. Zaki, applied for a patent on the genetic sequence of the virus.[75] This incensed the Saudi government who came out strongly against the patent, arguing that it violated their sovereign authority and inhibited scientific and public health research. In his analysis of the situation, Fidler noted:

> Saudi Arabia has not yet appealed to 'viral sovereignty,' the argument that Indonesia advanced during the 2007 controversy over sharing avian influenza A (H5N1) samples, namely that the state in which a virus is isolated has sovereign rights over that virus under international law, specifically the Convention on Biological Diversity. But Riyadh's complaints echo this reasoning: Zaki violated Saudi law, [the Saudi government] says, so Erasmus is benefiting from an illegal act. If Saudi Arabia has sovereign rights over the sample, moreover, Erasmus is ignoring these rights and engaging in a form of 'biopiracy' by exploiting a Saudi genetic resource without Saudi consent. This argument implicates the Dutch government because the Netherlands and Saudi Arabia are CBD parties, and the Dutch government has not intervened to protect Saudi Arabia's rights recognised by this treaty.[76]

---

[69]Zaki (2012).

[70]Joseph et al. (2013).

[71]Heymann and Rodier (2004).

[72]WHO Regional Office for the Eastern Mediterranean (2018).

[73]World Health Organisation (2017a).

[74]World Health Organisation (2018).

[75]Bartholomeus Leonardus Haagmans et al., 'Patent WO 2014/045254 A2'.

[76]Fidler (2013).

During the WHA in May 2013, Director General Margaret Chan denounced the actions of EMC, stating:

> Making deals between scientists because they want to take IP, because they want to be the world's first to publish in scientific journals, these are issues we need to address ... No IP will stand in the way of public health actions.[77]

That the Director General supported Saudi Arabia through this dispute riled many in the international health community. The way they saw it, the Saudis had not been forthcoming in reporting the initial cases (which the world heard about through ProMED-mail rather than through official channels as required by the IHR) or the extent of the outbreak.[78] There were reports that the Saudi government had rejected assistance from overseas collaborators and would not share virus samples.[79] The Saudis, for their part, were wary of scientists who had "taken back specimens from the Middle East to study in their own laboratories" and who had published data on these samples without the permission of the Saudi Ministry of Health.[80] The unco-ordinated response to MERS-CoV was disappointing when compared to the collaborative approach that was taken in dealing with SARS less than a decade earlier, and illustrated some of the tensions that had developed between the scientific community, nation states and the WHO in the intervening years, and as a consequence, the MERS-CoV continues to cost lives.

8   Ebola

On 8 August 2014, the International Health Regulations Emergency Committee regarding the Ebola virus disease outbreak in West Africa declared a Public Health Emergency of International Concern (PHEIC).[81] By the time the PHEIC was lifted on 29 March 2016, more than 28,000 cases of Ebola virus disease and 11,000 deaths had been recorded in Guinea, Liberia, and Sierra Leone.[82] Throughout the emergency, high volumes of biological samples were collected from sick and virus-exposed patients and sent to temporary pathology laboratories for diagnostic testing. Twenty-two laboratories were operated by various international government agencies and non-government organisations to augment the strained diagnostic capabilities of the West African countries in crisis.[83] As cases of Ebola in West Africa declined these

---

[77] Margaret Chan quoted in Edward Hammond, *Material Transfer Agreement Underlying the Controversy over Patent Rights and the Middle Eastern Respiratory Syndrome Virus* (2013) Third World Network, http://www.twn.my/title2/biotk/2013/biotk130502.htm.

[78] If true, this would constitute a violation of Article 6.1 of IHR (2005). World Health Organisation (2005b), above n 64.

[79] Youde (2015).

[80] Heymann et al. (2016).

[81] World Health Organisation (2014).

[82] World Health Organisation (2016a).

[83] Spengler et al. (2016).

international agencies started to close their temporary laboratories and return the personnel and equipment to their countries of origin. In the process, the biological samples that were collected throughout the crisis were destroyed, relocated to other laboratories in West Africa, or transferred to permanent laboratories in the nations that mounted the international response[84]:

West Africa became a playground for researchers allegedly appropriating and transporting specimens and data to their home laboratories, sometimes without the knowledge or permission of the countries in which they were collected.[85]

Prior to the viral sovereignty debate, this practice would not have raised too many eyebrows, and prior to the CBD, there would not have been a set of standards against which to dispute these sorts of activities. But the practice of "parachute research" has been a sore point for the governments of LMICs for decades.[86] The term refers to "fully equipped research teams from other countries arriv[ing] at the site where research is needed, conduct[ing] their research independently of others, and then leav[ing]".[87] Not only does this practice erode trust: it also denies host countries the opportunity to train local staff and otherwise build capacity to conduct future research themselves.[88] While international responders are becoming more aware of these sensitivities and trying to foster better relationships through partnerships and collaborations with host nations, the continued appropriation of biological samples illustrates the persistence of an exploitative dynamic.

At the time of the outbreak, the West African nations did not have adequate biobanking facilities to store large quantities of Ebola virus appropriately.[89] This was the justification for taking virus samples to international laboratories and biobanks. One doctor from Sierra Leonne noted in a *Nature* editorial that despite these "genuine reasons for circumventing bureaucracy … many of us who lived through the outbreak feel that data and samples from our people were used with little regard for our countries' or patients' sovereignty."[90] In their discussion about research ethics during the West Africa Ebola outbreak, Doris Schopper et al., went even further, saying:

While it may be tenable to claim that the urgency of a response trumped the necessity for appropriate collection of samples and that consent was not feasible in the context of the outbreak, given well-documented concerns around biopiracy and exploitation in the context of colonial past, it is a moral failure not to have considered how this issue may be addressed in other ways.[91]

The West African Nations, through the establishment of Global Emerging Pathogens Treatment (GET) Consortium, have started to build secure biobanking

[84]Abayomi et al. (2016).

[85]Heymann et al. above n 79.

[86]Costello and Zumla (2000).

[87]Heymann et al. above n 79, 1505.

[88]Costello and Zumla, above n 85.

[89]Conton (2017)

[90]Ibid., 143.

[91]Schopper et al. (2017)

infrastructure in Sierra Leone[92] and have made moves to "implement a sample rescue project"[93] to "take ownership and control of the [Ebolavirus] samples".[94] At a WHO Consultation on Biobanking in August 2015, international partners including Médecins Sans Frontières (MSF), Public Health England, and the U.S. National Institutes of Health (NIH) and Centers for Disease Control and Prevention (CDC) reported the status of their Ebola virus sample holdings.[95] The report from the meeting noted that "repatriation of some samples from some locations may be impractical".[96] It also stated:

> Countries from within the [West African] region expressed strong opinions that all the samples taken in their territory were their property and should not be destroyed without express permission.[97]

In 2015, Hinterberger and Porter conceptualised viral sovereignty as a "tether" connecting virus samples to the political territories within which they were isolated.[98] Up to now, the discussion about viral sovereignty has been about controlling access to viruses that are within the physical control of the nation state claiming sovereignty authority. In fact, regarding the MERS coronavirus dispute, one observer stated that "any claim by Saudi Arabia to viral sovereignty is essentially moot because [EMC] already possesses the MERS-CoV genome".[99] This statement implies that the existence of a nation state's sovereign rights over those resources is exhausted (legally or functionally) once those viruses are out of the physical control of that state. The WHO Consultation about the West African biobanks demonstrates that the sovereignty "tether" is more robust than that. Hinterberger and Porter note that the "tethering effect permits new modes of ownership and control to be exercised over biological entities as they circulate in transnational research arenas".[100] Thus, viral sovereignty is no longer a right that nation states must exercise prior to virus samples leaving their territorial borders in order for that right to be invoked,[101] and this further strengthens the notion of viral sovereignty as the new legal norm.

---

[92] Abayomi et al., 'African Civil Society Initiatives to Drive a Biobanking, Biosecurity and Infrastructure Development Agenda in the Wake of the West African Ebola Outbreak' 1. http://www.panafrican-med-journal.com/content/article/24/270/full/%0A©.

[93] Georgetown Global (2018).

[94] Abayomi et al., above n 91, 3; World Health Organisation (2015c).

[95] World Health Organisation, above n 93.

[96] Ibid.

[97] Ibid.

[98] Hinterberger and Porter (2015).

[99] Bollinger, above n 9, 7.

[100] Hinterberger and Porter, above n 97, 378.

[101] Viral sovereignty may even be extended to virus samples collected prior to the entry into force of the CBD in 1993, see Rourke (2018).

9 Zika

On 1 February 2016, the WHO declared PHEIC amid concerns that the outbreak of Zika virus occurring across the Caribbean and Latin America was linked to cases of congenital microcephaly and Guillain-Barré syndrome.[102] Just days later, news reporting indicated that Brazil, then "the epicenter of the ongoing Zika crisis" was not sharing vital epidemiological information or virus samples with the international public health community.[103] In 2015, the Brazilian government introduced new legislation regulating access to the country's genetic resources. Brazil's Biodiversity Law (Law No. 13,123), legislation implementing the CBD,[104] had only become effective on 17 November 2015 so there was still a great deal of confusion as to how to go about accessing and sharing genetic resources (including microorganisms) from Brazil.[105] One news report quoted the president of a state-run research institute as saying "[u]ntil the law is implemented, we're legally prohibited from sending samples abroad. Even if we wanted to send this material abroad, we can't because it's considered a crime".[106] This rankled U.S. and European scientists who were forced "to work with samples from previous outbreaks" or obtain virus samples surreptitiously.[107]

The experience with Zika in 2016 serves to demonstrate that the international regime on ABS created by the CBD and Nagoya Protocol is not the only set of rules that users of viral genetic resources have to navigate. This regime relies on the domestic implementation of national legislative, administrative or policy measures to regulate international transfers of genetic resources. Again, this illustrates the futility of arguing against the inclusion of pathogens within the definition of genetic resources under the CBD and Nagoya Protocol. Nation states have every right to include pathogens within their domestic ABS rules, and when accessing genetic resources from another country, the party accessing the resources must abide by the domestic laws of the provider nation.

10 H7N9 Influenza

The H7N9 avian influenza subtype emerged in China in March 2013, and to date there has been no evidence of sustained human-to-human transmission.[108] In August 2018 the *New York Times* reported that China had been withholding samples of H7N9

---

[102] World Health Organisation (2016b, p 1).

[103] Cheng et al. (2016).

[104] Note that Brazil is not party to the Nagoya Protocol. See https://www.cbd.int/countries/default.shtml?country=br.

[105] Brazilian Association of the Cosmetics Toiletry and Fragrance Industry (2018).

[106] Khaled (2016).

[107] Ibid.

[108] World Health Organisation (2017b).

influenza viruses from the U.S. CDC for more than a year. A separate report indicated that China was also withholding viruses from scientists in the UK.[109] This is the most recent viral sovereignty controversy, and it comes at a time when political tensions between China and the U.S. are ramping up.

One U.S. source in the *New York Times* was quoted as saying that "[c]ountries don't own their viral samples any more than they own the birds in their skies",[110] which, as this chapter has described, is not quite true. It turns out that countries do own their viruses in the very same sense that they own the birds in their skies (which are also within the purview of the CBD and Nagoya Protocol and therefore subject to the environmental laws of the nation state in whose territories those birds happen to be in at any given time). The U.S. is not a signatory to the CBD and is one of the last hold-outs on the issue of whether viral sovereignty is a legitimate claim under the CBD and Nagoya Protocol. The fact is, countries are exercising their sovereign authority over pathogens (which, granted, is not *exactly* the same thing as ownership).[111] The U.S. can resist the theory as much as it likes, but it must work within this new reality if it wants to secure access to virus samples from now on.

This is a particularly interesting case because China is exercising sovereign control over an influenza virus with human pandemic potential,[112] despite these viruses clearly being within the scope of the PIP Framework. Instead of accepting the terms and conditions outlined in the PIP Framework's Standard Material Transfer Agreements,[113] China is choosing instead to determine the terms of influenza sample sharing itself. This is its sovereign right, a right that the WHO has recognised repeatedly. While it does go against the object and intent of the PIP Framework, there are absolutely no direct legal ramifications for not sharing pandemic influenza viruses with the WHO. The PIP Framework was a political salve for a legal problem that persisted despite, and perhaps even because of, the PIP Framework. Put slightly differently, the CBD enables each nation to establish its own laws; the PIP Framework provides one possibility, although it is for the host country to decide whether to follow the PIP Framework or some other legal, administrative or policy arrangement. That is the basis of sovereignty.

11   Who Owns Data About Pathogens?

In addition to reaffirming sovereign authority over biological samples, the WHO has more recently stated that countries have sovereign authority over their public health data.[114] In the wake of the West African Ebola epidemic, the WHO convened a

---

[109]Majid (2018).

[110]Baumgaertner (2018).

[111]See Cullet (2001).

[112]See comments by Jonathan Van Tam and Ian Jones, Majid, above n 108.

[113]PIP Framework 2011, Arts. 5.4.1 and Annex 1 (SMTA 1), and 5.4.2 and Annex 2 (SMTA 2).

[114]World Health Organisation (2015d).

consultation with scientists, journal editors, industry and government officials on 1–2 September 2015 with the aim of creating global norms for "timely and transparent sharing of data and results during public health emergencies".[115] Although it is not explicitly stated, we can assume that this consultation dealt only with the sharing of information that is not already mandated under the IHR (2005).[116] An initial summary of the outcomes was released "immediately after the consultation" on the evening of the 2 September 2015[117]:

> It was recognised that epidemiologic data belong to the countries where they are generated, but there was consensus that the default option is that data should be shared (i.e. opt-out policy) to ensure that the knowledge generated becomes a global public good.[118] Some of the subsequent communications about this consultation saw the language about the state ownership of data soften. The only mention of the rights of nation states in a later Statement of Principles arising from the consultation stated:

> The legitimate needs of the originating country must be taken into account. These include acknowledgement in future research reporting, inclusion in decision-making before any next steps are taken with information arising from samples.[119]

There is no mention of originating countries owning the data, just an acknowledgement that their needs be taken into account. In 2016, Kayvon Modjarrad et al., published an article about the consultation in *PLOS Medicine*, stating:

> Although countries were recognised to be the key arbiters of the dissemination of data collected from their populations, it was also noted that data ultimately belong to the individuals from whom they are collected.[120]

So in three consecutive communications from the WHO about the same consultation, the stance changes from data belonging to the originating countries, to countries just being the arbiters of its dissemination. The WHO's outward stance on data ownership is muddled and adds to the confusion around whether the use of epidemiological data requires permissions or some form of benefit-sharing. Much like the pathogens themselves, the data are likely to have their greatest value when the risk to the rest of the world is high. Without clear rules as to who can control access to epidemiological data, there is the potential that the data, like physical samples, will be withheld in order to leverage benefits.

In the context of a public health emergency, the WHO's policy statement on data sharing encourages benefit-sharing:

> WHO underlines that countries should share benefits arising out of the utilization of the data received through WHO with the originating country in accordance with applicable international commitments.[121]

---

[115]Modjarrad et al. (2016).

[116]*International Health Regulations* (2005) Art. 6.

[117]World Health Organisation, above n 10.

[118]Ibid. This stance was repeated in World Health Organisation (2016c).

[119]World Health Organisation, above n 113.

[120]Modjarrad et al., above n 114, 3–4.

[121]World Health Organisation (2016c), above n 117, 238.

Although it is not at all clear which international commitments they are referring to here. They also apply the concept of ABS to genetic sequence data:

> WHO will advocate that pathogen genome sequences be made publicly available as rapidly as possible through relevant databases and that benefits arising out of the utilization of those sequences be shared equitably with the country from where the pathogen genome sequence originates. This refers only to the public sharing of sequences, not to biological samples, which will be subject to a separate WHO policy (in preparation).[122]

This separate policy document is not available at the time of writing—presumably it is still in preparation. But if we were to speculate based on their stance towards the ownership of epidemiological data and pathogen genetic sequence data, it is highly likely that more formal benefit-sharing will also be associated with the use of biological samples.

12   The New Norm

In 2007, Indonesia first connected the issue of accessing viruses to that of access to vaccines and antivirals using the language of ABS. The CBD gave Indonesia the legal backing to claim sovereignty over viruses as genetic resources. This was the one and only opportunity that the WHO had to make it clear that global health emergencies were one instance where the world should consider foregoing a measure of sovereignty to prioritise the outbreak and research response required in such instances. Undoubtedly this was an extremely difficult situation for the WHO to have to arbitrate. But with hindsight we can now see that Indonesia's sovereignty claim in 2007 may have been the WHO's only chance to take a firm stance on this issue and call for the broad exemption of all pathogens during a global health emergency. It is an oft-noted fact that pathogens pay no mind to the Westphalian principles of international law, and the WHO had reason to likewise sideline that system when lives are threatened by the international spread of infectious diseases. This would, however, undermine the sovereignty of nation states, and as a UN agency, the WHO could not endorse such a proposition.

This criticism ignores the fact that Indonesia's sovereignty claim in 2007 was situated in a global context where countries had been exercising sovereign control over virus samples and associated data since the early 2000s, though it was never referred to as such. Perhaps the writing was on the wall. But, as Kamradt-Scott and Lee have pointed out, the PIP Framework simply "papers over fundamental disagreements regarding authority in global health governance, the relationship between the WHO and governments, and the role of private industry".[123] And by papering over the issues rather than resolving them, the WHO legitimised "viral sovereignty" as a bargaining chip that could get LMICs a seat at the table to negotiate better health outcomes for their populations. This is a bargaining chip that has its greatest value precisely when

---

[122] Ibid., 239.

[123] Kamradt-Scott and Lee (2011).

the most lives are at stake, and it could just be the only option available to LMICs to redress some of the "embedded structural inequalities" of global health preparedness and response.[124] The CBD gave us the language of resource sovereignty; the Indonesians applied it to a human pathogen; and the PIP Framework locked it in as a legal norm. The transfer of pathogen samples, and now the epidemiological data related to the pathogen, must now be negotiated with reference to the principles of ABS: prior informed consent, mutually agreed terms, and benefit-sharing. The message from the WHO's handling of the Indonesia situation was clear: if your country happens to be the emergence site of a pathogen that is sufficiently interesting to scientists that it is deemed valuable, then your best bet is to control access to that pathogen to leverage some sort of benefit for your country.[125]

There is still resistance to the concept of viral sovereignty, often by those who romanticise research science as a global public good and fail to see that the benefits of scientific research generally accumulate to already powerful and wealthy nations.[126] Furthermore, invocations of viral sovereignty are hardly the only restrictions placed on access to pathogen samples or related data. Scientists are sometimes reluctant to share, sitting on samples and data until they can be guaranteed publication in peer review journals,[127] and, as seen with the MERS-CoV case, there are times when scientists seek intellectual property protections over virus genetic sequence data. Furthermore, biosecurity considerations are often the impetus to deny access to pathogen samples or sensitive data. Indeed, one 2012 influenza experiment branded "dual use research of concern" (DURC) led to a sovereignty-like claim by the Netherlands in an effort to supress publication of the experiment's results using export control laws.[128] Restricting access comes in many forms, not just sovereignty claims. One of the objectives of the Global Health Security Agenda (GHSA) is to "[s]trengthen the global norm of rapid, transparent reporting and sample sharing",[129] but as we have seen, this is no longer the norm.

---

[124]This quote is from ibid. 832 where the authors are specifically referring to the inequalities of "the existing market-based political economy surrounding influenza vaccine and procurement", but the term is quoted here as it applies equally well to the broader structural inequalities of global health preparedness and response.

[125]Bollinger, above n 9, 22.

[126]Hinterberger and Porter, above n 97, 372.

[127]There are various initiatives to address this practice, see e.g. the prepublication data sharing recommendations of the Toronto International Data Release Workshop, where "attendees endorsed the value of rapid pre-publication data release for large reference datasets in biology and medicine that have broad utility and agreed that pre-publication data release should go beyond genomics and proteomics studies to other datasets". Toronto International Data Release Workshop Authors, 'Prepublication Data Sharing' (2009) 461 *Nature* 168, 168.

[128]Hurlbut, above n 62, 10.

[129]Centers for Disease Control and Prevention (2016).

13 Conclusion

The legal concept of viral sovereignty is a phenomenon of the new millennium, and it is one we are stuck with. The international regime created by the CBD and Nagoya Protocol defaults to bilateral ABS negotiations on a case-by-case basis.[130] This default mode of ABS is extremely time consuming and not appropriate in global health emergencies where time costs lives. The PIP Framework uses an alternative mode: a multilateral agreement that might be considered a specialised ABS instrument under the Nagoya Protocol. But the PIP Framework has major flaws as an ABS instrument[131] and, as we have seen with H7N9 influenza in China, can be easily circumvented by any party not wishing to accept its standardised terms and conditions.

One option would be to amend the IHR (2005) to mandate the sharing of biological samples.[132] But this, like an overarching exemption to ABS for pathogen samples and epidemiological data during public health emergencies, is not an acceptable solution because it completely ignores the demands of LMICs for equitable benefit-sharing. While the IHR (2005) is a binding agreement, it is regularly criticised as being toothless. Any amendment to mandate sample sharing under the IHR (2005) would require a rider detailing sanctions if it is to affect any nations' cost-benefit analysis during a public health emergency. Attaching sanctions to the IHR (2005) is likely to be unpalatable for many countries, not just LMICs. Therefore, Article 4(4) of the Nagoya Protocol on specialised ABS instruments may provide the only avenue to deal with the issue of viral sovereignty. It would allow for the adoption of a multilateral agreement that, like the PIP Framework, would put the WHO at the centre of a constellation of stakeholders. Carter has argued "that the WHO must offer positive incentives so developing countries will have a compelling reason to share samples of newly discovered viruses with the international scientific and health communities",[133] and a multilateral instrument might be a mechanism through which to do that.

Benefit-sharing was a core component of all three of the CBD's objectives. The international community must come up with a solution to facilitate access to pathogen samples and epidemiological information that respects the sovereign rights of nation states and shares the benefits associated with the use of their resources. If we fail to find a solution that aligns with the object and purpose of the CBD, then individual nations will simply opt to negotiate access terms on an ad hoc basis, and lives will likely be lost in the process. As the examples here indicate, many of those lives are likely to be in the rich countries of the world. This suggests that a solution is possible because the consequences of inaction are not just the burden of the LMICs.

---

[130] Heymann et al., above n 79, 1505.

[131] Eccleston-Turner (2017), Rourke, 'Access by Design, Benefits If Convenient: A Closer Look at the Pandemic Influenza Preparedness Framework's Standard Material Transfer Agreements' *Milbank Quaterly* (2019).

[132] Carter (2010).

[133] Ibid.

References

Abayomi A et al (2016) Managing dangerous pathogens: challenges in the wake of the recent West African ebola outbreak. Glob Secur Health Sci Policy 9497:51

Bagley MA (2018) The morality of compulsory licensing as an access to medicines tool. Minnesota Law Rev 102:2463–2479

Baumgaertner E (2018) China has withheld samples of a dangerous flu virus. The New York Times (New York), 27 Aug 2018. https://www.nytimes.com/2018/08/27/health/china-flu-virus-samples.html?smtyp = cur&smid = tw-nythealth

Beck L (2006) China shares bird flu samples, denies new strain. Reuters Health E-Line, 10 Nov 2006

Bollinger AE (2015) E-MERS-GENCY: an application and evaluation of the pandemic influenza preparedness framework to the outbreak of MERS-CoV. Temple Int Comp Law J 29(1):21–22

Brazilian Association of the Cosmetics Toiletry and Fragrance Industry (2018) Guidebook on access to the brazilian biodiversity. Brazilian Association of the Cosmetics, Toiletry and Fragrance Industry. https://abihpec.org.br/site2016/wp-content/uploads/2018/04/Guidebook_biodiversity-ABIHPEC.pdf

Butler D (2005) "Refusal to share" leaves agency struggling to monitor bird flu. Nature 435(7039):131

Caplan AL, Curry DR (2007) Leveraging genetic resources or moral blackmail? Indonesia and avian flu virus sample sharing. Am J Bioeth 7(11):1–2

Carter J (2010) Who's virus is it anyway? How the world health organisation can protect against claims of "viral sovereignty". Georgia J Int Comp Law 38:717–721

Centers for Disease Control and Prevention (2016) The global health security agenda. CDC. https://www.cdc.gov/globalhealth/security/ghsagenda.htm

Cheng M, Satter R, Goodman J (2016) Few Zika samples are being shared by brazil, worrying international researchers. STAT, 3 Feb 2016. https://www.statnews.com/2016/02/03/zika-samples-brazil/

Conton B (2017) Build the ebola database in Africa. Nature 551(7679):143

Costello A, Zumla A (2000) Moving to research partnerships in developing countries existing research models in developing countries. Br Med J 321:827

Cullet P (2001) Property rights regimes over biological resources. Environ Plan C Govern Policy 19:651–652

Cyranoski D (2003) Taiwan left isolated in fight against SARS. Nature 422:652. http://www.nejm.org/doi/abs/10.1056/NEJMoa030781

Eccleston-Turner M (2017) The pandemic influenza preparedness framework: a viable procurement option for developing states? Med Law Int 17(4):227

Fidler DP (2008) Influenza virus samples, international law, and global health diplomacy. Emerg Infect Dis 14(1):88

Fidler DP (2013) Who owns MERS? The intellectual property controversy surrounding the latest pandemic. Foreign Aff. https://www.foreignaffairs.com/articles/saudi-arabia/2013-06-06/who-owns-mers

Georgetown Global (2018) Maloy distinguished lecture on global health—Dr. Akin Abayomi. Youtube. https://www.youtube.com/watch?v=J9mrOKzBKAI&t=123s

Gostin LO (2014) Global health law. Harvard University Press

Gostin LO, DeBartolo MC, Katz R (1918) The global health law trilogy: towards a safer, healthier, and fairer world. Lancet 390:1918–1923

Hameiri S (2014) Avian influenza, "viral sovereignty", and the politics of health security in Indonesia. Pac Rev 27(3):333

Heymann DL, Rodier G (2004) SARS: a global response to an international threat. Brown J World Aff 10(2):185–197

Heymann DL, Liu J, Lillywhite L (2016) Partnerships, not parachutists, for Zika research. New England J Med 374(16):1504–1505. https://doi.org/10.1056/NEJMp1515917

Hinterberger A, Porter N (2015) Genomic and viral sovereignty: tethering the materials of global biomedicine. Public Cult 27(2 76):361

Holbrooke R, Garrett L (2008) "Sovereignty" that risks global health. The Washington Post, 10 Aug 2008. http://www.washingtonpost.com/wp-dyn/content/article/2008/08/08/AR2008080802919. html

Hurlbut JB (2017) A science that knows no country: pandemic preparedness, global risk, sovereign science. Big Data Soc 4(2):1–6. http://doi.org/10.1177/2053951717742417

Joseph C et al (2013) Highlights and conclusions from the technical consultative meeting on novel coronavirus infection, Cairo, Egypt, 14–16 January 2013. Eastern Mediterr Health J 19(Supplement 1):68–69

Kamradt-Scott A, Lee K (2011) The 2011 pandemic influenza preparedness framework: global health secured or a missed opportunity? Polit Stud 59(4):831

Khaled SS (2016) Zika samples are scanty for preventive and curative research. The Financial Express (Bangladesh), 10 Feb 2016

Lange JE (2012) Negotiating issues related to pandemic influenza preparedness: the sharing of influenza viruses and access to vaccines and other benefits. In: Rosskam E, Kickbusch I (eds) Negotiating and navigating global health: case studies in global health diplomacy. World Scientific Publishing, Singapore

Majid A (2018) Disease X: China ignores UK request to share samples of flu virus with pandemic potential (August). The Telegraph (United Kingdom), 29 Aug 2018. https://www.telegraph.co. uk/news/2018/08/29/disease-x-china-ignores-uk-request-share-samples-flu-virus-pandemic/

Modjarrad K et al (2016) Developing global norms for sharing data and results during public health emergencies. PLoS Medicine 13(1):e1001935. http://journals.plos.org/plosmedicine/article?id= 10.1371/journal.pmed.1001935

Nebehay S (2006) WHO members elect bird flu expert chan as chief. Reuters, 10 Nov 2006

Ranga U (2009) The saga of the HIV controversy. Resonance 14(5):472–491

Rourke MF (2017) Viruses for sale: all viruses are subject to access and benefit-sharing obligations under the conventional on biological diversity. Eur Intellect Property Rev 39(2):79

Rourke MF (2018) Never mind the science, here's the convention on biological diversity: viral sovereignty in the smallpox destruction debate. J Law Med 25(2):429

Rourke MF (2019) Access by design, benefits if convenient: a closer look at the pandemic influenza preparedness framework's standard material transfer agreements. The Milbank Quarterly 97(1):91–112

Schopper D et al (2017) Research ethics governance in times of ebola. Public Health Ethics 10(1):49–56

Sedyaningsih ER et al (2008) Towards mutual trust, transparency and equity in virus sharing mechanism: the avian influenza case of Indonesia. Ann Acad Med Singapore 37(29):482–486

Seventieth World Health Assembly (2017) Review of the pandemic influenza preparedness framework. http://apps.who.int/gb/ebwha/pdf_files/WHA70/A70_17-en.pdf

Singer HL (1989) Institut Pasteur v United States: the AIDS patent dispute, the contract disputes act and the international exchange of scientific data. Am J Law Med 15:439

Smith FL (2012) Insights into surveillance from the influenza virus and benefit sharing controversy. Glob Change Peace Secur 24(1):71–80. https://doi.org/10.1080/14781158.2012.641292

Spengler JR et al (2016) Perspectives on West Africa ebola virus disease outbreak, 2013–2016. Emerg Inf Dis 22(6):956

Third World Network (2007) Briefing paper: sharing of avian influenza viruses. https://web. archive.org/web/20120822191210/, http://www.twnside.org.sg/title2/avian.flu/papers/avian.flu. twn.briefing.paper.may2007.doc

Vezzani S (2010) Preliminary remarks on the envisaged world health organisation pandemic influenza preparedness framework for the sharing of viruses and access to vaccines and other benefits. J World Intellect Property 13(6):675. https://doi.org/10.1111/j.1747-1796.2010.00400.x

Vietnam News Agency (2005) Vietnam, WHO denounce nature article on bird-flu countries' non-cooperation. BBC Monitoring Asia Pacific, 15 May 2005

WHO Regional Office for the Eastern Mediterranean (2018) MERS situation update, June 2018. http://www.emro.who.int/pandemic-epidemic-diseases/mers-cov/mers-situation-update-june-2018.html

World Health Organisation (2005) International Health Regulations. https://www.who.int/ihr/publications/9789241580496/en/

World Health Organisation (2005a) Strengthening pandemic-influenza preparedness and response. In: 58th World Health Assembly, WHA58.5. World Health Organisation

World Health Organisation (2005b) International health regulations, 3rd edn. http://apps.who.int/iris/bitstream/handle/10665/246107/9789241580496-eng.pdf;jsessionid=8F8ACF47BD824BBBAFC6E14053022B94?sequence=1

World Health Organisation (2006) Application of the International Health Regulations (2005). In: 59th World Health Assembly, WHA59.2. World Health Organisation

World Health Organisation (2014) Statement on the 1st meeting of the IHR emergency committee on the 2014 Ebola Outbreak in West Africa. http://www.who.int/mediacentre/news/statements/2014/ebola-20140808/en/

World Health Organisation (2015a) Developing global norms for sharing data and results during public health emergencies. WHO. http://www.who.int/medicines/ebola-treatment/data-sharing_phe/en/

World Health Organisation (2015b) Global influenza surveillance and response system (GISRS): technical and scientific resource for WHO public health policy making. http://www.who.int/csr/disease/OP_GISRS_FINAL.pdf

World Health Organisation (2015c) Report on the 2nd WHO consultation on biobanking: focus on West Africa. WHO. http://www.who.int/medicines/ebola-treatment/meetings/2nd_who_biobaking-consultation/en/

World Health Organisation (2015d) Developing global norms for sharing data and results during public health emergencies (statement of principles). WHO. http://www.who.int/medicines/ebola-treatment/blueprint_phe_data-share-results/en/

World Health Organisation (2016a) Ebola situation report, 30 Mar 2016. http://apps.who.int/ebola/current-situation/ebola-situation-report-30-march-2016

World Health Organisation (2016b) WHO Director-general summarizes the outcome of the emergency committee regarding clusters of microcephaly and guillain-barré syndrome. World Health Organisation. http://www.who.int/mediacentre/news/statements/2016/emergency-committee-zika-microcephaly/en/

World Health Organisation (2016c) Policy statement on data sharing by WHO in the context of public health emergencies (as of 13 April 2016). Wkly Epidemiol Rec 91(18):237. www.who.int/ictrp/results/reporting

World Health Organisation (2017a) Middle East respiratory syndrome coronavirus (MERS-CoV) WHO MERS-CoV global summary and assessment of risk (current situation 21 July 2017). http://www.who.int/emergencies/mers-cov/risk-assessment-july-2017.pdf?ua=1

World Health Organisation (2017b) Avian influenza A(H7N9) virus. http://www.who.int/influenza/human_animal_interface/influenza_h7n9/en/

World Health Organisation (2018) 2018 annual review of diseases prioritized under the research and development blueprint. http://www.who.int/emergencies/diseases/2018prioritisation-report.pdf?ua=1

Yasuda K (2004) Dispute over ownership of virus could cost lives. Yomiuri Shimbun (Tokyo), 2 Apr 2004

Youde J (2015) The 5 things you need to know about MERS (and global health). Washington Post, 12 June 2015. https://www.washingtonpost.com/news/monkey-cage/wp/2015/06/12/the-5-things-you-need-to-know-about-mers-and-global-health/

Zaki AM (2012) Novel coronavirus—Saudi Arabia: human isolate. ProMED-mail. http://www.promedmail.org/direct.php?id=1302733

Michelle F. Rourke is is a CSIRO Synthetic Biology Future Science Research Fellow at Griffith University's Law Futures Centre in Brisbane, Australia. She researches access and benefit-sharing for the Australian synthetic biology community.

Dual-Use and Infectious Disease Research

Nicholas G. Evans

Abstract Despite rapid advance in the prevention, diagnosis, and treatment, infectious diseases remain a central challenge for global health policy. In the twenty-first century, the life sciences—including microbiology, virology, and immunology—have been marshalled as key tools in the fight against infectious disease, and the promotion of global health. Rapid advance in these fields, however, has given rise to the "dual-use dilemma," when one and the same piece of scientific research or technology has the capacity to help or harm humanity. While not unique to fields that address infectious disease, contemporary cases of dual-use research are largely identified in the context of the life sciences. In this chapter I outline the debate about dual-use research in the life sciences, in particular the ethics of dual-use research. After a historical overview of the dual-use dilemma in the twenty-first century, I examine ethical issues in attempting to trade off the risks and benefits of dual-use research. I address how we select alternative, less risky experiments; translational issues arising for dual-use research; and political commitments to realise the benefits and mitigate the risks arising from such research. I then discuss the governance of dual-use research, before concluding with a brief discussion on priority setting in infectious disease research as a path forward for policymakers.

Keywords Scientific research · Dual-use · Gain of function · GOF

1 Introduction: Two Stories of Emerging Infectious Diseases

Infectious diseases present an important challenge for the health and security of modern communities. Despite staggering advances in medicine and public health through the twentieth century, common infectious diseases remain one of the top

---

[1]GBD 2016 Causes of Death Collaborators (2017).

N. G. Evans (✉)
Department of Philosophy, University of Massachusetts Lowell, Lowell, MA, USA
e-mail: Nicholas_evans@uml.edu

© Springer Nature Switzerland AG 2020
M. Eccleston-Turner and I. Brassington (eds.), *Infectious Diseases in the New Millennium*, International Library of Ethics, Law, and the New Medicine 82,
https://doi.org/10.1007/978-3-030-39819-4_9

193

five causes of years of life lost around the globe.[1] An important component of the continued fight against infectious diseases is recognised to be basic scientific research into the biology of infectious organisms: microbiology, virology, and immunology among others.

In the beginning of the twenty-first century, two significant events mobilised global attention on infectious diseases as both a *health* and *security* challenge. The first occurred in 2001, when letters containing *bacillus anthracis* were sent through the United States Postal Service, ultimately killing five people of twenty-two who were infected.[2] The so-called "amerithrax" attacks were decisive in pushing the threat of infectious into the national security spotlight.

In response to the amerithrax attacks, the United States Congress passed the Project Bioshield Act in 2004. Among other things, the act authorised the Secretary of Health and Human Services to conduct and support research and development activities for countermeasures in biological emergencies, and increased the capacity of the National Institutes of Health and National Institute of Allergy and Infectious Diseases to conduct research and respond to biological threats. In 2006, the Pandemic and All-Hazards Preparedness Act established the Biomedical Advanced Research and Development Authority, which would manage Project BioShield and guide research and development in aid of creating novel medical countermeasures against infectious diseases and Chemical, Biological Radiological, and Nuclear weapons.

In 2003, the emergence of severe acute respiratory syndrome (SARS) shocked the international community. While the threat of "emerging infectious diseases" (EID) had been flagged by the US and Canada in the 1990s,[3] SARS was frightening both for the pace at which it moved, and the unexpected nature of its emergence. After more than 8000 cases over 17 countries, and killing almost 10% of those infected, SARS was described as a "wake-up call" by then Director-General of the World Health Organisation (WHO) Margaret Chan. In 2005, in part as a response to SARS, the International health Regulations (IHR) entered into force. The IHR, among other things, coordinates the reporting of events to the WHO that may represent a "Public Health Emergency of International Concern," such as a major influenza pandemic. It also requires Parties to the IHR—the 196 members of the World Health Assembly—to ensure their national health surveillance and response capacities meet criteria set out in the Regulations.

These initiatives have thrown basic scientific research into the spotlight as a key weapon against the fight against infectious disease. As human and non-human animal communities become more interconnected, our climate changes, we encroach evermore into our remaining wilderness, and use existing drugs to fight diseases, our disease landscape is changing. As our mastery of biology changes, moreover, it becomes increasingly plausible that a malevolent actor, non-state group, or nation could create and deploy biological weapons. These dual biological threats—so-called naturally occurring and human-created—have situated modern biology as both a threat to human health and security, and its ultimate saviour.

---

[2]Inglesby et al. (2002).

[3]Weir (2012).

The name we give to this problem is the *dual-use dilemma*: when one and the same piece of scientific research or technology has the capacity to help or harm humanity. While much if not most scientific research is dual-use in some trivial sense, i.e. it has the capacity to inflict some harms and/or some benefits, the kind of dual-use research I am concerned with is research that has the capacity to inflict very great harms and/or benefits. Such a benefits might include, for example, the cure for a highly virulent infectious disease or "potential pandemic pathogen," such as avian influenza. A commensurate potential harm might be the creation of such a potential pandemic pathogen.[4] This research poses an ethical issue because the capacity of dual-use research to be used or misused invokes questions, *inter alia,* about the limits of scientific freedom, and kinds of values science promotes, or ought to promote, and the distribution of the risks and benefits of scientific innovation in society. Dual-use presents a dilemma because, in some cases, it is not clear where the balance of risks and benefits, or rights, lies.

In what follows, I outline the debate about dual-use research in the life sciences, beginning at the turn of the twenty-first century. I then examine ethical issues arising in the analysis of the balance of risks and benefits of dual-use research. I drill further into an inquiry into risks and benefits and examine how we select alternative experiments, translational issues arising for dual-use research, and political commitments to realise the benefits and mitigate the risks of dual-use research. I then turn to governance issues, and those of scientific freedom. I conclude with a brief discussion of priority setting, and how the foundational policies that promoted basic research in the life sciences may also compromise global health and security.

2   Dual-Use Research in the Life Sciences

The story of dual-use is now seventeen years in the making. For ease of reading, I will describe three broad phases of the debate: the early years (2001–2011); the "ferret flu" years (2011–2014); and the gain-of-function (GOF) debate (2014–present). Each phase is fascinating and worthy of a separate inquiry, but I restrict myself to the central points of each episode that are needed for the analysis to come.

2.1   *The Early Years: Mousepox, Polio, and Toxic Milk*

While the story of dual-use has, inevitably, come to revolve around the United States and its policies, the dual-use dilemma in the life sciences has its origins in Australia. Ronald Jackson and Ian Ramshaw worked as part of a team sponsored by the Australian Commonwealth Scientific and Industrial Research Organisation (CSIRO) and the Australian National University (ANU) to create a recombinant form of the

---

[4]Evans et al. (2015a).

myxoma virus, a poxvirus that infects rabbits. In the 1950s, *myxoma* had been used to control the plagues of rabbits that had devastated the Australian countryside since the late nineteenth century. While the initial release was almost totally successful, the small number of rabbits that survived inevitably did what they did best—bred like rabbits—back to their original population size.[5] Ramshaw, a student of Frank Fenner (better known for his work eradicating smallpox and a stunt in which he and two colleagues inoculated themselves with the *myxoma* virus, to demonstrate its safety in humans[6]), was along with Jackson charged with coming up for a cure to this resistance, and put an end to the plague.

The strategy Jackson and Ramshaw used was simple: use the viral machinery of *myxoma* to render rabbits infertile. In order to make their lives easier in the early stages of research—again, basic scientific research—they chose to use mice and the *ectromelia* or mousepox virus as their model organism. Rabbits are more expensive and larger than mice, making experiments with them less convenient to use; *ectromelia* is also a better-characterised poxvirus than *myxoma*. Their experiments with *ectromelia* showed some initial success: mice infected with the virus would remain infertile for between five and nine months.[7]

Jackson and Ramshaw wanted higher rates and durations of infertility, so they sought to further enhance the virus to express the interleukin-4 protein, a cytokine present in mammals that plays a key role in the immune system. By encouraging the production of interleukin-4, the hope was that the mouse's immune system would actually assist the virus in the attack against its host's reproductive system. The results, however, were unexpected. A paper in 2001 by the team in the *Journal of Virology* reported that more than sterilizing the mice, the virus outright killed its hosts. And not just sometimes: the virus killed 100% of the normal mice *and* vaccinated mice, and 60% of mice already genetically resistant to *ectromelia*.[8]

The central issue that arose from this research is that while mousepox doesn't infect humans, smallpox does. A disease that killed more humans than any other in history, smallpox was declared eradicated on May 8 of 1980 by Fenner, and humanity's victory over the virus is arguably one of the greatest triumphs in the history of modern medicine and public health. Few people today have been vaccinated against smallpox–why vaccinate against an extinct species?–and those who have lost their immunity long ago. Until 2014, when six vials of smallpox were discovered in a freezer in the old National Institutes of Health campus in Bethesda, MD [SZABO], it was thought that the virus only survived under lock and key at the Centers for Disease Control (CDC) in Atlanta, GA, and VECTOR, the Russian equivalent of the CDC in Sverdlosk.

The publication of the results of Jackson and Ramshaw's work coincided with the Amerithrax attacks, and in early 2002 the US Central Intelligence Agency released a report titled *The Darker Bioweapons Future,* listing the mousepox study as evidence

---

[5] Bartrip (2008).

[6] Henderson (2011).

[7] Jackson et al. (1998).

[8] Jackson et al. (2001).

that the capacity for state and non-state actors to build novel, sophisticated biological weapons already existed.[9] In response, the US Government commissioned a committee of the National Research Council to assess the risk of dual-use research in the life sciences. That committee's report, *Biotechnology Research in an Age of Terrorism,* later named the "Fink report" after the committee's chair Gerald Fink, recommended among other things the education of scientists on dual-use research, the establishment of the National Science Advisory Board for Biosecurity (NSABB), and the international harmonisation of biosecurity norms.[10] It also outlined seven "experiments of concern", which:

1. Would demonstrate how to render a vaccine ineffective;
2. Would confer resistance to therapeutically useful antibiotics or antiviral agents;
3. Would enhance the virulence of a pathogen or render a nonpathogen virulent;
4. Would increase transmissibility of a pathogen;
5. Would alter the host range of a pathogen;
6. Would enable the evasion of diagnostic/detection modalities;
7. Would enable the weaponisation of a biological agent or toxin;

A follow up report in 2006, *Globalisation, Biosecurity, and the Future of the Life Sciences,* (the "Lemon-Relman report") further recommended increased capacity for public health to respond to biological weapons, the promotion of a "culture of awareness" in the scientific community, increased biological expertise in the security community, and a broader assessment of what constituted a "threat" in dual-use than its predecessor. In the same year the NSABB was founded within the National Institutes of Health (NIH) as an advisory committee to the NIH and US Government on issues related to dual-use.

In the meantime, dual-use research continued to crop up. In 2002, scientists at State University of New York Stony Brook, funded by the US Defense Advanced Research Projects Agency (DARPA), successfully synthesised the poliovirus from its base sequence.[11] This marked the first time a virus had been synthesised, and was by all measure a scientific breakthrough. Yet while the polio had attenuated virulence due to difficulties in the synthesis process,[12] it opened the way to the synthesis of more complex and dangerous agents for use as biological weapons—again, such as smallpox.

In 2005, two researchers from Stanford modelled an attack on the US food supply, using the example of the release of the botulinum toxin in the milk supply.[13] Botulinum toxin is the most powerful toxin on earth, and widely used in clinical medicine for its paralytic properties. It, however, is a potent biochemical toxin, has been used in former biological weapons programmes (including the former Soviet

---

[9]Central Intelligence Agency (2003).
[10]National Research Council (2004a).
[11]Cello et al. (2002).
[12]Selgelid and Weir (2010).
[13]Wein and Liu (2005).

bioweapons program, which ran unknown to the world until 1992).[14] Moreover, it can be obtained, in bulk, online as part of discount or counterfeit cosmetic surgery products (where the toxin goes by the trade name Botox).[15] The research predicted that up to 200,000 people, mainly children and the elderly, would die if 1 kg of the toxin was released at the right point in the milk distribution system in the US. While a clear warning for government, it also was charged with providing a blueprint for terrorists, which led the US government into an unsuccessful plea to have the publication suppressed.[16]

At the same time, scientists at the CDC proceeded to piece together the genetic sequence for the 1918 H1N1 "Spanish Influenza" that killed 50–100 million people.[17] The scientists later synthesised the virus, and tested its virulence in nonhuman primates.[18] The NSABB was consulted on the dual-use aspects of the research: while on the one hand scientists argued that the reconstruction of the virus could give insight into what made it so devastating,[19] concerns remained that the creation of such a virus posed a risk if aspiring bioweaponeers were to do the same.[20]

In 2007, the NSABB released a draft framework for the oversight of dual-use life sciences research. In this, they codified the term "dual-use research of concern" (DURC), initially proposed by the Fink report but now defined as

> [r]esearch that, based on current understanding, can be reasonably anticipated to provide knowledge, products, or technologies that could be directly misapplied by others to pose a threat to public health and safety, agricultural crops and other plants, animals, the environment, or materiel.[21]

This framework maintained that, while regulation on the funding, conduct, or communication of dual-use research might be necessary, the judgement of researchers was still the dominant factor in preventing the misuse of emerging life sciences research and technology.[22] The framework recommended further awareness raising, education, and training in the responsible communication of research, defining a period of dual-use that centred on the self-governance of individual scientists.

2.2 Ferret Flu

The debate about dual-use calmed in the wake of the 1918 flu experiments. In 2011, this calm was disrupted with the announcement that two papers, slated for publication in *Science* and *Nature,* had described the creation of recombinant strains of highly

---

[14]Leitenberg et al. (2012).

[15]Coleman and Zilinskas (2010).

[16]Wein (2009).

[17]Tumpey (2005).

[18]Kobasa et al. (2007).

[19]Palese et al. (2006).

[20]Kennedy (2005).

[21]National Science Advisory Board for Biosecurity (2007).

[22]Ibid.

pathogenic avian influenza (HPAI) H5N1 that were transmissible via respiratory droplets (were "airborne") between ferrets.[23] The studies were significant because HPAI H5N1, up until 2016, only produced 854 recorded cases of H5N1 in humans, but 52% of those infected had died. In comparison, the 1918 flu pandemic had a case fatality rate of approximately 2.5%.[24] HPAI H5N1 only infected humans from birds, primarily poultry stocks, but had not undergone sustained transmission *between* humans in the wild. Ferrets are a common immunological model for flu pathogenesis and transmission in humans; the implications of the studies were that wild-type HPAI H5N1 could, in principle, develop the capacity to transmit between humans and thus trigger a potential pandemic with unprecedented lethality.

These "gain of function" (GOF) studies, so called because they followed a common virology practice of inducing novel mutations into viruses to modify their function, were conducted independently by groups at the University of Wisconsin-Madison in the US, and Erasmus University in the Netherlands. The NSABB was asked to review the studies, and recommended that both studies be redacted, suppressing the sequence information and key methods of the studies that would give individuals the capacity to reproduce the viruses.[25] Their reasoning followed the model for dual-use: while proponents of the work claimed that the research would improve surveillance efforts by identifying the mutations to look for that would signal an impending pandemic, and enhance efforts to create medical countermeasures against pandemic HPAI, critics noted that the same research offered a method to develop precisely such a virus for use on the human population.[26]

In 2012 the authors of the 2011 H5N1 studies and a group of colleagues declared a moratorium on GOFR on highly pathogenic H5N1 avian influenza strains in a letter to *Science*. They wrote the moratoria should last for 60 days, and include a meeting of experts to discuss how best to assure the public, provide room for discussion of the merits and risks of the studies, and find solutions to challenges posed by the research.[27] The moratorium ultimately lasted 9 months, after the US Government requested an indefinite extension on the moratorium to allow time to craft appropriate policy.[28] During this time, the World Health Organisation (WHO) held a meeting of experts in the manner suggested by the authors of the moratorium letter, which concluded with a rough scientific consensus that both studies should ultimately be published in full.[29] The NSABB subsequently reviewed and approved revised versions of the two papers, which included additional discussion of the public health benefits the authors believed could result from the work.[30]

---

[23] Enserink (2011).

[24] Taubenberger and Morens (2006).

[25] National Science Advisory Board for Biosecurity (2011).

[26] Evans (2013).

[27] Fouchier et al. (2012), Herfst (2012).

[28] Casadevall and Shenk (2012).

[29] Fouchier et al. (2012).

[30] National Science Advisory Board for Biosecurity (2012).

The papers were published in 2012,[31] and in January 2013 scientists declared the moratorium over, claiming "the aims of the voluntary moratorium have been met in some countries and are close to being met in others."[32] In February 2013, the Department of Health and Human Services published policy describing seven criteria that studies like the H5N1 studies would have to meet in order to be funded. These criteria included high significance for public health, the lack of feasible alternatives to answer the same scientific question, and the appropriate management of bio safety and Biosecurity risks.[33]

2.3 *Biosafety and Gain of Function*

From their final recommendations in 2012, the NSABB did not meet again until 2014.[34] That year, two sets of revelations reignited the GOF debate with a slight twist. First, it was revealed that gain of function studies involving the creation of novel, recombinant "potential pandemic pathogens" (PPPs) such as those in 2011 were being funded by the US, China,[35] the European Union,[36] private and public funders in the UK,[37] and the governments of Japan,[38] and the Netherlands.[39] The viruses had diversified, as well: in 2014, GOF had proliferated beyond HPAI H5N1 to H7N1,[40] H9N1,[41] and H7N9.[42]

Second, the debate about dual-use shifted from predominantly biosecurity concerns to those biosafety concerns, motivated by a number of problematic incidents involving US laboratories. First, the CDC announced that an accidental release of anthrax had occurred when an improperly inactivated sample had been moved out of a high containment laboratory, potentially exposing 70 employees to the bacterium.[43] Next, the United States Department of Agriculture (USDA) reported that a shipment of low pathogenicity avian influenza from the CDC had been contaminated with HPAI; the researchers at USDA discovered this when poultry inoculated with the samples began dying at an alarming rate.[44] Finally, a former Food and Drug

---

[31] Herfst et al. (2012), Imai et al. (2012).

[32] Fouchier et al. (2013).

[33] The United States Government (2013).

[34] Michael Osterholm and Paul Keim, personal communications, 2014.

[35] Zhang et al. (2013).

[36] Herfst and others (n 30).

[37] Shelton et al. (2013), Watanabe et al. (2014).

[38] Ibid.

[39] Herfst and others (n 30).

[40] Sutton et al. (2014).

[41] Kimble et al. (2014).

[42] Richard et al. (2013).

[43] Centers for Disease Control and Prevention (2014a).

[44] Centers for Disease Control and Prevention (2014b).

Administration (FDA) lab on the National institutes of Health Campus in Bethesda, Maryland, reported finding a shoe box full of dangerous viral samples, including a number of samples of smallpox.[45]

In response to these events, and the prompting of concerned scholars and scientists,[46] the US Government imposed a funding pause on 18 government funded GOF experiments on influenza, severe acute respiratory syndrome (SARS) coronavirus, and Middle East respiratory syndrome (MERS) coronavirus; paused the future funding of such research; and advised private funders to do the same. This pause came with the a "deliberative process" involving the National Academies of Science,[47] NSABB, a risk and benefit assessment of GOF,[48] and an ethics white paper on GOF research.[49]

The result of this process was a series of recommendations produced by the NSABB on the funding and conduct of GOF research. The NSABB acknowledged there was some GOF research that ought not to be conducted for security and safety reasons.[50] They provided a series of policy guidelines that would be reproduced, with minor amendments, in the White House Office of Science and Technology Policy's *Recommended Policy Guidance for Departmental Development of Review Mechanisms for Potential Pandemic Pathogen Care and Oversight (P3CO)*.[51] This guidance outlined the policy principles that should guide the funding and conduct of GOF research moving forward, and noted that an agency's adoption of policy consistent with *P3CO* would constitute the end of the funding pause. In December of 2017, the US Department of Health and Human Services released such a policy,[52] and the pause was deemed to be at an end.

This is only a sketch of the debate on dual-use research, a debate that has taken seventeen years and is still ongoing. For example, researchers in Canada in 2016 announced that they had successfully synthesised the horsepox virus, an extinct poxvirus that shares homology (genetic structure) with smallpox. This has scared some policymakers, but I set it aside here because while interesting, it shares enough features with the polio case and the 1918 flu case that it doesn't raise *novel* ethical issues. Rather, I use the above as context for detailing key ethical issues that will make up the rest of this chapter.

---

[45]Dennis and Sun (2014).

[46]For example, the *Cambridge Working Group Consensus Statement on the Creation of Potential Pandemic Pathogens (PPPs)*, of which the author is a founding member and author. http://www.cambridgeworkinggroup.org.

[47]National Academies of Sciences, Engineering and Medicine (2016), National Research Council Institute of Medicine (2015).

[48]Gryphon Scientific (2016).

[49]Selgelid (2016).

[50]National Science Advisory Board for Biosecurity (2016).

[51]Office of Science and Technology Policy (2017).

[52]Department of Health and Human Services (2017).

3 Risks and Benefits

Dual-use has, historically, been framed as a question of the balance of risks and benefits posed that inhere to scientific research. The literature on GOF research, in particular, focused on the question of whether the risks of GOF research, i.e. the accidental or deliberate release of a novel PPP causing a global pandemic, were outweighed by the potential benefits of the research in terms of contributions to science, disease surveillance, and medical countermeasures.[53] A preliminary question is, then, whether this is all that really matters for the purpose of dual-use.

To illustrate the pervasiveness of this framing, consider that the Fink report. When discussing the balance between scientific freedom and security, the committee focussed in the main on scientific freedom as instrumentally valuable to achieving scientific and material progress.[54] The Lemon-Relman report concurred, citing National Security Decision Directive 189 (NSDD-189) as the basis for maintaining policies and practices that promoted the free and open exchange of information in the life sciences. NSDD-189 is significant in US science policy: it makes a canonical distinction between "basic" and "applied" scientific research, and affirms the US national interest in the open communication of basic scientific research (i.e. free of government classification). The basis for this, in turn, is the strategic interest the US has in using basic science research to achieve its economic and security goals.[55]

But scientific freedom is more than an instrumental good. On the one hand, scientific freedom is important for its own sake—we might think that, all other things being equal, a scientific enterprise in which individual scientists make their own choices about which research to pursue (conduct, communicate, etc.) is better than one in which scientists are restrained in their activities.[56] Moreover, scientific research might be considered to be derivative of other important civil liberties, such as freedom of speech and/or inquiry.[57]

Any governance measure that purports to keep scientific research open in order to maximise the benefits of scientific research must also contend with a lack of necessary or sufficient connection between scientific freedom and scientific results. The physical sciences, in particular, have a strong tradition of achieving incredible progress in highly restrictive environments. The maintenance of "classified communities" in which scientists are free to communicate, but only within a small community, has created rapid scientific progress (though perhaps not always promoting the values we want).[58] While the life sciences does not currently adopt such a practice—or, at least, not widely—there is no in principle reason why scientific freedom is a necessary condition of scientific advancement.

---

[53]Casadevall and Imperiale (2014), Evans et al. (2015b).

[54]National Research Council (n 8).

[55]Hindin et al. (2017).

[56]Evans (n 24).

[57]Miller and Selgelid (2008).

[58]Evans (2000), Westwick (2000).

This case is illustrative of how the debate about dual-use frequently elides conceptual nuances about the ethics of pursuing research that poses serious, at times population-level risks and benefits to the public. In some cases, this may not make a difference to ultimate decisions. One could imagine, for example, an experiment outlining a recombinant strain of smallpox modified in the style of the mousepox experiment, and confirmation that this strain had the same transmissibility as wild-type smallpox, but with 100% lethality and the ability to overcome antivirals (which the Australian mousepox strain did).[59] We might think that in such an extreme case, whether or not there is some additional value to scientific freedom is a moot point.

In many if not most other cases, however, the risks are less than existential,[60] and the potential benefits less than beatific. These make up the paradigm cases of dual-use, though they may not in the future. In those cases, we need to account for other considerations. A preliminary issue is that the way we account for risks and benefits may differ. This was an acute challenge for the GOF risk and benefit assessment. While risk could be modelled numerically, the analysis of benefits was constrained to a qualitative examination of potential benefits, based in the main on open-ended interviews with subject matter experts in health, science, and security.[61]

This empirical issue points to a series of broader conceptual issue for dual-use research. We typically and perhaps justifiably tend to think of risks and benefits as straightforwardly comparable or commensurate. But this need not be the case. To begin, it isn't clear that the kinds of benefits we typically describe for dual-use infectious disease research—saving lives—are morally equivalent to the typical risks we assign to dual-use research in terms of lives lost. We could imagine a dual-use dilemma, for example, in which there was the expectation of some positive use saving 1000 lives, and the risks of misuse resulting in an expected 1000 lives taken by a malevolent user. It isn't clear that saving 1000 lives from an avoidable death that is not murder are morally equivalent to 1000 lives taken by a malevolent actor. Some might claim "justice delayed is justice denied" in the case of scientific progress; those same people may be reluctant to say that their failure to pursue one line of research is effectively the killing of those people.

This dovetails into a stronger issue around the pursuit of alternatives of dual-use research. Advocates for GOF research have argued that GOF as a methodology has unique epistemic merits. While other experiments may allow us to demonstrate the *potential* for a pathogen to alter its host range or experience enhanced transmissibility or virulence, advocates maintain that only GOF can *show* us this is possible. As such, a change to an alternate methodology deprives us of the one methodological tool we have to conclusively prove that a (wild-type) virus can acquire the potential to cause a human pandemic.[62]

---

[59]Robbins et al. (2005), Connell (2012).

[60]This is not to say that existential risks do not deserve nuanced analysis, just that in some cases the risks may outweigh all other benefits *a fortiori*. See e.g. Bostrom (2014).

[61]Gryphon Scientific (n 45).

[62]Casadevall et al. (2014).

Yet it isn't clear either that this is truly unique of GOF research, or that this unique benefit is the benefit that *matters* for an analysis of dual-use research. One alternate experiment that might be to choose specific parts of a viruses to investigate: to determine whether a virus with a substituted HA protein would bind to human receptors we could use an attenuated virus rather than its wild-type progenitor, rendering our experiment much safer. A more radical alternative might be cell-free study of single proteins—for example, H5 or H7 receptor binding to mammalian sialic acids—and eliminate the need for a live virus (at least, in initial research).[63]

These alternate experiments offer to potentially answer the same question. Yet why consider only these? We could offer a series of alternatives that accomplish the same benefit *qua* preventing the spread of some infectious disease through alternate means, even those that do not rely on further infectious disease research. We know, for example, that global health capacities are still sorely lacking in many nations, including the developed world. We could envisage abandoning potential dual-use research for a public health solution; simply allocating the funds we otherwise would have spent on that research to, say, public health surveillance. We could, alternatively, spend the same money in some totally other way to benefit human health—improving traffic safety, for example.[64]

This is still fairly simple; for other instances of dual-use, it is even less clear. In the case of the mousepox study, the claimed potential benefit was the eradication of rabbit plagues. As an Australian, I can confidently say that this would lead to improved wellbeing for humans in Australia, but there are also a range of important values that might be at stake: the value of the natural environment for its own sake; of biodiversity; of the well-being of intelligent non-human mammals (of which there are many) in the country; redressing environmental injustices imposed upon the indigenous human population of Australia, of whom those who live on their traditional lands are worst affected by the undermining of the Australian natural environment.

In principle, the kinds of harms about which we should be concerned are similarly subject to variation. What is commonly unacknowledged about the mousepox case is that even before the IL-4 mutation that made it so deadly, what is unrecognised about the research programme is that it was one in which scientists were on a quest for an *infectious contraceptive*. Conceivably, this could be used by some kind of malevolent actor to render humans infertile, which would undermine a serious, central life plan of many billions of people.[65] While there is some welfare component to this kind of harm, we might think that people's autonomy is undermined, as is their ability to flourish, in a way that is (dis)valuable for its own sake.[66]

Talk of flourishing identifies ways in which we might think about different timescales for risks. The central debate around dual-use revolves around the prospect of acute and extreme harms. The paper focusing on botulinum toxin in the US milk supply, for example, claimed that the use of 1 kg of botulinum toxin could cause

---

[63]Evans (2018).

[64]Evans (n 24).

[65]Pennings (2008).

[66]Kleinig and Evans (2013).

an expected 200,000 deaths. This is a large, single-source attack, comparable to a disease pandemic—between four and eight years of flu mortality in the US, rolled into a single attack. While these attacks undoubtedly arise from collective actions,[67] they culminate in an event that we can (and maybe should) treat in the singular.

In contrast, consider deaths from road fatalities, or something similar. Approximately 32,000 people die on American roads each year. They do so, however, a few (or one) at a time. Is such a thing possible in the context of dual-use, and should it feature in a scheme to weigh the risks and benefits of such research? To the former, the answer is a likely "yes." Consider, for example, that in the last year there have been three very public self-experiments in synthetic biology, a discipline that seeks to transform biology into a predictable and tractable engineering discipline, and which has been identified as a field with strong dual-use potential.[68] All three cases—two in which individuals injected themselves with CRISPR-Cas9 constructs,[69] another in which an individual with human immunodeficiency virus (HIV) discontinued his antiretroviral treatments and injected himself with an experimental gene therapy[70]— were done outside of laboratory conditions, without safety equipment. Or consider that in the last half decade there have been a slew of attempted ricin poisonings committed by individuals who distilled the compound in their homes.[71] While the last example is in chemistry and not biology, it seems clear that there are in principle malevolent, reckless, or otherwise problematic cases where biology is misused, but on a small scale. We should then be concerned that, as biology diffuses from the province of a few to totally ubiquitous, that even a low rate of individual or small group-harming misuses could lead to a large number of deaths.

Responses to these events might have different implications. On the one hand, it is possible that a large-scale biological attack will happen in the next decade: security experts to whom I have spoken often go further to say such an attack is likely.[72] But in the meantime, an unregulated market for biologics on the Internet, pursued by amateur biologists, could spark a rash of deaths that exceeds a large biological attack over the medium term to misadventure, lax biosafety, and the proliferation of biological technologies.[73]

On the other hand, companies and groups often have strong incentives to avoid predictable, statistically likely deaths. There are a serious of reputational and resource

---

[67]Evans (2015).

[68]Tucker (2011).

[69]Zhang (2018).

[70]Brown (2017).

[71]Evans (2015). A law enforcement agent, speaking on conditions of anonymity, has noted that the number of these cases is an order of magnitude larger than reaches news outlets; most of these attempts, however, are not as advanced as those attempts that do make headlines.

[72]These claims have been made at meetings subject to, or by speakers who invoked The Chatham House Rule: The first meeting of the 2015 class of the Emerging Leaders in Biosecurity Initiative Fellowship in Washington, DC., March 2015; The Australian National University meeting on dual-use research in 2008 funded under the auspices of the Wellcome Trust Grant "Building a Sustainable Capacity in Dual-Use Bioethics;" among others.

[73]Evans and Selgelid (2014).

incentives, for example, that might make a biotechnology startup likely to seek to avoid deaths caused by users buying inadequately quality-controlled products. On the other hand, the likelihood of a mass-casualty event being caused by that same firm, or the kind of cost it would incur on a limited-liability actor (who lacks the resources or is protected from full liability) might attenuate incentives to act. A world of private biological enterprise might under protect us from very large, very rare harms.[74]

4 Translation

The above discussion has focussed in the main on risks; a look at the literature will find this to be relatively normal for the dual-use dilemma. Benefits tend to receive much less explicit critical analysis, although all of the challenges described above arguably can all be said to occur if one were to look at the benefits side of the dilemma. Are there any issues that apply, however, uniquely, distinctly or first and foremost to benefits?

I would argue that a critical issue facing benefits is that of translation. The benefits most often identified in the context of dual-use research apply to human health. But it is common knowledge that human health outcomes are rarely produced as a result of a single experiment, or even a line of research. This is in part because translation from basic science—and dual-use, in the main, has been a problem for basic science—to clinical or public health practice is rarely straightforward.

With this in mind, it isn't clear what stock we should place in claims about the purported benefits of dual-use research. Of our paradigm cases, the mousepox and botulinum cases present the strongest and most direct benefits. In the case of mousepox, the central translational issue that remained was to apply what was learned in a mouse model to rabbits. The benefit of a recombinant *myxoma* virus to human health is indirect in the sense that the eradication of an invasive pest benefits humans in second or higher-order degrees, but the achievement of those benefits was largely contingent on the application of knowledge from one virus to a related virus. This work was confirmed in 2004.[75]

In the case of botulinum toxin, the benefits were arguably more straightforward. Wein and Liu presented, in the context of their initial paper, recommendations for securing the milk supply against a potential terror attack.[76] While Wein claimed the US Federal and State Governments ultimately never acted on those recommendations,[77] the benefits were there for the taking.

Other studies, however, are not so straightforward. GOF is both most salient to a discussion of infectious disease, and has received substantial attention in the context of the deliberative process. Some proponents have suggested that, for example, GOF

---

[74]Lipsitch et al. (2016).

[75]Kerr et al. (2004).

[76]Wein and Liu (n 11).

[77]Wein (n 14).

research involving the creation of novel pandemic influenza strains benefits human health by informing the selection of seasonal influenza strains for vaccine development.[78] However, it has been argued elsewhere that this claim conflates "gain-of-function," a relatively common virology technique in which novel mutations are introduced into *any* virus to determine which mutation leads to a change in phenotype, and GOF research involving the creation of novel variants of HPAI that have enhanced virulence, transmissibility, or host range. That is, folks who argue about the benefits of GOF research of concern tend to rely on their membership of a much larger set of experiments.[79] To date, evidence that the 2011 GOF studies contributed to the particular health goal of selecting seasonal influenza strains is slight, and that which does exist is controversial.[80]

In the development of pandemic vaccines, moreover, the situation looks even grimmer. GOF research may provide a benefit, for example, by identifying a potential pandemic strain against which we could start to develop a vaccine. But the chances that such a vaccine will target a naturally occurring pandemic strain have been argued to be relatively slight.[81] This is because what occurs in the wild is not necessarily the same as what occurs in the lab—the studies identify a path to potential pandemic status for flu, but it is not clear that this is *the* path, rather than one of many potential paths.[82]

This is not to say that GOF research, among others, does not have value for human health. Its value, however, might be more attenuated than is typically argued. GOF studies, like so much microbiological infectious disease research, are model organism studies. They use well-characterised strains of flu (e.g. the Erasmus GOF study used a strain isolated in Indonesia in 2004) as a model for the class of pathogens known as highly pathogenic avian influenza H5N1 viruses; they also use ferrets as a model for humans in terms of the way that the flu binds to receptors in their upper respiratory tracts.[83] These models could be *causal* models, in the sense that they purport to give accurate information about what really happens in humans (and HPAI viruses). But it is more likely, on the face of things, that they are hypothesis-generating tools that scientists use to ask questions about, for example, the nature of viral pathogenesis.[84] This is useful scientific research in the sense that it can ask and answer important questions, but it is not directly or self-evidently connected to human values.

This is not unique to the beneficial applications of dual-use research. The weaponisation of a pathogen is an exercise in translation, where a promising candidate for a biological weapon is developed into munitions of some kind (e.g. biological cluster

[78] Schultz-Cherry et al. (2014).

[79] Lipsitch (2016).

[80] Gryphon Scientific (2016).

[81] Enserink (n 21); Enserink (2012).

[82] Lipsitch and Galvani (2014).

[83] Herfst and others (n 30).

[84] LaFollette and Shanks (1995).

bombs).[85] It is, moreover, a complex activity that often requires serious infrastructure, up to and including a state driven weapons programme.[86] We can, and should, ask whether the risks posed by dual-use research are subject to the same translational problems as the benefits problematised above.

Where, I believe, benefits and harms differ is twofold. The first is that in many paradigm cases, the harms that are described are not vulnerable to the same translational issues as benefits. In GOF research of concern in particular, the potential harms associated with this research inhere to the recombinant viruses themselves. While weaponizing a flu virus is and would be very difficult, the harms about which we are concerned do not depend on weaponisation. The benefits of dual-use research, on the other hand, frequently require further translation.

The other reason is heuristic rather than conceptual or empirical. In documents on dual-use, there is frequently a distinction made between harms and benefits in which the benefits of dual-use research are regarded as likely and inevitable, while the risks or harms are (at least partially) discounted based on translational issues. The Fink report's discussion of the synthesis of poliovirus noted that the method was exceptionally laborious and technical, thus undermining its utility for bioterrorism; the report, however, at numerous points asserts the "great potential benefits" inhering to the life sciences without a more nuanced account of what these might be or how they might arise.[87] In 2010, the US President's Commission for the Study of Bioethical Issues released a report on synthetic biology[88]; in an interview with *The Scientist*, Amy Gutmann, the chair of that committee, set apart the "likely" benefits from the "prospective" risks of the field.[89] These two examples speak to a perceived tendency of advocates of a particular technology to omit the complex transitional issues facing prospective benefits, while framing risks in a way that is sceptical of their possibility. If we are going to be wary of one form of translation, we should be wary of both, and begin with an account of the difficulty of deriving benefits from emerging science and technology.

5   Political Commitments

Translation dovetails with political commitments. Let's assume that GOF research really did give knowledge we could use to create a vaccine against a HPAI H5N1 pandemic. And let's say that we had some reasonable expectation that this pandemic was going to be the next pandemic. Does this mean GOF research has potential benefits?

---

[85] Enemark (2005).

[86] Leitenberg et al. (2012), Jefferson et al. (2014), Ouagrham-Gormley (2012).

[87] National Research Council (2004b).

[88] Presidential Commission for the Study of Bioethical Issues (2010a).

[89] Akst (2010).

Not necessarily. Vaccines don't save lives; vaccinations save lives.[90] In particular, we need to move from basic science, to a candidate vaccine, to the distribution of that vaccine to patients. Even if we set aside all technical scientific obstacles to this outcome, there still comes a question of political will, and whether our institutions are designed to accomplish this kind of outcome.[91]

We ought to care about political and individual commitments to action, and we ought to do so *symmetrically*. By symmetrically, I mean that when thinking about dual-use, we ought to treat like commitments alike whether or not those commitments are toward the beneficial or malevolent uses of life sciences research and technology. This is something that has, until recently,[92] been overlooked in the debate on dual-use. In examining dual-use in synthetic biology, the President's Commission for the Study of Bioethical Issues frequently claimed that the benefits of synthetic biology were imminent and sought-after, while the harms were merely prospective and not intended.[93] Yet we know, for example, that global healthcare continues to labour with poor or poorly allocated resourcing, while non-state groups have explicitly advocated for the use of unconventional weapons. Given that commitments toward achieving health outcomes are frequently lacklustre or subject to weakness of will (political or otherwise), and that terrorists frequently mean what they say, it appears that we should take both at least as seriously as each other.

There are two possible approaches to how these kinds of commitments should feature into our decisions to act.[94] One, a *possibilist* explanation, would say that our appeal to potential benefits stands if it is possible that we can produce the will to act on our commitments. Here, we only need for it to be possible to act upon our stated commitments, even if we have reason to believe we won't actually muster the will to accomplish what we set out to do so.[95]

Another way we could think about this is an *actualist* account of our motivations to act. Here, the likelihood that we will actually commit to a certain action matters as much as the likelihood that such an action would succeed if taken. On this account, we must have some belief that an actor (or set of actors) will commit to act in certain way to classify it as a potential benefit or harm, and the strength of our belief in this potential benefit or harm would vary as a function of our belief in our actor's commitment to act. (This applies for a stochastic as well as a game theoretic account of actors).

It isn't immediately clear which of these is preferable or rational to accept. On the one hand, actualism appears to conform to an intuition that we ought to really believe that someone is going to X before forming a belief about X's relative goodness or badness. Our belief about "a nonstate group using recombinant smallpox to eradicate

---

[90] I'm grateful to Jason Schwartz for this aphorism.

[91] Evans (n 64).

[92] Evans and Selgelid (n 69).

[93] Presidential Commission for the Study of Bioethical Issues (2010b).

[94] Jackson and Pargetter (1986).

[95] While Jackson and Pargetter use a binary model, Holly Lawford Smith has offered a probabilistic model of accessibility of actions by individuals and collectives. See Lawford-Smith (2012).

the human race" should surely be action guiding if and only if we have reason to believe that someone genuinely intends to do so, and (in addition to technical considerations) has the will to carry out their plan. A risk that no one intends to take isn't a risk in some important sense.

On the other hand, actualism might give us a really bleak look on the potential benefits of science. Political commitments, especially—never mind the commitments of scientists who may change their research focuses or lose funding; or the public, whose concerns and focus might change—are highly responsive to acute incentives and unresponsive to long-term needs. The West African Ebola epidemic, which received attention in 2015 and 2016 as an extreme threat,[96] is now a distant memory for developed nations. Actualism might attenuate our priors about the chances of a catastrophic bioterror attack, given what such an attack would require of an actor,[97] but it might also attenuate our priors about the chances of any proposed benefits of dual-use research obtaining in practice.

6   Weighing Benefits and Risks, and Setting Priorities

The ethical issues that arise in the context of dual-use research in the basic life sciences, including the study of infectious disease, invoke considerations of important fundamental values. Utility, characterised as the aggregate well-being of a population (up to "global" utility, i.e. the welfare of all living humans or moral status-holders) is implicated in dual-use research because of the potential for harm or benefit *qua* health for populations. Liberty is implicated because the governance of dual-use research—such as the potential suppression or censorship of research—may infringe upon fundamental rights to inquiry and/or speech, and professional rights to scientific freedom. And equality is implicated because those who benefit from dual-use research may be distinct from those who are harmed; the distribution of well-being (and/or liberties) is potentially morally significant in addition to its aggregate.

None of these three values is absolute, or always prior to the others.[98] Scientific freedom presumably isn't assured just in cases where we expect science to benefit us, especially (as a classical utilitarian might require) a requirement to maximally benefit the globe. If this were the case, the landscape of scientific research might be completely different: for example, migraines have the same burden on health (in disability adjusted life years) as HIV/AIDS in the USA but receive 1/100th of the funding.[99] In the global context, depression and injuries (among others) are underfunded relative to their overall burden of disease.[100] Yet I suspect most would say that while it might be permissible to change funding priorities, mandating scientists

---

[96] Evans (2016).

[97] Carus (2015), Leitenberg, Zilinskas and Kuhn (n 12).

[98] Selgelid (2009).

[99] Kaiser (2015).

[100] Gillum et al. (2011).

conduct research only certain issues would be an unjustifiable burden on their freedom (in addition to any utilitarian assertions about the role of scientific freedom in promoting health outcomes).

On the other hand, some research, as the NSABB acknowledged, might simply be too dangerous to conduct or publish. Say scientists attempted to make a highly transmissible disease—say measles—engineered to become 100% lethal. Or consider when Vincent Racaniello, a virologist at Columbia University, posited that a study to confer respiratory transmission via respiratory droplets (colloquially, to "make airborne") on HIV would present an "interesting" study.[101] Arguably, both hypothetical studies pose so much risk that no appeal to liberty or equality would outweigh the value of preventing the potential harms of such research.

Finally, sometimes the conduct of risky research ought to be responsive to considerations of equality.[102] Biosafety regulations in the US and elsewhere, for very dangerous pathogens, aim to protect not just those in the lab but those outside the lab. Even in cases where the harms of dual-use research are fairly limited, it is *pro tanto* unethical to expose individuals to risk who do not stand to benefit from our risk-taking behaviour. Biosafety regulations on dual-use research should aim not (merely) to protect against absolute utility loss, but to protect those who do not stand to benefit (or benefit as much) from scientific research against its potential risks.[103]

All things considered, we should adopt a position of pluralism about the ethics of dual-use research. We should aim, where possible, to guide scientific research away from dual-use research through a commitment to funding research whose benefits clearly outweigh its risks, commensurate with scientific freedom. That is, we should "design in" our ethical considerations into the scientific process from the earliest stage.[104] This should be matched with institutional support to realise the benefits of dual-use research while mitigating its risks. This institutional support, moreover, should seek to distribute both risks and benefits fairly among a population, such that the risk-taking entailed by dual-use research represents a fair scheme of risk sharing within society.[105] In particularly acute cases of dual-use, where the potential risks out the purported benefits of particular research, government should be empowered to impose moratoria on research or communication of dual-use.[106]

---

[101] See the June 1, 2014 episode of *This Week in Virology*. http://www.microbe.tv/twiv/twiv-287-a-potentially-pandemic-podcast/. Accessed 25 March 2018.

[102] Considerations of justice might also enter into our equation; I set this aside here.

[103] Evans, Lipsitch and Levinson (n 50).

[104] Evans and Selgelid (n 69).

[105] Hansson (2011).

[106] Evans (n 24).

7   Conclusion

Dual-use research is a key issue in the ethics of basic scientific research, and a particularly acute concern for research into infectious diseases that have, or can be engineered to have high virulence and transmissibility in humans. Over 17 years, the debate about dual-use has progressed from one in which scientific self-governance was held to be sufficient for the management of dual-use concerns, to the acknowledgement that at times even ostensibly beneficial scientific research may entail risks to great to justify its pursuit or publication. Future work will no doubt focus on how the life sciences research enterprise can be best designed to identify dual-use potential early, and prevent the proliferation of risky research.

References

Akst J (2010, November 19) Q&A: ethics chair on synthetic biology. The Scientist. https://www.the-scientist.com/?articles.view/articleNo/29368/title/Q-A--Ethics-chair-on-synthetic-biology/. Accessed 27 Apr 2018

Bartrip PWJ (2008) Myxomatosis, vol 288. IBTauris

Bostrom N (2014) Superintelligence, vol 272. OUP, Oxford

Brown KV (2017, October 18) This guy just injected himself with a DIY HIV treatment on facebook live. Gizmodo. https://gizmodo.com/this-guy-just-injected-himself-with-a-diy-hiv-treatment-1819659724. Accessed 24 Mar 2018

Carus WS (2015) The history of biological weapons use: what we know and what we don't. Health Sec 13:219

Casadevall A, Imperiale MJ (2014) Risks and benefits of gain-of-function experiments with pathogens of pandemic potential, such as influenza virus: a call for a science-based discussion. mBio 5:e01730

Casadevall A, Shenk T (2012) The H5N1 moratorium controversy and debate. mBio 3:e00379

Casadevall A, Howard D, Imperiale MJ (2014) An epistemological perspective on the value of gain-of-function experiments involving pathogens with pandemic potential. mBio 5:e01875

Cello J, Paul AV, Wimmer E (2002) Chemical synthesis of poliovirus cDNA: generation of infectious virus in the absence of natural template. Science 297:1016

Centers for Disease Control and Prevention (2014a) Report on the potential exposure to anthrax

Centers for Disease Control and Prevention (2014b) Report on the inadvertent cross- contamination and shipment of a laboratory specimen with influenza virus H5N1

Central Intelligence Agency (2003) The darker bioweapons future. OTI SF 2003-108

Coleman K, Zilinskas RA (2010) Fake Botox, Real Threat. Sci Am 302:84

Connell N (2012) Immunological modulation. In Tucker JB (ed) Innovation, dual use, and security. MIT Press

Dennis B, Sun LH, FDA found more than smallpox vials in storage room. Washington Post, 16 July 2014. https://www.washingtonpost.com/national/health-science/fda-found-more-than-smallpox-vials-in-storage-room/2014/07/16/850d4b12-0d22-11e4-8341-b8072b1e7348_story.html. Accessed 12 Dec 2017

Department of Health and Human Services (2017) Framework for guiding funding decisions about proposed research involving enhanced potential pandemic pathogens (19 December 2017). https://www.phe.gov/s3/dualuse/Documents/P3CO.pdf. Accessed 19 Dec 2017

Enemark C (2004) United States biodefense, international law, and the problem of intent. Politics Life Sci 24:32

Enserink M (2011, November) Scientists brace for media storm around controversial flu studies. Science 23. http://www.sciencemag.org/news/2011/11/scientists-brace-media-storm-around-controversial-flu-studies. Accessed 28 Feb 2016

Enserink M (2012) Public at last, H5N1 study offers insight into virus's possible path to pandemic. Science 336:1494

Evans NG (2000) Contrasting dual-use issues in biology and nuclear science. In: Selgelid MJ, Rappert B (eds) (2013) On the dual uses of science and ethics

Evans NG (2013) Great expectation—ethics, avian flu and the value of progress. J Med Ethics 39:209

Evans NG (2015) Dual-use decision making: relational and positional issues. Monash Bioeth Rev 32:268

Evans NG (2016) Ebola: from public health crisis to national security threat. In: Lentzos F (ed) Biological threats in the 21st century. Imperial College Press, London

Evans NG (2018) Ethical and philosophical considerations for gain-of-function policy: the importance of alternate experiments. Front Bioeng Biotechnol 6:e1875

Evans NG, Selgelid MJ (2014) Biosecurity and open-source biology: the promise and peril of distributed synthetic biological technologies. Sci Eng Ethics 21:1065

Evans NG, Lipsitch M, Levinson M (2015) The ethics of biosafety considerations in gain-of-function research resulting in the creation of potential pandemic pathogens. J Med Ethics 41:901

Fouchier RAM et al. (2012) Pause on avian flu transmission research. Science 335:400

Fouchier RAM, Garcia-Sastre A, Kawaoka Y (2012) The pause on avian H5N1 influenza virus transmission research should be ended. mBio 3:e00358

Fouchier RAM et al (2013) Transmission studies resume for avian flu. Science 339:520

GBD 2016 Causes of Death Collaborators (2017) Global, regional, and national age-sex specific mortality for 264 causes of death, 1980–2016: a systematic analysis for the Global Burden of disease study 2016. The Lancet 390:1151

Gillum LA et al (2011) NIH disease funding levels and burden of disease. PLoS ONE 6:e16837

Gryphon Scientific (2016) Risk and benefit analysis of gain of function research. Grphyon Scientific

Hansson SO Ethical criteria of risk acceptance. Erkenntnis 59:291

Henderson DA (2011) Frank Fenner (1914–2010). Nature 469:35

Herfst S et al (2012) Airborne transmission of influenza a/H5N1 virus between ferrets. Science 336:1534

Herfst S, Osterhaus ADME, Fouchier RAM (2012) The future of research and publication on altered H5N1 viruses. J Inf Dis 205:1628

Hindin D, Strosnider K, Trooboff PD (2017, Jan 20) The role of export controls in regulating dual use research of concern: striking a balance between freedom of fundamental research and national security. http://sites.nationalacademies.org/cs/groups/pgasite/documents/webpage/pga_176436.pdf. Accessed 5 June 2017

Imai M et al (2012) Experimental adaptation of an influenza H5 HA confers respiratory droplet transmission to a reassortant H5 HA/H1N1 virus in ferrets. Nature 486:420

Inglesby TV et al (2002) Anthrax as a biological weapon, 2002: updated recommendations for management. JAMA 287:2236

Jackson F, Pargetter R (1986) Oughts, options, and actualism. Philos Rev 95:233

Jackson RJ et al (1998) Infertility in mice induced by a recombinant ectromelia virus expressing mouse zona pellucida glycoprotein 31. Biol Reprod 58:152

Jackson RJ et al (2007) Expression of mouse interleukin-4 by a recombinant ectromelia virus suppresses cytolytic lymphocyte responses and overcomes genetic resistance to mousepox. J Virol 75:1205

Jefferson C, Lentzos F, Marris C (2014) Synthetic biology and biosecurity: challenging the "Myths". Front Public Health 2:449

Kaiser J (2015) What does a disease deserve? Science 350:900

Kennedy D (2005) Better never than late. Science 310:195

Kerr PJ et al (2004) Expression of rabbit IL-4 by recombinant myxoma viruses enhances virulence and overcomes genetic resistance to myxomatosis. Virology 324:117

Kimble JB et al (2014) Alternative reassortment events leading to transmissible H9N1 influenza viruses in the ferret model. J Virol 88:66

Kleinig J, Evans NG (2013) Human flourishing, human dignity, and human rights. Law Philos 32:539

Kobasa D et al (2007) Aberrant innate immune response in lethal infection of macaques with the 1918 influenza virus. Nature 445:319

LaFollette H, Shanks N (1995) Two models of models in biomedical research. Philos Q (1950-) 45:141

Lawford-Smith H (2012) Non-ideal accessibility. Ethical Theory Moral Pract 16:653

Leitenberg M, Zilinskas RA, Kuhn JH (2012) The Soviet biological weapons program. Harvard University Press, Cambridge

Lipsitch M (2016) Comment on "Gain-of-function research and the relevance to clinical practice". J Inf Dis 214:1284

Lipsitch M, Galvani AP (2014) Ethical alternatives to experiments with novel potential pandemic pathogens. PLOS Med 11:e1001646

Lipsitch M, Evans NG, Cotton Barratt O (2016) Underprotection of unpredictable statistical lives compared to predictable ones. Risk Anal

Miller S, Selgelid MJ (2008) Ethical and philosophical consideration of the dual-use dilemma in the biological sciences, vol 76. Springer, Berlin

National Academies of Sciences, Engineering and Medicine (2016) Gain-of-Function Research: Summary of the Second Symposium. In: Millett P et al (eds) National Academies Press, Washington

National Research Council (2004) Biotechnology research in an age of terrorism. National Academies Press, Washington

National Research Council Institute of Medicine (2015) Potential risks and benefits of gain-of-function research, vol 130. National Academies Press, Washington

National Science Advisory Board for Biosecurity (2007) Proposed framework for the oversight of dual use life sciences research. National Institutes of Health, Bethesda

National Science Advisory Board for Biosecurity (2011, November 21) National science advisory board for biosecurity recommendations. National Institutes of Health, Bethesda

National Science Advisory Board for Biosecurity (2012, March 29–30) National science advisory board for biosecurity findings and recommendations

National Science Advisory Board for Biosecurity (2016) Recommendations for the evaluation and oversight of proposed gain-of-function research. Office of Science Policy

Office of Science and Technology Policy (2017, January 9) Recommended policy guidance for Departmental Development of Review Mechanisms for Potential Pandemic Pathogen Care and Oversight (P3CO). obamawhitehouse.archives.gov. https://obamawhitehouse.archives.gov/sites/default/files/microsites/ostp/p3co-finalguidancestatement.pdf. Accessed 27 Feb 2017

Ouagrham-Gormley SB (2012) Barriers to bioweapons: intangible obstacles to proliferation. Int Sec 36:80

Palese P, Tumpey TM, Garcia-Sastre A (2006) What can we learn from reconstructing the extinct 1918 pandemic influenza virus? Immunity 24:121

Pennings G (2008) Ethical issues of infertility treatment in developing countries. 2008 ESHRE Monographs, p 15

Presidential Commission for the Study of Bioethical Issues (2010, December) New directions: the ethics of synthetic biology and emerging technologies. https://bioethicsarchive.georgetown.edu/pcsbi/sites/default/files/PCSBI-Synthetic-Biology-Report-12.16.10_0.pdf. Accessed 25 Mar 2018

Presidential Commission for the Study of Bioethical Issues (2010, December) New directoins: the ethics of synthetic biology and emerging technologies. https://bioethicsarchive.georgetown.edu/pcsbi/sites/default/files/PCSBI-Synthetic-Biology-Report-12.16.10_0.pdf. Accessed 25 Mar 2018

Richard M et al (2013) Limited airborne transmission of H7N9 influenza a virus between ferrets. Nature 501:560

Robbins S et al (2005) The efficacy of cidofovir treatment of mice infected with ectromelia (mousepox) virus encoding interleukin-4. Antiviral Res 66:1

Schultz-Cherry S et al (2014) Influenza gain-of-function experiments: their role in vaccine virus recommendation and pandemic preparedness. mBio 5:e02430

Selgelid MJ (2009) A moderate pluralist approach to public health policy and ethics. Public Health Ethics 2:195

Selgelid MJ (2016) Gain-of-function research: ethical analysis. Sci Eng Ethics 22:923

Selgelid MJ, Weir L (2010) Reflections on the synthetic production of poliovirus. Bull At Sci 66:1

Shelton H et al (2013) Mutations in Haemagglutinin that affect receptor binding and pH stability increase replication of a PR8 influenza virus with H5 HA in the upper respiratory tract of ferrets and may contribute to transmissibility. J Gen Virol 94:1220 (PubMed—NCBI)

Sutton TC et al (2014) Airborne transmission of highly pathogenic H7N1 influenza in ferrets. J Virol 88. https://doi.org/10.1128/JVI.02765-13

Taubenberger JK, Morens DM (2006) 1918 influenza: the mother of all pandemics. Emerg Infect Dis 12:15

The United States Government (2013, February 21) A framework for guiding U.S. Department of Health and Human Services funding decisions about research proposals with the potential for generating highly pathogenic avian influenza H5N1 viruses that are transmissible among mammals by respiratory droplets. www.phe.gov. https://www.phe.gov/s3/dualuse/documents/funding-hpai-h5n1.pdf. Accessed 12 Dec 2017

Tucker JB (2011) Could terrorists exploit synthetic biology? New Atlantis

Tumpey TM (2005) Characterisation of the reconstructed 1918 Spanish Influenza Pandemic Virus. Science 310:77

Watanabe T et al (2014) Circulating avian influenza viruses closely related to the 1918 virus have pandemic potential. Cell Host Microbe 15:692

Wein LM (2009) Homeland security: from mathematical models to policy implementation: the 2008 Philip McCord morse lecture. Oper Res 57:801

Wein LM, Liu Y (2005) Analyzing a bioterror attack on the food supply: the case of botulinum toxin in milk. Proc Natl Acad Sci 102:9984

Weir L (2012) A genealogy of global health security. Int Polit Sociol 6:322

Westwick PJ (2000) Secret science: a classified community in the national laboratories. Minerva 38:363

Zhang Y et al (2013) H5N1 hybrid viruses bearing 2009/H1N1 virus genes transmit in Guinea Pigs by respiratory droplet. Science 340:1459 (PubMed—NCBI)

Zhang S (2018, February 20) A biohacker regrets publicly injecting himself with CRISPR. The Atlantic. https://www-theatlantic-com.libproxy.uml.edu/science/archive/2018/02/biohacking-stunts-crispr/553511/. Accessed 24 Mar 2018

Rights-Based Approaches to Preventing, Detecting, and Responding to Infectious Disease

Benjamin Mason Meier, Dabney P. Evans, and Alexandra Phelan

Policymakers have come to look to human rights law in framing national health policy and global health governance. Human rights law offers universal frameworks to advance justice in public health, codifying international standards to frame government obligations and facilitate accountability for realising the highest attainable standard of health. Addressing threats to individual dignity as 'rights violations' under international law, health-related human rights have evolved dramatically to offer a normative framework for public health. Yet, public health efforts to address infectious disease continue to employ mechanisms that infringe individual rights—from the recent Ebola epidemics in Sub-Saharan Africa to the ongoing COVID-19 pandemic that threatens the world—with public health laws violating individual bodily integrity through vaccination and treatment mandates, violating individual medical privacy through surveillance and reporting, and violating individual liberty through quarantine and isolation. This chapter examines the implementation of human rights law in infectious disease control, analysing rights-based approaches to prevent, detect, and respond to infectious disease outbreaks.

Part I outlines the theoretical framework for health and human rights and describes evolving efforts to balance individual rights protections against government public

B. M. Meier (✉)
Department of Public Policy, University of North Carolina at Chapel Hill, Chapel Hill, NC, USA
e-mail: bmeier@unc.edu

O'Neill Institute for National & Global Health Law, Georgetown University, Washington, DC, USA

D. P. Evans
Global Health at the Hubert Department of Health, Rollins School of Public Health, Emory University, Atlanta, GA, USA

A. Phelan
Department of Law, Georgetown University Law School, Washington, DC, USA

Assistant Professor, Center for Global Health Security, Georgetown University, Washington, DC, USA

© Springer Nature Switzerland AG 2020
M. Eccleston-Turner and I. Brassington (eds.), *Infectious Diseases in the New Millennium*, International Library of Ethics, Law, and the New Medicine 82,
https://doi.org/10.1007/978-3-030-39819-4_10

health practices. Where human rights were long neglected in international health debates, early government reactions to the HIV/AIDS pandemic catalysed human rights as a basis for public health, as advocates looked explicitly to human rights as being 'inextricably linked' to public health efforts. Amidst the heightened fear and emerging advocacy that structured the early years of the AIDS response, policymakers sought to implement human rights law in public health policy—viewing discrimination as counterproductive to public health goals, abandoning coercive tools of public health practice, and applying human rights to focus on the individual risk behaviours leading to HIV transmission. Moving towards a focus on collective rights, viewing public health itself as a human right, these human rights claims have sought to address underlying population-level determinants of health in a rapidly globalising world.

These human rights have since come to hold a central place in framing public health policy, and Part II examines the ways in which these health-related human rights have been applied to realise non-discrimination and equality; autonomy, bodily integrity, and informed consent; participation; and the right to health. By recognising an inextricable linkage between public health and human rights, the health and human rights movement could move away from its early focus on the conflicts between public health practice and individual human rights, employing human rights promotion to advance public health goals. However, infectious disease control efforts continue to challenge the notion that individual rights are always the best approach to support population health, with recent responses to Ebola and COVID-19 continuing to rely on national policies that unnecessarily limit individual rights to protect public health. The human rights infringements resulting from these violative national policies highlight the continuing need for rights-based global health governance in preventing, detecting and responding to infectious disease.

In the new millennium, global health governance has sought to balance infectious disease imperatives for the public's health with individual dignity protections in human rights, and Part III analyses how global health law has framed this balance between public health and human rights. International law has long been seen as essential to the international cooperation necessary to address the global threat of infectious disease, but human rights were never addressed under global health law until the 2005 revision of the International Health Regulations. This 2005 revision explicitly looked to human rights for the first time—as a basis to respect human dignity and bodily integrity across states in the national implementation of infectious disease control measures. Despite this recent promise of universal human rights in global health governance, the 2014 development of the Global Health Security Agenda reverts to the 'securitisation' of public health to frame national efforts to prevent, detect, and respond to infectious disease. As nations again resort to unnecessary human rights infringements, abandoning global solidarity and international law in their emergency responses to the COVID-19 pandemic, it remains unclear how human rights law will be implemented through global health governance to support the future of infectious disease control.

This chapter concludes that the rights-based approach to infectious disease control has evolved—under human rights law, as applied to national policy, and in the development of global health governance—yet there remains little assessment of how these approaches either realise or infringe upon human rights in the pursuit of public health. Calling for a human rights research agenda to assess infectious disease control policies, programmes, and practices throughout infectious disease responses, this chapter proposes human rights monitoring of infectious disease control as a basis to facilitate accountability for the implementation of international human rights under global health law.

1 Health and Human Rights

Human rights law offers international frameworks to facilitate accountability for social justice in efforts to prevent, detect, and respond to infectious disease. Instrumental to human dignity, human rights address basic needs and frame individual entitlements, conceptualising international imperatives to uphold a universal vision of global justice.[1] By addressing threats to dignity as 'rights violations,' international law offers global standards by which to frame government responsibilities and evaluate policies and outcomes under law, shifting the policy debate from political aspiration to legal obligation.[2] Empowering individuals to seek accountability for these government obligations rather than serving as passive recipients of government benevolence, human rights law identifies individual rights-holders and their entitlements and corresponding duty-bearers and their obligations.[3] The state becomes the principal duty-bearer of human rights upon ratification of the underlying international human rights treaty, with the government thereafter accepting resource-dependent obligations to 'progressively realise' a human right 'to the maximum of its available resources, with a view to achieving progressively the full realisation of the rights'.[4] Building upon state obligations to realise the public's health, human rights can be seen both to protect individual rights from infringement in the pursuit of infectious disease control and to promote collective rights to underlying determinants of health.

1.1 Responsibilities of the State for Public Health

Public health encompasses the policies, programmes, and practices of a government to realise the collective rights of its peoples to health. Rather than focusing on the health of individuals, public health focuses on the health of societies.[5] At its most

---

[1] Donnelly (2003).

[2] Gostin (2014).

[3] Steiner et al. (2008).

[4] UN General Assembly, 'International Covenant on Civil and Political Rights' (Res. 2200A (XXI), 16 December 1966) art. 2; Felner (2009).

[5] Rose et al. (1999).

basic, '[p]ublic health is what we, as a society, do collectively to assure the conditions for people to be healthy'.[6] States have long recognised a responsibility to protect their peoples from infectious disease threats,[7] developing varied approaches of what must be done at a population level to assure 'underlying determinants of health'.[8] Whereas medicine focuses primarily on individual curative treatments in clinical settings, public health actions protect and promote[9] the health of entire societies by using multi-disciplinary interventions and multi-sectoral approaches to address the economic, political, and social determinants that underlie the public's health.[10] Under this expansive view, public health responds to the fundamental underlying structures affecting health, involving, *inter alia*, disease outbreaks, demographic patterns, economic distributions, and deleterious behaviours. In meeting these collective challenges, public health approaches are often designed to achieve 'the greatest good for the greatest number', applying a utilitarian lens as a basis to control the spread of infectious disease.[11]

1.2   Individual Rights in Tension with Public Health

Where human rights protect the individual, these individual rights are often seen to be in tension with state responsibilities to protect the public's health. Public health, in ensuring that societies can be healthy, often includes government intervention to restrict individual rights to protect the general welfare. In this conflict between collective benefit and individual restrictions, policymakers have long grappled with the appropriate balance between individual rights protection and public health promotion. In the development of human rights law, World War II showed the world the horrors that could occur under the guise of public health, and human rights would be codified under the post-war United Nations (UN) as a means to prevent public health authorities from infringing individual human rights. Out of this UN development of human rights law to protect individuals from public health practices, scholars and practitioners in the 1980s came to recognise the 'inextricable linkages' between public health and human rights, examining the ways in which the public health lens and human rights paradigm can complement each other in preventing disease and promoting health.

---

[6]The Institute of Medicine (1988) 19; *see also* Brockington (1968).

[7]Fidler (2002).

[8]Gostin (2001).

[9]Raeburn and Macfarlane (2003).

[10]Beaglehole and Bonita (1997).

[11]Holland (2015).

1.2.1 Birth of Human Rights in Response to the Public Health State

The notion of human rights under international law as a basis for public health finds its roots in the horrors that occurred during World War II and the standards laid down by the war tribunals that followed.[12] International human rights law was seen as a direct response to public health actions that infringed on individual liberties during the war. In articulating health-related human rights, the so-called 'Doctors Trial' of Nazi health practitioners by the International Military Tribunal at Nuremberg formed a key foundation for early post-war human rights developments.[13]

The atrocities committed by Nazi physicians during World War II, enabled by the German public health establishment, reflected a complete disregard for the value of human life and the inherent dignity of research subjects.[14] Beginning in 1933, the German Reich advanced public health theories of eugenics as the basis for promulgating the Law for the Prevention of Genetically Diseased Offspring, which outlined processes for the voluntary and mandatory sterilization of myriad 'hereditary defects'.[15] Pursuant to these so-called 'racial hygiene' programmes, German public health physicians sterilized between 300,000 and 400,000 German citizens prior to the war.[16] At the onset of war, the Nazi medical establishment moved from the sterilization to the killing those deemed to be 'incurably ill'.[17] During the war, with eugenics holding widespread acceptance in the state medical establishment, German physicians voluntarily aided in theorizing, planning, and operating Nazi killing programmes, which had then expanded from patients of German state hospitals to inmates of Nazi concentration camps.[18] Founded upon debased notions of public health, physicians exterminated millions to prevent the spread of purported diseases and defects.[19] Rather than questioning the ethical propriety of their actions, Nazi physicians enthusiastically performed acts of genocide, acting under a strong, albeit perverse, belief that they were working in accordance with the sound medical principle of 'healing the state'.[20] The genocidal horrors and human experimentation of the Holocaust would not have been possible without the professional legitimation and direct participation of the public health establishment.

Given these wanton violations of individual life and liberty in the course of the War, human rights, inhering in every individual simply by virtue of being human, would become the cornerstone of the post-war world. The Doctors Trial of 1946–1947, in which U.S. judges at Nuremberg passed judgment on Nazi physicians and health workers, would mark the first international criminal prosecution of health

---

[12]Moyn (2010).

[13]Annas and Grodin (1992).

[14]See Taylor (1992).

[15]Lippman (1993).

[16]Sidel (1996).

[17]Lippman (1992).

[18]Barondess (1996).

[19]Lippman (1992).

[20]Malinowski (2003).

workers for 'crimes against humanity', uncovering widespread patient and subject harms that would come to be seen as violations of human rights.[21] Rebuilding a world out of the ashes of World War II, every human being would be seen as equal in dignity and rights, with these human rights serving as a protection against state public health actions.

1.2.2 Derogation from Individual Rights to Protect Public Health

Notwithstanding this primacy of individual dignity and rights, international law supports the derogation of certain individual rights to protect the public's health. Where a right is considered derogable (capable of being temporarily suspended), the protection of public health is seen as a legitimate reason for government interference to promote the general welfare.[22] In clarifying the derogation of human right to protect public health, the evolution of international human rights law has sought to: define which rights are derogable, limit the grounds for rights derogation, and outline the processes of derogating rights.

Beginning with the 1948 Universal Declaration of Human Rights (UDHR), states agreed that '[e]veryone shall be subject only to such limitations as are determined by law solely for the purpose of securing due recognition and respect for the rights and freedoms of others...'.[23] Translating this non-binding declaration into international treaty law, the 1966 International Covenant on Civil and Political Rights (ICCPR) articulated the grounds for human rights derogation, stipulating that an '[o]fficial proclamation of public emergency allows deviation from other obligations to the extent required'.[24] These derogable rights would be specified in the context of a public health emergency, noting that the 'right to liberty of movement is...subject to restrictions necessary to protect public health or morals or the rights and freedoms of others'.[25] The ICCPR would thus specify three principal grounds for derogation:

1. To secure due recognition and respect for the rights and freedoms of others;
2. To meet the just requirements of morality, public order, and the general welfare; or
3. In time of emergency, where there are threats to the vital interests of the nation.

---

[21] Annas and Grodin (1992).

[22] Gostin and Mann (1994).

[23] UN General Assembly, 'Universal Declaration of Human Rights' (Res. 217 A (III), 10 December 1948) art. 29.

[24] UN General Assembly, 'International Covenant on Civil and Political Rights' (Res. 2200A (XXI), 16 December 1966) art. 4.

[25] UN General Assembly, 'International Covenant on Civil and Political Rights' (Res. 2200A (XXI), 16 December 1966) art. 12.

As states came to recognise that 'public health may be invoked as a ground for limiting certain rights',[26] scholars developed a set of principles to assure that such limitations on rights occur only 'in narrowly defined circumstances', holding that such human rights infringements only be undertaken:

1. When applied as a last resort;
2. When prescribed by law (i.e., not imposed arbitrarily);
3. When related to a compelling public interest (e.g., protection of public health); and
4. When found to be necessary, proportional to the public interest, and without less intrusive or restrictive measures available.[27]

Balancing the societal benefit to public health against the state infringement of individual rights, various legal scholars have sought to develop balancing tests to understand the specific circumstances in which it is necessary to restrict human rights to protect public health. These 'human rights impact assessments' have sought to measure the human rights impacts of public health policies and scrutinise disease prevention efforts to:

1. Clarify the public health purpose, narrowing public health goals to avoid overburdening rights;
2. Evaluate likely policy effectiveness, questioning whether the means undertaken will achieve the public health purpose;
3. Determine whether the public health policy is well targeted, recognizing the dangers of over-inclusiveness; and
4. Examine each public health policy for possible human rights burdens, looking to (1) the nature of the human right, (2) the invasiveness of the intervention, (3) the frequency and scope of the infringement, and (4) its duration.[28]

1.2.3 Recognizing the "Inextricable Linkages" Between Public Health and Human Rights

Reversing a history of neglect for human rights in international health debates throughout the height of the Cold War, the advent of the AIDS response operationalised human rights as a foundation for public health, as scholars and advocates looked explicitly to human rights law in framing public health practice. Governments had initially sought to react to the emergent threat of AIDS through traditional infectious disease practices—including compulsory testing, named reporting,

[26]UN Commission on Human Rights, 'The Siracusa Principles on the Limitation and Derogation Provisions in the International Covenant on Civil and Political Rights (UN Doc E/CN.4/1985/4, 1984) art. 25.

[27]UN Commission on Human Rights, *The Siracusa Principles on the Limitation and Derogation Provisions in the International Covenant on Civil and Political Rights*, UN Doc. E/CN.4/1985/4, 28 September 1984.

[28]Gostin and Mann (1994).

travel restrictions, isolation and quarantine, and other rights derogations—yet human rights were seen as a protection against these intrusive government infringements on individual liberty and a bond for stigma-induced cohesion among HIV-positive activists.[29] In this period of emerging rights-based activism, Jonathan Mann's tenure at the World Health Organisation (WHO) marked a turning point in the application of individual human rights to public health policy, viewing discrimination and coercion as counterproductive to public health goals and applying human rights to focus attention on the individual risk behaviours leading to HIV transmission.[30] Mann's vocal leadership of the WHO Global Programme on AIDS, formally launched in 1987, shaped formative efforts to create a rights-based framework for global health governance and national health policy.[31] Drawing from international human rights standards, public health policies came to stress the need for risk reduction programs to respect and protect human rights as a means to achieve the individual behaviour change necessary to reduce HIV transmission.[32]

In looking beyond individual behaviours in the HIV/AIDS response, Mann sought to extend the promise of human rights in addressing underlying population-level determinants of health—viewing rights realisation as supportive of 'a broader, societal approach to the complex problem of human wellbeing'.[33] Mann cautioned that HIV would inevitably descend the social gradient, calling for the rights-based examination of socioeconomic, racial, and gender inequities in abetting the spread of the disease.[34] Through this consideration of the collective determinants of vulnerability to HIV infection—rejecting the paradigm of complete individual control for health behaviours, a basic premise of the individual rights framework—the health and human rights movement shifted away from its early focus on the conflicts between public health responsibilities and human rights obligations.[35] Out of this recognition of a mutually-reinforcing linkage between public health and human rights, Mann proposed a tripartite framework to describe the effects of (1) human rights violations on health, (2) public health policies on human rights violations, and (3) human rights protections on public health promotion.[36] Given this focus on population-level determinants of vulnerability, Mann argued that 'since society is an essential part of the problem, a societal-level analysis and action will be required', calling for a rights-based AIDS agenda that would frame policies for access to costly medical treatments while maintaining a commitment to infectious disease prevention efforts focused on education, health services, and underlying environments for the public's health.[37]

---

[29]Curran et al. (1987), Kirby (1988), Bayer (1991).

[30]Fee and Parry (2008).

[31]Gruskin et al. (2007).

[32]World Health Organization (1988), Mann and Tarantola (1998).

[33]Mann (1996).

[34]Mann (1992).

[35]Gruskin et al. (1996).

[36]Mann et al. (1999).

[37]Mann (1999).

1.3 Beyond the Individual/Public Health Divide

Where health-related human rights were largely framed through an individual rights-holder in the latter half of the twentieth century, these individual rights have increasingly proven incommensurate to the globalised public health threats of the new millennium, unable to speak with the collective voice through which infectious disease control efforts must be heard. Infectious disease control efforts represent a global public good, and public goods cannot easily be realised through the individualistic lens of human rights. Reframing the realization of the individual right to health, a collective right to public health has become necessary to give meaning to the health-related human rights of populations, addressing population-level public health interests in infectious disease prevention, detection, and response.

Legal discourses at the intersection of health and human rights have often failed to view public health itself as a human right. Although the tension between individual human rights obligations and governmental public health responsibilities dominated early health and human rights discourses,[38] an emphasis on this conflict undermines health-related human rights. Whereas many scholars continue to focus on individual negative rights—i.e., those that restrain government action from infringing upon individual liberties—a positive human rights framework acknowledges that governments must act affirmatively to fulfil the economic and social aspects of human rights.[39] Fulfilling these positive components of health-related human rights requires both an individual right to health and collective rights to public health.[40]

Normative concern for underlying determinants of public health has become a cornerstone of infectious disease control, laying a foundation for the modern health and human rights movement. This movement draws from social medicine—arising out of the industrial revolution in Prussia and France and revitalized during World War II in Great Britain—with social medicine long viewing public health as an interdisciplinary social science that can examine how socioeconomic inequalities shape the health of populations.[41] Finding that illnesses have multiple population-level causes, social medicine scholars have looked to multisectoral social and political reforms (i.e., underlying determinants of health) rather than medicine as a means of promoting health for the most vulnerable.[42] In the context of international relations, social medicine defined public health as an inherent matter of government concern, separate and apart from the historical role of international health law in the international projection of economic power and national protection of security interests. Incorporated into international law, such a normative focus on underlying determinants of health was elevated in the aftermath of World War II through the holistic goal proclaimed

---

[38]Childress and Bernheim (2003), King (1999), Gostin and Lazzarini (1997).
[39]Marks (2001).
[40]Meier and Mori (2005).
[41]Rosen (1974).
[42]Ryle (1948), Sand (1934).

by states in the WHO Constitution: 'health is a state of complete physical, mental and social wellbeing and not merely the absence of disease or infirmity'.[43]

Under this rights-based vision of social medicine to address underlying determinants of health, collective rights operate in ways similar to individual rights; however, rather than seeking to empower the individual, collective rights act at a population level to assure public benefits that cannot be fulfilled through individual rights mechanisms.[44] While Western scholars long presupposed an opposition between individual and collective human rights,[45] this distinction is inappropriate to infectious disease control in a globalizing world, where the goals of an individual right to health and a collective right to public health complement each other.[46] Combating the health disparities of a globalized world requires renewed human rights focus—in national policy and global governance—on these collective population-level concerns that underlie the spread of disease.

2   National Rights-Based Public Health Responses

In implementing these rights, national disease control policies frequently navigate between state responsibilities to protect the health of the public and obligations to respect the rights of individuals. Balancing tests now detail the rights, conditions, and processes that allow for the permissible derogation of some human rights towards the goal of protecting public health—where rights infringements should be, as reviewed above, based on justifiable limitations, responsive to a pressing social need, in pursuit of a legitimate aim, and proportionate to the health challenge.[47] State actors are responsible for most human rights infringements, whether permissible or not, and therefore national responses are of utmost importance.

States are in a position in which they have both the duty to respect, protect, and fulfil the right to health and other health-related rights and the power to legitimately restrict rights in order to protect public health.[48] Most frequently, it is the state's obligation to respect (or refrain from violating) the rights of individuals that is at odds with its responsibility to protect populations—highlighted by rights-infringing efforts to prevent, detect, and respond to infectious disease. This misalignment may create a

---

[43] World Health Assembly, 'Constitution of the World Health Organization' (signed on 22 July 1946, entered into force 7 April 1948) preamble.

[44] Marks (2004).

[45] VanderWal (1990).

[46] Meier (2006).

[47] UN Commission on Human Rights, *The Siracusa Principles on the Limitation and Derogation Provisions in the International Covenant on Civil and Political Rights*, UN Doc. E/CN.4/1985/4, 28 September 1984.

[48] UN Committee on Economic, Social and Cultural Rights (CESCR), 'General Comment No. 14: The Right to the Highest Attainable Standard of Health (Art. 12 of the Covenant)' (UN Doc. E/C.12/2000/4, 11 August 2000); UN General Assembly, 'International Covenant on Civil and Political Rights' (Res. 2200A (XXI), 16 December 1966) art. 11.

dual loyalty, where state obligations to respect individual rights may conflict with responsibilities for promoting public health. In order to appropriately balance competing interests, states may look to established international human rights norms and principles for guidance—either prospectively (to guide state public health actions) or retrospectively (to consider missed opportunities to respect rights). Applied in the context of national infectious disease control policies, such norms and principles include those necessary for (1) dignity, (2) non-discrimination, (3) participation, and (4) the right to health.

2.1 *Dignity: Bodily Integrity and Autonomy*

Although never explicitly defined within the human rights corpus, human dignity explicitly underpins all international human rights. The preambular text of the UN Charter states that one of the principal purposes of the UN is 'to reaffirm faith in fundamental human rights, in the dignity and worth of the human person'.[49] Scholars have long debated the precise conceptualisation of the relationship between human dignity and human rights.[50] Central to bodily integrity and autonomy, dignity is given concrete application in rights-based approaches to prevent, detect, and respond to infectious disease.

Public health practices of isolation and quarantine serve as paradigmatic examples of public health approaches to infectious disease control that may infringe upon individual autonomy via limitations on movement. In the case of isolation, infected individuals are contained to prevent the spread of disease; quarantine is used to confine healthy individuals who have been exposed to disease. The case of 'Typhoid Mary' (who was forcibly isolated after her repeated refusal to cooperate with public health authorities in preventing the spread of her asymptomatic typhoid) exemplifies the need, at times, for state intervention in restricting freedom of movement.[51] In the government exercise of isolation and quarantine—including the contemporary application of travel restrictions (both within a country and applied to travelers from other countries) in response to COVID-19—the individual right of free movement is in tension with the protection of public health; thus, the rights of the individual are infringed to protect the collective interests of the larger population.

Relatively recent responses to infectious disease outbreaks—particularly among new or previously unknown infections—have remained grounded in these age-old public health practices. In the early years of the HIV response, the Cuban government was strongly criticised for its use of HIV isolation facilities, known as sanatoriums.[52] This isolation practice undoubtedly infringed upon the dignity of people living with

---

[49]United Nations, 'Charter of the United Nations' (UN Doc. UNTS XVI, 24 October 1945) preamble.

[50]Donnelly (1982), McDougal et al. (1980).

[51]Marineli et al. (2013).

[52]Bayer and Healton (1989), Hoffman (2004).

HIV/AIDS (PLHA). However, those in the sanatoriums enjoyed access to higher food rations, specialized care for HIV, and relief from employment responsibilities, benefits that were seen as especially advantageous during Cuba's post-Cold War economic crisis, known as the 'special period'.[53] While the government has stepped away from these rights-infringing practices—employing the sanatoriums now as training centres for HIV diagnosis, education, and care management—Cuba continues to have one of the lowest rates of HIV/AIDS in the region, a public health outcome attributed their early rights-restricting HIV containment practices.[54] The 2014–16 Ebola Virus Disease epidemic similarly highlighted how well-intentioned public health efforts can infringe individual rights. In Liberia, residents of the West Point neighbourhood were quarantined despite a lack of evidence that the virus was more prevalent there than elsewhere in the country. In the United States, a nurse who tested negative for Ebola was nevertheless confined to isolation, although a court would later overturn this derogation of her rights and restriction on her movement.[55] Setting a precedent for current lockdowns during the rapidly spreading COVID-19 pandemic, these examples highlight the need for scientific evidence in public health decision making, even in the course of ongoing infectious disease outbreaks; where there is little scientific information related to new and emerging pathogens, research is warranted to understand the threats such pathogens pose to the public's health and the responses that are necessary to prevent disease. These data are critical in balancing risks and benefits to determine the most appropriate and least burdensome policy response, especially when individual rights restrictions include limitations on movement.

Such state restrictions on individual autonomy to protect public health may extend beyond limitations on physical movement to include mandatory treatment. Establishing a precedent for state vaccine mandates that stands to this day, the U.S. Supreme Court's 1905 decision in *Jacobson v. Massachusetts*[56] held that the state could enforce compulsory vaccination laws where individual autonomy was deemed subordinate to protecting the health of the population.[57] Recently, however, there has been an increase in vaccine-preventable diseases in high-income countries. Despite being officially eliminated from the United States in 2000, Measles outbreaks have been reoccurring sporadically throughout the country.[58] The resurgence of vaccine-preventable diseases in such settings has largely been attributed to vaccine opponents, who refuse vaccinations based upon religious or personal beliefs.[59] Notwithstanding the proven efficacy of vaccines, the result of this opposition has been to increase

---

[53]Reed (2011).

[54]Joint United Nations Programme on HIV/AIDS (UNAIDS), 'Global Report: UNAIDS Report on the Global AIDS Epidemic' (UNAIDS 2013).

[55]Price (2015).

[56]*Jacobson v Massachusetts* (1905) 197 US 11.

[57]Mariner et al. (2005).

[58]McCarthy (2015).

[59]Yang et al. (2015).

non-medical vaccine exemptions and, consequently, led to a higher incidence of vaccine-preventable disease in ways that threaten the public's health.[60]

Vaccine refusal highlights issues of individual responsibility. In the case of vaccine opposition (particularly for childhood vaccinations), parents must balance their perceived risk of vaccines against the potential negative outcomes of infection.[61] For many years, this debate was assuaged by broad acceptance of childhood vaccinations (bolstered by vaccine mandates for school enrollment), which led to substantial decreases in the incidence of vaccine-preventable diseases and the establishment of 'herd immunity' at the population level without the need for vaccine mandates.[62] In this way, childhood vaccination programmes have become a victim of their own success. The anti-vaccine movement—fuelled in recent years by false concerns about vaccine safety, coupled with religious and philosophical exemptions to school-based vaccine requirements—has provided an opening for the resurgence of vaccine-preventable diseases in places where they were previously rare.[63] As exemptions to school vaccine mandates have increased, there has been a waning of herd immunity (also known as 'community protection') against vaccine-preventable disease. Community protection relies on such population immunity. It is this herd immunity, not individual disease immunity, that protects a given population. Therefore, those choosing not to vaccinate remain individually vulnerable to infections, which can then be transmitted throughout the community. On the global scale, while vaccines are most frequently viewed as crucial to public health, erroneous perceptions about vaccine safety continue to undermine the potential of vaccines to prevent infectious disease.[64] This threat from individual refusal to adhere to public health guidelines is similarly seen among those flouting social distancing recommendations to prevent the spread of COVID-19. As a result, public health professionals must reexamine not only individual autonomy, but also individual responsibility towards the community—a concept which varies widely across cultural contexts.

Through the lens of human rights, individual responsibility to the community can be seen as a form of legal duty. Despite cultural variance towards individual and collective duties, the UDHR clarifies that restrictions of individual rights can be undertaken as a basis to respect the 'rights and freedoms of others' in the community.[65] In the case of exemptions from vaccination, policymakers have sought to make individual exemptions more rare as a basis to protect the public.[66] Beyond mandates, adherence to the principle of informed consent (including scientifically accurate information on the risks and benefits of vaccination) addresses misinformation and safety concerns while simultaneously supporting autonomy and informed

---

[60]Omer et al. (2006), Omer et al. (2012).

[61]Champion and Skinner (2008).

[62]Roush et al. (2007).

[63]Gust et al. (2008).

[64]Larson et al. (2016).

[65]UN General Assembly, 'Universal Declaration of Human Rights' (Res. 217 A (III), 10 December 1948) art. 29.

[66]Omer (2015).

decision making. Under this model for balancing individual rights and public health, receiving a vaccine exemption would be possible, but perhaps more difficult, in an effort to push individuals towards vaccination. This model could increase levels of individual vaccination and herd immunity—achieving a public health goal in balance with standards of human dignity.

2.2 Non-discrimination and Stigma

With this imperative for dignity through human rights requiring an emphasis on non-discrimination and equality, the attention to vulnerable populations in both human rights treaties and human rights institutions was born of the Holocaust experience of World War II, wherein the Nazi crimes against humanity implicated the discriminatory targeting of specific populations. Today, each core human rights treaty includes a non-discrimination clause that prohibits discrimination on the basis of, at a minimum, race, sex, language, and religion. At times, additional language has been used to expand beyond these categories, including prohibitions on discrimination on the basis of disability and health status. Although some of these characteristics were once viewed as both biologically-dictated and immutable, evolving notions of social constructions in the context of race and gender have allowed for flexibility and inclusiveness, rather than a rigid dogmatism linked to specific terms, in a more expansive view of human rights.

Human rights protections against stigma and discrimination are now seen as 'inextricably linked' to the realisation of public health goals. The emergence of HIV/AIDS exacerbated the social stigma, homophobia, and racism targeted against injection drug users, men who have sex with men (MSM), and racial minority groups. Furthering this discrimination through public health policy, the U.S. Centers for Disease Control and Prevention's '4H club' identified homosexuals, heroin users, haemophiliacs and Haitians as specific at-risk groups. This well-intentioned and catchy phrase led to devastating results, with vulnerable groups experiencing housing and employment discrimination, and the impoverished island of Haiti experiencing an 80% decrease in tourism.[67] Such stigma towards risk groups, rather than behaviours, is currently unfolding in the COVID-19 response, where individuals of Asian descent have been stigmatised by the label of the 'Chinese virus', facing discrimination, violence, and health care denial based upon racist demagoguery from nationalist politicians.

Through his work to advance human rights in WHO, Jonathan Mann sought to identify the linkages between human rights frameworks and the stigma and discrimination faced by vulnerable populations. Mann's vision of discrimination as harmful to public health and his understanding that individual behaviour change was key to disease prevention was prescient, giving rise to a health and human rights movement that would seek to end discrimination in public health practice. This discrimination,

---

[67] PBS Frontline (2006).

embodied by the longstanding US travel ban against HIV-positive individuals, was finally lifted only in 2010.[68] Rather than discussing risk groups or identity groups, policymakers now talk about risk behaviours underlying infection and key groups.

Where human behaviours and discriminatory attitudes may be exceedingly difficult to change, laws and policies provide a rights-based foundation upon which social norms may draw reference. The incorporation of human rights principles into legal and policy reforms has shown promise in reducing HIV/AIDS-related stigma and discrimination.[69] Legal protections for those infected or in groups at high risk of HIV infection (including MSM, injection drug users, and commercial sex workers) may prevent and mediate individual and institutionalised forms of stigma and discrimination.[70] These protections are inherently linked to the human rights principle of non-discrimination; related reductions in stigma surrounding risk behaviours, mother to child transmission of HIV, and HIV testing and treatment remain vital to both discrimination against vulnerable populations and reduction of disease transmission.[71] In the context of COVID-19, stigma and discrimination act as kindling for the spread of the infection among detained populations and homeless people who are vulnerable because of both their housing and their membership in socially stigmatized groups.

2.3 Participation

The participation of civil society and affected populations in holding duty bearers accountable for implementing these human rights obligations is a critical principle for the advancement of human rights. Such participation is necessary, in large part, because states are both duty-bearers and the most frequent violators of human rights.[72] This engagement in government processes is extremely important; in the case of health, participation in political debates may entail opportunities for direct action where community members are affected by health care goods, facilities, and services.[73] As such, participation plays a vitally important role in infectious disease control. In the South African case of the *Ministry of Health vs. Treatment Action Campaign (TAC)*, the South African Constitutional Court found that the state was responsible under the right to health for the provision of antiretroviral drugs to pregnant persons for the prevention of mother to child transmission of HIV.[74] TAC played a critical participatory role in both bringing the legal case and advocating publicly for the availability of antiretrovirals for all HIV-positive South Africans. Civil society

---

[68] Preston (2009).

[69] Mahajan et al. (2008).

[70] Rhodes et al. (2005).

[71] Mahajan et al. (2008).

[72] Potts (2008).

[73] Meier et al. (2012).

[74] Giliomee and Mbenga (2007).

groups, including non-governmental organizations, can also play an important formal role within international human rights mechanisms through the provision of shadow reports to the UN bodies responsible for monitoring human rights treaty compliance. While the UN Committee on Economic, Social and Cultural Rights is the primary treaty body responsible for monitoring the right to health, numerous other human rights bodies examine health-related human rights, incorporating participation from civil society actors in their assessments of national human rights implementation efforts.[75]

Community members can additionally be health agents locally, acting as health resources, improving governmental capacity for health, and supporting primary health care.[76] However, doctors, nurses, and public health professionals often face dual loyalty when, as in many countries, they work within national health systems.[77] Health professionals employed by such systems are state actors and have professional obligations to their employers, but at the same time, they have ethical obligations to those affected by health systems. While setting health policy, health professionals may also be directly providing health services at the community level.

Advancing their work as health agents, some community members may pursue formal medical and public health training, engaging in the health sector by becoming health practitioners while simultaneously representing the interests of their communities. Innovative models of medical and public education such as that of the Latin American School of Medicine (ELAM), which has the right to health mainstreamed throughout its curriculum, facilitate the training of disadvantaged groups who are most likely to return to serve their home communities.[78] The purposeful recruitment of marginalised populations into the health professions has shown demonstrated benefits for participation in the health system.[79]

It is not only those with clinical training who can participate in community level health delivery. The Chinese 'Barefoot Doctors' programme of the late 1960s established a framework for community based primary health care. Since 1970, *Where There Is No Doctor* has become one of the most widely used health care manuals, and both WHO and UNICEF use the text in their field offices, equipping readers with vital health information for personal and community based decision making.[80] The text has been credited with making basic health information, including information

---

[75] See, for example, United Nations (UN), 'NGO Participation at CEDAW sessions' (*UN Women*) http://www.un.org/womenwatch/daw/ngo/cedawngo.

[76] International Conference on Primary Health Care, 'Declaration of Alma-Ata' (6–12 September 1978).

[77] Physicians for Human Rights & School of Public Health and Primary Health Care, University of Cape Town, Health Sciences Faculty, 'Dual Loyalty & Human Rights in Health Professional Practice; Proposed Guidelines & Institutional Mechanisms' (2002) https://s3.amazonaws.com/PHR_Reports/dualloyalties-2002-report.pdf.

[78] Primer Hospital Popular Garifuna, 'Our History' (*Primer Hospital Popular Garifuna*) http://primerhospitalgarifuna.blogspot.com/p/ingles.html.

[79] Institute of Medicine (2003), Saha et al. (1999).

[80] Werner et al. (1992).

on hygiene and infectious diseases, globally accessible.[81] In accordance with community level health delivery, Community Health Workers (CHWs) play an extremely important role in the delivery of services[82] and the response to infectious disease.[83] Partners in Health (PIH), philosophically grounded in liberation theology, was an early adopter of community participation in infectious disease prevention and control. PIH successfully promoted the participation of affected communities in the early use of antiretroviral therapy in Haiti, resulting in improved compliance with what were then more rigorous medicine regimens.[84] Their success in this approach, coupled with rights-based advocacy efforts, has resulted in a sea change in thinking about the feasibility of antiretroviral therapy among populations in low-resource settings. The COVID-19 response highlights the continuing importance of participation, where adherence to social distancing, self-isolation, and shelter in place policies are designed to "flatten the curve"; yet, without widespread community participation, such critical policies are ineffective, if not meaningless.

2.4   The Right to Health

These rights-based approaches to infectious disease have been structured by the right to health, framed by attributes that examine the availability, accessibility, acceptability and quality (AAAQ) of health goods, facilities, and services. The UN Committee on Economic, Social and Cultural Rights outlined these four interconnected and essential attributes of the right to health,[85] which have specific application to infectious disease efforts, as highlighted by infectious disease prevention and response during the 2014–2016 Ebola Virus Disease epidemic and the ongoing COVID-19 pandemic.

Under this AAAQ framework, availability pertains to the quantity of health goods, facilities, and services available within a given country context; the concept includes essential medicines as defined by WHO and the underlying determinants of health like safe potable drinking water.[86] When Ebola emerged in 2014 in West Africa, the three affected countries (Guinea, Liberia, and Sierra Leone) were particularly vulnerable. Colonized by three different colonial powers, the countries share a history of military coups, dictatorship, civil war, and strife, which have resulted in the destruction of virtually all health care infrastructures, widespread poverty, and a lack of trust in

---

[81] Godlee et al. (2004).

[82] Figueroa-Downing et al. (2016).

[83] De Oliveria Chiang et al. (2015).

[84] Koenig et al. (2004).

[85] UN Committee on Economic, Social and Cultural Rights (CESCR), 'General Comment No. 14: The Right to the Highest Attainable Standard of Health (Art. 12 of the Covenant)' (UN Doc. E/C.12/2000/4, 11 August 2000).

[86] UN Committee on Economic, Social and Cultural Rights (CESCR), 'General Comment No. 14: The Right to the Highest Attainable Standard of Health (Art. 12 of the Covenant)' (UN Doc. E/C.12/2000/4, 11 August 2000).

public institutions.[87] Ebola capitalised upon these institutional weaknesses to create a perfect storm of public health, humanitarian, and human rights crises. The global community belatedly rushed to build Ebola Treatment Units (ETUs), as nations are seeking today to build hospitals to take in COVID-19 patients, but could offer little in terms of treatment. As seen in the early COVID-19 response, the shortage of surge capacity for face masks, ventilators, Personal Protective Equipment (PPE), and other essential medical equipment underscores that the global community has not yet learned the importance of public health preparedness. Key lessons from these public health emergencies relative to availability include the importance of investment in trained health professionals, facilities, and surveillance systems.[88]

Accessibility of health care and health care systems is operationalised in four ways. Facilities must be geographically and physically accessible, services must be affordable or economically accessible to users, care should be provided in a non-discriminatory manner (with vulnerable and marginalised populations prioritised), and both users and health personnel should be able to confidentially seek and receive health information.[89] Where health care facilities and personnel were extremely limited in the West African context at the start of the Ebola epidemic, infected people likely delayed seeking care due to poverty, and, later, ETUs were viewed as 'death centres'. Beyond care, it has been necessary in both the Ebola and COVID-19 response to have access to water, sanitation, and hygiene. Even where physically accessible, access to health information is critical to disease control, as seen where the availability of chlorine water buckets for handwashing was useless in the Ebola response without accompanying messaging about why and how to use them.[90]

Examining the acceptability of behaviour change relating to cultural practices—from mundane handshakes to sacred burials[91]—these practices were socially important and changing them was crucial to preventing Ebola transmission, as they will be necessary to understand and change the course of transmission during the COVID-19 pandemic. The concept of acceptability encompasses the oft-debated human rights notion of cultural relativism, requiring that health goods, facilities, and services are culturally appropriate.[92] In the case of Ebola in West Africa, nuanced approaches to behaviour change were necessary to ensure the prevention of disease, including engagement with religious and community leaders in the development of culturally

---

[87]Dabney P. Evans & Carlos del Rio, 'Ebola Virus Disease: An Evolving Epidemic.' (*Coursera*) https://www.coursera.org/learn/ebola-virus.

[88]Crawford et al. (2016).

[89]UN Committee on Economic, Social and Cultural Rights (CESCR), 'General Comment No. 14: The Right to the Highest Attainable Standard of Health (Art. 12 of the Covenant)' (UN Doc. E/C.12/2000/4, 11 August 2000).

[90]Dabney P. Evans & Carlos del Rio, 'Ebola Virus Disease: An Evolving Epidemic.' (*Coursera*) https://www.coursera.org/learn/ebola-virus.

[91]del Rio et al. (2014).

[92]UN Committee on Economic, Social and Cultural Rights (CESCR), 'General Comment No. 14: The Right to the Highest Attainable Standard of Health (Art. 12 of the Covenant)' (UN Doc. E/C.12/2000/4, 11 August 2000).

acceptable alternatives to traditional practices.[93] The concept of acceptability is also closely aligned with traditional discussions of medical ethics.[94] In accordance with such ethical principles, the lack of a cure and limited knowledge about effective Ebola treatment required that those treating cases in well-resourced settings rapidly share information with those in West Africa.[95]

Quality requires that health facilities, goods, and services are scientifically and medically appropriate.[96] Assuring such quality pursuant to the right to health requires, *inter alia*, unexpired drugs and equipment and appropriate training for health personnel. In the case of both Ebola and COVID-19, many early casualties of the disease were care givers, including health personnel. With respect to protecting care givers, the importance of correctly donning and doffing PPE is critical in slowing the spread of disease among those in direct contact with infected individuals. The practice was even successfully adopted by a nursing student who used garbage bags to protect herself from Ebola infection while caring for sick family members; in the absence of equipment in the COVID-19 response, seamstresses everywhere have coalesced to sew needed face masks for medical personnel.[97]

This examination of efforts to address Ebola and COVID-19 through the AAAQ lens provides useful insights into missed opportunities for the application of the right to health to infectious disease control policy and future directions for public health responses.

National governments are only beginning to apply health-related human rights in addressing infectious disease—including the right to health, health-related human rights, and cross-cutting rights-based principles of dignity, non-discrimination, and participation—but despite the control of some infectious diseases, there is more that must be done.[98] Tuberculosis (TB) kills millions each year,[99] yet lack of access to treatment for key populations remains a challenge, worsened for those marginalised by HIV co-infection or Multi Drug Resistant TB (MDR-TB). HIV/AIDS, now in its fourth decade as a global pandemic, continues to disproportionately affect impoverished populations, racial and ethnic minorities, the incarcerated, and sexual minorities. Inadequate attention to vector-borne diseases like Zika have resulted in devastating consequences for marginalized populations, including among poor

---

[93]Dabney P. Evans & Carlos del Rio, 'Ebola Virus Disease: An Evolving Epidemic.' (*Coursera*) https://www.coursera.org/learn/ebola-virus.

[94]UN Committee on Economic, Social and Cultural Rights (CESCR), 'General Comment No. 14: The Right to the Highest Attainable Standard of Health (Art. 12 of the Covenant)' (UN Doc. E/C.12/2000/4, 11 August 2000).

[95]Lyon et al. (2014); Dabney P. Evans & Carlos del Rio, 'Ebola Virus Disease: An Evolving Epidemic.' (*Coursera*) https://www.coursera.org/learn/ebola-virus.

[96]UN Committee on Economic, Social and Cultural Rights (CESCR), 'General Comment No. 14: The Right to the Highest Attainable Standard of Health (Art. 12 of the Covenant)' (UN Doc. E/C.12/2000/4, 11 August 2000).

[97]Dabney P. Evans & Carlos del Rio, 'Ebola Virus Disease: An Evolving Epidemic.' (*Coursera*) https://www.coursera.org/learn/ebola-virus.

[98]Barrett et al. (1998).

[99]World Health Organization (2016).

Afro-Brazilian populations. COVID-19 has already descended the social gradient to become a disease of the poor and marginalised, exposing the continuing weaknesses of national efforts to see individual rights as inextricably linked with public health efforts. Despite the challenges posed by existing and emerging infectious diseases, human rights-based approaches offer a framework for advancing national disease control efforts. However, the continuing limitations of these national policies highlight the need for rights-based global health governance.

3 Development of Rights-Based Global Health Governance for Infectious Disease Prevention, Detection, and Response

Globalisation has channelled the spread of disease, connected societies in shared vulnerability, and highlighted the risks posed by inadequate national policies.[100] Yet if globalisation has presented challenges to infectious disease control, globalised institutions offer the promise of bridging national boundaries to alleviate these common threats through global health governance for infectious disease prevention, detection, and response. Global collective action through international law is essential to develop the rights-based governance structures for realizing global solidarity in dealing with global infectious disease threats that are outside the control of individual states.[101]

3.1 Infectious Disease Control Gives Birth to Global Health Governance

Collective international governance for infectious disease control has evolved over the past two centuries. Propelled by the steam of industrialisation, migration from rural to urban areas, and cross-border travel and trade challenged nation-states in the nineteenth century to cooperate in the prevention, detection, and control of infectious diseases. As cholera spread throughout Europe in the early-to-mid nineteenth century, individual states, still unaware of modern principles of epidemiology or microbiology, responded by imposing burdensome restrictions on merchants and travellers, including the quarantine of travellers, the disabling of ships, and the destruction of cargo.

Given the constraints of these national restrictions on international commerce,[102] international health law would seek to coordinate national public health responses

---

[100]Taylor (2004).

[101]Slaughter (1997).

[102]Howard-Jones (1975).

to protect international economic and security interests against infectious disease threats. In 1851, twelve nations met for the first of fourteen International Sanitary Conferences, seeking to stem the spread of infectious disease across Europe without unduly hindering commerce.[103] While a lack of scientific understanding and international consensus stymied international agreement during early conferences,[104] evolving understanding of infectious disease epidemiology finally led to the development in 1892 of a binding agreement: the International Sanitary Convention (ISC).[105] Driven by national security and economic interests rather than a desire to protect the public's health—as either a public good or a human right[106]—states agreed under the ISC to notify each other urgently of outbreaks of specific diseases within their territories, and that the only goods subject to any restrictions would be clothes, bed linen, and rags. There would be no land quarantine, but travellers with cholera or cholera-like symptoms could be detained in isolation.[107] Over the next thirty years, nations adopted additional conventions under the ISC, and by 1926, international law covered three main diseases: cholera, plague, and yellow fever.[108] When WHO was established in 1948 to facilitate post-war international health cooperation, oversight and management of the ISC was incorporated into the Organisation's mandate.[109]

Under the WHO Constitution, the World Health Assembly (WHA), the annual meeting of WHO member states, would have authority to adopt sanitary, quarantine, and other regulations designed to prevent the international spread of diseases.[110] These international regulations would be automatically binding on all WHO member states unless they expressly opt-out within a specified period.[111] In 1951, the WHA renamed the ISC the 'International Sanitary Regulations' and expanded their scope to include smallpox, typhus, and relapsing fever. The WHA removed the latter two diseases in 1969 and renamed these regulations the International Health Regulations (IHR). In 1981, smallpox was also removed following its global eradication, returning the IHR to the initial three diseases that sparked international health diplomacy: cholera, plague, and yellow fever. Yet, as the world faced a continuous stream of emerging and re-emerging diseases, the principal international law for preventing, detecting, and responding to infectious disease outbreaks was increasingly seen as inadequate.

---

[103] Ibid., 12. The participating nations in the first International Sanitary Conference were France, Austria, the Two Sicilies, Spain, the Papal States, Great Britain, Greece, Portugal, Russia, Sardinia, Tuscany, and Turkey.

[104] Ibid., 17–57, 65.

[105] Ibid., 65.

[106] Gostin and Katz (2016).

[107] Ibid., 70.

[108] Ibid.

[109] World Health Organization (1958).

[110] World Health Assembly, 'Constitution of the World Health Organization' (signed on 22 July 1946, entered into force 7 April 1948) art. 21(a).

[111] Ibid., art. 22.

In addition to its under-inclusivity in addressing the expanding range of infectious disease threats, the IHR also failed to incorporate individual human rights protections. Under the 1969 IHR, states were expressly prohibited from requiring vaccinations against plague upon entry and subjecting individuals to rectal swabbing to test for cholera; however, neither prohibition of these bodily intrusions was couched as a protection of human rights. This neglect of human rights is surprising given the parallel development of UN human rights treaties during this period and the explicit inclusion of the right to health in the 1948 WHO Constitution, placing human rights at the centre of international health law.[112] Despite calls for the revision of the IHR to address these perceived weaknesses, it took the emergence of a previously unknown infectious disease to prompt international action.

Severe acute respiratory syndrome (SARS) emerged in Guangdong, China in late 2002. Concerned that international travel and trade restrictions would be imposed to control this infectious disease, thereby hampering national economic growth, China did not inform the international community of this emerging disease—as SARS was not one of the three diseases that states were specifically obligated to report to WHO under the IHR.[113] In February, 2003, SARS began to spread internationally,[114] prompting the Chinese government for the first time to report cases to WHO and allow previously-obstructed WHO officials and epidemiologists into the country. China's delays in accurately reporting the SARS outbreak—compounded by prohibitions on local Chinese government officials from disclosing public health outbreaks, deemed state secrets, until announced by the Ministry of Health in Beijing[115]—drew widespread international condemnation, including from the WHO Director-General.[116] Only once the international community was formally aware of the outbreak did Chinese officials begin to impose strict *cordons sanitaires* and quarantines, swiftly closing universities, villages, and apartment buildings and imposing mass quarantines affecting more than 30,000 people in Beijing alone.[117] China's judiciary thereafter issued an edict that existing laws criminalising the intentional spread of disease applied to SARS, carrying a punishment from 10 years imprisonment to execution.[118] Yet these public health measures were criticised as being applied arbitrarily and in a discriminatory manner[119] and thus inconsistent with the legitimate public health use of quarantines or isolation measures. While these state

---

[112]Pannenborg (1979).

[113]United States Congressional-Executive Commission on China (CECC) (2003).

[114]Huang (2004).

[115]Gill (2003).

[116]Fleck (2003).

[117]Huang (2004), Centers for Disease Control and Prevention (CDC) (2003).

[118]Eckholm (2003).

[119]'US Criticised China over Death Penalty for SARS Quarantine Violations' (*Agence France-Presse* 16 May 2003) http://global.factiva.com/redir/default.aspx?P=sa&an=afpr000020030516dz5g00mri&cat=a&ep=ASE.

measures were consistent with international health law, they risked violating inter-national human rights law, including protections of the right to life, right to health, freedom of movement, and freedom of speech.[120]

With SARS highlighting the weaknesses of international law for infectious disease control, the international community would commit not only to update the breadth, scope, and notification obligations under the IHR, but also to address the absence of human rights protections under international health law.

3.2   The Revised International Health Regulations (2005)

On 23 May 2005, the 58th WHA adopted the revised IHR, marking a significant shift in the relationship between human rights and the prevention, detection, and response to infectious disease under international law. Adopted under Articles 21 and 22 of the WHO Constitution, the IHR became automatically binding on all WHO member states and entered into force in July 2007. The purpose of the revised IHR is to prevent, protect against, control, and respond to the international spread of infec-tious disease through public health measures that avoid unnecessary interference with international traffic and trade.[121] Much like the International Sanitary Conven-tions of the nineteenth century, merchants and travellers are the primary focus of these provisions, which aim to respond to any Public Health Emergency of Inter-national Concern (PHEIC), including the introduction and spread of a disease from one country into another. Implemented by national governments, state sovereignty continues to be a central tenet of the IHR, reflected in principles that provide states the sovereign responsibility to develop health legislation to address a specific public health risk. However, this domestic legislation 'should uphold the purpose' of the IHR,[122] reinforcing international commitments under both international health law and international human rights law.

3.2.1   Domestic Implementation of Human Rights Through the IHR

Human rights are at the forefront of principles underpinning the IHR, requiring that the domestic implementation of the IHR shall be guided by the UN Charter and the WHO Constitution and 'shall be with the full respect for the dignity, human rights and fundamental freedoms of persons'.[123] Reflecting this new rights-based focus, the IHR's general health measures (i.e., those not specific to travellers) reinforce the centrality of human rights to the global governance of infectious disease. As a cornerstone principle of human rights, any health measure taken by a country in

---

[120] Fidler (2003).

[121] World Health Organization, 'International Health Regulations (2005)' (2008) art. 2.

[122] Ibid., art. 4.

[123] Ibid., art. 3(1).

accordance with the IHR must be applied in a transparent and non-discriminatory manner.[124] The IHR do not preclude countries from implementing health measures within their territory in response to a PHEIC; however, such measures must be in accordance with both national and international law. Thus, national measures must achieve at least the same level of health protection as WHO recommendations and must not be more restrictive of international traffic, or more invasive or intrusive to individuals, than reasonably available alternatives.[125]

Crucially, the IHR provide that an imminent public health risk does not displace a state's non-derogable obligations under human rights law. These include respecting, protecting, and fulfilling the right to life, freedom from torture, cruel, inhuman, or degrading treatment, and freedom from non-consensual medical experimentation. In addition to limits on the domestic health measures that a WHO member state may take, the IHR additionally limit the nature of health measures governments may take with respect to travellers, requiring that states treat travellers with respect for their dignity, human rights, and fundamental freedoms as well as minimise any discomfort or distress arising from the health measures taken.[126] Protecting the rights of travellers in the implementation of health measures, the IHR require that states consider the gender, sociocultural, ethnic, or religious concerns of travellers.[127]

Yet states have not always complied with these human rights principles in the implementation of the IHR. During the 2014–2016 Ebola epidemic, Liberia, Sierra Leone, and Guinea implemented a triangular, regional *cordon sanitaire* where the three national borders meet.[128] This cross-border area already had a long history of restrictive health responses, having faced prior colonial campaigns of cordoning entire villages affected by infectious diseases.[129] Responding to these Ebola restrictions, the WHO spokesperson stated that while WHO would not be against the use of a *cordon sanitaire*, 'human rights have to be respected'.[130] The effective implementation of a *cordon sanitaire* invariably impacts the right to movement, yet during an extraordinary public health event, it may be the least restrictive option based upon scientific evidence and principles. However, if not implemented in accordance with human rights, *cordons sanitaires* may additionally lead to the deprivation of other health-related human rights, including the right to health, the right to food, the right to water, and the non-derogable right to life.[131] Compounding these rights violations, the Liberian government additionally imposed an expansive quarantine over the West Point area of Monrovia in August 2014, contradicting public health recommendations and forcing at least 75,000 people to remain in overcrowded and

[124] Ibid., art. 42.
[125] Ibid., art. 43(2).
[126] Ibid., art. 32.
[127] Ibid., art. 32(b).
[128] McNeil Jr (2014).
[129] Commission on a Global Health Risk Framework for the Future (2016).
[130] McNeil Jr (2014).
[131] Zidar (2015).

unsanitary conditions.[132] After ten days of restrictions on access to food, water, and other determinants of health—resulting in deadly clashes between residents and the military—the government was forced to remove the quarantine order.[133] Tested by the 2014–2016 Ebola epidemic, the public health and human rights safeguards contained in the IHR remained insufficient to prevent the use of unnecessary and IHR-non-compliant domestic health measures, setting a precedent that would be vastly expanded amidst the rights violations accompanying *cordons sanitaires* employed by China in the early COVID-19 response.[134]

3.2.2 Human Rights Protections for Travellers

The IHR additionally establish normative standards for the health measures states may take to mitigate the international spread of disease, including express consideration of the human rights of travellers to protect individual dignity. Upon arrival or departure, states may gather information on a traveller's travel history or destination for the purpose of contact tracing (to assess possible exposure to an infectious disease) or require a non-invasive medical examination (provided that it is the least intrusive examination required to achieve the relevant public health aim).[135] Such non-invasive medical examinations can include visual examination of the ear, nose, and mouth, temperature assessment using an ear, mouth, or skin thermometer or thermal imaging, measurement of blood pressure, or the external collection of urine, faeces, or saliva samples.[136] If the initial examination shows a public health risk exists, countries may, on a case-by-case basis, apply additional health measures on the affected or suspected traveller; however, such measures must be the least intrusive and least invasive means to prevent the international spread of disease, must be consistent with the IHR, and as a result, must avoid unnecessary infringements of human rights.[137] Respecting human dignity and bodily integrity, no medical examination (invasive or non-invasive), vaccination, prophylaxis, or other health measure can be performed on travellers without their prior express informed consent or, for individuals without capacity to give fully informed consent, parental or guardian consent.[138] However, if a traveller fails to consent to invasive medical examinations or provide information necessary for contact tracing, the country may, where there is an imminent public health risk, compel or advise the traveller to undergo the least invasive and intrusive medical examination necessary, vaccination or prophylaxis, or other health measures such as quarantine or isolation.[139] For travellers that are

---

[132]Onishi (2014).

[133]Amon (2014a).

[134]Habibi et al. (2020).

[135]World Health Organization, 'International Health Regulations (2005)' (2008) art. 23.1(a).

[136]Ibid., art. 1.

[137]Ibid., art. 23(2).

[138]Ibid., art. 23(3).

[139]Ibid., art. 31(2).

quarantined, isolated, or subjected to medical examination or other public health procedures, countries must provide (in accordance with human rights obligations) adequate food and water, accommodation, and clothing, protection of possessions, medical treatment, and means of communication in a language the traveller can understand.[140]

Facilitating accountability for these standards through WHO monitoring, a state must notify WHO if it implements any additional health measure that significantly interferes with international travel, such as refusing entry or prohibiting departure of travellers for more than 24 hours, providing WHO with its public health rationale and scientific basis for these travel restrictions.[141] In response, WHO can request that the state reconsider its measures; however, there is no formal IHR enforcement mechanism or process if human rights are being violated or unduly burdened. Further limiting accountability through WHO, this international monitoring mechanism is not activated if state measures are domestically focused and do not have a significant impact on international travel. Where countries engage in exclusively domestic health measures that may violate human rights, the IHR remain silent, with states bound only by independent international human rights obligations and any normative influence found through the 'temporary recommendations' process during a PHEIC.

3.2.3   PHEICs and Temporary Recommendations

The revised IHR take an 'all-hazards' approach to PHEICs. No longer limited to specific infectious diseases, the obligations under the IHR apply to 'any illness or medical condition, irrespective of origin or source, that presents or could present significant harm to humans'.[142] Requiring states to notify WHO of any and all events that may potentially constitute a PHEIC,[143] the revised IHR were also updated to allow WHO to receive information about possible events from a broad range of sources beyond member states, such as through the media, civil society, and countries that are not WHO member states.[144] This new provision filled a critical gap in previous versions of the IHR in cases where a government, as seen during SARS, fails to comply with its notification obligation.[145] Despite addressing this gap, the implementation of this provision has been negated in practice, with scientists and civil society denied the use of this right to share information, and the media, as seen in the COVID-19 outbreak, facing imprisonment for reporting necessary public health information.[146]

---

[140] Ibid., art. 33(c).

[141] Ibid., art. 43(3).

[142] Ibid., art. 1.

[143] Ibid., art. 6.

[144] Ibid., art. 9.

[145] Baker and Fidler (2006).

[146] Davies (2017).

Upon notification, the WHO Director-General, advised by an Expert Committee, independently declares whether such an event constitutes a PHEIC,[147] and may then issue temporary recommendations to WHO member states on the measures they should, or should not, implement to address the public health threat.[148] These recommended measures may include how persons and goods are to be treated by countries, including recommendations either for or against restrictions at points of entry (land borders, airports, and ports), the use of quarantine or isolation, the requirements of medical examinations, treatments, or vaccinations, contact tracing, access to medical records, or travel and trade restrictions.

These WHO recommendations under the IHR are intended to guide IHR implementation with full respect for the dignity, human rights, and fundamental freedom of persons. The protection of human rights is enshrined in the factors that the WHO Director-General may consider in issuing, modifying, or terminating recommendations, which include health measures that (on the basis of a risk assessment) are not more intrusive to persons than reasonably available alternatives.[149] While these temporary WHO recommendations are non-enforceable under international law, they are intended to carry the normative weight of WHO authority in global health governance, prescribe best practices in public health, and provide an informal basis for accountability where countries do not follow them.

Yet, in spite of the authority of these WHO recommendations, countries around the world have implemented health measures contrary to WHO recommendations during the H1N1 influenza PHEIC, the 2014–2016 Ebola PHEIC, and the ongoing COVID-19 PHEIC.[150] For example, WHO's temporary recommendations during the Ebola PHEIC advised that there should be no restrictions on international travel or trade—recommending against the banning of flights from affected countries or other border restrictions—as such travel restrictions infringe upon the freedom of movement and correspondingly limit life-saving humanitarian provisions and critically needed medical professionals from reaching the affected countries. Despite this, nearly 30 countries had imposed travel bans by November 2014, including Australia and Canada, both high-income countries with developed public health systems.[151] To assure greater compliance with future recommendations, WHO Director-General Margaret Chan called in October 2015 for accountability mechanisms under the IHR, including sanctions for countries that restrict international travel and trade.[152] This was echoed in the report of the Ebola Interim Assessment Panel, tasked with reviewing the IHR and WHO in response to the Ebola epidemic.[153] However, other independent reviews such as the Harvard-LSHTM Independent Panel on the Global Response to Ebola concluded that economic incentives and the use of existing WHO

---

[147] World Health Organization, 'International Health Regulations (2005)' (2008) art. 12.

[148] Ibid., art. 15.

[149] Ibid., art. 7(d).

[150] World Health Organization (2009, 2014).

[151] Taylor (2014).

[152] De Bode (2015).

[153] Ebola Interim Assessment Panel (2015).

powers to publicly examine countries' rationales for their health measures may be more effective.[154] Notwithstanding these universal recommendations to curtail unnecessary travel restrictions, nations have largely disregarded these WHO recommendations again in the COVID-19 response, with nationalist governments rapidly enacting emergency travel bans that have divided the world and threatened global governance while providing only marginal health benefits.[155]

The implementation of the IHR is intended to be carried out with full respect for human rights and fundamental freedoms, and the laws, structures, and procedures that countries employ to meet their IHR obligations must be compatible with international human rights obligations. By extension, satisfactory implementation of the IHR domestically should ensure that human rights are respected, protected, and fulfilled—not only for travellers but for all residents. Where the Ebola epidemic and COVID-19 pandemic have highlighted the practical limitations of the IHR temporary recommendations, there remain accountability challenges in assuring rights-based approaches to PHEICs.

3.3 Implementation of the IHR and the Global Health Security Agenda

The limitations of IHR implementation over the past decade have forced countries to develop new forms of global governance for infectious disease control. While states are required to report to WHO on their progress in achieving a set of core capacities deemed necessary for fulfilment of their IHR obligations to detect, report, and respond to public health threats,[156] only 22% of countries reported by their 2012 deadline that they had met these capacity requirements.[157] In an effort to independently assess state progress in implementing the IHR, WHO in 2016 formally adopted a joint external evaluation (JEE) tool that established an independent expert review process to assess national progress against IHR core capacities, find gaps in implementation, and identify best practices.[158] Given the slow and inconsistent implementation of the IHR, states additionally looked to develop new institutions of global governance to prevent, detect, and respond to public health emergencies. A partnership of forty countries and international organisations came together in February 2014 to launch the Global Health Security Agenda (GHSA) to assist countries to develop and meet their IHR capacities for 'a world safe and secure from infectious disease threats'.

The GHSA is centred around three pillars of infectious disease: prevention (to preemptively protect against threats), detection (to determine when a threat arises) and

---

[154]Moon et al. (2015).

[155]Meier et al. (2020).

[156]World Health Organization, 'International Health Regulations (2005)' (2008) art. 44.

[157]Kerry et al. (2014).

[158]World Health Organization (2018).

response (to address threats as they are occurring).[159] Under these pillars are eleven 'action packages', or areas of specific focus, to give effect to these pillars of prevention, detection, and response. The action packages—including, *inter alia*, preventing zoonotic diseases, ensuring biosafety and biosecurity, establishing real-time surveillance and developing medical countermeasures—set out targets, measurements, and specific action items for states to realise infectious disease control. National governments under the GHSA are urged to build their capacities to support these action packages, including through specific legislative and policy reforms.[160]

Despite the centrality of human rights to the revision of the IHR, and the opportunity to use the IHR implementation process to incorporate human rights protections into public health policies, the GHSA shifts away from an explicit consideration of human rights. The right to health is implicitly realised through the work of the GHSA, improving infectious disease surveillance and outbreak response capacities; however, the GHSA does not incorporate the lessons that led to the inclusion of human rights language in the revision of the IHR, such as the role of civil society, scientists, and the media as surveillance sources.[161] The realisation of human rights is not expressly included at all in the text of the GHSA action packages. While the action packages require participating countries to implement policy reforms, there is no requirement that countries ensure that such reforms are consistent with human rights obligations under international health law or international human rights law. Many of the action packages will influence health-related human rights—on issues of surveillance and privacy rights, bodily integrity and freedom of movement, and interventions that may raise procedural rights issues—yet the GHSA includes no safeguards that such activities are conducted in ways that respect, protect, or fulfill human rights.

3.4 The Securitisation of Infectious Disease and Implications for Human Rights

Given the absence of explicit human rights language and obligations, the GHSA risks neglecting—or even undermining—the public health benefits of a rights-based approach to infectious disease prevent, detection, and response. Rather than the traditional public health paradigm, the GHSA is framed through a 'securitisation' approach to disease, which views threats to public health as existential threats to national and international security, 'requiring emergency measures and justifying actions outside the normal bounds of political procedure'.[162] Conceptually, the process of securitising socio-economic issues is not inherently in conflict with human rights. For example, the concept of 'human security' arose from human rights-based

---

[159]Centers for Disease Control and Prevention (CDC) (2014).

[160]Meier et al. (2017).

[161]Davies (2017).

[162]Buzan et al. (1998); as cited in Elbe (2006).

approaches to development.[163] WHO has described global health security as addressing 'vulnerabilities to acute public health events',[164] and this description is consistent with how international human rights law frames the right to health. However, global health security is rarely presented in current policy discourse through the lens of human rights.[165] As seen in the modern history of infectious disease control—from HIV to Ebola to COVID-19—governments have used public health emergencies to rationalise limitations on, or in some cases derogations from, their obligations under international human rights law. Framing certain infectious diseases as risks to security can normalise what would otherwise be extraordinary measures, undermining the justifications behind necessary limitations of human rights under international law. Further, if an infectious disease arises that is deemed a threat to national or international security, there is a risk that primary decision-making authority can shift from public health decision-makers to national security institutions.[166] For example, during the 2014–2016 Ebola outbreak in West Africa, the UN Security Council stepped into the realm of global health through the adoption of Resolution 2177, which determined that the 'unprecedented extent of the Ebola outbreak in Africa constitutes a threat to international peace and security'.[167] This resolution highlighted the potential for 'forum shopping' global health threats—from health governance to security governance—leading to security-based policies that may conflict with health and human rights goals, as seen in autocratic emergency responses to COVID-19 that have drawn the scrutiny of the UN High Commissioner for Human Rights, public health professional societies, and human rights non-governmental organizations.[168] Rather than supporting infectious disease control efforts, such conflicts can undermine effective collaboration between domestic public health and national security authorities responsible for the infectious disease response.[169]

The GHSA has demonstrated that the reframing of global public health as an international security issue has the power to mobilize high-income countries to invest financial and technical resources into capacity building for infectious disease prevention, detection, and response in low-income countries. Through the JEE process, more than sixty countries have undergone external evaluations of their IHR core capacity compliance to highlight gaps in capacities and set priorities for full IHR implementation.[170] However, such a securitization approach funded by high-income countries

---

[163] Amon (2014b), 293.

[164] World Health Organization (2007).

[165] Amon (2014b), 293.

[166] Buzan et al. (1998); as cited in Elbe (2006), 119, 127–28.

[167] United Nations Security Council, 'Security Council resolution 2177 (2014) [on the outbreak of the Ebola virus in, and its impact on, West Africa]' 18 September 2014, S/RES/2177 (2014).

[168] Human Rights Watch. Human Rights Dimensions of COVID-19 Response (2020).

[169] Crawford et al. (2016).

[170] World Health Organization, 'Join External Evaluation (JEE) mission reports', available at: http://www.who.int/ihr/procedures/mission-reports/en/.

inherently prioritises threats to high-income countries.[171] Neglected diseases or diseases that do not pose a security threat to wealthy nations are unlikely to trigger the financing and capacity building necessary for infectious disease governance, forcing low-income countries to rely solely on traditionally underfunded humanitarian approaches to some pressing infectious disease threats. The securitization approach imparts obligations on low-income countries that prioritises surveillance of emerging or re-emerging infectious diseases, which may not reflect the immediate public health priorities of that country.[172] Despite this, the strengthening of public health systems for emerging or re-emerging diseases is hoped to have flow-on effects that benefit infectious diseases that do not fit within the securitisation paradigm. This was demonstrated in the reverse (i.e., humanitarian investment advancing health security) in Nigeria during the 2014–2016 Ebola epidemic, when polio surveillance and response systems were able to transform quickly to detect cases and conduct subsequent contact tracing, and now as Ebola surveillance and response systems are being repurposed for COVID-19 control.[173]

With the GHSA distorting political priority-setting in infectious disease governance, the securitisation of infectious disease further risks undermining rights-based approaches to health where emergency measures test the permissible limitations on human rights to protect public health. Through a securitisation lens, what would otherwise be an unauthorised limitation of a right may be legitimised in circumstances where the legitimacy derives from emergency authorities. This risks removing infectious disease control from 'routine democratic considerations'[174] in ministries of health or departments of public health to less transparent parts of government under police or military authorities. This securitisation of public health has been pervasive in the COVID-19 response. Inherent in the securitisation of public health is the risk that national security concerns drive a country's response to an infectious disease in ways that harm both human rights and public health. It is imperative that any risk that an infectious disease poses to the economic or political integrity of the nation does not override parallel risks to human rights. This balance between infectious disease control and human rights realisation in the context of a pandemic was carefully examined in the drafting of the IHR; however, countries that have not implemented human rights frameworks under law—whether constitutional, legislative, or regulatory—risk implementing infectious disease prevention, detection, and response without these important rights-based safeguards.

The IHR brought human rights explicitly into the realm of global governance for infectious diseases. While implementation of the IHR's traditional public health core competencies has been the focus of programmes to accelerate domestic implementation, greater attention must be paid to ensuring the implementation of the IHR's human rights provisions. To re-centre and reiterate human rights protections within

---

[171] Davies (2008), 295, 298–302.

[172] Ibid., 309.

[173] Vaz et al. (2016).

[174] Elbe (2006), 119, 127.

global health law, it will be necessary to continue to recognise the inextricable link-ages between human rights and public health. As seen in the limited influence of rights-violating efforts to contain and mitigate the COVID-19 pandemic, it remains clear that the lack of respect for human rights in a global health security response can hobble efforts to prevent, detect, and respond to infectious disease.[175] Correspond-ingly, the realisation of human rights principles—including non-discrimination, par-ticipation, transparency, and accountability—remain critical for an effective public health response that ensures the highest attainable standard of health.

4 Conclusion

Notwithstanding the robust development of international human rights frameworks to codify health-related human rights, it remains uncertain whether human rights will continue to influence infectious disease control. Assuring the continuing realisation of human rights—even amidst this unprecedented COVID-19 pandemic response—it will be necessary to assess whether infection control policies, programmes, and practices pose the least threat of infringing on human rights while presenting the greatest opportunity to realise health-related human rights. Human rights scholars can provide this human rights impact assessment as a basis to monitor infectious disease control actions in national health policy and global health governance. There must be accountability for human rights in national policy and global governance, codified through the adoption of: interpretive general comments on infectious disease control from human rights treaty bodies; WHO human rights guidance for IHR implementation that is assessed through the IHR Review Process; and revised human rights derogation standards prepared by an independent body of experts, involving civil society, global health lawyers, and other public health experts in the field. Given that such human rights derogation and realisation must be assessed on a case-by-case basis, global governance systems can provide necessary assessments of state actions, recognizing the connections between national policy and global governance and facilitating human rights accountability in preventing, detecting, and responding to infectious disease through global health law.

References

Amon J (2014a) What turns a few cases of disease into thousands? Human Rights Watch. https://www.hrw.org/news/2014/09/12/what-turns-few-cases-disease-thousands (12 Sept)
Amon JJ (2014b) Health security and/or human rights? In: Rushton S, Youde J (eds) Routledge handbook of global health security. Routledge
Annas G, Grodin M (1992) The Nazi doctors and the Nuremberg code: human rights in human experimentation. Oxford University Press, Oxford

---

[175] Amon (2014b), 293, 300.

Baker MG, Fidler DP (2006) Global public health surveillance under new international health regulations. Emerg Infect Dis 12(7):1058–1062

Barondess JA (1996) Medicine against society: lessons from the Third Reich. JAMA 276(20):1657–1660

Barrett R, Kuzawa C, McDade T, Armelagos G (1998) Emerging and re-emerging infectious diseases: the third epidemiologic transition. Annu Rev Anthropol 27:247–271

Bayer R (1991) Public health policy and the AIDS epidemic. An end to HIV exceptionalism? N Engl J Med 324(21):1500–1504

Bayer R, Healton C (1989) Controlling AIDS in Cuba. N Engl J Med 320(15):1022–1024

Beaglehole R, Bonita R (1997) Public health at the crossroads: achievements and prospects. Cambridge University Press, Cambridge

Brockington F (1968) World health, 2nd edn. Churchill Livingstone, Harcourt Brace, p 131

Buzan B, Wæver O, de Wilde J (1998) Security: a new framework for analysis. Lynne Rienner Publishers, Boulder

Centers for Disease Control and Prevention (CDC) (2003) Efficiency of quarantine during an epidemic of severe acute respiratory syndrome—Beijing, China, 2003. MMWR Morb Mortal Wkly Rep 52(43):1037

Centers for Disease Control and Prevention (CDC) (2014) Global health security agenda: action packages. CDC. https://www.cdc.gov/globalhealth/healthprotection/ghs/pdf/ghsa-action-packages_24-september-2014.pdf

Champion VL, Skinner CS (2008) The health belief model. In Glanz K, Rimer BK, Viswanath K (eds) Health behavior and health education. Jossey-Bass, pp 45–65

Childress JF, Bernheim RG (2003) Beyond the liberal and communitarian impasse: a framework and vision for public health. Fla Law Rev 55(5):1191–1193

Commission on a Global Health Risk Framework for the Future (2016) The neglected dimension of global security: a framework to counter infectious disease crises. National Academies Press

Crawford R, Rutz D, Evans DP (2016) "Between Combat Boots and Birkenstocks"—lessons from HIV/AIDS, SARS, H1N1 and Ebola. Public Health 141:186–191

Curran WJ, Clark ME, Gostin L (1987) AIDS: legal and policy implications of the application of traditional disease control measures. J Law Med Ethics 15(1–2):27–35

Davies SE (2008) Securitizing infectious disease. Int Aff 84(2):295–313

Davies SE (2017) Infectious disease outbreak response: mind the rights gap. Med Law Rev 25(2):270–292

De Bode L (2015) WHO wants sanctions against countries for mishandling epidemic. Al Jazeera America. http://america.aljazeera.com/articles/2015/10/22/health-sanctions-against-countries-misguided.html (22 Oct)

De Oliveria Chiang ED, Baker ML, Figueroa-Downing D, Baggio ML, Villa LL, Neto JE, Hadley C, Bednarczyk RA, Evans DP (2015) "Those who love, vaccinate": parental perceptions of HPV vaccination. J Hum Growth Dev 25(3):341–350

del Rio C, Mehta AK, Lyon M III, Guarner J (2014) Ebola hemorrhagic fever in 2014: the tale of an evolving epidemic. Ann Intern Med 161:746–748

Donnelly J (1982) Human rights and human dignity: an analytic critique of non-Western conceptions of human rights. Am Polit Sci Rev 76(2):303–316

Donnelly J (2003) Universal human rights in theory and practice, 2nd edn. Cornell University Press, London

Ebola Interim Assessment Panel (2015) Report of the Ebola Interim Assessment Panel. World Health Organization, p 12. http://www.who.int/csr/resources/publications/ebola/report-by-panel.pdf?ua=1 (7 July)

Eckholm E (2003) China threatens execution in intentional spreading of SARS. The New York Times. https://www.nytimes.com/2003/05/15/international/asia/china-threatens-execution-in-intentional-spreading-of.html (15 May)

Elbe S (2006) Should HIV/AIDS be securitized? The ethical dilemmas of linking HIV/AIDS and security. Int Stud Q 50(1):119–144

Fee E, Parry M (2008) Jonathan Mann, HIV/AIDS, and human rights. J Public Health Policy 29(1):54–71

Felner E (2009) Closing the "Escape Hatch": a toolkit to monitor the progressive realisation of economic, social, and cultural rights. J Hum Rights Pract 1:402–404

Fidler DP (2002) A globalized theory of public health law. J Law Med Ethics 30(2):150–156

Fidler D (2003) SARS and international law. ASIL Insights 8(7)

Figueroa-Downing D, Baggio ML, Baker ML, De Oliveria Chiang ED, Villa LL, Neto JE, Evans DP, Bednarczyk RA (2016) Factors influencing HPV vaccine delivery by healthcare professionals at public health posts in São Paulo, Brazil. Int J Gynecol Obstet 136(1):33–39

Fleck F (2003) How SARS changed the world in less than six months. Bull World Health Organ 81(8):625–626

Giliomee H, Mbenga B (2007) New history of South Africa, 1st edn. Tafelberg Publishers, Cape Town

Gill B (2003) China and SARS: lessons, implications and future steps: presentation to the Congressional-Executive Commission on China. CECC. http://www.cecc.gov/sites/chinacommission.house.gov/files/documents/roundtables/2003/CECC%20Roundtable%20Testimony%20-%20Bates%20Gill%20-%205.12.03.pdf

Godlee F, Pakenham-Walsh N, Ncayiyana D, Cohen B, Packer A (2004) Can we achieve health information for all by 2015? Lancet 364(9430):295–300

Gostin LO (2001) Public health, ethics, and human rights: a tribute to the Late Jonathan Mann. J Law Med Ethics 29(2):121–130

Gostin LO (2014) Global health law. Harvard University Press, Cambridge

Gostin LO, Katz R (2016) The International Health Regulations: the governing framework for global health security. Milbank Q 94:264–266

Gostin L, Lazzarini Z (1997) Human rights and public health in the AIDS pandemic. Oxford University Press, Oxford

Gostin L, Mann J (1994) Towards the development of a human rights impact assessment for the formulation and evaluation of health policies. Health Hum Rights 1(1):58, 70–71

Gruskin S, Hendriks A, Tomasevski K (1996) Human rights and responses to HIV/AIDS. In: Mann J, Tarantola D (eds) AIDS in the World II: global dimensions, social roots, and responses. Oxford University Press, Oxford

Gruskin S, Mills EJ, Tarantola D (2007) History, principles, and practice of health and human rights. Lancet 370(9585):449–455

Gust D, Darkling N, Kennedy A, Schwartz B (2008) Parents with doubts about vaccines: which vaccines and reasons why. Pediatrics 122(4):718–725

Habibi R et al (2020) Do not violate the international health regulations during the COVID-19 Outbreak. Lancet 395(10225):664–666

Hoffman SZ (2004) HIV/AIDS in Cuba: a model for care or an ethical dilemma? Afr Health Sci 4(3):208–209

Holland S (2015) Public health ethics. Polity Press, Cambridge

Howard-Jones N (1975) The scientific background of the international sanitary conferences. World Health Organization. http://apps.who.int/iris/bitstream/10665/62873/1/14549_eng.pdf

Huang Y (2004) The SARS epidemic and its aftermath in China: a political perspective. National Academies Press, Washington, D.C.

Institute of Medicine (2003) Unequal treatment: confronting racial and ethnic disparities in health care. The National Academies Press, Washington, D.C.

Kerry J, Sebelius K, Monaco L (2014) Why global health security is a national priority. CNN. http://www.cnn.com/2014/02/12/opinion/kerry-sebelius-health-security/index.html (12 Feb)

King S (1999) Vaccination policies: individual rights v. community health. Br Med J 319(7223)

Kirby M (1988) The new AIDS virus—ineffective and unjust laws. J Acquir Immune Defic Syndr 1(3):304–305

Koenig S, Léandre F, Farmer PE (2004) Scaling-up HIV treatment programmes in resource-limited settings: the rural Haiti experience. AIDS (Lond) 18:S21–S25

Larson H, de Figueiredo A, Xiahong Z, Schulz W, Verger P, Johnston I, Cook A, Jones N (2016) The state of vaccine confidence 2016: global insights through a 67-country survey. EBioMedicine 12:295–301

Lippman M (1992) The other Nuremberg: American prosecutions of Nazi war criminals in occupied Germany. Indiana Int Comp Law Rev 3(1):1–22

Lippman M (1993) The Nazi doctors trial and the international prohibition on medical involvement in torture. Loyola Los Angeles Int Comp Law J 15(2):395–406

Lyon M, Mehta A, Varkey JB, Brantly K, Plyler L, McElroy A, Kraft C et al (2014) Clinical care of two patients with Ebola virus disease in the United States. N Engl J Med 371:2402–2409 (18 Dec)

Mahajan AP, Sayles J, Patel VA, Remien RH, Sawires SR, Ortiz DJ, Szekeres G, Coates TJ (2008) Stigma in the HIV/AIDS epidemic: a review of the literature and recommendations for the way forward. AIDS (Lond Engl) 22(Suppl 2):S67

Malinowski MJ (2003) Choosing the genetic makeup of children: our eugenics past, present, and future? Conn Law Rev 36(1):125, 152–154

Mann J (1992) AIDS: the second decade: a global perspective. J Infect Dis 165(2):245–250

Mann J (1996) Health and human rights. Br Med J 312(7036)

Mann J (1999) Human rights and AIDS. In: Mann J, Gruskin S, Grodin M, Annas G (eds) Health and human rights: a reader. Routledge, New York

Mann J, Tarantola D (1998) Responding to HIV/AIDS: a historical perspective. Health Hum Rights 2(4):5–8

Mann J, Gostin L, Gruskin S, Brennan T, Lazzarini Z, Fineberg H (1999) Health and human rights. In: Mann J, Gruskin S, Grodin M, Annas G (eds) Health and human rights: a reader. Routledge, New York

Marineli F, Tsoucalas G, Karamanou M, Androutsos G (2013) Mary Mallon (1869–1938) and the history of typhoid fever. Ann Gastroenterol 26(2)

Mariner WK, Annas G, Glantz LH (2005) Jacobson v Massachusetts: it's not your great-great-grandfather's public health law. Am J Public Health 95(4):581–590

Marks SP (2001) Jonathan Mann's legacy to the 21st century: the human rights imperative for public health. J Law Med Ethics 29(2):131–136

Marks S (2004) The human right to development: between rhetoric and reality. Harvard Hum Rights J 17:137–138

McCarthy M (2015) Measles outbreak linked to Disney theme parks reaches five states and Mexico. Br Med J 350

McDougal MS, Lasswell HD, Chen L (1980) Human rights and world public order: the basic policies of an international law of human dignity. Yale University Press, p 29

McNeil DG Jr (2014) Using a tactic unseen in a century, countries cordon off Ebola-racked areas. The New York Times. https://www.nytimes.com/2014/08/13/science/using-a-tactic-unseen-in-a-century-countries-cordon-off-ebola-racked-areas.html?mcubz=1 (12 Aug)

Meier BM (2006) Employing health rights for global justice: the promise of public health in response to the insalubrious ramifications of globalisation. Cornell Int Law J 39(3):711–778

Meier BM, Mori LM (2005) The highest attainable standard: advancing a collective human right to public health. Columbia Hum Rights Law Rev 37(1):101–147

Meier BM, Pardue C, London L (2012) Implementing community participation through legislative reform: a study of the policy framework for community participation in the Western Cape province of South Africa. BMC Int Health Hum Rights 12(1):15

Meier BM, Tureski K, Bockh E, Carr D, Ayala A, Roberts A, Cloud L, Wilhelm N, Burris S (2017) Examining national public health law to realize the global health security agenda. Med Law Rev 25(2):240–243

Meier BM, Habibi R, Yang YT (2020) Travel restrictions violate international law. Science 367:1436

Moon S, Sridhar D, Pate M, Jha A, Clinton C, Delaunay S, Edwin V et al (2015) Will Ebola change the game? Ten essential reforms before the next pandemic. The report of the Harvard-LSHTM Independent Panel on the Global Response to Ebola. Lancet 386(10009):2204–2221

Moyn S (2010) The last utopia: human rights in history. Harvard University Press, Cambridge

Omer SB (2015) How to handle vaccine skeptics. New York Times. https://www.nytimes.com/2015/02/06/opinion/how-to-handle-the-vaccine-skeptics.html?_r=0 (6 Feb)

Omer SB, Pan WKY, Halsey NA (2006) Nonmedical exemptions to school immunisation requirements: secular trends and association off state policies with pertussis incidence. JAMA 296(14):1757–1763

Omer SB, Richards JL, Bednarczyk RA (2012) Vaccination policies and rates of exemption from immunisation, 2005–2001. N Engl J Med 367:1170–1171

Onishi N (2014) Quarantine for Ebola lifted in Liberia slum. The New York Times. https://www.nytimes.com/2014/08/30/world/africa/quarantine-for-ebola-lifted-in-liberia-slum.html (29 Aug)

Pannenborg CO (1979) A New International Health Order: An Inquiry into the International Relations of World Health and Medical Care. Sijthoff & Noordhoff, Alphen aan den Rijn, The Netherlands

PBS Frontline (2006) Haiti, the high price of stigma. PBS Frontline: The Age of AIDS. http://www.pbs.org/wgbh/pages/frontline/aids/countries/ht.html

Potts H (2008) Participation and the right to the highest attainable standard of health. University of Essex

Preston J (2009) Obama lifts a ban on entry into U.S. by H.I.V.-positive people. New York Times. http://www.nytimes.com/2009/10/31/us/politics/31travel.html (30 Oct)

Price PJ (2015) Ebola and the Law in the United States: a short guide to public health authority and practical limits. Emory Legal Studies Research Paper No. 14-299. https://ssrn.com/abstract=2538187

Raeburn J, Macfarlane S (2003) Putting the public into public health: towards a more people-centred approach. In: Beaglehole R (ed) Global public health: a new era. Oxford University Press, pp 243–245

Reed G (2011) The human dimension of AIDS in Cuba: Jorge Perez MD, MS Director, Pedro Kourí Tropical Medicine Institute. MEDICC Rev 13(2):14–19

Rhodes T, Singer M, Bourgois P, Friedman S, Strathdee S (2005) The social structural production of HIV risk among injecting drug users. Soc Sci Med 61(5):1026–1044

Rose G, Navarro V, Krieger N, Zierler S (1999) Population perspective. In: Beauchamp DE, Steinbock B (eds) New ethics for the public's health. Oxford University Press, Oxford

Rosen G (1974) From medical police to social medicine: essays on the history of health care. Science History Publications, New York

Roush S, Murphy T, The Vaccine-Preventable Disease Table Working Group (2007) Historical comparisons of morbidity and morality for vaccine-preventable disease in the United States. 298(18):2155–2163

Ryle JA (1948) Changing disciplines: lectures on the history, method, and motives of social pathology. Oxford University Press, Oxford

Saha S, Komaromy M, Koepsell TD, Bindman AB (1999) Patient-physician racial concordance and the perceived quality and use of health care. Arch Intern Med 159(9):997–1004

Sand R (1934) L'Économie humaine par la médicine sociale. Rieder, Paris

Sidel VW (1996) The social responsibilities of health professionals: lessons from their role in Nazi Germany. JAMA 276(20):1679

Slaughter A-M (1997) The real new world. Foreign Aff 76:183–184

Steiner HJ, Alston P, Goodman R (2008) International human rights in context: law, politics, morals, 3rd edn. Oxford University Press, Oxford

Taylor T (1992) Opening statement of the prosecution, December 9, 1946. In: Annas G, Grodin M (1992) The Nazi doctors and the Nuremberg code: human rights in human experimentation. Oxford University Press, Oxford

Taylor AL (2004) Governing the globalization of public health. J Law Med Ethics 32:500–501

Taylor A (2014) Why are Australia and Canada following North Korea's lead on Ebola? Washington Post. https://www.washingtonpost.com/news/worldviews/wp/2014/11/06/why-are-australia-and-canada-following-north-koreas-lead-on-ebola/?utm_term=.b1efeb356ecc (6 Nov)

The Institute of Medicine (1988) The future of public health. The National Academies Press, Washington, D.C.

United States Congressional-Executive Commission on China (CECC) (2003) Information control and self-censorship in the PRC and the spread of SARS. CECC. https://www.cecc.gov/publications/issue-papers/information-control-and-self-censorship-in-the-prc-and-the-spread-of-sars

VanderWal K (1990) Collective human rights: a Western view. In: Bertin J, Baeher P, Herman Burgers J, Flinterman C, de Klerk B, Kroes R, van Minnen CA, VanderWal K (eds) Human rights in a pluralist world: individuals and collectivities. Meckler, London

Vaz RG, Mkanda P, Banda R, Komkech W, Ekundare-Famiyesin OO, Onyibe R, Abidoye S et al (2016) The role of the polio program infrastructure in response to Ebola virus disease outbreak in Nigeria 2014. J Infect Dis 213(Suppl 3):S140–S146

Werner D, Thuman C, Maxwell J (1992) Where there is no doctor: a village health care handbook. Hesperian Press

World Health Organization (1958) The first ten years of the World Health Organization. World Health Organization, Geneva

World Health Organization (1988) AIDS prevention and control: invited presentations and papers from the World Summit of Ministers of Health on Programmes for AIDS Prevention. World Health Organization and Pergamon Press

World Health Organization (2007) The world health report 2007—a safer future: global public health security in the 21st century. World Health Organization, Geneva

World Health Organization (2009) No rationale for travel restrictions. World Health Organization. http://www.who.int/csr/disease/swineflu/guidance/public_health/travel_advice/en/ (1 May)

World Health Organization (2014) Statement on the 1st meeting of the IHR Emergency Committee on the 2014 Ebola outbreak in West Africa. World Health Organization. http://www.who.int/mediacentre/news/statements/2014/ebola-20140808/en/ (8 Aug)

World Health Organization (2016) Global tuberculosis report 2016. World Health Organization. http://apps.who.int/iris/bitstream/10665/250441/1/9789241565394-eng.pdf?ua=1

World Health Organization (2018). IHR (2005) Monitoring and evaluation framework: Joint External Evaluation tool (JEE tool) second edition. WHO, Geneva

Yang YT, Barraza L, Weidenaar K (2015) Measles outbreak as a catalyst for stricter vaccine exemption legislation. JAMA 314(12):1229–1230

Zidar A (2015) WHO International Health Regulations and human rights: from allusions to inclusion. Int J Hum Rights 19:505–526

Printed in Great Britain
by Amazon